ADVANCED PROGRAMMING

LANGUAGE DESIGN

Raphael A. Finkel

UNIVERSITY OF KENTUCKY

Addison-Wesley Publishing Company

Menlo Park, California • Reading, Massachusetts
New York • Don Mills, Ontario • Harlow, U.K. • Amsterdam
Bonn • Paris • Milan • Madrid • Sydney • Singapore • Tokyo
Seoul • Taipei • Mexico City • San Juan, Puerto Rico

Acquisitions Editor: J. Carter Shanklin
Editorial Assistant: Christine Kulke
Senior Production Editor: Teri Holden
Copy Editor: Nick Murray
Manufacturing Coordinator: Janet Weaver
Printer: The Maple-Vail Book Manufacturing Group
Composition and Film Coordinator: Vivian McDougal

Proofreader: Holly McLean-Aldis
Text Designer: Peter Vacek, Eigentype
Film Preparation: Lazer Touch, Inc.
Cover Designer: Yvo Riezebos

Library of Congress Cataloging-in-Publication Data

```
Finkel, Raphael A.
      Advanced programming languages / Raphael A. Finkel.
      p.    cm.
      Includes index.
      ISBN 0-8053-1191-2
      1.  Programming languages (Electronic computers)   I. Title.
QA76.7.F56  1995                                                    95-36693
005.13--dc20                                                           CIP
```

1 2 3 4 5 6 7 8 9—MA—99 98 97 96 95

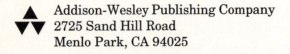
Addison-Wesley Publishing Company
2725 Sand Hill Road
Menlo Park, CA 94025

Dedicated to the memory of my father, Asher J. Finkel, who first tickled my interest in programming languages by announcing that he was learning a language that could be read and written, but not pronounced.

Contents

Preface

This book stems in part from courses taught at the University of Kentucky and at the University of Wisconsin–Madison on programming language design. There are many good books that deal with the subject at an undergraduate level, but there are few that are suitable for a one-semester graduate-level course. This book is my attempt to fill that gap.

The goal of this course, and hence of this book, is to expose first-year graduate students to a wide range of programming language paradigms and issues, so that they can understand the literature on programming languages and even conduct research in this field. It should improve the students' appreciation of the art of designing programming languages and, to a limited degree, their skill in programming.

This book does not focus on any one language, or even on a few languages; it mentions, at least in passing, over seventy languages, including well-known ones (Algol, Pascal, C, C++, LISP, Ada, FORTRAN), important but less known ones (ML, SR, Modula-3, SNOBOL), significant research languages (CLU, Alphard, Linda), and little-known languages with important concepts (Io, Gödel). Several languages are discussed in some depth, primarily to reinforce particular programming paradigms. ML and LISP demonstrate functional programming, Smalltalk and C++ demonstrate object-oriented programming, and Prolog demonstrates logic programming.

Students are expected to have taken an undergraduate course in programming languages before using this book. The first chapter includes a review of much of the material on imperative programming languages that would be covered in such a course. This review makes the book self-contained, and also makes it accessible to advanced undergraduate students.

Most textbooks on programming languages cover the well-trodden areas of the field. In contrast, this book tries to go beyond the standard territory, making brief forays into regions that are under current research or that have been proposed and even rejected in the past. There are many fascinating constructs that appear in very few, if any, production programming languages. Some (like power loops) should most likely not be included in a programming language. Others (like Io continuations) are so strange that it is not clear how to program with them. Some (APL arrays) show alternative ways to structure languages. These unusual ideas are important even though they do not pass the test of current usage, because they elucidate important aspects of programming language design, and they allow students to evaluate novel concepts.

Certain themes flow through the entire book. One is the interplay between what can be done at compile time and what must be deferred to runtime. Actions performed at compile time make for more efficient and less error-prone execution. Decisions deferred until runtime lead to greater flexibility. Another theme is how patterns and pattern matching play a large role in many ways in programming languages. Pattern matching is immediately important for string manipulation, but it is also critical in steering logic programming, helpful for extracting data from structures in ML, and for associating caller and callee in CSP. A third theme is the quest for uniformity. It is very much like the mathematical urge to generalize. It can be seen in polymorphism, which generalizes the concept of type, and in overloading, which begins by unifying operators and functions and then unifies disparate functions under one roof. It can be seen in the homoiconic forms of LISP, in which program and data are both presented in the same uniform way.

Two organizing principles suggest themselves for a book on programming languages. The first is to deal separately with such issues as syntax, types, encapsulation, parallelism, object-oriented programming, pattern matching, dataflow, and so forth. Each section would introduce examples from all relevant languages. The other potential organizing principle is to present individual languages, more or less in full, and then to derive principles from them.

This book steers a middle course. I have divided it into chapters, each of which deals primarily with one of the subjects mentioned above. Most chapters include an extended example from a particular language to set the stage. This section may introduce language-specific features not directly relevant to the subject of the chapter. The chapter then introduces related features from other languages.

Because this book covers both central and unusual topics, the instructor of a course using the book should pick and choose whatever topics are of personal interest. In general, the latter parts of chapters delve into stranger and more novel variants of material presented earlier. The book is intended for a one-semester course, but it is about 30 percent too long to cover fully in one semester. It is not necessary to cover every chapter, nor to cover every section of a chapter. Only Chapter 1 and the first seven sections of Chapter 3 are critical for understanding the other chapters. Some instructors will want to cover Chapter 4 before the discussion of ML in Chapter 3. Many instructors will decide to omit dataflow (Chapter 6). Others will wish to omit denotational semantics (in Chapter 10).

I have not described complete languages, and I may have failed to mention your favorite language. I have selected representative programming languages that display particular programming paradigms or language features clearly. These languages are not all generally available or even widely known. The appendix lists all the languages I have mentioned and gives you some pointers to the literature and to implementations and documentation available on the Internet through anonymous ftp (file-transfer protocol).

The exercises at the end of each chapter serve two purposes. First, they allow students to test their understanding of the subjects presented in the text by working exercises directly related to the material. More importantly, they push students beyond the confines of the material presented to consider new situations and to evaluate new proposals. Subjects that are only hinted at in the text are developed more thoroughly in this latter type of exercise.

In order to create an appearance of uniformity, I have chosen to modify the syntax of presented languages (in cases where the syntax is not the crucial issue), so that language-specific syntax does not obscure the other points that I am trying to make. For examples that do not depend on any particular language, I have invented what I hope will be clear notation. It is derived largely from Ada and some of its predecessors. This notation allows me to standardize the syntactic form of language, so that the syntax does not obscure the subject at hand. It is largely irrelevant whether a particular language uses **begin** and **end** or { and } . On the other hand, in those cases where I delve deeply into a language in current use (like ML, LISP, Prolog, Smalltalk, and C++), I have preserved the actual language. Where reserved words appear, I have placed them in **bold monospace**. Other program excerpts are in monospace font. I have also numbered examples so that instructors can refer to parts of them by line number. Each technical term that is introduced in the text is printed in **boldface** the first time it appears. All boldface entries are collected and defined in the glossary. I have tried to use a consistent nomenclature throughout the book.

In order to relieve the formality common in textbooks, I have chosen to write this book as a conversation between me, in the first singular person, and you, in the second person. When I say *we*, I mean you and me together. I hope you don't mind.

Several supplemental items are available to assist the instructor in using this text. Answers to the exercises are available from the publisher (ISBN: 0-201-49835-9) in a disk-based format. The figures from the text (in Adobe Acrobat format), an Adobe Acrobat reader, and the entire text of this book are available from the following site:

`ftp://aw.com/cseng/authors/finkel`

Please check the `readme` file for updates and changes. The complete text of this book is intended for on-screen viewing free of charge; use of this material in any other format is subject to a fee.

There are other good books on programming language design. I can particularly recommend the text by Pratt [Pratt 96] for elementary material and the text by Louden [Louden 93] for advanced material. Other good books include those by Sebesta [Sebesta 93] and Sethi [Sethi 89].

I owe a debt of gratitude to the many people who helped me write this book. Much of the underlying text is modified from course notes written by Charles N. Fischer of the University of Wisconsin–Madison. Students in my classes have submitted papers which I have used in preparing examples and text; these include the following:

Subject	Student	Year
C++	Feng Luo	1992
	Mike Rogers	1992
Dataflow	Chinya Ravishankar	1981
Gödel	James Gary	1992
Lynx	Michael Scott	1985
Mathematics languages	Mary Sue Powers	1994
Miranda	Manish Gupta	1992
Post	Chinya Ravishankar	1981
	Rao Surapaneni	1992
CLP	William Ralenkotter	1994
Russell	Rick Simkin	1981
	K. Lakshman	1992
	Manish Gupta	1992
Smalltalk/C++	Jonathan Edwards	1992

Jonathan Edwards read an early draft of the text carefully and made many helpful suggestions. Michael Scott assisted me in improving Chapter 7 on concurrency. Arcot Rajasekar provided important feedback on Chapter 8 on logic programming. My editor, J. Carter Shanklin, and the reviewers he selected, made a world of difference in the presentation and coverage of the book. These reviewers were David Stotts (University of North Carolina at Chapel Hill), Spiro Michaylov (Ohio State University), Michael G. Murphy (Southern College of Technology), Barbara Ann Greim (University of North Carolina at Wilmington), Charles Elkan (University of California, San Diego), Henry Ruston (Polytechnic University), and L. David Umbaugh (University of Texas at Arlington). The University of Kentucky provided sabbatical funding to allow me to pursue this project, and Metropolitan College in Kuala Lumpur, Malaysia, provided computer facilities that allowed me to work on it. This book was prepared on the Linux version of the Unix operating system. Linux is the result of work by Linus Torvalds and countless others, primarily at the Free Software Foundation, who have provided an immense suite of programs I have used, including text editors, document formatters and previewers, spelling checkers, and revision control packages. I would have been lost without them. Finally, I would like to thank my wife, Beth L. Goldstein, for her support and patience, and my daughter, Penina, and son, Asher, for being wonderful.

Raphael A. Finkel
University of Kentucky

Chapter 1

Introduction

The purpose of this book is to study the principles and innovations found in modern programming languages. We will consider a wide variety of languages. The goal is not to become proficient in any of these languages, but to learn what contributions each has made to the "state of the art" in language design.

I will discuss various programming paradigms in this book. Some languages (such as Ada, Pascal, Modula-2) are **imperative**; they use variables, assignments, and iteration. For imperative languages, I will dwell on such issues as flow of control (Chapter 2) and data types (Chapter 3). Other languages (for example, LISP and FP) are **functional**; they have no variables, assignments, or iteration, but model program execution as expression evaluation. I discuss functional languages in Chapter 4. Other languages (for example, Smalltalk and C++), represent the **object-oriented** paradigm, in which data types are generalized to collections of data and associated routines (Chapter 5). **Dataflow languages** (Val, Sisal, and Post, Chapter 6) attempt to gain speed by simultaneous execution of independent computations; they require special computer architectures. A more common way to gain speed is by **concurrent** programming (typified by languages such as SR and Lynx, discussed in Chapter 7). Another major paradigm constitutes the **declarative** languages such as Prolog and Gödel (Chapter 8); they view programming as stating what is wanted and not necessarily how to compute it. **Aggregate languages** (Chapter 9) form a a final loosely knit paradigm that includes languages with special-purpose data formats, such as strings (SNOBOL and Icon), arrays (APL), databases (dBASE and SQL), and mathematical formulas (Mathematica and Maple).

In addition to studying actual programming language constructs, I will present formal semantic models in Chapter 10. These models allow a precise specification of what a program means, and provide the basis for reasoning about the correctness of a program.

1 ◆ PROGRAMMING LANGUAGES AS SOFTWARE TOOLS

Programming languages fit into a larger subject that might be termed **software tools**. This subject includes such fields as interactive editors (text, picture, spreadsheet, bitmap, and so forth), data transformers (compilers, assemblers, stream editors, macro processors, text formatters), operating systems, database management systems, and tools for program creation, testing, and maintenance (script files, source-code management tools, debuggers).

In general, software tools can be studied as interfaces between clients, which are usually humans or their programs, and lower-level facilities, such as files or operating systems.

Figure 1.1   Software tools

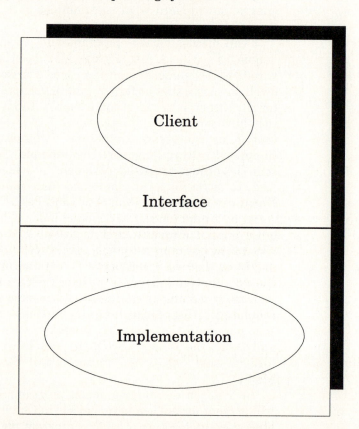

Three questions arising from Figure 1.1 are worth discussing for any software tool:

1. What is the nature of the interface?
2. How can the interface be implemented by using the lower-level facilities?
3. How useful is the interface for humans or their agents?

When we deal with programming languages as software tools, these questions are transformed:

1. What is the structure (syntax) and meaning (semantics) of the programming language constructs? Usually, I will use informal methods to show what the constructs are and what they do. However, Chapter 10 presents formal methods for describing the semantics of programming languages.
2. How does the compiler writer deal with these constructs in order to translate them into assembler or machine language? The subject of compiler construction is large and fascinating, but is beyond the scope of this book. I will occasionally touch on this topic to assure you that the constructs can, in fact, be translated.
3. Is the programming language good for the programmer? More specifically, is it easy to use, expressive, readable? Does it protect the programmer from programming errors? Is it elegant? I spend a significant amount of effort trying to evaluate programming languages and their constructs in this way. This subject is both fascinating and difficult to be objective about. Many languages have their own fan clubs, and discussions often revolve about an ill-defined sense of elegance.

Programming languages have a profound effect on the ways programmers formulate solutions to problems. You will see that different paradigms impose very different programming styles, but even more important, they change the way the programmer looks at algorithms. I hope that this book will expand your horizons in much the same way that your first exposure to recursion opened up a new way of thinking. People have invented an amazing collection of elegant and expressive programming structures.

2 ◆ EVALUATING PROGRAMMING LANGUAGES

This book introduces you to some unusual languages and some unusual language features. As you read about them, you might wonder how to evaluate the quality of a feature or an entire language. Reasonable people disagree on what makes for a great language, which is why so many novel ideas abound in the arena of programming language design. At the risk of oversimplification, I would like to present a short list of desiderata for programming languages [Butcher 91]. Feel free to disagree with them. Another excellent discussion of this topic is found in Louden [Louden 93].

- **Simplicity.** There should be as few basic concepts as possible. Often the job of the language designer is to discard elements that are superfluous, error-prone, hard to read, or hard to compile. Many people consider PL/I, for example, to be much too large a language. Some criticize Ada for the same reason.

- **Uniformity.** The basic concepts should be applied consistently and universally. We should be able to use language features in different contexts without changing their form. Non-uniformity can be annoying. In Pascal, constants cannot be declared with values given by expressions, even though expressions are accepted in all other contexts when a value is needed. Non-uniformity can also be error-prone. In Pascal, some **for** loops take a single statement as a body, but **repeat** loops can take any number of statements. It is easy to forget to bracket multiple statements in the body of a **for** loop.

- **Orthogonality.** Independent functions should be controlled by independent mechanisms. (In mathematics, independent vectors are called "orthogonal.")

- **Abstraction.** There should be a way to factor out recurring patterns. (Abstraction generally means hiding details by constructing a "box" around them and permitting only limited inspection of its contents.)

- **Clarity.** Mechanisms should be well defined, and the outcome of code should be easily predictable. People should be able to read programs in the language and be able to understand them readily. Many people have criticized C, for example, for the common confusion between the assignment operator (=) and the equality test operator (==).

- **Information hiding.** Program units should have access only to the information they require. It is hard to write large programs without some control over the extent to which one part of the program can influence another part.

- **Modularity.** Interfaces between programming units should be stated explicitly.

- **Safety.** Semantic errors should be detectable, preferably at compile time. An attempt to add values of dissimilar types usually indicates that the programmer is confused. Languages like Awk and SNOBOL that silently convert data types in order to apply operators tend to be error-prone.

- **Expressiveness.**   A   wide   variety   of   programs   should   be expressible.[1] Languages with coroutines, for example, can express algorithms for testing complex structures for equality much better than languages without coroutines. (Coroutines are discussed in Chapter 2.)

- **Efficiency.** Efficient code should be producible from the language, possibly with the assistance of the programmer. Functional programming languages that rely heavily on recursion face the danger of inefficiency, although there are compilation methods (such as eliminating tail recursion) that make such languages perfectly acceptable. However, languages that require interpretation instead of compilation (such as Tcl) tend to be slow, although in many applications, speed is of minor concern.

3 ♦ BACKGROUND MATERIAL ON PROGRAMMING LANGUAGES

Before showing you anything out of the ordinary, I want to make sure that you are acquainted with the fundamental concepts that are covered in an undergraduate course in programming languages. This section is intentionally concise. If you need more details, you might profitably refer to the fine books by Pratt [Pratt 96] and Louden [Louden 93].

3.1 Variables, Data Types, Literals, and Expressions

I will repeatedly refer to the following example, which is designed to have a little bit of everything in the way of types. A **type** is a set of values on which the same operations are defined.

Figure 1.2

```
variable                                                     1
    First : pointer to integer;                              2
    Second : array 0..9 of                                   3
        record                                               4
            Third: character;                                5
            Fourth: integer;                                 6
            Fifth : (Apple, Durian, Coconut, Sapodilla,      7
                Mangosteen)                                  8
        end;                                                 9
```

---

[1] In a formal sense, all practical languages are Turing-complete; that is, they can express exactly the same algorithms. However, the ease with which a programmer can come up with an appropriate program is part of what I mean by expressiveness. Enumerating binary trees (see Chapter 2) is quite difficult in most languages, but quite easy in CLU.

```
begin                                                        10
    First := nil;                                            11
    First := &Second[1].Fourth;                              12
    Firstˆ := 4;                                             13
    Second[3].Fourth := (Firstˆ + Second[1].Fourth) *       14
        Second[Firstˆ].Fourth;                               15
    Second[0] := [Third : 'x'; Fourth : 0;                   16
        Fifth : Sapodilla];                                  17
end;                                                         18
```

Imperative languages (such as Pascal and Ada) have **variables**, which are named memory locations. Figure 1.2 introduces two variables, First (line 2) and Second (lines 3–9). Programming languages often restrict the values that may be placed in variables, both to ensure that compilers can generate accurate code for manipulating those values and to prevent common programming errors. The restrictions are generally in the form of type information. The **type** of a variable is a restriction on the values it can hold and what operations may be applied to those values. For example, the type integer encompasses numeric whole-number values between some language-dependent (or implementation-dependent) minimum and maximum value; values of this type may act as operands in arithmetic operations such as addition. The term integer is not set in bold monospace type, because in most languages, predefined types are not reserved words, but ordinary identifiers that can be given new meanings (although that is bad practice).

Researchers have developed various taxonomies to categorize types [ISO/IEC 94; Meek 94]. I will present here a fairly simple taxonomy. A **primitive type** is one that is not built out of other types. Standard primitive types provided by most languages include integer, Boolean, character, real, and sometimes string. Figure 1.2 uses both integer and character. Enumeration types are also primitive. The example uses an enumeration type in lines 7–8; its values are restricted to the values specified. Enumeration types often define the order of their enumeration constants. In Figure 1.2, however, it makes no sense to consider one fruit greater than another.[2]

Structured types are built out of other types. Arrays, records, and pointers are structured types.[3] Figure 1.2 shows all three kinds of standard structured types. The building blocks of a structured type are its **components**. The component types go into making the structured type;

---

[2] In Southeast Asia, the durian is considered the king of fruits. My personal favorite is the mangosteen.

[3] Whether to call pointers primitive or structured is debatable. I choose to call them structured because they are built from another type.

component values go into making the value of a structured type. The pointer type in line 2 of Figure 1.2 has one component type (integer); a pointer value has one component value. There are ten component values of the array type in lines 3–9, each of a record type. Arrays are usually required to be **homogeneous**; that is, all the component values must be of the same type. Arrays are indexed by elements of an **index type**, usually either a subrange of integers, characters, or an enumeration type. Therefore, an array has two component types (the base type and the index type); it has as many component values as there are members in the index type.

Flexible arrays do not have declared bounds; the bounds are set at runtime, based on which elements of the array have been assigned values. **Dynamic-sized** arrays have declared bounds, but the bounds depend on the runtime value of the bounds expressions. Languages that provide dynamic-sized arrays provide syntax for discovering the lower and upper bounds in each dimension.

Array **slices**, such as Second[3..5], are also components for purposes of this discussion. Languages (like Ada) that allow array slices usually only allow slices in the last dimension. (APL does not have such a restriction.)

The components of the record type in lines 4–9 are of types character and integer. Records are like arrays in that they have multiple component values. However, the values are indexed not by members of an index type but rather by named **fields**. The component values need not be of the same type; records are not required to be homogeneous. Languages for systems programming sometimes allow the programmer to control exactly how many bits are allocated to each field and how fields are packed into memory.

The **choice** is a less common structured type. It is like a record in that it has component types, each selected by a field. However, it has only one component value, which corresponds to exactly one of the component types. Choices are often implemented by allocating as much space as the largest component type needs. Some languages (like Simula) let the programmer restrict a variable to a particular component when the variable is declared. In this case, only enough space is allocated for that component, and the compiler disallows accesses to other components.

Which field is active in a choice value determines the operations that may be applied to that value. There is usually some way for a program to determine at runtime which field is active in any value of the choice type; if not, there is a danger that a value will be accidentally (or intentionally) treated as belonging to a different field, which may have a different type. Often, languages provide a **tagcase** statement with branches in which the particular variant is known both to the program and to the compiler. Pascal allows part of a record to be a choice and the other fields to be active in any variant. One of the latter fields indicates which variant is in use. It doesn't make sense to modify the value of that field without modifying the variant part as well.

A **literal** is a value, usually of a primitive type, expressly denoted in a program. For example, 243 is an integer literal and Figure 1.2 has literals 0, 1, 3, 4, 9, and 'x'. Some values are provided as predeclared constants (that is, identifiers with predefined and unchangeable values), such as false (Boolean) and nil (pointer).

A **constructor** expressly denotes a value of a structured type. Figure 1.2 has a record constructor in lines 16–17.

An **expression** is a literal, a constructor, a constant, a variable, an invocation of a value-returning procedure, a conditional expression, or an operator with operands that are themselves expressions. Figure 1.2 has expressions in lines 11–17. An **operator** is a shorthand for an invocation of a value-returning procedure whose parameters are the operands. Each operator has an **arity**, that is, the number of operands it expects. Common arities are unary (one operand) and binary (two operands). Unary operators are commonly written before their operand (such as -4 or &myVariable), but some are traditionally written after the operand (such as ptrVariable^). Sometimes it is helpful to consider literals and constants to be nullary (no-operand) operators. For example, true is a nullary operator of type **Boolean**.

Operators do not necessarily take only numeric operands. The **dereferencing** operator (^), for example, produces the value pointed to by a pointer. This operator is unary and **postfix**, that is, it follows its expression. You can see it in Figure 1.2 in lines 13, 14, and 15. Some languages, such as Gedanken, Ada, and Oberon-2, coerce pointers (repeatedly, if needed) to the values they dereference if the context makes it clear which type is required. The unary prefix **referencing** operator (&) in line 12 generates a pointer to a value.

Common operators include those in the table on the next page. Many operators are **overloaded**; that is, their meaning depends on the number and types of the operands. It is easiest to understand overloaded operators as multiply defined procedures, from which the compiler chooses the one with the appropriate number and type of parameters.

Each operator has an assigned **precedence**, which determines the way the expression is grouped in the absence of parentheses. In Figure 1.2, lines 14–15, the meaning would probably be different without the parentheses, because multiplication is usually given a higher precedence than addition.

Operator	Left type	Right type	Result type	Comments
+ - *	integer	integer	integer	
+ - * /	real	real	real	
/	integer	integer	real	or integer
div mod	integer	integer	integer	
-	numeric	none	same	
**	integer	integer	integer	exponentiation
**	numeric	real	real	exponentiation
=	any	same	Boolean	
< > >= <=	numeric	same	Boolean	
+	string	string	string	concatenation
~	string	pattern	Boolean	string match
and	Boolean	Boolean	Boolean	
or	Boolean	Boolean	Boolean	
not	Boolean	none	Boolean	
^	pointer	none	component	
&	any	none	pointer	

Expressions evaluate to **R-values**. Variables and components of variables of structured types also have an **L-value**, that is, an address where their R-value is stored. The assignment statement (lines 11–17 in Figure 1.2) requires an L-value on the left-hand side (*L* stands for "left") and an R-value on the right-hand side (*R* stands for "right"). In Figure 1.2, lines 11 and 12 show a variable used for its L-value; the next lines show components used for their L-values.

The types of the left-hand side and the right-hand side must be **assignment-compatible**. If they are the same type, they are compatible. (What it means to have the same type is discussed in Chapter 3.) If they are of different types, the language may allow the value of the right-hand side to be implicitly converted to the type of the left-hand side. Implicit type conversions are called **coercions**. For example, Pascal will coerce integers to reals, but not the reverse. Coercions are error-prone, because the target type may not be able to represent all the values of the source type. For example, many computers can store some large numbers precisely as integers but only imprecisely as reals.

Converting types, either explicitly (**casting**) or implicitly (**coercing**) can sometimes change the data format. However, it is sometimes necessary to treat an expression of one type as if it were of another type without any data-format conversion. For example, a message might look like an array of characters to one procedure, whereas another procedure must understand it as a record with header and data fields. Wisconsin Modula introduced a nonconverting casting operator **qua** for this pur-

pose. In C, which lacks such an operator, the programmer who wishes a
nonconverting cast must cast a pointer to the first type into a pointer to
the second type; pointers have the same representation no matter what
they point to (in most C implementations). The following code shows
both methods.

Figure 1.3

```
type                                                      1
    FirstType = ... ;                                     2
    SecondType = ... ;                                    3
    SecondTypePtr = pointer to SecondType;                4
variable                                                  5
    F : FirstType;                                        6
    S : SecondType;                                       7
begin                                                     8
    ...                                                   9
    S := F qua SecondType; -- Wisconsin Modula            10
    S := (SecondTypePtr(&F))^; -- C                       11
end;                                                      12
```

Line 10 shows how F can be cast without conversion into the second type
in Wisconsin Modula. Line 11 shows the same thing for C, where I use
the type name SecondTypePtr as an explicit conversion routine. The
referencing operator & produces a pointer to F. In both cases, if the two
types disagree on length of representation, chaos may ensue, because
the number of bytes copied by the assignment is the appropriate number
for SecondType.

The Boolean operators **and** and **or** may have **short-circuit** semantics; that is, the second operand is only evaluated if the first operand
evaluates to true (for **and**) or false (for **or**). This evaluation strategy is
an example of **lazy evaluation**, discussed in Chapter 4. Short-circuit
operators allow the programmer to combine tests, the second of which
only makes sense if the first succeeds. For example, I may want to first
test if a pointer is nil, and only if it is not, to test the value it points to.

Conditional expressions are built with an **if** construct. To make
sure that a conditional expression always has a value, each **if** must be
matched by both a **then** and an **else**. The expressions in the **then** and
else parts must have the same type. Here is an example:

Figure 1.4

```
write(if a > 0 then a else -a);
```

3.2 Control Constructs

Execution of imperative programming languages proceeds one **statement** at a time. Statements can be **simple** or **compound**. Simple statements include the assignment statement, procedure invocation, and **goto**. Compound statements enclose other statements; they include conditional and iterative statements, such as **if**, **case**, **while**, and **for**. Programming languages need some syntax for delimiting enclosed statements in a compound statement. Some languages, like Modula, provide closing syntax for each compound statement:

Figure 1.5
```
while First^ < 10 do                                            1
    First^ := 2 * First^;                                      2
    Second[0].Fourth := 1 + Second[0].Fourth;                 3
end;                                                            4
```

The **end** on line 4 closes the **while** on line 1. Other languages, like Pascal, only allow a single statement to be included, but it may be a **block statement** that encloses multiple statements surrounded by **begin** and **end**.

Syntax for the **if** statement can be confusing if there is no trailing **end** syntax. If an **if** statement encloses another **if** statement in its **then** clause, the **else** that follows might refer to either **if**. This problem is called the "dangling-**else**" problem. In the following example, the **else** in line 4 could match either the one in line 1 or line 2. Pascal specifies that the closer **if** (line 2) is used.

Figure 1.6
```
if IntVar < 10 then                                            1
if IntVar < 20 then                                           2
    IntVar := 0                                               3
else                                                           4
    IntVar := 1;                                              5
```

On the other hand, if **if** statements require a closing **end**, the problem cannot arise:

Figure 1.7
```
if IntVar < 10 then                                            1
    if IntVar < 20 then                                       2
        IntVar := 0;                                          3
    end                                                        4
else                                                           5
    IntVar := 1;                                              6
end;                                                           7
```

Here, the **else** in line 5 unambiguously matches the **if** in line 1. Closing syntax is ugly when **if** statements are deeply nested in the **else** clause:

Figure 1.8

```
if IntVar < 10 then                                          1
    IntVar := 0                                              2
else                                                         3
    if IntVar < 20 then                                      4
        IntVar := 1                                          5
    else                                                     6
        if IntVar < 30 then                                  7
            IntVar := 2                                      8
        else                                                 9
            IntVar := 3;                                     10
        end;                                                 11
    end;                                                     12
end;                                                         13
```

The **elsif** clause clarifies matters:

Figure 1.9

```
if IntVar < 10 then                                          1
    IntVar := 0                                              2
elsif IntVar < 20 then                                       3
    IntVar := 1                                              4
elsif IntVar < 30 then                                       5
    IntVar := 2                                              6
else                                                         7
    IntVar := 3;                                             8
end;                                                         9
```

All the examples in this book use a closing **end** for compound statements. You don't have to worry about language-specific syntax issues when you are trying to concentrate on semantics.

Some languages, like Russell and CSP, allow conditionals to have any number of branches, each with its own Boolean condition, called a **guard**. The guards may be evaluated in any order, and execution chooses any branch whose guard evaluates to true. These conditionals are called **nondeterministic**, since running the program a second time with the same input may result in a different branch being selected. In such languages, **else** means "when all the guards are false."

A wide range of iterative statements (loops) is available. An iterative statement must indicate under what condition the iteration is to terminate and when that condition is tested. The **while** loop tests an arbitrary Boolean expression before each iteration.

When **goto** statements became unpopular because they lead to unreadable and unmaintainable programs, languages tried to avoid all control jumps. But loops often need to exit from the middle or to abandon the current iteration and start the next one. The **break** and **next** statements were invented to provide these facilities without reintroducing unconstrained control jumps. An example of exiting the loop from the middle is the "*n*-and-a-half-times loop":

Figure 1.10

```
loop                                            1
      read(input);                              2
      if input = 0 then break end;              3
      if comment(input) then next end;          4
      process(input);                           5
end;                                            6
```

The **break** in line 3 terminates the loop when a sentinel indicating the end of input is read. The **next** in line 4 abandons the current iteration if the input is not to be processed. A similar statement found in Perl is **redo**, which restarts the current iteration without updating any loop indices or checking termination conditions. The **break**, **next**, and **redo** statements can also take an integer or a loop label to specify the number of levels of loop they are to terminate or iterate. In this case, they are called **multilevel** statements.

Many loops require control variables to be initialized before the first iteration and updated after each iteration. Some languages (like C) provide syntax that includes these steps explicitly, which makes the loops more readable and less error-prone. However, such syntax blurs the distinction between definite (**for**) and indefinite (**while**) iteration:

Figure 1.11

```
for a := 1; Ptr := Start -- initialization       1
while Ptr ≠ nil -- termination condition          2
updating a := a+1; Ptr := Ptr^.Next; -- after each iter.   3
do                                                4
      ... -- loop body                            5
end;                                              6
```

Russell and CSP generalize the nondeterministic **if** statement into a nondeterministic **while** loop with multiple branches. So long as any guard is true, the loop is executed, and any branch whose guard is true is arbitrarily selected and executed. The loop terminates when all guards are false. For example, the algorithm to compute the greatest common divisor of two integers a and b can be written as follows:

Figure 1.12

```
while                                                    1
    when a < b => b := b - a;                            2
    when b < a => a := a - b;                            3
end;                                                     4
```

Each guard starts with the reserved word **when** and ends with the symbol => . The loop terminates when a = b.

The **case** statement is used to select one of a set of options on the basis of the value of some expression.[4] Most languages require that the selection be based on a criterion known at compile time (that is, the case labels must be constant or constant ranges); this restriction allows compilers to generate efficient code. However, conditions that can only be evaluated at runtime also make sense, as in the following example:

Figure 1.13

```
case a of                                                1
    when 0 => Something(1); -- static unique guard       2
    when 1..10 => Something(2); -- static guard          3
    when b+12 => Something(3); -- dynamic unique guard   4
    when b+13..b+20 => Something(4); -- dynamic guard    5
    otherwise Something(5); -- guard of last resort      6
end;                                                     7
```

Each guard tests the value of a. Lines 2 and 4 test this value for equality with 0 and b+12; lines 3 and 5 test it for membership in a range. If the guards (the selectors for the branches) overlap, the **case** statement is erroneous; this situation can be detected at compile time for static guards and at runtime for dynamic guards. Most languages consider it to be a runtime error if none of the branches is selected and there is no **otherwise** clause.

3.3 Procedures and Parameter Passing

Figure 1.14 will be discussed in detail in this section. For clarity, I have chosen a syntax that names each formal parameter at the point of invocation; Ada and Modula-3 have a similar syntax.

---

[4] C. A. R. Hoare, who invented the **case** statement, says, "This was my first programming language invention, of which I am still most proud." [Hoare 73]

Figure 1.14

```
procedure TryAll(                                            1
    ValueInt : value integer;                                2
    ReferenceInt : reference integer;                        3
    ResultInt : result integer;                              4
    ReadOnlyInt : readonly integer := 10;                    5
    NameInt : name integer;                                  6
    MacroInt : macro integer) : integer;                     7
variable                                                     8
    LocalInt : integer;                                      9
begin                                                        10
    LocalInt := 10; -- affects only TryAll's LocalInt        11
    ValueInt := 1 + ValueInt; -- formal becomes 16           12
    ReferenceInt := 1 + ValueInt;                            13
        -- actual and formal become 17                       14
    ResultInt := 1 + ReferenceInt + ReadOnlyInt + NameInt;   15
        -- 47                                                16
    return 2*MacroInt; -- 40                                 17
end; -- TryAll                                               18

variable                                                     19
    LocalInt : integer;                                      20
    A, B : integer;                                          21

begin -- main program                                        22
    LocalInt := 3;                                           23
    B := TryAll(                                             24
        ValueInt : 15,                                       25
        ReferenceInt : LocalInt,                             26
        ResultInt : A, -- becomes 47                         27
        ReadOnlyInt  : 12,                                   28
        NameInt : LocalInt,                                  29
        MacroInt : 2*LocalInt)                               30
    );                                                       31
    -- Final values: LocalInt = 17, A = 47, B = 40           32
end; -- main program                                         33
```

Procedures (often called **functions** if they return values) are usually declared with a header, local declarations, and a body. The **header** (lines 1–7) indicates the procedure name and the parameters, if any, along with their types and modes. If the procedure is to return a value, the type of the value is also declared. If not, the predeclared type void is used in some languages to indicate that no value at all is returned. The declarations (lines 8 and 9) introduce local meanings for identifiers. Together, the parameters and the local identifiers constitute the **local referencing environment** of the procedure. Identifiers appearing within the procedure are interpreted, if possible, with respect to the local referencing environment. Otherwise, they are interpreted with respect to parts of the program outside the procedure. The nonlocal referencing environment is more complicated, so I will discuss it later.

The **body** of the procedure (lines 10–18) is composed of the statements that are to be executed when the procedure is invoked. The header need not be adjacent to the declarations and body; they may be separated for the purpose of modularization (discussed in Chapter 3). Most programming languages allow **recursion**; that is, procedures may invoke themselves, either directly or indirectly.

Parameters are inputs and outputs to procedures. The identifiers associated with parameters in the header are called **formal parameters**; the expressions passed into those parameters at the point of invocation (lines 24–31) are the **actual parameters**. There are many parameter-passing **modes**, each with different semantics specifying how formal parameters are bound to actual parameters.

- **Value.** The value of the actual parameter is copied into the formal parameter at invocation. In the example, the assignment in line 12 modifies the formal, but not the actual parameter; the expression in line 13 uses the modified value in the formal. Value mode is the most common parameter-passing mode. Some languages, like C, provide only this mode.

- **Result.** The value of the formal parameter is copied into the actual parameter (which must have an L-value) at procedure return. In the example, the assignment in line 15 gives the formal a value, which is copied into the actual parameter A (line 27) when the procedure TryAll returns. It is usually invalid to provide actual parameters with the same L-value to two different result parameters, because the order of copying is undefined. However, this error cannot always be caught by the compiler, because it cannot always tell with certainty that two identifiers will have different L-values at runtime.

- **Value result.** The parameter is treated as in value mode during invocation and as in result mode during return.

- **Reference.** The L-value of the formal parameter is set to the L-value of the actual parameter. In other words, the address of the formal parameter is the same as the address of the actual parameter. Any assignment to the formal parameter immediately affects the actual parameter. In the example, the assignment in line 13 modifies both the formal parameter (ReferenceInt) and the actual parameter (LocalInt of the main program), because they have the same L-value. Reference mode can be emulated by value mode if the language has a referencing operator (I use &), which produces a pointer to an expression with an L-value, and a dereferencing operator (I use ^), which takes a pointer and produces the value pointed to. The program passes the pointer in value mode and dereferences the formal parameter every time it is used. FORTRAN only has reference mode; expressions, which have no L-value, are evaluated and placed in temporary locations in order to acquire an L-value for the duration of the procedure.[5] Large arrays are usually passed in reference mode instead of value mode to avoid the copying otherwise required.

- **Readonly.** Either value or reference mode is actually used, but the compiler ensures that the formal parameter is never used on the left-hand side of an assignment. The compiler typically uses value mode for small values (such as primitive types) and reference mode for larger values. In the example, it would be invalid for `ReadOnly-Int` to be used on the left-hand side of the assignment on line 15.

The following modes have been proposed and used in the past, but are no longer in favor due to their confusing semantics and difficult implementation.

- **Name.** Every use of the formal parameter causes the actual parameter to be freshly evaluated in the referencing environment of the invocation point. If the formal parameter's L-value is needed (for example, the parameter appears on the left-hand side of an assignment), the actual parameter's L-value must be freshly evaluated. If the formal parameter's R-value is needed, the actual parameter's R-value must be freshly evaluated. This mode is more complex than reference mode, because the actual parameter may be an expression, and the procedure may modify one of the variables that make up that expression. Such a modification affects the value of the formal parameter. In the example, `NameInt` in line 15 evaluates to `LocalInt` of the main program, which was modified by the assignment in line 13. Name mode was invented in Algol 60, caused a certain amount of consternation among compiler writers, who had to invent an implementation, and proved to be not very useful and fairly error-prone.[6] Modern languages don't usually provide name mode.

- **Macro.** Every use of the formal parameter causes the text of the actual parameter to be freshly evaluated in the referencing environment of the use point. That is, if the actual parameter is a variable, `IntVar`, and the procedure declares a new variable with the same name, then reference to the formal parameter is like reference to the new, not the old, `IntVar`. In the example, `MacroInt` in line 17 expands to `2*LocalInt`, the actual parameter (line 30), but `LocalInt` is

---

[5] Some implementations of FORTRAN store all literals in a data region at runtime. A literal actual parameter is at risk of being modified by the procedure, after which the literal will have a new value!

[6] J. Jensen invented a clever use for name-mode parameters that is called "Jensen's device", but its cleverness is outweighed by its lack of clarity.

interpreted as referring to the variable belonging to `TryAll`, not to the main program. Macro mode is extremely error-prone, not very useful, and almost never provided. It opens the possibility of run-time parsing, because the actual parameter could be an expression fragment, such as `+ LocalInt`, which would need to be understood in the syntactic context of each use of the formal parameter.

Procedures themselves may be passed as parameters. In this case, we generally don't talk about the parameter-passing mode.[7] The formal parameter declaration may indicate the number and types of the parameters to the passed procedure. The formal parameter may be used in any way that a procedure can be used: it can be invoked or passed again as an actual parameter.

Goto labels may also be passed as parameters. The formal parameter may then be the target of a **goto** or may be passed again as an actual parameter. If it is the target of a **goto**, the referencing environment of the original invoker is restored, and intervening referencing environments are closed. (I will discuss referencing environments shortly.) Implementing these semantics correctly is complex, and few languages with block structure allow labels to be passed as parameters.

Sometimes the programmer cannot predict how many parameters will be provided. This situation arises particularly for input and output routines. If there may be an arbitrary number of actual parameters of the same type, they may be packaged into an array (perhaps an anonymous dynamic-sized array built by a constructor). The formal parameter can be queried to discover how many elements were passed.

Ada, C++, and Common LISP provide default values, so that formal parameters that have no matching actuals can still have values; line 5 in Figure 1.14 provides a default value of 10 for parameter `ReadOnlyInt` in case it is not provided by the call. A call can just omit an actual parameter to indicate that it is missing. Only trailing parameters (that is, the parameters at the end of the parameter list) may be omitted, so that the compiler can determine which ones are missing. Other syntax is possible. For example, the procedure call could still delimit missing parameters with commas (such as `myProcedure(paramA,,paramC)`). Alternatively, the call may explicitly associate formal and actual parameters in any order. Lines 24–31 in Figure 1.14 use this **keyword** (as opposed to **positional**) parameter-passing syntax for specifying actuals. Keyword parameters make it easy to omit an actual parameter.

---

[7] You might say that the procedure is passed by value, but in fact, no copy is made. Instead, a closure is passed; this concept is elaborated below and in Chapter 3.

Languages differ in the syntax they use to return a value to the caller. Line 17 of Figure 1.14 shows **explicit return**, in which the **return** statement includes the value. The compiler can check that all returns specify a value of the appropriate type and that the procedure does not terminate without returning a value. Often the programmer introduces a local variable to construct and manipulate the value before returning it; the actual return results in an extra copy step. **Implicit return** uses the procedure identifier as a write-only pseudovariable that is automatically returned when the procedure finishes. The compiler cannot check that all execution paths set this variable, and the programmer must be careful not to use the procedure identifier as an ordinary variable, because such use may be misunderstood as a recursive procedure invocation. If the procedure needs to manipulate the value before it is finalized, programmers usually introduce a local variable and copy it into the write-only variable. Finally, **identifier return** introduces a new identifier or identifiers in the procedure header to represent the returned values, as in the following example:

Figure 1.15

```
procedure Double(                                              1
     ValueInt : value integer) : integer RetVal;              2
begin                                                          3
     RetVal := ValueInt * 2;                                   4
     if RetVal < 0 then RetVal := 0; end;                      5
end; -- Double                                                 6
```

Line 2 introduces the new identifier RetVal, and line 4 assigns it a value. Line 5 treats it as an ordinary integer variable. Neither the program nor the compiled code needs to copy the values from the new identifiers into return-value cells.

The new-identifier method makes it easy to describe procedures that return multiple values. Such procedures are invoked in a context of multiple assignment, as in Figure 1.16. Here, procedure TwoVals returns two results, which are assigned simultaneously to two variables in the multiple assignment of line 8.

Figure 1.16

```
procedure TwoVals : integer Answer1, Answer2;                 1
begin                                                         2
     Answer1 := 3;                                            3
     Answer2 := 9;                                            4
end;                                                          5

variable a, b : integer;                                     6
```

```
begin                                                      7
    a, b := TwoVals;                                       8
end;                                                       9
```

3.4 Block Structure

I will describe classic Algol block structure here; it has been adopted, with modification, in many programming languages. A program is divided into nested **blocks**, each of which introduces a new name scope. A **name scope** is a region of program in which particular declarations of identifiers are in effect. A declaration **maps** an identifier to a meaning. We also say that it **binds** the meaning to the identifier. The meanings can be variables, types, constants, labels, procedures, or other concepts discussed elsewhere in the book, such as modules (Chapter 3), classes (Chapter 5), and monitors (Chapter 7). Traditionally, each nested name scope inherits all bindings from the surrounding scope, except that if the same identifier is redefined in the nested scope, the new declaration **overrides** the old declaration for the duration of the nested scope. Some languages, such as Ada and C++, allow declared procedures to be overloaded; that is, the same name is bound to multiple declarations at the same time, and the compiler chooses which is meant by the number and types of the parameters.

The new declarations can be defined to take effect from the beginning of the block (so that an earlier declaration, say of a variable, can refer to a later declaration, perhaps of a type). More commonly, they take effect (are **elaborated**) from the point in the block where the declaration appears. In the following example, I could define B in line 8 to be either real or integer, depending on whether the outer declaration of T is hidden yet by the declaration in line 10. Usually, languages either disallow such references or let the new declaration take effect only after the point at which it appears. This decision makes one-pass compilers easier to write.

Figure 1.17

```
type -- introduces outer block                            1
    T : real;                                             2
variable -- continues outer block                         3
    A : integer;                                          4
```

```
begin -- statements start                                         5
    A := 4;                                                       6
    variable -- introduces nested block                           7
        B : T; -- real or integer?                                8
    type                                                          9
        T : integer; -- overrides outer declaration of T         10
    begin                                                        11
        B := 3; -- coercion needed?                              12
    end -- nested block ends                                     13
end -- block ends                                                14
```

I use **type**, **variable**, or **constant** to introduce a new block, which in-cludes a new name scope (lines 1 and 7). After declarations introduce new identifiers (including multiple instances of **type**, **variable**, or **con-stant**), the statements in the name scope are delimited by **begin** and **end**.

Variables may be initialized to the value of some expression at the same time they are declared. Pascal restricts initialization expressions to literals and constants. Some languages allow arbitrary initialization expressions to be evaluated at elaboration time; these expressions may even invoke procedures.

Entering a new block just to introduce temporary declarations can be helpful in structuring programs. More commonly, though, blocks are found as the bodies of procedures. The identifiers introduced in the new block are all the formal parameters and any types, constants, variables, labels, and procedures defined within the procedure. A language is con-sidered **block-structured** if procedures introducing name scopes can nest. By this criterion, C is not block-structured, but Pascal is.

An identifier is considered **local** to a name scope if it is introduced in that name scope. Identifiers inherited from surrounding scopes are called **nonlocal**. An identifier is **global** if it belongs to the outermost block of the program. In FORTRAN, there are no global identifiers, and name scopes do not nest. These restrictions help make FORTRAN effi-cient at runtime.

Although the *declaration* of an identifier may be clear from its defin-ing name scope, the *instance* of the identifier may not be. Every invoca-tion of a procedure introduces not only a new name scope, but also new instances of variables themselves.[8] A procedure may have many simul-taneous instances, because it may be invoked recursively. For local identifiers and global identifiers, it is always clear which instance to

---

[8] Although this discussion centers on variables, it also applies to labels and types, because types may depend on runtime values. For example, an array type may have lim-its that are taken from runtime values.

use. For nonlocal identifiers, the **nonlocal referencing environment**
refers to the set of identifier bindings dynamically in force during program execution. This set changes at every procedure invocation and return, as well as when the program enters and exits blocks, as illustrated
in the following example.

Figure 1.18

```
procedure ProcA(value AParam : integer);                      1
type AType : array 1..AParam of integer;                      2
variable AVar1, AVar2 : integer;                              3
    procedure ProcB(value BParam : integer);                  4
    variable BVar1 : AType;                                   5
    begin -- ProcB                                            6
        ... -- some statements                                7
    end; -- ProcB                                             8
begin -- ProcA                                                9
    ... -- some statements                                   10
end; -- ProcA                                                11
```

When ProcA is invoked, the new instance of ProcA elaborates a new set
of formal parameters (AParam), types (AType), variables (AVar1 and
AVar2), and procedures (ProcB), which are inherited by nested procedure
ProcB. When ProcB is invoked, its new instance elaborates a new formal
parameter (BParam) and variable (BVar1), the latter of a type inherited
from ProcA. ProcB may be invoked many times by ProcA and ProcB;
each time, its new instance inherits identifiers from the ProcA instance
that elaborates the particular ProcB that is invoked.

The situation becomes surprisingly complex when procedures (and
labels) are passed as parameters. They carry with them their nonlocal
referencing environment, so that when they are invoked, they may access nonlocal variables that are otherwise inaccessible in the program.
A procedure in combination with its nonlocal referencing environment is
called a **closure**.

Because this idea is unfamiliar to students who mainly use C (which
has no nested procedures, and therefore no nonlocal referencing environments), I will present several examples.

Figure 1.19

```
procedure A(procedure X());                                   1
variable Z : integer;                                         2
begin -- A                                                    3
    X();                                                      4
end; -- A                                                     5
```

```
procedure B(S : integer);                                    6
variable Z : integer;                                        7
    procedure C();                                           8
    begin -- C                                               9
        write(Z); -- from lexical parent B                  10
    end; -- C                                               11
begin -- B                                                  12
    Z := S;                                                 13
    C();                                                    14
    A(C);                                                   15
end; -- B                                                   16

B(3);                                                       17
```

When B is called in line 17, it sets its local variable Z (line 7) to 3, the value of formal parameter S. It then calls nested procedure C two times. The first time is a direct call (line 14), and the second is indirect through a helper procedure A, which just relays the call (lines 15 and 4). In both cases, B is still present, in the sense that its activation record is still on the central stack. Procedure C needs B's activation record, because C refers to B's local variable Z, which is only to be found in B's activation record. In fact, C must access B's copy of Z during the second call, even though the intermediate procedure A also has declared a local variable Z. In other words, C's nonlocal referencing environment is B, which elaborated C. When C is passed as an actual parameter to A in line 15, a closure must be passed, so that when A invokes its formal parameter X (which is actually C), the procedure it invokes can properly access its nonlocal variables.

Figure 1.20 shows the stack of invocations at the point C is invoked via A. The first row shows that the main program has declarations for A and B. The second row shows that B has been invoked, and that it has local identifiers S (the formal parameter, with actual value 3), Z (a locally declared integer), and C (a locally declared procedure). The third row shows that A has been invoked (from line 15 of the program). It has a formal parameter X (bound to the actual parameter C) and a local integer variable Z. The last row shows that A has called its formal parameter, which we know is procedure C from row 2. The arrows to the left of the box indicate the nonlocal referencing environment of each invocation. Rows 2 and 3 (B and A) both use the main program as their nonlocal referencing environment. Row 4, however, shows that C uses B as its nonlocal referencing environment. This is because C was elaborated first in B, as the connecting lines indicate. That is why when C finally refers to Z in line 10, it accesses the Z of the second row, the one belonging to B.

Figure 1.20 Referencing environments

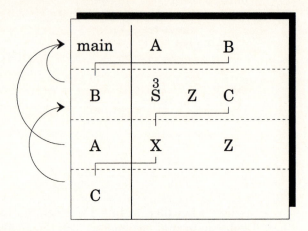

The following example shows a more complicated situation.

Figure 1.21

```
procedure A(                                         1
    readonly AParam : integer;                       2
    AProc : procedure()                              3
);                                                   4
    procedure B();                                   5
    begin -- B                                       6
        write(AParam); -- writes 2                   7
    end; -- B                                        8
begin -- A                                           9
    case AParam of                                   10
        when 2 => A(1, B);                           11
        when 1 => A(0, AProc);                       12
        when 0 => AProc();                           13
    end; -- case                                     14
end; -- A                                            15

procedure Dummy(); begin end;                        16
    -- never called; same type as B                  17

begin -- main program                                18
    A(2, Dummy);                                     19
end;                                                 20
```

The referencing environments of each instance of each procedure are shown in Figure 1.22.

Figure 1.22 Referencing
environments

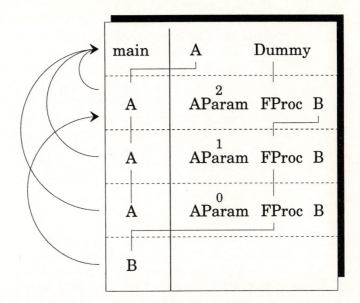

Each row again shows an invocation of some procedure, starting with
main. The entries on the row indicate the local referencing environment
elaborated by that invocation. The arrows on the left indicate the nonlocal referencing environments. Here, main introduces A and Dummy. The
instance of A that main invokes is the one it elaborated, as shown by the
connecting line. Procedure A elaborates its parameters, AParam and
AProc, and its nested procedure, B. When A invokes itself recursively, it
uses the meaning of A in its nonlocal referencing environment, that is,
the first row. It passes the closure of its own elaborated B as an actual
parameter. This closure of B includes the nonlocal referencing environment of the first A, so when it is finally invoked, after being passed once
more as a parameter to the third instance of A, it still owns the first A as
its nonlocal referencing environment. When B prints AParam, therefore,
it prints 2.

Binding the nonlocal referencing environment of a procedure at the
time it is elaborated is called **deep binding**. Under deep binding, when
a procedure is passed as a parameter, its closure is actually passed. The
opposite, **shallow binding**, is to bind the nonlocal referencing environment of a procedure at the time it is invoked. Shallow binding does not
pass closures. Descendents of Algol use deep binding; original LISP
used shallow binding, although it provided a way for the programmer to
explicitly build a closure.

Another difference between the Algol family and original LISP is the
scope rules they follow to determine which syntactic entity is bound to
each identifier. Languages in the Algol family are statically scoped,

whereas original LISP was dynamically scoped.[9] Under **static scope rules**, the compiler can determine the declaration (although not necessarily the instance, as you have seen) associated with each identifier. The strict compile-time nesting of name scopes in Algol makes it a statically scoped language. In contrast, **dynamic scope rules** make identifiers accessible in a procedure if they were accessible at the point of invocation; therefore, different invocations can lead to different sets of accessible identifiers. The compiler cannot tell which identifiers are accessible to any procedure. The trend in programming language design has been away from dynamic scope rules, because they are often confusing to the programmer, who cannot tell at a glance which declaration is associated with each use of a variable. However, some recent languages, such as Tcl, use dynamic scope rules.

3.5 Runtime Store Organization

Programmers usually don't care how runtime store is organized. They expect the compiler or interpreter to arrange the program and data for efficient execution. They are only interested if some language constructs are likely to use large amounts of space or time. However, language designers are definitely interested in runtime store organization because it affects the efficient implementation of the language.

Runtime store is typically divided into several regions. The first region holds the compiled program instructions, which I will just call **code**. This region contains each procedure in the program as well as runtime libraries. Under some operating systems, the libraries may be shared among processes and may be brought into store dynamically when they are first referenced.

A second region holds global variables. Because the compiler knows the identity, type, and size of these variables, it can allocate precise amounts of store and can generate code that accesses global variables very efficiently.

A third region is the **central stack**. It holds an activation record for each active procedure instance. Because procedures are invoked and return in last-in, first-out order, a stack is appropriate. Each **activation record** stores the return address, a pointer to the activation record of its invoker (forming the **dynamic chain**), a pointer to the activation record of its nonlocal referencing environment (forming the **static chain**), its parameters, its local variables, and temporary locations needed during expression evaluation. It is possible to represent the

---

[9] More recent LISP languages, such as Common LISP and Scheme, are statically scoped.

static chain in various ways; for simplicity, I will just assume that it is a linked list of activation records. Dynamic-sized arrays are typically represented by a fixed-size type descriptor (the size depends only on the number of dimensions of the array, which is known by the compiler) and a pointer to the value, which is placed in the activation record after all static-sized local variables.

The central stack allows the compiler to generate efficient access code for the variables stored there in a statically scoped language. Let me abbreviate the phrase "accessed at a statically known offset" by the simpler but less precise "found." Static-sized local variables are found in the current activation record. Nonlocal variables are found in an activation record a certain distance from the front of the static chain; the compiler knows how many steps to take in that chain. Pointers to the values of dynamic-sized local variables are found in the current activation record; the values are interpreted according to type descriptors found either in the current record (if the type is declared locally) or in an activation record deeper on the static chain (for a nonlocal type).

The fourth region of runtime store, called the **heap**, is used for dynamic allocation of values accessed through pointers.[10] These values do not follow a stack discipline. This region of store expands as needed, getting increments from the operating system when necessary. To avoid ever-increasing store requirements for long-running programs, values are deallocated when they are no longer needed. The space can later be reallocated to new values. Deallocation can be triggered by explicit program requests (such as Pascal's `dispose` procedure) or by automatic methods such as reference counts and garbage collection. Reference counts indicate how many pointers are referencing each value. Each assignment and parameter binding modifies these counts, and each exit from a name scope reduces the counts for those variables that are disappearing. When a count is reduced to 0, the value may be deallocated and its space used for something else. Unfortunately, circular lists are never deallocated, even when they are no longer accessible. Garbage collection takes place when the store allocator notices that not much room is left. All accessible structures are recursively traversed and marked, and then all unmarked values are deallocated. The user often notices a distinct pause during garbage collection. There are incremental and concurrent garbage collection algorithms that reduce this interruption.

---

[10] Don't confuse the heap with the treelike data structure of the same name.

4 ◆ FINAL COMMENTS

This chapter has attempted to introduce the study of programming languages by placing it in the context of software tools in general. The background material on programming languages is, of necessity, very concise. Its aim is to lay the foundation for the concepts developed in the rest of this book.

The language concepts introduced here are in some sense the classical Algol-like structures. They are developed in various directions in the following chapters, each of which concentrates first on one programming language and then shows ideas from a few others to flesh out the breadth of the topic. Where appropriate, they end with a more mathematical treatment of the subject. Chapter 2 shows nonclassical control structures. Chapter 3 investigates the concept of data type. It presents a detailed discussion of ML, which shows how polymorphism can be incorporated in a statically typed language. Because ML is mostly a functional language, you may want to read Chapter 4 before the section on ML in Chapter 3.

The next chapters are devoted to nonclassical paradigms, that is, languages not descended from Algol. Chapter 4 discusses functional programming, concentrating on LISP. The concept of abstract data type is generalized in several ways in the next three chapters. Chapter 5 introduces object-oriented programming, concentrating on Smalltalk and C++. Chapter 6 discusses dataflow languages, concentrating on Val. Chapter 7 shows some of the wide range of development of languages for concurrent programming. A very different view of programming is presented in Chapter 8, which is is devoted to logic programming, concentrating on Prolog. Languages dealing with special-purpose data aggregates, such as strings, arrays, databases, and mathematical formulas, are discussed in Chapter 9. Finally, Chapter 10 shows several mathematical approaches to formalizing the syntax and semantics of programming languages; although it uses imperative languages as its model, such approaches have been used for the other language paradigms as well.

EXERCISES

Review Exercises

1.1 In what ways does C (or pick another language) fall short of the criteria in Section 2 for excellence?

1.2 How would you define the **mod** operator?

1.3 Show a code fragment in which short-circuit semantics for **or** yield a different result than complete-evaluation semantics.

1.4 Why do most languages with **case** statements prefer that the conditions have compile-time values?

1.5 Write a procedure that produces different results depending on whether its parameters are passed by value, reference, or name mode.

1.6 FORTRAN only passes parameters in reference mode. C only passes parameters in value mode. Pascal allows both modes. Show how you can get the effect of reference mode in C and how you can get the effect of value mode in FORTRAN by appropriate programming techniques. In particular, show in both FORTRAN and C how to get the effect of the following code.

Figure 1.23

```
variable X, Y : integer;                                        1

procedure Accept                                                2
    (A : reference integer; B: value integer);                  3
begin                                                           4
    A := B;                                                     5
    B := B+1;                                                   6
end; -- Accept                                                  7

X := 1;                                                         8
Y := 2;                                                         9
Accept(X, Y);                                                  10
-- at this point, X should be 2, and Y should be 2            11
```

1.7 If a language does not allow recursion (FORTRAN II, for example, did not), is there any need for a central stack?

1.8 C does not allow a procedure to be declared inside another procedure, but Pascal does allow nested procedure declarations. What effect does this choice have on runtime storage organization?

Challenge Exercises

1.9   Why are array slices usually allowed only in the last dimension?

1.10 Write a program that prints the index of the first all-zero row of an
$n \times n$ integer matrix M [Rubin 88]. The program should access each
element of the matrix at most once and should not access rows beyond the first all-zero row and columns within a row beyond the
first non-zero element. It should have no variables except the matrix M and two loop indices Row and Column. The program may not
use **goto**, but it may use multilevel **break** and **next**.

1.11 What is the meaning of a **goto** from a procedure when the target is
outside the procedure?

1.12 Why do **goto** labels passed as parameters require closures?

1.13 Rewrite Figure 1.21 (page 24) so that procedure A takes a label instead of a procedure. The rewritten example should behave the
same as Figure 1.21.

1.14 What rules would you make if you wanted to allow programmers to
mix positional and keyword actual parameters?

1.15 The C language allows new name scopes to be introduced. However, C is not generally considered a block-structured language.
Why not?

1.16 The text claims that the compiler knows the size of all global variables. Is this claim true for global dynamic-sized arrays?

Chapter 2

Control Structures

Assembler language only provides **goto** and its conditional variants. Early high-level languages such as FORTRAN relied heavily on **goto**, three-way arithmetic branches, and many-way indexed branches. Algol introduced control structures that began to make **goto** obsolete. Under the banner of "structured programming," computer scientists such as C. A. R. Hoare, Edsger W. Dijkstra, Donald E. Knuth, and Ole-Johan Dahl showed how programs could be written more clearly and elegantly with **while** and **for** loops, **case** statements, and loops with internal exits [Knuth 71; Dahl 72]. One of the tenets of structured programming is that procedures should be used heavily to modularize effort. In this chapter we will explore control structures that are a little out of the ordinary.

1 ◆ EXCEPTION HANDLING

If a procedure discovers that an erroneous situation (such as bad input) has arisen, it needs to report that fact to its caller. One way to program this behavior is to have each procedure provide an error return and to check for that return on each invocation. SNOBOL allows an explicit failure **goto** and success **goto** on each statement, which makes this sort of programming convenient. However, using a **goto** to deal with errors does not lead to clear programs, and checking each procedure invocation for error returns makes for verbose programs.

A control construct for dealing with error conditions was first proposed by Goodenough [Goodenough 75] and has found its way into languages like Ada, Mesa, CLU, ML, Eiffel, and Modula-3. I will use a syntax like Ada's for describing this control structure.

When a procedure needs to indicate failure, it **raises** an **exception**. This action causes control to transfer along a well-defined path in the program to where the exception is **handled**. To embed this concept in programming languages, identifiers can be declared to be of type **exception**. Each such identifier represents a distinct exception; the programmer usually names exception identifiers to indicate when they are to be raised, such as StackOverflow. Some built-in operations may raise exceptions on some arguments. For example, division by zero raises the predefined exception DivByZero. Converting an integer to a float in such a way that precision is lost might raise the exception PrecisionLoss. Trying to extract the head of an empty list might raise the exception ListEmpty.

A raised exception causes control to exit from the current expression, statement, and procedure, exiting outward until either the entire program is exited or control reaches a place where the program is explicitly prepared to handle the raised exception. For example:

Figure 2.1

```
variable                                        1
    A, B : integer;                             2
begin                                           3
    B := 0;                                     4
    A := (4 / B) + 13;                          5
    write(A);                                   6
handle                                          7
    when DivByZero => A := 0;                   8
    when PrecisionLoss => B := 2;               9
end;                                            10
```

When control reaches line 5, a divide error occurs, raising DivByZero. Control exits from the expression (no addition of 13 occurs) and from the body of the block (line 6 is not executed). It would exit entirely from the block, but this block has a handler (lines 7–9) that includes this particular exception (line 8). Control therefore continues on line 8, setting A to 0. After that, the block exits (and A disappears, but let's ignore that.) If an exception had been raised that this block does not handle (even if it handles other exceptions), control would have continued to exit outward. If the raised exception causes the program to terminate, the runtime library might print a message indicating the exception name and a backtrace showing where the program was executing when the exception was raised.

It is also possible to associate an exception handler directly with an expression:

Figure 2.2

```
if ((A / B) handle when DivByZero => return 0) = 3      1
then ...                                                2
```

Here I have used **return** instead of **do** to indicate that the handler yields a value to be used in the larger expression.

Languages that provide for exception handling usually allow the programmer to define new exceptions and explicitly raise them.

Figure 2.3

```
variable                                                          1
    BadInput : exception;                                         2
    A : integer;                                                  3
begin                                                             4
    read(A);                                                      5
    if A < 0 then                                                 6
        raise BadInput                                            7
    end;                                                          8
    ...                                                           9
handle                                                           10
    when BadInput =>                                             11
        write("Negative numbers are invalid here.");            12
        raise BadInput;                                         13
end;                                                            14
```

BadInput is a programmer-defined exception declared in line 2, raised in line 7, and handled in lines 11–13. This example also shows that a handler can reraise the same exception (or raise a different one) in order to propagate the raised exception further.

Perhaps I want all divide errors to yield 0 for the entire program. It is tedious to place a handler on each expression; instead, a language might allow execution to resume from a handler.

Figure 2.4

```
variable                                                          1
    A, B : integer;                                               2
begin                                                             3
    B := 0;                                                       4
    A := (4 / B) + 13;                                            5
    write(A);                                                     6
handle                                                            7
    when DivByZero => resume 0;                                   8
end;                                                              9
```

In this example, line 6 will be executed and will print 13. The DivByZero exception is raised in the middle of an expression, so it makes sense to resume the expression with a given value.

Unfortunately, resuming computation can be ill-defined. It is not always clear where to resume computation: at the point at which **raise** occurred or at some intermediate point along the exit path from that point to where the exception is handled. For example,

Figure 2.5

```
A := (GetInput() handle when BadInput => resume 0);
```

Does **resume** 0 mean that GetInput should return 0, or does it mean that computation should continue inside GetInput (perhaps at a **raise** statement, where 0 makes no sense)?

Luckily, programmers can usually manage quite well without needing to resume computation. A statement that might fail can be surrounded by a handler in a loop. If the statement fails, the handler can print diagnostic information, and the loop can try again.

Exceptions introduce several scope problems. First, the name scope that handles a raised exception generally has no access to the name scope that raised it. Therefore, there is no way for the handler to manipulate variables local to the raising scope in order to compute alternative answers or even to generate error messages that convey exactly which values were erroneous. This problem is ameliorated in Modula-3, in which exceptions can take value-mode parameters. The actual parameters are provided by the **raise** statement, and the formal parameters are defined by the **handle** clause. Parameters can be used to indicate where in the program the exception was raised and what values led to the exceptional situation.

Second, programmer-defined exceptions may be visible in the raising scope but not in the handling scope. The problem arises for programmer-defined exceptions that exit the entire program (to a scope where only predefined exceptions exist) and for "don't-care" exception-handler patterns within the program, as in line 4 below:

Figure 2.6

```
begin                                                    1
    ...                                                  2
handle                                                   3
    when _ => ...                                        4
end;                                                     5
```

Such a handler might not be able to raise the exception further (unless the programming language provides a predefined exception identifier Self that holds the exception that was raised).

In some ways, **raise** statements are like **goto** statements to labels passed as parameters. However, exceptions are far more disciplined than **goto**s, and they do not require that the programmer pass targets as parameters.

Exceptions reduce the clarity of loop constructs. Every loop has an implicit exit caused by an unhandled exception wresting control out of the loop. Modula-3 unifies loops and exceptions by treating **break** as equivalent to **raise** ExitException. Loop statements implicitly handle this exception and exit the loop. Similarly, Modula-3 considers the

return statement as equivalent to **raise** ReturnException. The value returned by a function becomes the parameter to ReturnException.

The exception mechanism I have shown binds exception handlers to blocks. An alternative is to let raised exceptions throw the computation into a failure state [Wong 90]. In failure state, ordinary statements are not executed. Procedures can return while execution is in failure state, however. Only the **handle** statement is executed in failure state; after it completes, failure state is no longer in force unless **handle** reraises an exception. The programmer may place **handle** statements in the middle of blocks, interspersed with ordinary statements. The execution cost for this scheme may be fairly high, however, because every statement must be compiled with a test to see if execution is in failure state.

Exceptions are useful for more than handling error conditions. They also provide a clean way for programs to exit multiple procedure invocations. For example, an interactive editor might raise an exception in order to return to the main command loop after performing a complex action.

Exceptions are not the only reasonable way to handle error conditions. Sometimes it is easier for the programmer to have errors set a global variable that the program may inspect later when it is convenient. For example, the standard library packaged with C has a global variable errno that indicates the most recent error that occurred in performing an operating-system call. The programmer can choose to ignore return values and inspect errno well into the calculation, redirecting further effort if an error has occurred. The program is likely to be more efficient and clearer than a program that surrounds code with exception handlers. This point is especially important in numerical computations on large data sets on highly pipelined computers. Putting in the necessary tests to handle exceptions can slow down such computations so much that they become useless, whereas hardware that sets a flag when it discovers overflow, say, allows such computations to run at full speed and lets the program notice rare problems after the fact.

Another way to treat errors is by generating **error values**, such as undefined and positive_overflow, that are an integral part of arithmetic types. Similarly, null_pointer_dereference and array_range_-error can be error values generated by the related mistakes. Expressions can evaluate to an error value instead of their normal results. These error values are propagated (using specific rules) to produce a final result. For example, 1/0 yields the value zero_divide, while 0*(1/0) yields undefined. Any operation involving zero_divide yields undefined. Error values render the results of all computations well defined, guaranteeing that all valid evaluation orders produce the same result.[1] They also provide for a degree of error repair, since the program can test for error values and perhaps transform them into something meaningful. However, because the program can continue computing with error values, the error values finally produced may provide no indication of the original errors. It can be quite difficult to debug programs when errors propagate in this way. It would be far more helpful if the error value contained extra information, such as the source file and line number where the error occurred, which could propagate along with the error value itself.

2 ⬥ COROUTINES

Consider the problem of comparing two binary trees to see if their nodes have the same values in symmetric (also called in-order) traversal. For example, the trees in Figure 2.7 compare as equal.

Figure 2.7 Equivalent binary trees

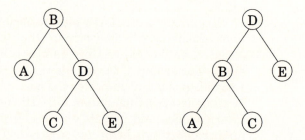

We could use a recursive procedure to store the symmetric-order traversal in an array, call the procedure for each tree, and then compare the arrays, but it is more elegant to advance independently in each tree, comparing as we go. Such an algorithm is also far more efficient if the trees are unequal near the beginning of the traversal. The problem is that each traversal needs its own recursion stack. In most programming languages, this solution requires an explicit stack for each tree and a program that replaces recursion with iteration.

2.1 Coroutines in Simula

Simula provides explicit coroutines that have just the effect we need. Simula classes are introduced in Chapter 3 as a way to implement abstract data types. Here I will show you another use.

A class is a data type much like a record structure, but it may also contain procedures and initialization code. When a variable is declared

---

[1] An error algebra with good numeric properties is discussed in [Wetherell 83].

of that class type, or when a value is created at runtime from the heap using a new call, an instance of the class is created. This instance is often called an **object**; in fact, the concept of object-oriented programming, discussed in Chapter 5, is derived largely from Simula classes. After space is allocated (either on the stack or the heap), the initialization code is run for this object. Programmers usually use this facility to set up the object's data fields. However, the initialization code may suspend itself before it completes. I will call an object that has not completed its initialization code an **active object**. An active object's fields may be inspected and modified, and its procedures may be called. In addition, its initialization code can be resumed from the point it suspended.

Because the initialization can invoke arbitrary procedures that may suspend at any point during their execution, each object needs its own stack until its initialization has completed. An active object is therefore a **coroutine**, that is, an execution thread that can pass control to other coroutines without losing its current execution environment, such as its location within nested name scopes and nested control structures.

Simula achieves this structure by introducing two new statements. The **call** statement specifies a suspended active object, which is thereby allowed to continue execution in its saved execution environment. The callers are saved on a runtime stack. The **detach** statement suspends the current object and returns control to the most recent object that invoked **call**. (This object is found on the stack just mentioned.) The main program is treated as an object for this purpose, but it must not invoke **detach**.

The program of Figure 2.8 solves the binary-tree equality puzzle. Simula syntax is fairly similar to Ada syntax; the following is close to correct Simula, although I have modified it somewhat so I don't confuse syntactic with semantic issues.

Figure 2.8

```
class Tree; -- used as a Pascal record           1
    Value : char;                                2
    LeftChild, RightChild : pointer to Tree;     3
end; -- Tree                                     4
```

```
class TreeSearch; -- used as a coroutine                   5
    MyTree : pointer to Tree;                              6
    CurrentNode : pointer to Tree;                         7
    Done : Boolean; -- true when tree exhausted            8

    procedure Dive                                         9
            (readonly Node : pointer to Tree);            10
    begin                                                 11
        if Node ≠ nil then                                12
            Dive(Node^.LeftChild);                        13
            CurrentNode := Node;                          14
            detach;                                       15
            Dive(Node^.RightChild);                       16
        end;                                              17
    end; -- Dive                                          18

begin -- TreeSearch: initialization and coroutine         19
    Done := false;                                        20
    CurrentNode := nil;                                   21
    detach; -- wait for initial values                    22
    Dive(MyTree); -- will detach at each node             23
    Done := true;                                         24
end; -- TreeSearch                                        25

variable -- main                                          26
    A, B : pointer to Tree;                               27
    ASearch, BSearch : pointer to TreeSearch;             28
    Equal : Boolean;                                      29
begin -- main                                             30
    ... -- initialize A and B                             31
    new(ASearch); ASearch^.MyTree := A;                   32
    new(BSearch); BSearch^.MyTree := B;                   33
    while not (ASearch^.Done or BSearch^.Done or          34
            ASearch^.CurrentNode ≠ BSearch^.CurrentNode)  35
    do                                                    36
        call ASearch^; -- continues coroutine             37
        call BSearch^; -- continues coroutine             38
    end;                                                  39
    Equal := ASearch^.Done and BSearch^.Done;             40
end;                                                      41
```

The new calls in lines 32–33 create new instances of TreeSearch and assign them to ASearch and BSearch. Each of these instances detaches during initialization (line 22) to allow their local variables MyTree to be set (lines 32–33). Then they are repeatedly resumed by the main program (lines 37–38). The **call** statements in lines 37–38 are invalid after the coroutines have finished (that is, after the initialization code of the class instances ASearchˆ and BSearchˆ has finished line 24), but line 34 prevents such a mistake from occurring. The class instances for both the trees and the coroutines are deallocated after control exits from the block at line 41, since all pointers to those instances disappear at that point. (Garbage collection is used for deallocation.)

2.2 Coroutines in CLU

The CLU language, designed by Barbara Liskov at MIT, provides a generalized **for** loop [Liskov 81]. The control variable takes on successive values provided by a coroutine called an **iterator**. This iterator is similar in most ways to an ordinary procedure, but it returns values via a **yield** statement. When the **for** loop requires another value for the control variable, the iterator is resumed from where it left off and is allowed to execute until it encounters another **yield**. If the iterator reaches the end of its code instead, the **for** loop that relies on the iterator terminates. CLU's **yield** is like Simula's **detach**, except that it also passes back a value. CLU's **for** implicitly contains the effect of Simula's **call**.

A naive implementation of CLU would create a separate stack for each active iterator instance. (The same iterator may have several active instances; it does, for example, if there is a **for** nested within another **for**.) A coroutine linkage, much like Simula's **call** and **detach**, would ensure that each iterator instance maintains its own context, so that it may be resumed properly.

The following program provides a simple example. CLU syntax is also fairly close to Ada syntax; the following is almost valid CLU.

Figure 2.9

```
iterator B() : integer; -- yields 3, 4            1
begin                                             2
    yield 3;                                      3
    yield 4;                                      4
end; -- B                                         5

iterator C() : integer; -- yields 1, 2, 3         6
begin                                             7
    yield 1;                                      8
    yield 2;                                      9
    yield 3;                                     10
end; -- C                                        11
```

```
iterator A() : integer; -- yields 10, 20, 30              12
variable                                                  13
    Answer : integer;                                     14
begin                                                     15
    for Answer := C() do -- ranges over 1, 2, 3           16
        yield 10*Answer;                                  17
    end;                                                  18
end; -- A                                                 19

variable                                                  20
    x, y : integer;                                       21
begin                                                     22
    for x := A() do -- ranges over 10, 20, 30             23
        for y := B() do -- ranges over 3, 4               24
            P(x, y); -- called 6 times                    25
        end;                                              26
    end;                                                  27
end;                                                      28
```

The loop in line 23 iterates over the three values yielded by iterator A (lines 12–19). For each of these values, the loop in line 24 iterates over the two values yielded by iterator B (lines 1–5). Iterator A itself introduces a loop that iterates over the three values yielded by iterator C (lines 6–11).

Happily, CLU can be implemented with a single stack. As a **for** loop begins execution, some activation record (call it the *parent*) is active (although not necessarily at the top of the stack). A new activation record for the iterator is constructed and placed at the top of the stack. Whenever the body of the loop is executing, the parent activation record is current, even though the iterator's activation record is higher on the stack. When the iterator is resumed so that it can produce the next value for the control variable, its activation record again becomes current. Each new iterator invocation gets a new activation record at the current stack top. Thus an activation record fairly deep in the stack can be the parent of an activation record at the top of the stack. Nonetheless, when an iterator terminates, indicating to its parent **for** loop that there are no more values, the iterator's activation record is certain to be at the top of the stack and may be reclaimed by simply adjusting the top-of-stack pointer. (This claim is addressed in Exercise 2.10.)

For Figure 2.9, each time P is invoked, the runtime stack appears as follows. The arrows show the dynamic (child-parent) chain.

Figure 2.10 Runtime CLU stack during iterator execution

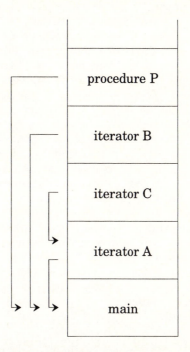

CLU iterators are often trivially equivalent to programs using ordinary **for** loops. However, for some combinatorial algorithms, recursive CLU iterators are much more powerful and allow truly elegant programs. One example is the generation of all binary trees with n nodes. This problem can be solved without CLU iterators, albeit with some complexity [Solomon 80]. Figure 2.11 presents a natural CLU implementation.

Figure 2.11

```
type Tree =                                            1
    record                                             2
        Left, Right : pointer to Node;                 3
    end; -- Tree;                                       4

iterator TreeGen(Size : integer) : pointer to Tree;    5
-- generate all trees with Size nodes                  6
variable                                               7
    Answer : Tree;                                     8
    Root : integer; -- serial number of the root       9
```

```
begin                                              10
    if Size = 0 then                               11
        yield nil; -- only the empty tree          12
    else -- answer not empty                       13
        for Root := 1 to Size do                   14
            for Answer.Left := TreeGen(Root-1) do  15
                for Answer.Right := TreeGen(Size-Root) 16
                do                                 17
                    yield &Answer;                 18
                end; -- for Right                  19
            end; -- for Left                       20
        end; -- for Root                           21
    end -- answer not empty                        22
end -- TreeGen                                     23

variable -- sample use of TreeGen                  24
    T : pointer to Tree;                           25
begin                                              26
    for T := TreeGen(10) do                        27
        TreePrint(T);                              28
    end;                                           29
end;                                               30
```

This marvelously compact program prints all binary trees of size 10. The **for** loop in lines 27–29 invokes the iterator TreeGen(10) until no more values are produced. TreeGen will produce 16,796 values before it terminates. It works by recursion on the size of tree required. The simple case is to generate a tree of size 0; the **yield** in line 12 accomplishes this. If an instance of TreeGen(0) is resumed after line 12, it falls through, thereby terminating its parent loop. The other case requires that TreeGen iterate through all possibilities of the root of the tree it will generate (line 14). Any one of the Size nodes could be root. For each such possibility, there are Root-1 nodes on the left and Size-Root nodes on the right. All combinations of the trees meeting these specifications must be joined to produce the trees with Size nodes. The nested loops starting in lines 15 and 16 iterate through all such combinations; for each, **yield** in line 18 passes to the parent a reference to the solution. The storage for the solution is in the local activation record of the iterator. As iterators terminate, their storage is released, so there is no need to explicitly allocate or deallocate any storage for the resulting tree.

2.3 Embedding CLU Iterators in C

Surprisingly, it is possible to implement CLU iterators using only the constructs available to a C programmer. This implementation clarifies CLU and shows some interesting aspects of C.

The only machine-independent way to manipulate activation records in C is to use the library routines `setjmp` and `longjmp`. They are intended to provide the equivalent of exception handling; they allow many levels of activation records to be terminated at once, jumping from an activation record at the top of the stack directly back to one deep within the stack. I apply these routines in a way probably unintended by their inventors: to resume an activation record higher on the stack than the invoker.

Setjmp(Buf) takes a snapshot of the current environment — registers, stack pointers, program counter, and such — and places it in the `Buf` data structure. Longjmp(Buf, ReturnValue) restores the registers from `Buf`, effectively restoring the exact context in which the `setjmp` was called. In fact, it creates another return from the original `setjmp` call. In order to let the program distinguish whether `setjmp` is returning the ordinary way or because of a `longjmp`, `setjmp` returns a 0 in the former case and `ReturnValue` in the latter case. For this reason, `setjmp` is usually embedded in a conditional or case statement to identify these cases and take appropriate action.

This facility is very like jumping to a label passed as a parameter, which has the effect of unwinding the stack to the right activation record for the target of the **goto**. Setjmp can capture the situation before a procedure call, and `longjmp` can be invoked from within a procedure; the call unwinds the stack to its position when `setjmp` recorded the situation. Unbridled use of `setjmp` and `longjmp` can be worse than an unconstrained **goto**. It allows such activities as jumping into a control structure (after all, the `setjmp` can be in the middle of a loop or a branch of a conditional) or even jumping back to a procedure that has exited.

This ability to break the rules makes it possible to implement CLU iterators within the C language. My implementation is packaged as a set of C macros, primarily `iterFOR` and `iterYIELD`. Whenever `iterFOR` is about to invoke an iterator, it performs `setjmp` to allow the iterator to come back to the `iterFOR` via `longjmp`. Likewise, each `iterYIELD` performs `setjmp` to allow its parent `iterFOR` to resume it via `longjmp`. The macros use a single global variable (not visible to the programmer) to store a pointer to the associated `Buf` structures in both these cases.

Now that the linkage between `iterFOR` and its iterator can be established, two problems remain. They both concern managing space on the stack. Unfortunately, new activation records are placed on the stack immediately above the invoker's activation record, even if other activation records have been placed there.

The first problem is that even in the simplest situation, with a single iterFOR invoking a single iterator, we need padding on the stack between their respective activation records. If there is no padding, then attempts by iterFOR to resume the iterator fail. After all, iterFOR calls longjmp, and this invocation places an activation record on the stack (since longjmp is also a procedure). This activation record coincides with the iterator's activation record, destroying at least the arguments and quite likely other information as well. Furthermore, any ordinary procedure calls invoked by the body of the iterFOR need a place to put their activation records. I solve this problem by invoking iterators via a Helper routine, which declares a local array just for padding and then calls the iterator by a normal procedure invocation.

The second problem arises with nested iterFOR loops, which are, after all, the interesting ones. Consider again Figure 2.9 introduced on page 39. Once the outer **for** in line 23 has established an instance of A, and A in line 16 has established an instance of C, the inner **for** in line 24 needs to put its instance of B at the top of the stack. Main can't directly invoke Helper, because that would place the activation record for B exactly where the A is residing. I therefore keep track of the iterator instance (in this case, C) that is currently at the top of the stack so that I can resume it, not so it will yield its next value, but so it will call Helper on my behalf to start B.

Figure 2.12   Runtime
C stack during
iterator execution

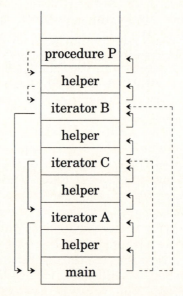

Figure 2.12 demonstrates the appearance of the runtime stack at the same stage as the previous figure. Solid arrows pointing downward show to which activation record each activation record returns control via `longjmp`. Dotted arrows pointing downward show ordinary procedure returns. Solid arrows pointing upward show which activation record actually started each new activation record. Dotted arrows pointing upward show the direction of `longjmp` used to request new invocations.

Choosing to build iterators as C macros provides the ability to express CLU coroutines at the cost of clarity. In particular, I made the following decisions:

1. The value returned by an `iterYIELD` statement must be placed in a global variable by the programmer; the macros do not attempt to transmit these values.

2. The programmer must write the `Helper` routine. In the usual case, the helper just declares a dummy local array and invokes the iterator procedure, passing arguments through global variables. If there are several different iterators to be called, `Helper` must distinguish which one is intended.

3. Any routine that includes an `iterFOR` and every iterator must invoke `iterSTART` at the end of local declarations.

4. Instead of falling through, iterators must terminate with `iterDONE`.

5. The `Helper` routine does not provide enough padding to allow iterators and their callers to invoke arbitrary subroutines while iterators are on the stack. Procedures must be invoked from inside `iterFOR` loops by calling `iterSUB`.

The macro package appears in Figure 2.13. (Note for the reader unfamiliar with C: the braces { and } act as **begin** and **end**; void is a type with no values; declarations first give the type (such as int or jmp_buf *) and then the identifier; the assignment operator is = ; the dereferencing operator is * ; the referencing operator is & .)

Figure 2.13

```
#include <setjmp.h>                                         1
#define ITERMAXDEPTH 50                                     2
jmp_buf   *GlobalJmpBuf;  /* global pointer for linkage */  3
jmp_buf   *EnvironmentStack[ITERMAXDEPTH] = {0},            4
    **LastEnv = EnvironmentStack;                           5
```

```
/* return values for longjmp */                                6
#define J_FIRST 0 /* original return from setjmp */            7
#define J_YIELD 1                                              8
#define J_RESUME 2                                             9
#define J_CALLITER 3                                          10
#define J_DONE 4                                              11
#define J_CALLSUB 5                                           12
#define J_RETURN 6                                            13


/*   iterSTART must be invoked after all local declarations  14
     in any procedure with an iterFOR and in all iterators.  15
*/                                                            16
#define iterSTART \                                           17
    jmp_buf MyBuf, CallerBuf; \                               18
    if (GlobalJmpBuf) \                                       19
        bcopy((char *)GlobalJmpBuf, (char *)CallerBuf, \      20
            sizeof(jmp_buf)); \                               21
    LastEnv++; \                                              22
    *LastEnv = &MyBuf;                                        23


/*   Initialization gives global args to Helper.             24
     Body is the body of the for loop.                       25
*/                                                            26
#define iterFOR(Initialization, Body) \                       27
    switch (setjmp(MyBuf)) { \                                28
        case J_FIRST: \                                       29
            GlobalJmpBuf = MyBuf; \                            30
            Initialization; \                                 31
            if (*LastEnv != MyBuf)\                            32
                longjmp(**LastEnv, J_CALLITER); \             33
            else Helper(); \                                  34
        case J_YIELD: \                                       35
            {   jmp_buf *Resume = GlobalJmpBuf; \             36
                Body; \                                       37
                longjmp(*Resume, J_RESUME); \                 38
            } \                                               39
        case J_DONE: break; \                                 40
    }                                                         41
```

```
/*      No arguments; the value yielded must be passed          42
        through globals.                                        43
*/                                                              44
#define iterYIELD \                                             45
    switch (setjmp(MyBuf)) { \                                  46
        case J_FIRST: \                                         47
            GlobalJmpBuf = &MyBuf; \                            48
            longjmp(CallerBuf, J_YIELD); \                      49
        case J_CALLITER: \                                      50
            Helper();  /* won't return */ \                     51
        case J_CALLSUB: \                                       52
            {   jmp_buf *Return = GlobalJmpBuf; \               53
                Helper(); \                                     54
                longjmp(*Return, J_RETURN); \                   55
            } \                                                 56
        case J_RESUME: break; \                                57
    }                                                           58


/*      Every iterator must return via iterDONE;                59
        a direct return is meaningless.                         60
*/                                                              61
#define iterDONE \                                              62
    LastEnv--; \                                                63
    longjmp(CallerBuf, J_DONE)                                  64


/*      iterSUB(Initialization) invokes Helper to perform       65
        subroutine work from an iterator or its user.           66
*/                                                              67
#define iterSUB(Initialization) \                               68
    {   jmp_buf SubBuf; \                                       69
        switch (setjmp(SubBuf)) { \                             70
            case J_FIRST: \                                     71
                Initialization; \                               72
                if (*LastEnv != &MyBuf) { \                     73
                    GlobalJmpBuf = &SubBuf; \                   74
                    longjmp(**LastEnv, J_CALLSUB); \            75
                } \                                             76
                else Helper(); \                                77
                break; \                                        78
            case J_RETURN: \                                    79
                break; \                                        80
        } \                                                     81
    }                                                           82
```

The variables used to remember the stack of environments are
EnvironmentStack and LastEnv (lines 4 and 5). When an iterator starts,
it must save a copy of its parent's Buf (lines 20–21); this code is in a

conditional, since iterStart is also called by noniterators that happen
to invoke iterators. An iterator is invoked through Helper (line 34) or by
asking a more deeply nested iterator to assist (line 33). Such calls for
assistance always appear as resumptions from iterYIELD (line 50).

iterSUB (line 68) invokes Helper from the top of the stack but expects a normal return. Helper needs to be able to identify which subroutine is actually to be called by inspecting global variables. The flow of
control travels to the top of the stack (line 75), where it invokes Helper
(line 54) and then returns via a longjmp (line 55).

Figure 2.14 shows how to code Figure 2.9 (on page 39) using the C
macros.

Figure 2.14

```
int AValue, BValue, CValue, mainX, mainY;                     1
enum {CallA, CallB, CallC, CallPrint} HelpBy;                 2

void Helper(){                                                3
    switch (HelpBy) {                                         4
        case CallA: A(); break;                               5
        case CallB: B(); break;                               6
        case CallC: C(); break;                               7
        case CallPrint:                                       8
            printf("%d %d0, mainX, mainY); break;             9
    }                                                        10
}                                                            11

int B(){                                                     12
    iterSTART;                                               13
    BValue = 3; iterYIELD;                                   14
    BValue = 4; iterYIELD;                                   15
    iterDONE;                                                16
}                                                            17

int C(){                                                     18
    iterSTART;                                               19
    CValue = 1; iterYIELD;                                   20
    CValue = 2; iterYIELD;                                   21
    CValue = 3; iterYIELD;                                   22
    iterDONE;                                                23
}                                                            24
```

```
int A(){                                                        25
    int Answer;                                                 26
    iterSTART;                                                  27
    iterFOR ({HelpBy = CallC;} , {                             28
        Answer = 10 * CValue;                                   29
        AValue = Answer; iterYIELD;                             30
    });                                                         31
    iterDONE;                                                   32
}                                                               33

void main(){                                                    34
    iterSTART;                                                  35
    iterFOR({HelpBy = CallA;} , {                              36
        mainX = AValue;                                         37
        iterFOR ({HelpBy = CallB;} , {                         38
            mainY = BValue;                                     39
            iterSUB( HelpBy = CallPrint );                      40
        });                                                     41
    });                                                         42
}                                                               43
```

Line 1 introduces all the variables that need to be passed as parameters or as results of **yield** statements. Lines 2–11 form the Helper routine that is needed for invoking iterators as well as other routines, such as printf.

I cannot entirely recommend using these C macros; it is far better to use a language that provides iterators directly for those situations (admittedly rare) when recursive iterators are the best tool. After all, CLU iterators are not at all hard to compile into fine code.

The C macros can be used (I have used them on several occasions), but they leave a lot of room for errors. The programmer must pass parameters and results to and from the iterators through global variables. All calls to iterators (via iterFOR) and to routines (via iterSUB) are funneled through a single Helper routine. Helper needs to reserve adequate space (experience shows that not much is needed) and must use global variables to distinguish the reason it is being called. The programmer must be careful to use iterSUB instead of direct calls inside iterFOR. The resulting programs are certainly not elegant in appearance, although with some practice, they are not hard to code and to read.

The C macros have other drawbacks. In some C implementations, longjmp refuses to jump up the stack. Compile-time and hand-coded optimizations that put variables in registers typically render them invisible to setjmp, so iterators and routines that contain iterFOR must not be optimized. There is a danger that interrupts may cause the stack to become garbled, because a program written in C cannot protect the top of the stack.

2.4 Coroutines in Icon

Icon is discussed in some detail in Chapter 9. It generalizes CLU iterators by providing expressions that can be reevaluated to give different results.

3 ◆ CONTINUATIONS: IO

FORTRAN demonstrates that is possible to build a perfectly usable programming language with only procedure calls and conditional **goto** as control structures. The Io language reflects the hope that a usable programming language can result from only a single control structure: a **goto** with parameters. I will call the targets of these jumps procedures even though they do not return to the calling point. The parameters passed to procedures are not restricted to simple values. They may also be **continuations**, which represent the remainder of the computation to be performed after the called procedure is finished with its other work. Instead of returning, procedures just invoke their continuation. Continuations are explored formally in Chapter 10; here I will show you a practical use.

Io manages to build remarkably sophisticated facilities on such a simple foundation. It can form data structures by embedding them in procedures, and it can represent coroutines.

Io programs do not contain a sequence of statements. A program is a procedure call that is given the rest of the program as a continuation parameter. A statement continuation is a closure; it includes a procedure, its environment, and even its parameters.

Io's syntax is designed to make statement continuations easy to write. If a statement continuation is the last parameter, which is the usual case, it is separated from the other parameters by a semicolon, to remind the programmer of sequencing. Continuations and procedures in other parameter positions must be surrounded by parentheses. I will present Io by showing examples from [Levien 89].

Figure 2.15

```
write 5;                                                      1
write 6;                                                      2
terminate                                                     3
```

As you expect, this program prints 5 6. But I need to explain how it works. The predeclared `write` procedure takes two parameters: a number and a continuation. The call in line 1 has 5 as its first parameter and `write 6; terminate` as its second. The `write` procedure prints 5 and then invokes the continuation. It is a call to another instance of `write` (line 2), with parameters 6 and `terminate`. This instance prints 6 and then invokes the parameterless predeclared procedure terminate. This procedure does nothing. It certainly doesn't return, and it has no continuation to invoke.

Procedures can be declared as follows:

Figure 2.16

```
declare writeTwice: → Number;                              1
    write Number; write Number; terminate.                 2
```

That is, the identifier writeTwice is associated with an anonymous procedure (introduced by →) that takes a single formal parameter Number (the parameter list is terminated by the first ;) and prints it twice. The period, . , indicates the end of the declaration. This procedure is not very useful, because execution will halt after it finishes. Procedures do not return. So I will modify it to take a continuation as well:

Figure 2.17

```
declare writeTwice: → Number Continuation;                 1
    write Number; write Number; Continuation.              2

writeTwice 7;                                              3
write 9;                                                   4
terminate                                                  5
```

Lines 1–2 declare writeTwice, and line 3 invokes it with a 7 and a continuation composed of lines 4–5. Here is a trace of execution:

Figure 2.18

```
writeTwice 7 (write 9; terminate) -- called on line 3      1
    Number := 7                                            2
    Continuation := (write 9; terminate)                   3
write 7 (write 7; write 9; terminate) -- called on line 2  4
    -- writes 7                                            5
write 7 (write 9; terminate) -- called by write            6
    -- writes 7                                            7
write 9 (terminate) -- called by write                     8
    -- writes 9                                            9
terminate  -- called by write                              10
```

Indented lines (such as lines 2–3) indicate the formal-actual bindings. I surround parameters in parentheses for clarity.

Even arithmetic operations are built to take a continuation. The difference between a statement and an expression is that an expression continuation expects a parameter, namely, the value of the expression. Consider the following code, for example:

Figure 2.19

```
+ 2 3 → Number;                                                1
write Number;                                                  2
terminate                                                      3
```

The + operator adds its parameters 2 and 3 and passes the resulting value 5 to its last parameter (→ Number; write Number; terminate), which prints the 5 and terminates. This expression continuation is an anonymous procedure; that is, it is declared but not associated with an identifier. In general, an expression continuation is a procedure expecting a single parameter. The syntax conspires to make this program look almost normal. The result of the addition is apparently assigned to a variable Number, which is used in the following statements. In fact, the result of the addition is bound to the formal parameter Number, whose scope continues to the end of the program.

Conditional operators are predeclared to take two statement continuations corresponding to the two Boolean values true and false. For example, the following code will print the numbers from 1 to 10.

Figure 2.20

```
declare Count: → Start End Continuation;                       1
     write Start;                                              2
     = Start End (Continuation); -- "then" clause              3
     + Start 1 → NewStart; -- "else clause"                    4
     Count NewStart End Continuation.                          5
Count 1 10; terminate                                         6
```

Here is a trace of execution:

Figure 2.21

```
Count 1 10 terminate -- called on line 6                      1
     Start := 1                                                2
     End := 10                                                 3
     Continuation := terminate                                 4
write 1 (= 1 10 terminate A:(+ 1 1 → NewStart;                5
     Count NewStart 10; terminate)                             6
     -- writes 1                                               7
= 1 10 terminate A                                            8
     -- called by write                                        9
A -- called by '='                                           10
+ 1 1 B:(→ NewStart; Count NewStart 10; terminate)           11
B 2 -- called by '+'                                         12
Count 2 10 terminate -- called by B                          13
...
Count 10 10 terminate                                        14
```

```
write 10 (= 10 10 terminate C:(                               15
    + 1 1 → NewStart; Count NewStart 10; terminate.)         16
    -- writes 10                                              17
= 10 10 terminate C                                           18
terminate                                                     19
```

I have introduced the shorthand forms A (line 5), B (line 11), and C (line 15) for conciseness.

Procedures can contain constants that are made available later:

Figure 2.22
```
declare TwoNumbers: → Client;                                 1
    Client 34 53.                                             2
declare WritePair: → PairProc Continuation;                  3
    PairProc → x y;                                           4
    write x;                                                  5
    write y;                                                  6
    Continuation.                                             7
WritePair TwoNumbers;                                         8
terminate                                                     9
```

Line 8 invokes WritePair with two parameters: the first is a procedure (twoNumbers), and the second is a continuation (terminate). WritePair invokes its first parameter (line 4), passing the remainder of its body (lines 4–7) as a procedure parameter with local variable Continuation bound to terminate. TwoNumbers applies that procedure to parameters 34 and 53, causing these numbers to be printed and then terminate to be called. Procedure TwoNumbers can be generalized to contain any two numbers:

Figure 2.23
```
declare MakePair: → x y User Continuation;                    1
    User (→ Client; Client x y); Continuation.               2

MakePair 12 13 (WritePair);                                   3
terminate.                                                    4
```

The execution trace is as follows:

Figure 2.24
```
MakePair 12 13 WritePair terminate                            1
    x := 12                                                   2
    y := 14                                                   3
    User := WritePair                                         4
    Continuation := terminate                                 5
```

```
WritePair A:(→ Client; Client 12 13) terminate        6
    PairProc := A                                     7
    Continuation := terminate                         8
A B:(→ x y; write x; write y; terminate);             9
    Client := G                                       10
B 12 13 -- writes "12 13" then terminates.            11
```

Linked lists can be implemented by suitable cleverness as functions with two parameters, both procedures. An empty list calls its first parameter, which is a continuation. Other lists call the second parameter, passing two new parameters that represent the first number in the list and the remainder of the list. Here are the relevant declarations:

Figure 2.25

```
declare WriteList: → List Continuation;               1
    List (Continuation) → First Rest;                 2
    write First;                                      3
    WriteList Rest;                                   4
    Continuation.                                     5

declare EmptyList: → Null NotNull;                    6
    Null.                                             7

declare Cons: → Number List EContinuation;            8
    EContinuation → Null NotNull;                     9
    NotNull Number List.                              10

Cons 1 EmptyList → List;                              11
Cons 2 List → List;                                   12
WriteList List;                                       13
terminate                                             14
```

Here, Cons (the name is taken from LISP, described in Chapter 4) is meant to combine a header element with the rest of a list to create a new list. Again, the execution trace clarifies what happens:

Figure 2.26

```
Cons 1 EmptyList A:(                                  1
    → List; Cons 2 List → List; WriteList List;       2
        terminate)                                    3
    Number := 1                                       4
    List := EmptyList                                 5
    EContinuation := A                                6
A B:(→ Null NotNull; NotNull 1 EmptyList)             7
    List := B                                         8
```

```
Cons 2 B C:(→ List; WriteList List; terminate)          9
        Number := 2                                      10
        List := B                                        11
        EContinuation := C                               12
C D:(→ Null NotNull; NotNull 2 B)                       13
        List := D                                        14
WriteList D terminate                                    15
        List := D                                        16
        Continuation := terminate                        17
D terminate E:(→ First Rest; write First;               18
        WriteList Rest; terminate)                       19
        Null := terminate                                20
        NotNull := E                                      21
E 2 B                                                    22
        First := 2                                        23
        Rest := B                                         24
        -- writes 2                                       25
WriteList B terminate                                    26
        List := B                                         27
        Continuation := terminate                         28
B terminate F:(→ First Rest; write First;                29
        WriteList Rest; terminate)                        30
        Null := terminate                                 31
        NotNull := F                                       32
F 1 EmptyList                                             33
        First := 1                                         34
        Rest := EmptyList                                  35
        -- writes 1                                        36
WriteList EmptyList terminate                             37
        List := EmptyList                                 38
        Continuation := terminate                         39
EmptyList terminate G:(→ First Rest; write First;        40
        WriteList Rest; terminate)                        41
        Null := terminate                                 42
        NotNull := G                                       43
terminate                                                 44
```

Similar cleverness can produce a set of declarations for binary trees. Empty trees call their first parameter. Other trees call their second parameter with the key, left subtree, and the right subtree. Other data structures can be built similarly.

Continuations are perfectly capable of handling coroutines. For example, a global variable could hold the continuation of the thread that is not currently executing. I could define a switch procedure that saves its continuation parameter in the global and invokes the old value of the global. It would be more elegant to redesign statement continuations. Instead of being a single closure, they could be a list of closures (using the list mechanisms I have already introduced). The switch procedure would take the appropriate element from the list and sort it to the front of the list. Ordinary procedures use the front of the list as the current thread.

Instead of showing the gory details of coroutines, I will show how Io can build infinite data structures that are evaluated only when necessary. (Lazy evaluation is discussed in Chapter 4.)

Figure 2.27

```
declare Range: → First EContinuation;                       1
        EContinuation First → Null NotNull;                 2
        + First 1 → NewFirst;                               3
        Range NewFirst EContinuation.                       4
declare FullRange: → Null NotNull;                          5
        Range 0 NotNull.                                    6

WriteList FullRange; -- writes 0 1 2 3 ...                  7
terminate                                                   8
```

I leave it to you as an exercise to trace the execution.

Given that continuations are very powerful, why are they not a part of every language? Why do they not replace the conventional mechanisms of control structure? First, continuations are extremely confusing. The examples given in this section are almost impossible to understand without tracing, and even then, the general flow of control is lost in the details of procedure calls and parameter passing. With experience, programmers might become comfortable with them; however, continuations are so similar to **goto**s (with the added complexity of parameters) that they make it difficult to structure programs.

Second, continuations are not necessarily pleasant to implement. Procedures may be referenced long after they are created, and allocation does not follow a stack discipline, so it appears that activation records must be created in the heap. Luckily, circularities will not exist, so reference counts can govern reclamation of activation records. The implementation and the programmer must be able to distinguish functions that have not yet been bound to parameters (classical closures) from those that are so bound. Both are present in Io. In Figure 2.25 (on page 54), the anonymous procedure in lines 2–5 is a classical closure, whereas the subsidiary call to write in line 3 includes its parameters (First and WriteList Rest; Continuation).

Even though continuations will never be a popular programming method, I like them because they combine several ideas you will see elsewhere in this book. The examples abound with higher-level functions (discussed in Chapter 3) and anonymous functions (also Chapter 3). Continuations can implement coroutines and LISP-style lists

(Chapter 4). Finally, denotational semantic definitions of programming languages use continuations directly (Chapter 10).

4 ◆ POWER LOOPS

Although the programmer usually knows exactly how deeply loops must nest, there are some problems for which the depth of nesting depends on the data. Programmers usually turn to recursion to handle these cases; each level of nesting is a new level of recursion. However, there is a clearer alternative that can generate faster code. The alternative has recently[2] been called **power loops** [Mandl 90]. The idea is to have an array of control variables and to build a loop that iterates over all control variables.

For example, the n-queens problem is to find all solutions to the puzzle of placing n queens on an $n \times n$ chessboard so that no queen attacks any other. Here is a straightforward solution:

Figure 2.28

```
variable                                            1
    Queen : array 1 .. n of integer;                2

nest Column := 1 to n                               3
    for Queen[Column] := 1 to n do                  4
        if OkSoFar(Column) then                     5
            deeper;                                 6
        end; -- if OkSoFar(Column)                  7
    end; -- for Queen[Column]                       8
do                                                  9
    write(Queen[1..n]);                             10
end;                                                11
```

Any solution will have exactly one queen in each column of the chessboard. Line 2 establishes an array that will describe which row is occupied by the queen in each column. The OkSoFar routine (line 5) checks to make sure that the most recent queen does not attack (and therefore is not attacked by) any of the previously placed queens. Line 3 introduces a set of nested loops. It effectively replicates lines 4–8 for each value of Column, placing the next replica at the point marked by the **deeper** pseudostatement (line 6). There must be exactly one **deeper** in a **nest**. Nested inside the innermost instance is the body shown in line 10. If n = 3, for example, this program is equivalent to the code of Figure 2.29.

---

[2] The Madcap language had power loops in the early 1960s [Wells 63].

Figure 2.29

```
for Queen[1] := 1 to n do                              1
    if OkSoFar(1) then                                 2
        for Queen[2] := 1 to n do                      3
            if OkSoFar(2) then                         4
                for Queen[3] := 1 to n do              5
                    if OkSoFar(3) then                 6
                        write(Queen[1..3])             7
                    end; -- if 3                       8
                end; -- for 3                          9
            end; -- if 2                               10
        end; -- for 2                                  11
    end; -- if 1                                       12
end; -- for 1                                          13
```

Nesting applies not only to loops, as Figure 2.30 shows.

Figure 2.30

```
nest Level := 1 to n                                   1
    if SomeCondition(Level) then                       2
        deeper;                                        3
    else                                               4
        write("failed at level", Level);               5
    end;                                               6
do                                                     7
    write("success!");                                 8
end;                                                   9
```

Of course, a programmer may place a **nest** inside another **nest**, either in the replicated part (as in lines 2–6 of Figure 2.30) or in the body (line 8), but such usage is likely to be confusing. If **nest** can be nested in the replicated part, each **deeper** must indicate which **nest** it refers to.

It is not hard to generate efficient code for **nest**. Figure 2.31 is a flowchart showing the generated code, where i is the **nest** control variable. The labels t and f are the true and false exits of the conditionals. Label d is the exit from the replicated part when it encounters **deeper**, and r is the reentry after **deeper**. The fall-through exit from the replicated part is called e. If execution after **deeper** will just fall through (as in Figure 2.30), decrementing i and checking i < init can be omitted.

Although power loops are elegant, they are subsumed by recursive procedures, albeit with a loss of elegance and efficiency. Power loops are so rarely helpful that languages should probably avoid them. It doesn't make sense to introduce a construct in a general-purpose language if it will only be used in a handful of programs.

Figure 2.31 Flowchart for **nest**

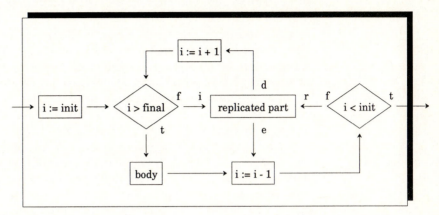

5 ◆ FINAL COMMENTS

This chapter has introduced a variety of control constructs that have a mixed history of success. Exception-handling mechanisms are enjoying increasing popularity. General coroutines are found to some extent in concurrent programming languages (discussed in Chapter 7). CLU iterators and power loops never caught on in mainstream languages. Io continuations have no track record, but appear unlikely to catch on.

We can often see good reason for these results. Chapter 1 presented a list of characteristics of good programming languages. Among them were simplicity (using as few concepts as possible), clarity (easily understood code semantics), and expressiveness (ability to describe algorithms). Exception handling scores well on all these fronts. The mechanism introduces only one additional concept (the exception, with the **raise** statement and the **handle** syntax). The semantics are clear when an exception is raised, especially if no resumption is possible and if all exceptions must be declared at the global level. The only confusion might come from the fact that the handler is determined dynamically, not statically; dynamic binding tends to be more confusing to the programmer, because it cannot easily be localized to any region of the program. The mechanism serves a real need in expressing multilevel premature procedure return.

Coroutines are less successful by my measures. The set of concepts is not too large; Simula manages with per-object initialization code and two new statements: **detach** and **call**. However, the dynamic nature of the **call** stack and the fact that each object needs its own private stack make coroutines harder to understand and less efficient to implement. The additional expressiveness they provide is not generally useful;

programmers are not often faced with testing traversals of trees for equality.

CLU iterators are truly elegant. They are clear and expressive. They provide a single, uniform way to program all loops. They can be implemented efficiently on a single stack. Perhaps they have not caught on because, like general coroutines, they provide expressiveness in an arena where most programs do not need it. The only application I have ever found for which CLU iterators give me just what I need has been solving combinatorial puzzles, and these don't crop up often.

Power loops have less to recommend them. They are not as clear as ordinary loops; if you don't believe this, consider what it means to **nest** a structure other than **for**. They don't provide any expressiveness beyond what recursion already provides. There are very few situations in which they are the natural way to pose an algorithm. However, the mathematical concept of raising a function to a power is valuable, and APL (discussed in Chapter 9), in which manipulation by and of functions is central, has an operator much like the power loop.

Io continuations provide a lot of food for thought. They spring from an attempt to gain utter simplicity in a programming language. They seem to be quite expressive, but they suffer from a lack of clarity. No matter how often I have stared at the examples of Io programming, I have always had to resort to traces to figure out what is happening. I think they are just too obscure to ever be valuable.

EXERCISES

Review Exercises

2.1 In what way is raising an exception like a **goto**? It what way is it different?

2.2 Write a CLU iterator upto(a,b) that yields all the integer values between a and b. You may use a **while** loop, but not a **for** loop, in your implementation.

2.3 Write a CLU iterator that generates all Fibonacci numbers, that is, the sequence 1, 1, 2, 3, 5, 8, . . . , where each number is the sum of the previous two numbers.

2.4 Write a Simula class Fibonacci with a field Value that the initialization code sets to 1 and then suspends. Every time the object is resumed, Value should be set to the next value in the Fibonacci sequence.

2.5   What does the following Io program do?

Figure 2.32

```
declare foo: → Number Continuation;        1
        + Number 1 → More;                 2
        write More;                        3
        Continuation .                     4

foo 7;                                     5
foo 9;                                     6
terminate                                  7
```

2.6   Use power loops to initialize a $10 \times 10 \times 10$ integer array A to ze-roes.

2.7   If I have power loops, do I need **for** loops?

Challenge Exercises

2.8   In Figure 2.3 (page 33), I show how a handler can reraise the same exception (or raise a different one) in order to propagate the raised exception further. Would it make sense to define a language in which exceptions were handled by the handler that raised them, not propagated further?

2.9   What are the ramifications of letting exceptions be first-class val-ues? (First-class values are discussed in Chapter 3.)

2.10 Prove the contention on page 40 that when a CLU iterator termi-nates, indicating to its parent **for** loop that there are no more val-ues, the iterator's activation record is actually at the top of the stack.

2.11 Use CLU iterators to write a program that takes a binary tree and prints all distinct combinations of four leaves.

2.12 Prove that in Figure 2.11 (page 41) the references to Answer gener-ated in line 18 are always valid. In particular, prove that by the time an instance of Answer is deallocated, there are no remaining pointers to that instance. Actually, CLU requires that control vari-ables, such as T in line 25, have a scope that only includes the loop they control. You may make use of this restriction in your proof.

2.13 Show how to use the C iterator macros to write a program that enumerates binary trees.

2.14 Are CLU iterators as powerful as Simula coroutines? In particular, can the binary-tree equality puzzle be solved in CLU?

2.15 In Figure 2.17 (page 51), could I replace the 9 in line 4 with the identifier Number?

2.16 What sort of runtime storage organization is appropriate for Io?

2.17 Does Io support recursion?

2.18 Show the execution trace of Figure 2.27 (page 56).

2.19 What is the meaning of a power loop for which the range is empty?

2.20 Figure 2.31 (page 59) has one potential inefficiency. What is it?

2.21 Power loops are modeled on **for** loops. Can I model them on **while** loops instead? That is, can they look like the following?

Figure 2.33

```
nest Boolean expression                                    1
        replicated part                                    2
do                                                         3
        body                                               4
end;                                                       5
```

2.22 Does it make sense to place declarations inside the replicated part or the body of a power loop?

Chapter 3

Types

The evolution of modern programming languages is closely coupled with the development (and formalization) of the concept of data type. At the machine-language level, all values are untyped (that is, simply bit patterns). Assembler-language programmers, however, usually recognize the fundamental differences between addresses (considered relocatable) and data (considered absolute). Hence they recognize that certain combinations of addresses and data (for example, the sum of two addresses) are ill defined.

This assembler-language view of typing is flawed, however, because it views type as a property of a datum rather than a property of the cell containing the datum. That is, whether or not an operation is meaningful can usually be determined only at runtime when the actual operand values are available. An assembler will probably recognize the invalidity of an expression that adds two labels, while it will accept a code sequence that computes exactly the same thing! This weakness has led to the introduction of tagged architectures that include (at runtime) type information with a datum. Such architectures can detect the label-addition error, because the add instruction can detect that its operands are two addresses. Unfortunately, the type information included with data is usually limited to the primitive types provided by the architecture. Programmer-declared data types cannot receive the same sort of automatic correctness checking.

FORTRAN and later high-level languages improved upon assembler languages by associating type information with the locations holding data rather than the data itself. More generally, languages associate type information with identifiers, which may be variables or formal parameters. When an attribute such as a type is associated with an identifier, we say the the identifier is **bound** to the attribute. Binding that takes place at compile time is usually called **static**, and binding that takes place at runtime is called **dynamic**. **Static-typed** languages are those that bind types to identifiers at compile time. Since types are known at compile time, the compiler can detect a wide range of type errors (for example, an attempt to multiply two Boolean variables).

High-level languages prior to Pascal usually limited their concepts of data types to those provided directly by hardware (integers, reals, double precision integers and reals, and blocks of contiguous locations). Two objects had different types if it was necessary to generate different code to manipulate them. Pascal and later languages have taken a rather different approach, based on the concept of abstract data types. In Pascal, the programmer can give two objects different types even if they have the same representation and use the same generated code. Type rules have shifted from concentrating on what makes sense to the computer to what makes sense to the programmer.

1 ◆ DYNAMIC-TYPED LANGUAGES

It is possible to delay the binding of types to identifiers until runtime, leading to dynamic-typed languages. Interpreted languages (like SNOBOL, APL, and Awk) often bind types only at runtime. These languages have no type declarations; the type of an identifier may change dynamically. These are different from **typeless** languages, such as Bliss or BCPL, which have only one type of datum, the cell or word.

Delaying the binding of a type to an identifier gains expressiveness at the cost of efficiency, since runtime code must determine its type in order to manipulate its value appropriately. As an example of expressiveness, in dynamic-typed languages, arrays need not be homogeneous. As an example of loss of efficiency, even in static-typed languages, the values of choice types require some runtime checking to ensure that the expected variant is present.

2 ◆ STRONG TYPING

One of the major achievements of Pascal was the emphasis it placed on the definition of data types. It viewed the creation of programmer-declared data types as an integral part of program development. Pascal introduced the concept of strong typing to protect programmers from errors involving type mismatches. A **strongly typed language** provides rules that allow the compiler to determine the type of every value (that is, every variable and every expression).[1] Assignments and actual-formal parameter binding involving inequivalent types are invalid, except for a limited number of automatic conversions. The underlying

---

[1] Actually, Pascal is not completely strongly typed. Procedure-valued parameters do not specify the full procedure header, so it is possible to provide an actual parameter that does not match the formal in number or type of parameters. Untagged record variants are another loophole.

philosophy is that different types represent different abstractions, so they ought to interact only in carefully controlled and clearly correct ways.

3 ◆ TYPE EQUIVALENCE

The concept of strong typing relies on a definition of exactly when types are equivalent. Surprisingly, the original definition of Pascal did not present a definition of type equivalence. The issue can be framed by asking whether the types T1 and T2 are equivalent in Figure 3.1:

Figure 3.1

```
type                                               1
    T1, T2 = array[1..10] of real;                 2
    T3 = array[1..10] of real;                     3
```

Structural equivalence states that two types are equivalent if, after all type identifiers are replaced by their definitions, the same structure is obtained. This definition is recursive, because the definitions of the type identifiers may themselves contain type identifiers. It is also vague, because it leaves open what "same structure" means. Everyone agrees that T1, T2, and T3 are structurally equivalent. However, not everyone agrees that records require identical field names in order to have the same structure, or that arrays require identical index ranges. In Figure 3.2, T4, T5, and T6 would be considered equivalent to T1 in some languages but not others:

Figure 3.2

```
type                                               1
    T4 = array[2..11] of real; -- same length      2
    T5 = array[2..10] of real; -- compatible index type   3
    T6 = array[blue .. red] of real; -- incompatible      4
           -- index type                           5
```

Testing for structural equivalence is not always trivial, because recursive types are possible. In Figure 3.3, types TA and TB are structurally equivalent, as are TC and TD, although their expansions are infinite.

Figure 3.3

```
type                                                       1
    TA = pointer to TA;                                    2
    TB = pointer to TB;                                    3
    TC =                                                   4
        record                                             5
            Data : integer;                                6
            Next : pointer to TC;                          7
        end;                                               8
    TD =                                                   9
        record                                            10
            Data : integer;                               11
            Next : pointer to TD;                         12
        end;                                              13
```

In contrast to structural equivalence, **name equivalence** states that two variables are of the same type if they are declared with the same type name, such as integer or some declared type. When a variable is declared using a **type constructor** (that is, an expression that yields a type), its type is given a new internal name for the sake of name equivalence. Type constructors include the words **array**, **record**, and **pointer to**. Therefore, type equivalence says that T1 and T3 above are different, as are TA and TB. There are different interpretations possible when several variables are declared using a single type constructor, such as T1 and T2 above. Ada is quite strict; it calls T1 and T2 different. The current standard for Pascal is more lenient; it calls T1 and T2 identical [ANSI 83]. This form of name equivalence is also called **declaration equivalence**.

Name equivalence seems to be the better design because the mere fact that two data types share the same structure does not mean they represent the same abstraction. T1 might represent the batting averages of ten members of the Milwaukee Brewers, while T3 might represent the grade-point average of ten students in an advanced programming language course. Given this interpretation, we surely wouldn't want T1 and T3 to be considered equivalent!

Nonetheless, there are good reasons to use structural equivalence, even though unrelated types may accidentally turn out to be equivalent. Applications that write out their values and try to read them in later (perhaps under the control of a different program) deserve the same sort of type-safety possessed by programs that only manipulate values internally. Modula-2+, which uses name equivalence, outputs both the type name and the type's structure for each value to prevent later readers from accidentally using the same name with a different meaning. Anonymous types are assigned an internal name. Subtle bugs arise if a programmer moves code about, causing the compiler to generate a different internal name for an anonymous type. Modula-3, on the other hand, uses structural equivalence. It outputs the type's structure (but not its name) with each value output. There is no danger that rearranging a program will lead to type incompatibilities with data written by a previous version of the program.

A language may allow assignment even though the type of the expression and the type of the destination variable are not equivalent; they only need to be **assignment-compatible**. For example, under name equivalence, two array types might have the same structure but be inequivalent because they are generated by different instances of the **array** type constructor. Nonetheless, the language may allow assignment if the types are close enough, for example, if they are structurally equivalent. In a similar vein, two types may be compatible with respect to any operation, such as addition, even though they are not type-equivalent. It is often a quibble whether to say a language uses name equivalence but has lax rules for compatibility or to say that it uses structural equivalence. I will avoid the use of "compatibility" and just talk about equivalence.

Modula-3's rules for determining when two types are structurally equivalent are fairly complex. If every value of one type is a value of the second, then the first type is a called a "subtype" of the second. For example, a record type TypeA is a subtype of another record type TypeB only if their fields have the same names and the same order, and all of the types of the fields of TypeA are subtypes of their counterparts in TypeB. An array type TypeA is a subtype of another array type TypeB if they have the same number of dimensions of the same size (although the range of indices may differ) and the same index and component types. There are also rules for the subtype relation between procedure and pointer types. If two types are subtypes of each other, they are equivalent. Assignment requires that the value being assigned be of a subtype of the target variable.[2]

After Pascal became popular, a weakness in its type system became apparent. For example, given the code in Figure 3.4,

Figure 3.4

```
type                                                                          1
     natural = 0 .. maxint;                                                   2
```

you would expect natural numbers (which are a subrange of integers) to be equivalent to integers, so that naturals and integers might be added or assigned. On the other hand, given the code of Figure 3.5,

---

[2] The actual rule is more complex in order to account for range types and to allow pointer assignments.

Figure 3.5

```
type                                                  1
    feet   = 0 .. maxint;                             2
    meters = 0 .. maxint;                             3
```

you would probably expect feet and meters to be inequivalent. It turns out in Pascal that subranges of an existing type (or a type identifier defined as equal to another type identifier) are equivalent (subject to possible range restrictions). But I don't want feet and meters to be equivalent.

Successors to Pascal (especially Ada) have attempted to generalize type rules to allow types derived from an existing type to be considered inequivalent. In such languages, one can declare a type to be a **subtype** of an existing type, in which case the subtype and original type are type-equivalent. One can also declare a type to be **derived** from an existing type, in which case the derived and original types are not type equivalent. To implement feet and meters as inequivalent, I could therefore create types as follows:

Figure 3.6

```
type                                                  1
    feet = derived integer range 0..maxint;           2
    meters = derived integer range 0..maxint;         3
variable                                              4
    imperial_length : feet;                           5
    metric_length   : meters;                         6
begin                                                 7
    metric_length := metric_length * 2;               8
end;                                                  9
```

In order to make sure that values of a derived type that are stored by one program and read by another maintain their type, Modula-3 **brands** each derived type with a string literal. Branded values may only be read into variables with the same brand. In other words, the programmer may control which derived types are considered structurally equivalent to each other.

There is a slight problem in line 8 in Figure 3.6. The operator * is defined on integer and real, but I intentionally made meters a new type distinct from integer. Similarly, 2 is a literal of type integer, not meters. Ada solves this problem by overloading operators, procedures, and literals associated with a derived type. That is, when meters was created, a new set of arithmetic operators and procedures (like sqrt) was created to take values of type meters. Similarly, integer literals are allowed to serve also as meters literals. The expression in line 8 is valid, but `metric_length * imperial_length` involves a type mismatch.[3]

The compiler determines which version of an overloaded procedure, operator, and literal to use. Intuitively, it tries all possible combinations of interpretations, and if exactly one satisfies all type rules, the expression is valid and well defined. Naturally, a smart compiler won't try all possible combinations; the number could be exponential in the length of the expression. Instead, the compiler builds a collection of subtrees, each representing a possible overload interpretation. When the root of the expression tree is reached, either a unique overload resolution has been found, or the compiler knows that no unique resolution is possible [Baker 82]. (If no appropriate overloaded procedure can be found, it may still be possible to coerce the types of the actual parameters to types that are accepted by a declared procedure. However, type coercion is often surprising to the programmer and leads to confusion.)

The concept of subtype can be generalized by allowing **extensions** and **reductions** to existing types [Paaki 90]. For example, array types can be extended by increasing the index range and reduced by decreasing the index range. Enumeration types can be extended by adding new enumeration constants and reduced by removing enumeration constants. Record types can be extended by adding new fields and reduced by removing fields. (Oberon allows extension of record types.) Extending record types is very similar to the concept of building subclasses in object-oriented programming, discussed in Chapter 5.

The resulting types can be interconverted with the original types for purposes of assignment and parameter passing. Conversion can be either by casting or by coercion. In either case, conversion can ignore array elements and record fields that are not needed in the target type and can set elements and fields that are only known in the target type to an error value. It can generate a runtime error if an enumeration value is unknown in the target type.

The advantage of type extensions and reductions is much the same as that of subclasses in object-oriented languages, discussed in Chapter 5: the new type can make use of the software already developed for the existing type; only new cases need to be specifically addressed in new software. A module that extends or reduces an imported type does not force the module that exports the type to be recompiled.

---

[3] In Ada, a programmer can also overload operators, so one can declare a procedure that takes a metric unit and an imperial unit, converts them, and then multiplies them.

4 ◆ DIMENSIONS

The example involving meters and feet shows that types alone do not prevent programming errors. I want to prohibit multiplying two feet values and assigning the result back into a feet variable, because the type of the result is square feet, not feet.

The AL language, intended for programming mechanical manipulators, introduced a typelike attribute of expressions called **dimension** to prevent such errors [Finkel 76]. This concept was first suggested by C. A. R. Hoare [Hoare 73], and it has been extended in various ways since then. Recent research has shown how to include dimensions in a polymorphic setting like ML [Kennedy 94]. (Polymorphism in ML is discussed extensively later in this chapter.) AL has four predeclared base dimensions: time, distance, angle, and mass. Each base dimension has predeclared constants, such as second, centimeter, and gram. The values of these constants are with respect to an arbitrary set of units; the programmer only needs to know that the constants are mutually consistent. For example, 60*second = minute. New dimensions can be declared and built from the old ones. AL does not support programmer-declared base dimensions, but such an extension would be reasonable. Other useful base dimensions would be electrical current (measured, for instance, in amps), temperature (degrees Kelvin), luminous intensity (lumens), and currency (florin). In retrospect, angle may be a poor choice for a base dimension; it is equivalent to the ratio of two distances: distance along an arc and the radius of a circle. Figure 3.7 shows how dimensions are used.

Figure 3.7	

```
dimension                                              1
    area = distance * distance;                        2
    velocity = distance / time;                        3
constant                                               4
    mile = 5280 * foot; --  foot is predeclared        5
    acre = mile * mile / 640;                          6
variable                                               7
    d1, d2 : distance real;                            8
    a1 : area real;                                    9
    v1 : velocity real;                               10
```

```
begin                                                    11
    d1 := 30 * foot;                                     12
    a1 := d1 * (2 * mile) + (4 * acre);                  13
    v1 := a1 / (5 * foot * 4 * minute);                  14
    d2 := 40; -- invalid: dimension error                15
    d2 := d1 + v1; -- invalid: dimension error           16
    write(d1/foot, "d1 in feet",                         17
          v1*hour/mile, "v1 in miles per hour");         18
end;                                                     19
```

In line 13, a1 is the area comprising 4 acres plus a region 30 feet by 2 miles. In line 14, the compiler can check that the expression on the right-hand side has the dimension of velocity, that is, distance/time, even though it is hard for a human to come up with a simple interpretation of the expression.

In languages lacking a dimension feature, abstract data types, introduced in the next section, can be used instead. The exercises explore this substitution.

5 ◆ ABSTRACT DATA TYPES

An **abstract data type** is a set of values and a set of procedures that manipulate those values. An abstract data type is analogous to a built-in type, which is also a set of values (such as integers) and operations (such as addition) on those values. Once a program has introduced an abstract data type, variables can be declared of that type and values of the type can be passed to the procedures that make up the type. The **client** of an abstract data type (that is, a part of a program that uses that type, as opposed to the part of the program that defines it) can create and manipulate values only by using procedures that the abstract data type allows. The structure of an abstract data type (usually a **record** type) is hidden from the clients. Within the definition of the abstract data type, however, procedures may make full use of that structure.

An abstract data type can be seen as having two parts: the specification and the implementation. The specification is needed by clients; it indicates the name of the type and the headers of the associated procedures. It is not necessary for the client to know the structure of the type or the body of the procedures. The implementation includes the full description of the type and the bodies of the procedures; it may include other procedures that are used as subroutines but are not needed directly by clients.

This logical separation allows a programmer to concentrate on the issues at hand. If the programmer is coding a client, there is no need to worry about how the abstract data type is implemented. The implementer may upgrade or even completely redesign the implementation, and the client should still function correctly, so long as the specification still holds.

A popular example of an abstract data type is the stack. The procedures that manipulate stacks are push, pop, and empty. Whether the implementation uses an array, a linked list, or a data file is irrelevant to the client and may be hidden.

Abstract data types are used extensively in large programs for modularity and abstraction. They put a barrier between the implementor of a set of routines and its clients. Changes in the implementation of an abstract data type will not influence the clients so long as the specification is preserved. Abstract data types also provide a clean extension mechanism for languages. If a new data type is needed that cannot be effectively implemented with the existing primitive types and operations (for example, bitmaps for graphics), it can be still specified and prototyped as a new abstract data type and then efficiently implemented and added to the environment.

In order to separate the specification from the implementation, programming languages should provide a way to hide the implementation details from client code. Languages like C and Pascal that have no hiding mechanism do not cater to abstract data types, even though they permit the programmer to declare new types. CLU, Ada, C++, and Modula-2 (as well as numerous other languages) provide a name-scope technique that allows the programmer to group the procedures and type declarations that make up an abstract data type and to give clients only a limited view of these declarations. All declarations that make up an abstract data type are placed in a **module**.[4] It is a name scope in which the programmer has control over what identifiers are imported from and exported to the surrounding name scope. Local identifiers that are to be seen outside a module are **exported**; all other local identifiers are invisible outside the module, which allows programmers to hide implementation details from the clients of the module. Identifiers from surrounding modules are not automatically inherited by a module. Instead, those that are needed must be explicitly **imported**. These features allow name scopes to selectively import identifiers they require and provide better documentation of what nonlocal identifiers a module will need. Some identifiers, like the predeclared types integer and Boolean, may

---

[4] You can read a nice overview of language support for modules in [Calliss 91]. Modules are used not only for abstract data types, but also for nesting name scopes, separate compilation, device control (in Modula, for example), and synchronization (monitors are discussed in Chapter 7).

be declared **pervasive**, which means that they are automatically imported into all nested name scopes.

Languages that support abstract data types often allow modules to be partitioned into the specification part and the implementation part. (Ada, Modula-2, C++, and Oberon have this facility; CLU and Eiffel do not.) The **specification part** contains declarations intended to be visible to clients of the module; it may include constants, types, variables, and procedure headers. The **implementation part** contains the bodies (that is, implementations) of procedures as well as other declarations that are private to the module. Typically, the specification part is in a separate source file that is referred to both by clients and by the implementation part, each of which is in a separate source file.

Partitioning modules into specification and implementation parts helps support libraries of precompiled procedures and separate compilation. Only the specification part of a module is needed to compile procedures that use the module. The implementation part of the module need not be supplied until link time. However, separating the parts can make it difficult for implementation programmers to find relevant declarations, since they might be in either part. One reasonable solution is to join the parts for the convenience of the implementor and extract just the specification part for the benefit of the compiler or client-application programmer.

Figure 3.8 shows how a stack abstract data type might be programmed.

Figure 3.8

```
module Stack;                                         1

export                                                2
    Push, Pop, Empty, StackType, MaxStackSize;        3

constant                                              4
    MaxStackSize = 10;                                5

type                                                  6
    private StackType =                               7
        record                                        8
            Size : 0..MaxStackSize := 0;              9
            Data : array 1..MaxStackSize of integer;  10
        end;                                          11
```

```
        -- details omitted for the following procedures        12
        procedure Push(reference ThisStack : StackType;        13
            readonly What : integer);                          14
        procedure Pop(reference ThisStack) : integer;          15
        procedure Empty(readonly ThisStack) : Boolean;         16

    end; -- Stack                                              17
```

In Figure 3.8, line 3 indicates that the module exports the three procedures. It also exports the constant MaxStackSize, which the client may wish to consult, and StackType, so the client may declare variables of this type. I assume that integer and Boolean are pervasive. The code does not export enumeration types or record types. Generally, exporting these types implies exporting the enumeration constants and the record field names as well.

In Ada, the programmer can control to what extent the details of an exported type are visible to the module's clients. By default, the entire structure of an exported type, such as its record field names, is visible. If the exported type is declared as **private**, as in line 7, then only construction, destruction, assignment, equality, and inequality operations are available to the client. Even these can be hidden if the exported type is declared **limited private**. The only way the client can manipulate objects of **limited private** types is to present them as actual parameters to the module's procedures. The programmer of the implementation may change the details of private types, knowing that the change will not affect the correctness of the clients. In Oberon, record types can be partly visible and partly private.

Languages differ in how programmers restrict identifier export. In some languages, like Simula, all identifiers are exported unless explicitly hidden. Others, like Eiffel, provide for different clients (which are other modules) to import different sets of identifiers from the same module. The **export** line for Eiffel might look as shown in Figure 3.9:

Figure 3.9

```
export                                                         1
    Push, Pop, Empty, StackType {ModuleA},                     2
        MaxStackSize {ModuleA, ModuleB};                       3
```

Here, Push, Pop, and Empty are exported to all clients. Only ModuleA may import StackType, and only two modules may import MaxStackSize. The module can thereby ensure that no client makes unauthorized use of an exported identifier. However, this approach of restricting exports requires that a module be recompiled any time its client set changes, which can be cumbersome.

An alternative, found in Modula-2, is for client modules to selectively import identifiers, as in Figure 3.10.

Figure 3.10

```
from Stack import                                                              1
      Push, Pop, Empty, StackType;                                             2
```

This client has chosen not to import `MaxStackSize`. This approach of restricting imports is not as secure but requires less recompilation when programs change.[5]

Very large programs sometimes face confusion when importing from several modules; the same identifier may be imported from more than one module. Languages often permit or require qualified identifiers to be used in order to remove any ambiguity.

The **principle of uniform reference** suggests that clients should not be able to discover algorithmic details of exporting modules. In particular, they should not be able to distinguish whether an exported identifier is a constant, a variable, or a parameterless function. However, in many languages, the client *can* distinguish these identifiers. In C++, for example, parameterless functions are special because they are invoked with parentheses surrounding an empty list. Variables are special in that only they may be used on the left-hand side of an assignment. In Eiffel, however, the syntax is the same for all three, and exported variables are readonly, so the principle of uniform reference is upheld.

6 ◆ LABELS, PROCEDURES, AND TYPES AS FIRST-CLASS VALUES

You are used to thinking of integers as values. But to what extent is a label or a procedure a value? Can a type itself be a value? One way to address these questions is to categorize values by what sort of manipulation they allow. The following chart distinguishes **first**, **second**, and **third-class values**.

---

[5] The difference between restricting exports and restricting imports is identical to the difference between access lists and capability lists in operating systems.

Manipulation	Class of value		
	First	Second	Third
Pass value as a parameter	yes	yes	no
Return value from a procedure	yes	no	no
Assign value into a variable	yes	no	no

Languages differ in how they treat labels, procedures, and types. For example, procedures are third-class values in Ada, second-class values in Pascal, and first-class values in C and Modula-2. Labels are generally third-class values, but they are second-class values in Algol-60.

Labels and procedures are similar in some ways. If a label is passed as a parameter, then jumping to it must restore the central stack to its situation when the label was elaborated. The value of a label passed as a parameter must therefore include a reference to the central stack as well as a reference to an instruction. In other words, a label is passed as a closure. Similarly, procedures that are passed as parameters generally are passed as closures, so that when they are invoked, they regain their nonlocal referencing environments. In both cases, the closure points to an activation record deeper on the central stack than the called procedure's activation record. Jumping to a passed label causes the central stack to be unwound, removing intermediate activation records. Invoking a passed procedure establishes its static chain to point somewhere deep in the central stack.

Allowing labels and procedures to be first-class values is trickier. Such values may be stored in variables and invoked at a time when the central stack no longer contains the activation record to which they point. Figure 3.11 demonstrates the problem.

Figure 3.11

```
variable                                        1
    ProcVar : procedure();                      2

procedure Outer();                              3
    variable OuterVar : integer;                4
    procedure Inner();                          5
    begin -- Inner                              6
        write(OuterVar);                        7
    end; -- Inner                               8
begin -- Outer                                  9
    ProcVar := Inner; -- closure is assigned    10
end; -- Outer                                   11
```

```
begin -- main program                                           12
    Outer();                                                    13
    ProcVar();                                                  14
end;                                                            15
```

By the time Inner is invoked (as the value of the procedure variable ProcVar in line 14), its nonlocal referencing environment, the instance of Outer, has been deactivated, because Outer has returned. I call this the **dangling-procedure problem**. Languages take various stances in regard to the dangling-procedure problem:

1. Treat any program that tries to invoke a closure with a dangling pointer as erroneous, but don't try to discover the error.
2. Prevent the bad situation from arising by language restrictions. Top-level procedures do not need a nonlocal referencing environment. In C, all procedures are top-level, so bad situations cannot arise. Modula-2 disallows assigning any but a top-level procedure as a value to a variable; it forbids the assignment in line 10 above. Neither language treats labels as first-class values.
3. Prevent the bad situation from arising by expensive implementation. The nice aspect of a central stack is that allocation and deallocation are inexpensive and occur in a strict stack order as procedures are invoked and return. This inexpensive mechanism can be replaced by activation records that are allocated from the heap and are linked together. A reference-count mechanism suffices for reclamation, since there will be no cycles. Activation, deactivation, and access to referencing environments is likely to be slower than if a stack were used.

Labels as first-class values are frightening for another reason: they can be stored in a variable and repeatedly invoked. Therefore, the procedure that elaborates a label (that is, that defines the label) can return more than once, because that label may be invoked repeatedly. Multiply-returning procedures are certain to be confusing.

So far, I have only dealt with labels and procedures, but the same questions can also be asked about types. Types as parameters, type variables and procedures that return types could be very useful. For example, an abstract data type implementing stacks really ought to be parameterized by the type of the stack element, rather than having it simply "wired in" as integer, as in Figure 3.8 (page 73). Ada and C++ allow a limited form of **type polymorphism**, that is, the ability to partially specify a type when it is declared and further specify it later. They implement polymorphism by permitting modules (that is, the name scopes that define abstract data types) to accept type parameters. Such modules are called **generic modules**.[6] A declaration of a generic module creates a template for a set of actual modules. The stack example can be rewritten as in Figure 3.12.

Figure 3.12

```
generic(type ElementType) module Stack;                           1

export                                                            2
    Push, Pop, Empty, StackType, MaxStackSize;                    3

constant                                                          4
    MaxStackSize = 10;                                            5

type                                                              6
    private StackType =                                           7
        record                                                    8
            Size : 0..MaxStackSize := 0;                          9
            Data : array 1..MaxStackSize of ElementType;         10
        end;                                                     11
                                                                 12

    -- details omitted for the following procedures             13
    procedure Push(reference ThisStack : StackType;             14
        readonly What : ElementType);                           15
    procedure Pop(reference ThisStack) : ElementType;           16
    procedure Empty(readonly ThisStack) : Boolean;              17

end; -- Stack                                                   18

module IntegerStack = Stack(integer);                           19
```

To create an instance of a generic module, I **instantiate** it, as in line 19. Instantiation of generic modules in Ada and C++ is a compile-time, not a runtime, operation — more like macro expansion than procedure invocation. Compilers that support generic modules need to store the module text in order to create instances.

The actual types that are substituted into the formal generic parameters need not be built-in types like integer; program-defined types are also acceptable. However, the code of the generic module may require that the actual type satisfy certain requirements. For example, it might only make sense to include pointer types, or array types, or numeric types. Ada provides a way for generic modules to stipulate what sorts of types are acceptable. If the constraint, for example, is that the actual type be numeric, then Ada will permit operations like + inside the

---

[6] Ada and C++ allow generic procedures in addition to generic modules.

generic module; if there the constraint only requires that assignment work, Ada will not allow the + operation. Now, program-defined types may be numeric in spirit. For example, a complex number can be represented by a record with two fields. Both Ada and C++ allow operators like + to be overloaded to accept parameters of such types, so that generic modules can accept these types as actual parameters with a "numeric" flavor.

More general manipulation of types can also be desirable. Type constructors like **array** or **record** can be viewed as predeclared, type-valued procedures. It would be nice to be able to allow programmers to write such type constructors. Although this is beyond the capabilities of today's mainstream languages, it is allowed in Russell, discussed later in this chapter. A much fuller form of polymorphism is also seen in the ML language, the subject of the next section.

7 ♦ ML

Now that I have covered some issues surrounding types, I will present a detailed look at one of the most interesting strongly typed languages, ML [Harper 89; Paulson 92]. ML, designed by Robin Milner, is a functional programming language (the subject of Chapter 4), which means that procedure calls do not have any **side effects** (changing values of variables) and that there are no variables as such. Since the only reason to call a procedure is to get its return value, all procedures are actually functions, and I will call them that. Functions are first-class values: They can be passed as parameters, returned as values from procedures, and embedded in data structures. **Higher-order functions** (that is, functions returning other functions) are used extensively. Function application is the most important control construct, and it is extremely uniform: all functions take exactly one parameter and return exactly one result. Parameters and results can, however, be arbitrary structures, thereby achieving the effect of passing many parameters and producing many results. Parameters to functions are evaluated before invocation and are passed in value mode.

ML is an **interactive** language. An ML session is a dialogue of questions and answers. Interaction is achieved by an **incremental compiler**, which translates new code (typically new functions) and integrates it into already-compiled code. Incremental compilers have some of the advantages of interpreted languages (fast turnaround for dialogues) and of compiled languages (high execution speed).

ML is statically scoped. All identifiers are associated with meanings according to where they occur in the program text, not according to run-time execution paths. This design avoids name conflicts in large programs, because identifier names can be hidden in local scopes, and it prevents accidental damage to existing programs. Static scoping greatly improves the security and, incidentally, the efficiency of an interactive language.

ML is strongly typed. Every ML expression has a statically determined type. The type of an expression is usually inferred from the way it is used so that type declarations are not necessary. This **type inference** property is very useful in interactive use, when it would be distracting to have to provide type information. However, it is always possible for the programmer to specify the type of any value. Adding redundant type information can be a good documentation practice in large programs. Strong typing guarantees that expressions will not generate type errors at runtime. Static type checking promotes safety; it detects at compile time a large proportion of bugs in programs that make extensive use of the ML data-structuring capabilities (type checking does not help so much in numerical or engineering programs, since there is no concept of dimension). Usually, only truly "logical" bugs are left after compilation.

ML has a **polymorphic type** mechanism. Type expressions may contain **type identifiers**, which stand for arbitrary types. With such expressions, the ML programmer can express the type of a function that behaves uniformly on a class of parameters of different (but structurally related) types. For example, the `length` function, which computes the length of a list, has type `'a` **list** `-> int`, where `'a` is a type identifier standing for any type. Length can work on lists of any type (lists of integers, lists of functions, lists of lists, and so forth), because it disregards the elements of the list. The polymorphic type mechanism gives ML much of the expressiveness of dynamic-typed languages without the conceptual cost of runtime type errors or the computational cost of runtime type checking.

ML has a rich collection of data types, and the programmer can define new abstract data types. In fact, arrays are not part of the language definition; they can be considered as a predeclared abstract data type that just happens to be more efficient than its ML specification would lead one to believe.

ML has an exception-handling mechanism that allows programs to uniformly handle predeclared and programmer-declared exceptions. (Exception handling is discussed in Chapter 2.) Exceptions can be selectively trapped, and handlers can be specified.

ML programs can be grouped into separately compiled modules. Dependencies among modules can be easily expressed, and the sharing of common submodules is automatically guaranteed. ML keeps track of module versions to detect compiled modules that are out of date.

I will describe some (by no means all!) of the features of SML, the Standard ML of New Jersey implementation [Appel 91]. I should warn you that I have intentionally left out large parts of the language that do not pertain directly to the concept of type. For example, programming in the functional style, which is natural to ML, is discussed in Chapter 4. If you find functional programming confusing, you might want to read Chapter 4 before the rest of this chapter. In addition, I do not discuss how ML implements abstract data types, which is mostly similar to what I have covered earlier. I do not dwell on one very significant type constructor: **ref**, which represents a pointer to a value. Pointer types introduce variables into the language, because a program can associate an identifier with a pointer value, and the object pointed to can be manipulated (assigned into and accessed). ML is therefore not completely functional. The examples are syntactically correct SML program fragments. I mark the user's input by in and ML's output by out.

7.1 Expressions

ML is an expression-based language; all the standard programming constructs (conditionals, declarations, procedures, and so forth) are packaged as expressions yielding values. Strictly speaking, there are no statements: even operations that have side effects return values.

It is always meaningful to supply an arbitrary expression as the parameter to a function (when the type constraints are satisfied) or to combine expressions to form larger expressions in the same way that simple constants can be combined.

Arithmetic expressions have a fairly conventional appearance; the result of evaluating an expression is presented by ML as a value and its type, separated by a colon, as in Figure 3.13.

Figure 3.13
```
in:  (3 + 5) * 2;                                                          1
out: 16 : int                                                              2
```

String expressions are straightforward (Figure 3.14).

Figure 3.14
```
in:  "this is it";                                                         1
out: "this is it" : string                                                 2
```

Tuples of values are enclosed in parentheses, and their elements are separated by commas. The type of a tuple is described by the type constructor * .[7]

---

[7] The * constructor, which usually denotes product, denotes here the set-theoretic Cartesian product of the values of the component types. A value in a Cartesian product is a compound formed by selecting one value from each of its underlying component types. The number of values is the product of the number of values of the component types, which is one reason this set-theoretic operation is called a product.

Figure 3.15

```
in:   (3,4);                                              1
out:  (3,4) : int * int                                  2

in:   (3,4,5);                                            3
out:  (3,4,5) : int * int * int                          4
```

Lists are enclosed in square brackets, and their elements are separated by commas, as in Figure 3.16. The list type constructor is the word **list** after the component type.

Figure 3.16

```
in:   [1,2,3,4];                                         1
out:  [1,2,3,4] : int list                               2

in:   [(3,4),(5,6)];                                     3
out:  [(3,4),(5,6)] : (int * int) list                   4
```

Conditional expressions have ordinary **if** syntax (as usual in expression-based languages, **else** cannot be omitted), as in Figure 3.17.

Figure 3.17

```
in:   if true then 3 else 4;                             1
out:  3 : int                                            2

in:   if (if 3 = 4 then false else true)                 3
           then false else true;                         4
out:  false : bool                                       5
```

The **if** part must be a Boolean expression. Two predeclared constants true and false denote the Boolean values; the two binary Boolean operators **orelse** and **andalso** have short-circuit semantics (described in Chapter 1).

7.2 Global Declarations

Values are bound to identifiers by **declarations**. Declarations can appear at the top level, in which case their scope is global, or in blocks, in which case they have a limited local scope spanning a single expression. I will first deal with global declarations.

Declarations are not expressions. They establish bindings instead of returning values. Value bindings are introduced by the keyword **val**; additional value bindings are prefixed by **and** (Figure 3.18).

Figure 3.18

```
in:   val   a = 3 and                                                        1
            b = 5 and                                                        2
            c = 2;                                                           3
out:  val c = 2 : int                                                        4
      val b = 5 : int                                                        5
      val a = 3 : int                                                        6

in:   (a + b) div c;                                                         7
out:  4 : int                                                               8
```

In this case, I have declared the identifiers a, b, and c at the top level; they will be accessible from now on unless I redeclare them. Value bindings printed by ML are always prefixed by **val**, to distinguish them from type bindings and module bindings.

Identifiers are not variables; they are named constants. All identifiers must be initialized when introduced. The initial values determine their types, which need not be given explicitly.

Value declarations are also used to declare functions, with the syntax shown in Figure 3.19.

Figure 3.19

```
in:   val f = fn x => x + 1;                                                1
out:  val f = fn : int -> int                                              2

in:   val g = fn (a,b) => (a + b) div 2;                                    3
out:  val g = fn : (int * int) -> int                                      4

in:   (f 3, g(8,4));                                                        5
out:  (4,6) : int * int                                                    6
```

The function f declared in line 1 has one formal parameter, x. The result of a function is the value of its body, in this case x+1. The arrow -> (lines 2 and 4) is a type constructor that takes two types (the left operand is the type of the parameter of the function, and the right operand is the type of its return value) and returns the type that describes a function that takes such a parameter and returns such a result. In other words, functions have types that can be described by a constructor syntax, which is necessary if functions are to be first-class values and if all values are to have describable types. The function g declared in line 3 has a single parameter, the tuple of integers formally named a and b.

Parameters to functions do not generally need to be parenthesized (both in declarations and applications): the simple juxtaposition of two expressions is interpreted as a **function application**, that is, as invoking the function (the first expression) with the given parameter (the second expression). Function application is an invisible, high-precedence, binary operator; expressions like f 3 + 4 are parsed like (f 3) + 4 and not like f (3 + 4). Parentheses are needed in line 5, because g 8,4 would be interpreted as (g 8),4.

The identifiers f and g are bound to functions. Since functions are first-class values, they can stand alone, without being applied to parameters (Figure 3.20).

Figure 3.20

```
in:  (f, f 3);                                  1
out: (fn,4) : (int -> int) * int               2

in:  val h = g;                                 3
out: val h = fn : (int * int) -> int           4
```

In line 1, f is both presented alone and applied to 3. Functional values, shown in line 2, are always printed **fn** without showing their internal structure. In line 3, h is mapped to the function g. I could also have written line 3 as **val** h = **fn** (a,b) => g(a,b).

Identifiers are statically scoped, and their values cannot change. When new identifiers are declared, they may override previously declared identifiers having the same name, but those other identifiers still exist and still retain their old values. Consider Figure 3.21.

Figure 3.21

```
in:  val a = 3;                                 1
out: val a = 3 : int                            2

in:  val f = fn x => a + x;                     3
out: val f = fn : int -> int                    4

in:  val a = [1,2,3];                           5
out: val a = [1,2,3] : int list                 6

in:  f 1;                                       7
out: 4 : int                                    8
```

The function f declared in line 3 uses the top-level identifier a, which was bound to 3 in line 1. Hence f is a function from integers to integers that returns its parameter plus 3. Then a is redeclared at the top level (line 5) to be a list of three integers; any subsequent reference to a will yield that list (unless it is redeclared again). But f is not affected at all: the old value of a was frozen in f at the moment of its declaration, and f continues to add 3 to its actual parameter. The nonlocal referencing environment of f was bound when it was first elaborated and is then fixed. In other words, ML uses deep binding.

Deep binding is consistent with static scoping of identifiers. It is quite common in block-structured programming languages, but it is rarely used in interactive languages like ML. The use of deep binding at the top level may sometimes be counterintuitive. For example, if a function f calls a previously declared function g, then redeclaring g (for example, to correct a bug) will not change f, which will keep calling the old version of g.

The **and** keyword is used to introduce sets of independent declarations: None of them uses the identifiers declared by the other bindings in the set; however, a declaration often needs identifiers introduced by previous declarations. The programmer may introduce such declarations sequentially, as in Figure 3.22.

Figure 3.22

```
in:   val a = 3; val b = 2 * a;                                    1
out:  val a = 3 : int                                              2
      val b = 6 : int                                              3
```

A function that expects a pair of elements can be converted to an infix operator for convenience, as seen in line 2 of Figure 3.23.

Figure 3.23

```
in:   val plus = fn (a,b) => a + b : int;                          1
in:   infix plus;                                                  2
in:   4 plus 5;                                                    3
out:  9 : int;                                                     4
```

7.3 Local Declarations

Declarations can be made local by embedding them in a block (see Figure 3.24), which is formed by the keywords **let** (followed by the declarations), **in** (followed by a single expression, the body), and **end**. The scope of the declaration is limited to this body.

Figure 3.24

```
in:   let                                                         1
          val a = 3 and b = 5                                     2
      in                                                          3
          (a + b) div 2                                           4
      end;                                                        5
out:  4 : int                                                     6
```

Here the identifiers a and b are mapped to the values 3 and 5 respectively for the extent of the expression (a + b) **div** 2. No top-level binding is introduced; the whole **let** construct is an expression whose value is the value of its body.

Just as in the global scope, identifiers can be locally redeclared, hiding the previous declarations (whether local or not). It is convenient to think of each redeclaration as introducing a new scope. Previous declarations are not affected, as demonstrated in Figure 3.25.

Figure 3.25

```
in:  val a = 3 and b = 5;                               1
out: val b = 5 : int;                                   2
     val a = 3 : int;                                   3

in:  (let val a = 8 in a + b end, a);                   4
out: (13,3) : int * int                                 5
```

The body of a block can access all the identifiers declared in the surrounding environment (like b), unless they are redeclared (like a).

Declarations can be composed sequentially in local scopes just as in the global scope, as shown in Figure 3.26.

Figure 3.26

```
in:  let                                                1
         val a = 3;                                     2
         val b = 2 * a                                  3
     in                                                 4
         (a,b)                                          5
     end;                                               6
out: (3,6) : int * int                                  7
```

7.4 Lists

Lists are homogeneous; that is, all their components must have the same type. The component type may be anything, such as strings, lists of integers, and functions from integers to Booleans.

Many functions dealing with lists can work on lists of any kind (for example to compute the length); they do not have to be rewritten every time a new kind of list is introduced. In other words, these functions are naturally polymorphic; they accept a parameter with a range of acceptable types and return a result whose type depends on the type of the parameter. Other functions are more restricted in what type of lists they accept; summing a list makes sense for integer lists, but not for Boolean lists. However, because ML allows functions to be passed as parameters, programmers can generalize such restricted functions. For example, summing an integer list is a special case of a more general function that accumulates a single result by scanning a list and applying a commutative, associative operation repeatedly to its elements. In particular, it is not hard to code a polymorphic accumulate function that can be used to sum the elements of a list this way, as in Figure 3.27.

Figure 3.27

```
in:     accumulate([3,4,5], fn (x,y) => x+y, 0);     1
out:    12 : int                                       2
```

Line 1 asks for the list [3,4,5] to be accumulated under integer summation, whose identity value is 0. Implementing the accumulate function is left as an exercise.

The fundamental list constructors are nil, the empty list, and the right-associative binary operator :: (pronounced "cons," based on LISP, discussed in Chapter 4), which places an element (its left operand) at the head of a list (its right operand). The square-brackets constructor for lists (for example, [1,2,3]) is an abbreviation for a sequence of cons operations terminated by nil: 1 :: (2 :: (3 :: nil)). Nil itself may be written []. ML always uses the square-brackets notation when printing lists.

Expression	Evaluates to
nil	[]
1 :: [2,3]	[1,2,3]
1 :: 2 :: 3 :: nil	[1,2,3]

Other predeclared operators on lists include
- null, which returns true if its parameter is nil, and false on any other list.
- hd, which returns the first element of a nonempty list.
- tl, which strips the first element from the head of a nonempty list.
- @ (append), which concatenates lists.

Hd and tl are called **selectors**, because they allow the programmer to select a component of a structure. Here are some examples that use the predeclared operators.

Expression	Evaluates to
null []	true
null [1,2,3]	false
hd [1,2,3]	1
tl [1,2,3]	[2,3]
[1,2] @ []	[1,2]
[] @ [3,4]	[3,4]
[1,2] @ [3,4]	[1,2,3,4]

Lists are discussed in greater depth in Chapter 4, which discusses functional languages. They are interesting to us in this chapter because of their interaction with ML's type rules and with patterns.

7.5 Functions and Patterns

Because all functions take exactly one parameter, it is often necessary to pass complicated structures in that parameter. The programmer may want the formal parameter to show the structure and to name its components. ML patterns provide this ability, as shown in Figure 3.28.

Figure 3.28

```
in:   val plus = fn (a,b) => a + b;
```

I need to say a + b : int, as I will show later. Here, the function plus takes a single parameter, which is expressed as a pattern showing that the parameter must be a tuple with two elements, which are called formally a and b.[8] This pattern does not force the actual parameter to be presented as an explicit tuple, as Figure 3.29 shows.

Figure 3.29

```
in:   plus(3,4)                              1
out:  7 : int                                2

in:   let                                    3
            val x = (3,4)                     4
      in                                      5
            plus x                            6
      end;                                    7
out:  7 : int                                8
```

The first example (line 1) builds the actual parameter to plus explicitly from two components, 3 and 4. The comma between them is the tuple constructor. The syntax is contrived to remind the programmer that the intent is to provide two parameters.[9] The second example presents a single variable x as the actual parameter (line 6); the compiler can tell that it has the right type, namely int * int.

Figure 3.30 shows how the declaration of plus can be written in single-parameter form.

---

[8] The declaration is actually ambiguous; ML cannot determine which meaning of + is meant.

[9] In practice, a compiler can usually optimize away the extra pair constructions.

Figure 3.30

```
in:   val plus = fn x =>                           1
            let                                     2
                 val (a,b) = x                      3
            in                                      4
                 a + b                              5
            end;                                    6
out:  val plus = fn : int * int -> int
```

This example avoids a pattern for the formal parameter, now called x (line 1). However, it introduces a pattern in line 3 to produce the same effect. This pattern constrains x (retroactively) to be a pair, and it binds a and b to the two components. Figure 3.31 also uses patterns, both in specifying formal parameters and in declaring identifiers.

Figure 3.31

```
in:   val f = fn [x,y,z] => (x,y,z);               1
out:  val f = fn : 'a list -> 'a * 'a * 'a         2

in:   val (a,b,c) = f[1,2,3];                      3
out:  val c = 3 : int                              4
      val b = 2 : int                              5
      val a = 1 : int                              6
```

The function f (line 1) returns three values packaged as a tuple. The pattern a,b,c in line 3 is used to unpack the result of f[1,2,3] into its components.

Patterns in ML come in many forms. For example, a pattern [a,b,c] matches a list of exactly three elements, which are mapped to a, b, and c; a pattern first::rest matches a nonempty list with its first element associated with first, and its other elements to rest. Similarly, first::second::rest matches a list with at least two elements, and so forth. The most common patterns are tuples like (a,b,c), but more complicated patterns can be constructed by nesting, such as ([a,b],c,(d,e)::_). The don't-care pattern _ matches any value without establishing any binding. Patterns can conveniently replace selector operators for unpacking data.

Patterns allow functions to be coded using **case analysis**, that is, testing the value of the parameter to determine which code to execute. This situation is most common in recursive functions, which must first test if the parameter is the base case, which is treated differently from other cases. ML programs seldom need to use the **if** expression for this purpose. Instead, pattern alternatives are used, as in Figure 3.32.

Figure 3.32

```
in:  val rec summation =                                    1
         fn nil => 0                                        2
          | (head :: tail) => head + summation tail;        3
out: val summation = fn : int list -> int                  4
```

The **rec** declaration in line 1 indicates that the scope of the declaration of summation starts immediately, not after the declaration. This wide scope allows the invocation of summation in line 3 to refer to this function itself. The formal parameter is presented as a series of alternatives separated by the | symbol. Each alternative gives a different pattern, thereby restricting the allowable values of the actual parameter and naming its formal components. The patterns are evaluated sequentially when the function is invoked. If a pattern matches the actual parameter, the identifiers in the pattern act as formal parameters that are bound to the respective parts of the actual parameter, and the corresponding action is executed. If several patterns match the actual parameter, only the first matching one is activated. If all patterns fail to match the actual parameter, a runtime exception occurs. In this case, the first pattern requires that the parameter be an empty list; the second matches any nonempty list and names its components head and tail.[10]

Patterns used for case analysis should obey several properties. First, they must all be of the same type. In Figure 3.32, both nil and (head :: tail) are of a list type with unspecified component type. ML disallows a declaration in which the formal-parameter patterns cannot be unified into a single type. Second, they should be exhaustive, covering all possible cases. The ML compiler will issue a warning if it detects a nonexhaustive match. (In the example, omitting either of the two cases elicits such a warning.) Invoking a function with a nonexhaustive match can lead to a Match exception being raised (exceptions are discussed in Chapter 2). Third, good style dictates that they should not overlap. The ML compiler issues a warning if it detects a redundant match. The first matching pattern will be used when the function is invoked.

Patterns are found in other languages as well. CSP (Chapter 7) and Prolog (Chapter 8) use patterns both for unpacking parameters and for introducing restrictions on their values. String-processing languages (Chapter 9) use patterns for testing data and extracting components.

---

[10] The parentheses in the second pattern are not needed; I put them in for the sake of clarity. Parentheses are required in tuples, however.

7.6 Polymorphic Types

A function is **polymorphic** when it can work uniformly over parameters of different data types. For example, the function in Figure 3.33 computes the length of a list.

Figure 3.33

```
in:   val rec length =                                          1
         fn nil => 0                                            2
          | (_ :: tail) => 1 + length tail;                     3
out:  val length = fn : 'a list -> int                          4

in:   (length [1,2,3], length ["a","b","c","d"]);              5
out:  (3,4) : int * int                                        6
```

The type of length inferred by the compiler (line 4) contains a type identifier ('a), indicating that any kind of list can be used, such as an integer list or a string list. A type identifier is any ordinary identifier prefixed by one or more tic marks ('). For convenience, we can pronounce 'a as "alpha" and 'b as "beta."

A type is **polymorphic** if it contains type identifiers; otherwise it is **monomorphic**. A type identifier can be mapped to any ML type and thereby form an instance of that type. For example, int **list** is a monomorphic instance of 'a **list**. Instances of polymorphic types may themselves be polymorphic. For example, ('b * 'c) **list** is a polymorphic instance of 'a **list**.

Several type identifiers can be used in a type, and each identifier can appear several times, expressing contextual relationships between components of a type. For example, 'a * 'a is the type of all pairs having components of the same type. Contextual constraints can also be expressed between parameters and results of functions, as in the identity function, which has type 'a -> 'a, or the function in Figure 3.34, which swaps pairs:

Figure 3.34

```
in:   val swap = fn (x,y) => (y,x);                            1
out:  val swap = fn : ('a * 'b) -> ('b * 'a)                   2

in:   swap ([],"abc");                                         3
out:  ("abc",[]) : string * ('a list)                         4
```

The empty list [] is a polymorphic expression of type 'a **list**, because it can be considered an empty integer list, an empty string list, or some other empty list.

In printing out polymorphic types, ML uses the type identifiers 'a, 'b, and so on in succession, starting again from 'a at every new top-level declaration.

Several primitive functions are polymorphic. For example, you have already encountered the list operators, whose types appear in the following table.

Operator	Type
nil	'a list
::	('a * 'a list) -> 'a list
null	('a list) -> bool
hd	('a list) -> 'a
tl	('a list) -> ('a list)
@	('a list * 'a list) -> ('a list)

If these operators were not polymorphic, a program would need different primitive operators for all possible types of list elements. The 'a shared by the two parameters of :: (cons) prevents any attempt to build lists containing expressions of different types.

The user can always determine the type of any ML function or expression by typing its name at the top level; the expression is evaluated and, as usual, its type is printed after its value, as in Figure 3.35.

Figure 3.35

```
in:   [];                                              1
out:  [] : 'a list                                     2

in:   hd;                                              3
out:  fn : ('a list) -> 'a                             4
```

7.7 Type Inference

A type can be a type identifier ('a, 'b, ...), or it can be constructed with type constructors. Predeclared type constants, like int and bool, are actually nullary type constructors. Polymorphic type constructors include -> , * , and **list**.

As a simple example of type inference, if I declare Identity = **fn** x => x, then Identity has type 'a -> 'a, because it returns unchanged expressions of any type. If I have the application Identity 0, then since 0 is of type int, this application of Identity is specialized to int -> int, and hence the value of the application is of type int.

The following table summarizes the types assumed for a variety of literals and operators, some of which are naturally polymorphic.

Expression	Type
true	bool
false	bool
1	int
+	(int * int) -> int
=	('a * 'a) -> bool
nil	'a list
::	('a * 'a list) -> 'a list
hd	'a list -> 'a
tl	'a list -> 'a list
null	'a list -> bool

A type expression may contain several occurrences of the same type identifier, allowing the programmer to specify type dependencies. Thus 'a -> 'a represents a function whose parameter and result type are the same, although it does not specify what that type is. In a type expression, all occurrences of a type identifier must represent the same type. Discovering that type is done by an algorithm called **unification**; it finds the strongest common type constraint for (possibly polymorphic) types. For example, int -> int and (int -> bool) -> (int -> bool) can be unified to 'a -> 'a. They can also be unified to 'a -> 'b, but that is a weaker constraint. In fact, they can be unified to the weakest possible type, 'a.

To perform polymorphic type inference, ML assigns a type identifier to each expression whose type is unknown and then solves for the type identifiers. The algorithm to solve for the type identifiers is based on repeatedly applying constraints:

1. All occurrences of the same identifier (under the scoping rules) have the same type.
2. In a **let rec** declaration, all free occurrences of the declared identifier (that is, those that are not bound by new declarations in nested name scopes) have the same type.
3. In a conditional expression such as **if** B **then** branch1 **else** branch2, B must have type bool, and branch1, branch2, and the total expression have the same type. A shorthand expression for this constraint would be **if** bool **then** 'a **else** 'a : 'a.
4. Function application: ('a -> 'b) 'a : 'b. This means that applying a function to a parameter yields a result of the appropriate type. This constraint can be used to derive the type of the parameter, the type of the result, or the type of the function.
5. Function abstraction: **fn** 'a => 'b : 'a -> 'b. This means that an anonymous function has a type based on the type of its parameter

and its result. Again, this constraint can be used to derive the type of the parameter, the type of the result, or the type of the function.

Let me now illustrate type inference based on the code in Figure 3.36.

Figure 3.36

```
in:   val rec length = fn AList =>                        1
              if null AList then                          2
                    0                                      3
              else                                         4
                    1 + length(tl AList);                  5
out:  val length = fn : 'a list -> int
```

To begin, the following type constraints hold:

Expression	Type
length	't1 -> 't2
AList	't3
null AList	bool
1 + length(tl AList))	int

Using the type of null, that is, 'a **list** -> bool, it must be that 't3 = 'a **list**, and because + returns int, it must be that length(tl AList) : int; hence 't2 = int. Now tl : 'a **list** -> 'a **list**, so tl AList : 'a **list**. Therefore, length : 'a **list** -> int, which agrees with the intuitive declaration of a length function.

Although type inference may appear trivial, interesting problems can arise. Consider first self-application, as shown in Figure 3.37.

Figure 3.37

```
in:   val F = fn x => x x;                                 1
out:  Type clash  in:   (x x)                              2
      Looking  for a:   'a                                  3
      I have found a:   'a -> 'b                            4
```

Here, F : 'a -> 'b, so x : 'a. Since (x x) : 'b, therefore x : 'a -> 'b, which leads to the conclusion that 'a = 'a -> 'b, which has no (finite) solution. Under the type inference rules, F has an invalid type.

Another interesting problem is illustrated in Figure 3.38.

Figure 3.38

```
in:   val f1 = fn x => (x 3, x true);                    1
out:  Type clash in:  (x true)                           2
      Looking for a:  int                                3
      I have found a:  bool                              4
```

The problem is how to type the parameter x, which clearly is a function. ML treats functions as first-class values, so passing a function as a parameter isn't a problem. The first application of x to 3 suggests a type of int -> 'a, while the second application to true suggests bool -> 'b. You might be tempted to generalize the type of x to 'c -> 'a, so any function would be valid as a parameter to f. But, for example, not (of type bool -> bool) matches 'c -> 'a, but not can't take an integer parameter, as required in the first application of x. Rather, ML must conclude that f can't be typed using the rules discussed above and hence is invalid.

Now consider the valid variant of f1 shown in Figure 3.39.

Figure 3.39

```
in:   let                                                1
          val f2 = fn x => x                             2
      in                                                 3
          ((f2 3), (f2 true))                            4
      end;                                               5
out:  (3,true) : int * bool                              6
```

Now f2's type is 'a -> 'a, so both calls of f2 are valid. The significance is that a parameter to a function, like x in f1, must have a single type that works each time it appears. In this case, neither int -> 'a nor bool -> 'a works. On the other hand, polymorphic functions like f2 can acquire different inferred types each time they are used, as in line 4 of Figure 3.39.

Even with its polymorphism, ML is strongly typed. The compiler knows the type of every value, even though that type may be expressed with respect to type identifiers that are not yet constrained. Furthermore, ML is **type-safe**; that is, whenever a program passes the compile-time type-checking rules, no runtime type error is possible. This concept is familiar in monomorphic languages, but not in polymorphic languages.

The type mechanism of ML could be enhanced to allow f1 in Figure 3.3456 to be typed. ML could provide a choice type, composed of a fixed number of alternatives, denoted by **alt**. Then f1 could be typed as ((int **alt** bool) -> 'a) -> ('a * 'a). I could use **datatype** for this purpose, but it would not be as elegant.

7.8 Higher-Order Functions

ML supports higher-order functions, that is, functions that take other functions as parameters or deliver functions as results. Higher-order functions are particularly useful to implement **partial application**, in which an invocation provides only some of the expected parameters of a function, as in Figure 3.40.

Figure 3.40

```
in:   val times = fn a => (fn b : int => a * b);          1
out:  val times = fn : int -> (int -> int)               2

in:   times 3 4;                                          3
out:  12 : int                                           4

in:   val twice = times 2;                               5
out:  val twice = fn : int -> int                        6

in:   twice 4;                                           7
out:  8 : int                                            8
```

The type of times (lines 1–2) is unexpectedly complex, because I have chosen to split the two parameters. (I explicitly indicate that b is of type int to resolve the * operator.) In line 3, times 3 4 is understood as (times 3) 4. Times first takes the actual parameter 3 and returns a function from integers to integers; this anonymous function is then applied to 4 to give the result 12. This unusual definition allows me to provide only the first parameter to times if I wish, leading to partial application. For example, I declare twice in line 5 by calling times with only one parameter. When I wish to supply the second parameter, I can do so, as in line 7.

The function-composition function, declared in Figure 3.41, is a good example of partial application. It also has an interesting polymorphic type.

Figure 3.41

```
in:   val compose = fn (f,g) => (fn x => f (g x));        1
out:  val compose = fn :                                  2
          (('a -> 'b) * ('c -> 'a)) -> ('c -> 'b)         3

in:   val fourTimes = compose(twice,twice);              4
out:  val fourTimes = fn : int -> int                    5

in:   fourTimes 5;                                       6
out:  20 : int                                           7
```

Compose takes two functions f and g as parameters and returns a function that when applied to a parameter x returns f (g x). Composing twice with itself, by partially applying compose to the pair (twice, twice), produces a function that multiplies numbers by four. Function composition is actually a predeclared binary operator in ML written as o. The composition of f and g can be written f o g.

Suppose now that I need to partially apply a function f that, like plus, takes a pair of parameters. I could redeclare f as in Figure 3.42.

Figure 3.42

val f = **fn** a => (**fn** b => f(a,b))

Since I did not say **rec**, the use of f inside the declaration refers to the preexisting function f. The new f can be partially applied and uses the old f as appropriate.

To make this conversion more systematic, I can write a function that transforms any function of type ('a * 'b) -> 'c (that is, it requires a pair of parameters) into a function of type 'a -> ('b -> 'c) (that is, it can be partially applied). This conversion is usually called **currying** the function.[11] Figure 3.43 declares a curry function.

Figure 3.43

```
in:   val curry = fn f => (fn a => (fn b => f(a,b)));      1
out:  val curry = fn :                                      2
          (('a * 'b) -> 'c) -> ('a -> ('b -> 'c))           3

in:   val curryPlus = curry plus;                           4
out:  val curryPlus = fn : int -> (int -> int)              5

in:   val successor = curryPlus 1;                          6
out:  val successor = fn : int -> int                       7
```

The higher-order function curry (line 1) takes any function f defined on pairs and two parameters a and b, and applies f to the pair (a,b). I have declared curry so that it can be partially applied; it needs to be provided at least with f, but not necessarily with a or b. When I partially apply curry to plus (line 4), I obtain a function curryPlus that works exactly like plus, but which can be partially applied, as in line 6.

---

[11] Haskell B. Curry was a logician who popularized this idea.

7.9 ML Types

The type of an expression indicates the set of values it may produce. Types include primitive types (integer, real, Boolean, string) and structured types (tuples, lists, functions, and pointers). An ML type only gives information about attributes that can be computed at compile time and does not distinguish among different sets of values having the same structure. Hence the set of positive integers is not a type, nor is the set of lists of length 3. In contrast, Pascal and Ada provide subtypes that restrict the range of allowable values.

On the other hand, ML types can express structural relations within values, for example, that the right part of a pair must have the same type as the left part of the pair, or that a function must return a value of the same type as its parameter (whatever that type may be).

Types are described by recursively applied type constructors. Primitive types like int are type constructors that take no parameters. Structured types are built by type constructors like * (Cartesian product, for tuples), **list**, -> (for functions), and **ref** (for pointers). Type constructors are usually infix or suffix: int * int, int **list**, int -> int, and int **ref** are the types of integer pairs, lists, functions, and pointers. Type constructors can be arbitrarily nested. For example, (int -> int) **list** is the type of lists of integer-to-integer functions.

Type identifiers can be used to express polymorphic types. Polymorphic types are mostly useful as types of functions, although some non-functional expressions, like [], of type 'a **list**, are also polymorphic. A typical example of a polymorphic function is hd, of type 'a **list** -> 'a. The type of hd indicates that it can accept any list and that the type of the result is the same as the type of the elements of the list.

Every type denotes a **type domain**, which is the set of all values of the given type. For example, int * int denotes the domain of integer pairs, and int -> int denotes the domain of all integer functions. An expression can have several types; that is, it can belong to several domains. For example, the identity function **fn** x => x has type int -> int, because it maps any expression of type integer to itself, but it also has the type bool -> bool for a similar reason. The most general polymorphic type for the identity function is 'a -> 'a, because all the types of identity are instances of it. This last notation gives more information than the others, because it encompasses all the types that the identity function can have and thus expresses all the ways that the identity function can be used. Hence it is preferable to the others, although the others are not wrong. The ML type checker always determines the most general type for an expression, given the information contained in that expression.

The programmer may append a type expression to a data expression in order to indicate a **type constraint**, as in Figure 3.44.

Figure 3.44	in: 3 : int;	1
	out: 3 : int	2
	in: [(3,4), (5,6) : int * int];	3
	out: [(3,4),(5,6)] : (int * int) **list**	4

In this example, the type constraint has no effect. The compiler independently infers the types and checks them against the given constraints. Any attempt to constrain a type incorrectly will result in a type error, as shown in Figure 3.45.

Figure 3.45	in: 3 : bool;	1
	out: Type clash in: 3 : bool	2
	Looking for a: bool	3
	I have found a: int	4

However, a type constraint can restrict the types inferred by ML by constraining polymorphic expressions or functions, as in Figure 3.46.

Figure 3.46	in: [] : int **list**;	1
	out: [] : int **list**	2
	in: (**fn** x => x) : int -> int;	3
	out: **fn** : int -> int	4

The type normally inferred for [] is 'a **list**, and for **fn** x => x, it is 'a -> 'a.

Type constraints can be used in declarations, as in Figure 3.47.

Figure 3.47	in: **val** (a : int) = 3;	1
	in: **val** f = **fn** (a : int, b : int) => a+b;	2
	in: **val** f = **fn** (a : int, b) => a+b;	3
	in: **val** f = **fn** ((a,b) : int * int) => (a + b) : int;	4

The examples in lines 2, 3, and 4 are equivalent.

7.10 Constructed Types

A **constructed type** is a type for which constructors are available. Constructors can be used in patterns later to decompose data. You have already seen examples of this dual usage with the tuple constructor and the list constructors nil and :: (cons).

A constructed type and its constructors should be considered as a single conceptual unit. Whenever a new constructed type is declared, its constructors are declared at the same time. Wherever a constructed type is known, its constructors are also known.

The programmer can introduce new constructed types in a type declaration. A type declaration introduces a new type name and the names of the constructors for that type. Each of those constructors leads to a component, whose type is also presented. The components together make up a choice type, that is, a type whose values cover all the components. Syntactically, components are separated by | . Each component starts with its constructor name, followed by the keyword **of** and then the type of the component. The keyword **of** and the component type can be omitted; in this case the constructor is a constant of the new type.

For example, money can be a coin of some value (in cents), a bill of some value (in dollars), a check drawn on some bank for some amount (in cents), or the absence of money (see Figure 3.48).

Figure 3.48

```
in:  datatype money =                               1
         nomoney |                                  2
         coin of int |                              3
         bill of int |                              4
         check of string * int; -- (bank, cents)    5
out: datatype money =                               6
         bill of int |                              7
         check of string * int |                    8
         coin of int |                              9
         nomoney                                   10
     con nomoney : money                           11
     con coin = fn int -> money                    12
     con check = fn : (string * int) -> money      13
     con bill = fn : int -> money                  14
```

Here nomoney, coin, bill, and check are money constructors; nomoney is also a money constant. Constructors can be used as ordinary functions in expressions, as in Figure 3.49.

Figure 3.49

```
in:  val                                            1
         nickel = coin 5 and                        2
         dime = coin 10 and                         3
         quarter = coin 25;                         4
out: val                                            5
         quarter = coin 25 : money                  6
         dime = coin 10 : money                     7
         nickel = coin 5 : money                    8
```

Figure 3.50 shows that they can also be used in patterns.

Figure 3.50

```
in:  val amount =                                           1
            fn nomoney => 0                                 2
            | (coin cents) => cents                         3
            | (bill dollars) => 100 * dollars              4
            | (check(bank,cents)) => cents;                5
out: val amount = fn : money -> int                         6
```

Quarter is not a constructor, but an identifier with value coin 25 of type
money. I cannot add, say after line 4, a clause saying quarter => 25, because quarter would be interpreted as a formal parameter, like cents.

A constructed type can be made entirely of constants, in which case it
is similar to an enumeration type, except there is no ordering relation
among the individual constants. A type can be composed of a single constructor, in which case the type declaration can be considered as an abbreviation for the type following **of**. Both these possibilities are shown
in Figure 3.51.

Figure 3.51

```
in:  datatype color = red | blue | yellow;                 1
out: datatype color = blue | red | yellow                  2
     con yellow : color                                     3
     con red : color                                        4
     con blue : color                                       5

in:  datatype point = point of int * int;                  6
out: datatype point = point of int * int                   7
     con point = fn : (int * int) -> point                 8
```

In the second example, I have overloaded the identifier point, which is
both the name of a type and a constructor that builds values of that
type. Such overloading is conventional in ML if there is only one constructor for a type. There is no risk of ambiguity, since ML can always
tell by context if a constructor or a type is intended.

A constructed-type declaration may involve type identifiers, in which
case the constructed type is polymorphic. All the type identifiers used
on the right side of the declaration must be listed on the left side as type
parameters, as shown in Figure 3.52.

Figure 3.52

```
in:  datatype 'a predicate =                                1
            predicate of 'a -> bool;                        2
out: datatype 'a predicate = predicate of 'a -> bool        3
     con predicate = fn : ('a -> bool) -> ('a predicate)    4

in:  predicate null;                                        5
out: predicate null : ('a list) predicate;                  6
```

```
in:    datatype ('a,'b) leftProjection =                      7
           leftProjection of ('a * 'b) -> 'a;                 8
out:   datatype ('a,'b) leftProjection =                      9
           leftProjection of ('a * 'b) -> 'a                 10
       con leftProjection = fn :                             11
           (('a * 'b) -> 'a) -> ('a,'b) leftProjection       12
```

In lines 1–2, predicate is declared as a type with one constructor, also
called predicate. This constructor turns Boolean-valued functions into
objects of type predicate. An example is shown in line 5, which applies
the constructor to null, which is a Boolean-valued function. The result,
shown in line 6, is in fact a predicate, with the polymorphic type somewhat constrained to 'a list. In lines 7–8, leftProjection is declared
as a type with one constructor, also called leftProjection. This type is
doubly polymorphic: it depends on two type parameters. This constructor turns functions of type ('a * 'b) -> 'a into objects of type leftProjection.

ML also allows recursive constructed types. Figure 3.53 shows how
the predeclared list type and the hd selector are declared:

Figure 3.53

```
in:    datatype 'a list =                                     1
           nil |                                              2
           :: of 'a * ('a list);                             3
out:   datatype 'a list =                                     4
           nil |                                              5
           :: of 'a * ('a list)                              6
       con nil : 'a list                                      7
       con :: = fn : ('a * ('a list)) -> ('a list)           8

in:    val hd = fn ::(head, rest) => head;                    9
out:   val hd = fn : ('a list) -> 'a                         10
```

The pattern in line 9 indicates that hd may only be called on lists constructed with the :: constructor; it is invalid to call it on nil.

In addition to constructed types, ML provides abstract data types
through a module mechanism. It permits the specification and the implementation parts to be separated. Modules can be parameterized by
types, in much the same way as generic modules in Ada and C++.

Before leaving the subject of types, I will turn briefly to two other
programming languages that are closely related to ML but show how
one might extend its treatment of types.

8 ◆ MIRANDA

The Miranda language, designed by David Turner of the University of Kent, shares many features with ML [Turner 85a, 86; Thompson 86]. It is strongly typed, infers types from context, provides for abstract data types, and has higher-order functions. It provides tuples and homogeneous lists, and components of tuples are extracted by patterns. Operators are provided for cons and append, as well as for list length, selection from a list by position, and set difference.

Miranda differs from ML in some minor ways. It is purely functional; there are no pointer types. Functions of more than one parameter are automatically curried unless parentheses explicitly indicate a tuple. (ML also has a declaration form that automatically curries, but I have not shown it.) The scope rules in Miranda are dynamic, which means that functions may be referenced textually before they are declared. All declarations implicitly allow recursion; there is no need for a **rec** keyword. Binary operators may be passed as actual parameters in Miranda; they are equivalent to curried functions that take two parameters.

Miranda has a nontraditional syntax in which indentation indicates grouping and conditionals look like the one in Figure 3.54.

Figure 3.54

```
max  = a, a>=b                                                        1
     = b, otherwise                                                   2
```

However, my examples will follow ML syntax (modified as necessary) for consistency.

Miranda provides some novel extensions to ML. First, evaluation is normally lazy. I discuss **lazy evaluation** in detail in Chapter 4; for now, let me just say that expressions, particularly actual parameters, are not evaluated until they must be, and then only as much as necessary. As Figure 3.55 shows, I can declare a function cond that does not need to evaluate all its parameters.

Figure 3.55

```
in:  val cond =                                                       1
         fn true, x, y => x                                           2
         | false, x, y => y;                                          3
out: val cond = fn : bool -> ('a -> ('a -> 'a))                       4

in:  let val x=0 in cond x=0 0 1/x end                                5
out: 0 : int                                                          6
```

If cond evaluated all its parameters, the invocation in line 5 would generate an exception as the program tries to divide 1 by 0. However, lazy evaluation prevents the suspicious parameter from being evaluated until it is needed, and it is never needed.

Miranda provides a concise syntax for specifying lists by enumerating their components. Most simply, one can build a list by a shorthand, as in Figure 3.56.

Figure 3.56

```
in:  [1..10];                                          1
out: [1, 2, 3, 4, 5, 6, 7, 8, 9, 10] : int list       2
```

Infinite lists (Figure 3.57) are a bit more sophisticated.

Figure 3.57

```
in:  [0..];                                            1
out: [0, 1, 2, ...] : int list                         2

in:  val ones = 1 :: ones;                             3
out: [1, 1, 1, ...] : int list                         4
```

Line 3 declares ones recursively. I have arbitrarily decided to let the expression printer evaluate only the first three components of an infinite list.

The next step is to filter objects, whether finite or infinite, to restrict values. ZF-expressions (named after Zermelo and Fraenkel, founders of modern set theory), also called list comprehensions, are built out of filters, as shown in Figure 3.58.

Figure 3.58

```
in:  [n*n | n <- [1..5] ];                             1
out: [1, 4, 9, 16, 25] : int list                      2

in:  [ (a,b,c,n) | a,b,c,n <- [3..]; a^n + b^n = c^n ]; 3
out: [ ... ] : (int * int * int * int) list            4

in:  val QuickSort =                                   5
     fn [] => []                                       6
     | (a :: rest) =>                                  7
         QuickSort [ b | b <- rest; b <= a ] @         8
         [a] @                                         9
         QuickSort [ b | b <- rest; b > a];            10
out: val QuickSort = fn : 'a list -> 'a list           11
```

Line 1 evaluates to a list of 5 squares. Line 3 evaluates to an empty list (most likely), but will take forever to compute. However, if the expression is evaluated lazily, the infinite computation need not even start. Lines 5–10 represent the Quicksort algorithm concisely.

Infinite lists can be used to create lookup tables for caching the values of a function. Caching allows a programmer to use a recursive algorithm but apply caching (also called dynamic programming and memoization) to change an exponential-time algorithm into a linear-time one. For example, Fibonacci numbers can be computed efficiently as shown in Figure 3.59.

Figure 3.59

```
in:   val map =                                                          1
          fn function, [] => []                                         2
          | function, [a :: rest] =>                                    3
              (function a) :: (map function rest);                      4
out:  val map = fn : ('a -> 'b) -> ('a list -> 'b list)                 5

in:   val cache = map fib [0..]                                         6
      and fib =                                                         7
          fn 0 = 1                                                      8
          | 1 => 1                                                      9
          | n => cache at (n-1) + cache at (n-2)                        10
out:  val fib = fn : int -> int                                        11
```

The map function (lines 1–4) applies a function to each member of a list, producing a new list. The fib function (lines 7–10) uses the infinite object cache (line 6), which is not evaluated until necessary. Line 10 calls for evaluating just those elements of cache that are needed. (The at operator selects an element from a list on the basis of its position.) The chart in Figure 3.60 shows the order of events in evaluating fib 4.

Figure 3.60

```
fib 4                                                                   1
    cache at 3                                                         2
        cache at 0                                                     3
            fib 0 returns 1; cache at 0 becomes 1                      4
        cache at 1                                                     5
            fib 1 returns 1; cache at 1 becomes 1                      6
        cache at 2                                                     7
            fib 2                                                      8
                    cache at 1 returns 1                              9
                    cache at 0 returns 1                              10
                    fib 2 returns 2; cache at 2 becomes 2             11
        fib 3                                                         12
            cache at 2 returns 2                                      13
            cache at 1 returns 1                                      14
            returns 3; cache at 3 becomes 3                           15
    cache at 2 returns 2                                              16
    returns 5                                                         17
```

Another way to express dynamic programming for computing Fibonacci numbers is described in Chapter 9 in the section on mathematics languages.

Lazy evaluation also makes it fairly easy to generate an infinite binary tree with 7 at each node, as in Figure 3.61.

Figure 3.61			
	in:	**datatype** 'a tree =	1
		nil |	2
		node **of** 'a * ('a tree) * ('a tree);	3
	out:	**datatype** 'a tree =	4
		nil |	5
		node **of** 'a * ('a tree) * ('a tree)	6
		con nil : 'a tree	7
		con node = **fn** : 'a ->	8
		(('a tree) -> (('a tree) -> ('a tree)))	9
	in:	**val** BigTree = node 7 BigTree BigTree;	10
	out:	node 7 ... ... : int tree	11

In Miranda, the programmer may introduce a named polymorphic type much like ML's **datatype** construct but without specifying constructors, as Figure 3.62 shows.

Figure 3.62			
	in:	**type** 'a BinOp = 'a -> ('a -> 'a);	1
	out:	**type** 'a BinOp = 'a -> ('a -> 'a)	2
	in:	BinOp int;	3
	out:	int -> (int -> int)	4
	in:	**type** 'a Matrix = 'a list list;	5
	out:	**type** 'a Matrix = 'a list list	6
	in:	**type** BoolMatrix = Matrix bool;	7
	out:	**type** BoolMatrix = bool list list	8
	in:	**val** AMatrix = [[true, false] [false, false]]	9
		: BoolMatrix;	10
	out:	**val** AMatrix = [[true, false] [false, false]]	11
		: bool list list	12
	in:	**val** FirstRow = **fn**	13
		[RowOne :: OtherRows] : BoolMatrix => RowOne;	14
	out:	**val** FirstRow = **fn** :	15
		bool list list -> bool list	16

In line 1, BinOp is declared as a polymorphic type with one type parameter, 'a. Line 3 demonstrates that BinOp can be invoked with a parameter int, leading to the type int -> (int -> int). Types derived from polymorphic types may be used to constrain declarations, as seen trivially in lines 9–10 and not so trivially in lines 13–14.

Recursively defined types sometimes need to provide multiple ways of deriving the same object. For example, if I wish to declare integers as a recursive data type with constructors succ and pred, I need to indicate that zero is the same as succ(pred zero). Miranda allows the programmer to specify simplification laws, as shown in Figure 3.63.

Figure 3.63

```
in:   datatype MyInt =                                    1
          zero |                                          2
          pred of MyInt |                                 3
          succ of MyInt                                   4
      laws                                                5
          pred(succ n) => n and succ(pred n) => n;        6

in:   pred(pred(succ(zero)));                             7
out:  pred zero : MyInt                                   8
```

Simplification laws also allow the programmer to declare a rational-number data type that stores numbers in their canonical form (see Figure 3.64).

Figure 3.64

```
in:   datatype Rational = ratio of num * num             1

      laws ratio (a,b) =>                                 2
          if b = 0 then                                   3
              error "zero denominator"                    4
          elsif b < 0 then                                5
              ratio (-a,-b)                               6
          else                                            7
              let                                         8
                  val gcd = fn (x,y) =>                   9
                      if a < b then gcd (a,b-a)          10
                      elsif b < a then gcd (a-b,b)       11
                      else a;                            12
                  CommonPart = gcd (abs a, abs b)        13
```

```
            in                                          14
                if CommonPart > 1 then                  15
                    ratio (a div CommonPart,            16
                    b div CommonPart);                  17
                else                                    18
                    nosimplify                          19
            end;                                        20

    in:   ratio (3,2);                                  21
    out:  ratio (3,2) : Rational                        22

    in:   ratio (12,-3);                                23
    out:  ratio (-4,1) : Rational                       24
```

In line 19, **nosimplify** indicates that no law applies in that case.

9 ◆ RUSSELL

The Russell language predates ML but is quite similar in general flavor [Demers 79; Boehm 86]. It was developed to explore the semantics of types, in particular, to try to make types first-class values. Russell is strongly typed, infers types from context, provides for abstract data types, and has higher-order functions.

Russell differs from ML in some minor ways. Although it is statically scoped, new function declarations do not override old ones of the same name if the types differ; instead, the name becomes overloaded, and the number and type of the actual parameters are used to distinguish which function is meant in any particular context. (Redeclaration of identifiers other than functions is not allowed at all.) Functions may be declared to be invoked as prefix, suffix, or infix operators. Functions that take more than two parameters may still be declared to be invoked with an infix operator; a given number of the parameters are placed before the operator, and the rest after. ML only allows infix notation for binary functions. To prevent side effects in the presence of variables (**ref** types), functions do not import identifiers mapped to variables.

Russell's nomenclature is nonstandard; what ML calls a type is a signature in Russell; an abstract data type (a collection of functions) is a type in Russell. So when Russell succeeds in making types first-class values, it doesn't accomplish quite as much as we would expect. Russell's syntax is quite different from ML. For consistency, I will continue to use ML terminology and syntax as I discuss Russell.

The principal difference between Russell and ML is that in Russell abstract data types are first-class values, just like values, pointers, and functions. That is, abstract data types may be passed as parameters, returned from functions, and stored in identifiers. Abstract data type values can also be manipulated after they have been constructed.

More specifically, Russell considers an abstract data type to be a collection of functions that may be applied to objects of a particular domain. The `Boolean` abstract data type includes the nullary functions `true` and `false`, binary operators such as **and** and **or**, and even statements such as **if** and `while`, which have Boolean components. Manipulation of an abstract data type means deleting or inserting functions in its definition.

The border between data and program becomes quite blurred if we look at the world this way. After all, we are not used to treating control constructs like `while` as functions that take two parameters, a Boolean and a statement, and return a statement. We don't usually consider a statement to be data at all, since it cannot be read, written, or manipulated.[12]

The components of an abstract data type may be quite different from each other. I could declare an abstract data type MyType that includes the Boolean **false** as well as the integer 3 (both nullary functions). If I wish to distinguish which `false` is meant, I can qualify it by saying `bool.false` or MyType.false. (The . operator is a selector that extracts a given component of a given abstract data type.)

I might declare a simple abstract data type of small integers as shown in Figure 3.65.

---

[12] Some languages, like SNOBOL and APL, let strings be converted at runtime into statements and then executed. Only LISP, discussed in Chapter 4, and Tcl, discussed in Chapter 9, actually build programs out of the same stuff as data.

Figure 3.65

```
val SmallInt =                                                      1
    type New = fn : void -> SmallInt -- constructor                 2
    and ":=" = fn : (SmallInt ref, SmallInt) -> SmallInt            3
            -- assignment                                           4
    and ValueOf = fn : SmallInt ref -> SmallInt -- deref            5
    and alias = fn : (SmallInt ref, SmallInt ref) -> bool           6
            -- pointer equality                                     7
    and "<" = fn : (SmallInt,SmallInt) -> Boolean                   8
    ... -- other comparisons, such as <= , =, >, >=, ≠             9
    and "-" = fn : (SmallInt, SmallInt) -> SmallInt                 10
    ... -- other arithmetic, such as +, *, div, mod                11
    and "0" : SmallInt -- constant                                 12
    ... -- other constants 1, 2, ... , 9                           13
            -- the rest are built by concatenation                 14
    and "^" = fn : (SmallInt,SmallInt) -> SmallInt                 15
            -- concatenation                                        16
    ;                                                               17
```

I use void in line 2 to indicate that the New function is nullary. The function declarations are all missing their implementations.

Generally, one builds abstract data types with shorthand forms that expand out to such lists. For example, there are shorthands for declaring enumerations, records, choices, and new copies of existing abstract data types. The lists generated by the shorthands contain functions with predefined bodies.

Since abstract data types can be passed as parameters, the programmer can build polymorphic functions that behave differently on values of different abstract data types. It is common to pass both value-containing parameters and type-containing parameters to functions. Figure 3.66 shows how to declare a polymorphic Boolean function least that tells if a given value is the smallest in its abstract data type.

Figure 3.66

```
val least =                                                        1
    fn (value : bool, bool) => value = false                       2
    | (value : SmallInt, SmallInt) => value = SmallInt."0"         3
    | (value : Other, Other : type) => false;                      4
```

Line 2 applies when the first parameter is Boolean and the second parameter so indicates. It returns true only if the first parameter has value false. Line 3 applies when the first parameter is of type SmallInt. Line 4 applies to all other types, so long as the type of the first parameter matches the value of the second parameter. A call such as least("string", int) would fail because none of the alternatives would match.

Manipulations on an abstract data type include adding, replacing, and deleting its functions. The programmer must provide a body for all replacement functions. For example, I can build a version of the integer type that counts how many times an assignment has been made on its values (Figure 3.67).

Figure 3.67

```
val InstrumentedInt =                                        1
    record (Value : int, Count : int)                        2
        -- "record" expands to a list of functions           3
    adding                                                    4
        Alloc = fn void =>                                    5
            let                                               6
                val x = InstrumentedInt.new                   7
            in                                                8
                count x := 0;                                 9
                x -- returned from Alloc                      10
            end                                               11
    and                                                       12
        Assign = fn                                           13
            (IIVar : InstrumentedInt ref,                     14
             IIValue : InstrumentedInt) ->                    15
            (     -- sequence of several statements           16
                count IIValue := count IIValue + 1;           17
                Value IIVar := Value IIValue;                 18
            )                                                 19
    and                                                       20
        GetCount = fn (IIValue : InstrumentedInt) ->          21
            count IIValue                                     22
    and                                                       23
        new = InstrumentedInt.Alloc -- new name               24
    and                                                       25
        ":=" = InstrumentedInt.Assign -- new name             26
    and                                                       27
        ValueOf = ValueOf Value                               28
    hiding                                                    29
        Alloc, Assign, -- internal functions                  30
        Value, Count, -- fields (also functions);             31
```

Two abstract data types are considered to have the same type if they contain the same function names (in any order) with equivalent parameter and result types. This definition is a lax form of structural equivalence.

10 ◆ DYNAMIC TYPING IN STATICALLY TYPED LANGUAGES

It seems strange to include dynamic typing in otherwise statically typed languages, but there are situations in which the types of objects cannot be predicted at compile time. In fact, there are situations in which a program may wish to create a new type during its computation.

An elegant proposal for escaping from static types is to introduce a predeclared type named dynamic [Abadi 91]. This method is used extensively in Amber [Cardelli 86]. Values of this type are constructed by the polymorphic predeclared function makeDynamic. They are implemented as a pair containing a value and a type description, as shown in Figure 3.68 (in an ML-like syntax).

Figure 3.68

```
val A = makeDynamic 3;                                          1
val B = makeDynamic "a string";                                2
val C = makeDynamic A;                                         3
```

The value placed in A is 3, and its type description is int. The value placed in B is "a string", and its type description is string. The value placed in C is the pair representing A, and its type description is dynamic.

Values of dynamic type can be manipulated inside a **typecase** expression that distinguishes the underlying types and assigns local names to the component values, as in Figure 3.69.

Figure 3.69

```
val rec Stringify = fn Arg : dynamic =>                          1
    typecase Arg                                                2
    of   s : string => '"' + s + '"'                            3
    |    i : int => integerToString(i)                          4
    |    f : 'a -> 'b => "function"                             5
    |    (x, y) => "(" + (Stringify makeDynamic x) +            6
                   ", " + (Stringify makeDynamic y) + ")"       7
    |    d : dynamic => Stringify d                             8
    |    _ => "unknown";                                        9
```

Stringify is a function that takes a dynamic-typed parameter Arg and returns a string version of that parameter. It distinguishes the possible types of Arg in a **typecase** expression with patterns both to capture the type and to assign local identifiers to the components of the type. If the underlying type is itself dynamic, Stringify recurses down to the underlying type (line 8). In lines 6–7, makeDynamic is invoked to ensure that the parameters to Stringify are of the right type, that is, dynamic.

Figure 3.70 shows a more complicated example that nests **typecase** expressions. The function Apply takes two curried dynamic parameters and invokes the first one with the second one as a parameter, checking that such an application is valid.

Figure 3.70

```
val rec Apply =                                          1
    fn Function : dynamic =>                             2
        fn Parameter : dynamic =>                        3
            typecase Function                            4
            of f : 'a -> 'b =>                           5
                typecase Parameter                       6
                of p : 'a => makeDynamic f(p);           7
```

Line 5 explicitly binds the type identifiers 'a and 'b so that 'a can be used later in line 7 when the program checks for type equivalence. Line 7 needs to invoke makeDynamic so that the return value of Apply (namely, dynamic) is known to the compiler. In each **typecase** expression, if the actual type at runtime is not matched by the guard, a type error has occurred. I could use an explicit **raise** statement in a language with exception handling.

The dynamic type does not violate strong typing. The compiler still knows the type of every value, because all the otherwise unknown types are lumped together as the dynamic type. Runtime type checking is needed only in evaluating the guards of a **typecase** expression. Within each branch, types are again statically known.

It is possible to allow compile-time coercion of dynamic types. If a dynamic value is used in a context where the compiler does not have any applicable meaning, it may implicitly supply a **typecase** that distinguishes the meanings that it knows how to handle, as shown in Figure 3.71.

Figure 3.71

```
in:  write makeDynamic (4 + makeDynamic 6)               1
out: 10 : int                                            2
```

In line 1, the + operator has no overloaded meaning for integers plus dynamic values. The compiler realizes this fact and inserts an explicit **typecase** to handle the one meaning it knows, integers plus integers. The predeclared write function cannot handle dynamic types, either, so another **typecase** is inserted for all the types that it can handle. In other words, the input is expanded to that shown in Figure 3.72.

Figure 3.72

```
typecase makeDynamic 4 +                                  1
    typecase makeDynamic 6                                2
    of i : int => i                                       3
    end;                                                  4
of                                                        5
    i : int => write i                                    6
    r : real => write r                                   7
    ...                                                   8
end;                                                      9
```

The **typecase** expression in lines 2–4 has type int, so the + in line 1 is well defined. In order to give write's parameter a compile-time type, I had to draw the write function into the outer **typecase** (in lines 6–8). Drawing functions into the implicit **typecase** expressions can lead to an explosion of code.

It is much better to coerce at runtime, when the actual type is known for each dynamic type. The program in Figure 3.72 would clearly use integer addition and printing of integers. Runtime coercion is still perfectly type-safe, although some type errors won't be discovered until runtime.

11 ⬩ FINAL COMMENTS

The discussion of derived types and dimensions is part of a larger issue about how restrictive a programming language needs to be in order to permit the art of programming. One way to look at this question [Gauthier 92] is to notice that on the one hand the real world is very restrictively typed, as students of physics realize. One should not add apples and oranges, much less volts and calories. On the other hand, the memory of most computers is completely untyped; everything is represented by bits (organized into equally untyped bytes or words). The programming language represents a platform for describing the real world via the computer, so it properly lies somewhere between these extremes. It needs to balance type security with simplicity. Type security demands that each different kind of value have its own type in order to match the real world. For example, lists of exactly three elements are different from lists of four elements. Integers constrained to even numbers are different from unconstrained integers. Simplicity demands that types be easy to specify and that types be efficiently checked, preferably at compile time. It is not so easy to include lengths or number-theoretic considerations in the type description of lists and integers, respectively.

It is largely a matter of personal taste where this platform should be on the spectrum ranging from restrictively typed, using strong typing and perhaps providing derived types with dimensions, to lax, with dynamic typing and easy coercion. Proponents of the restrictive style point with pride to the clarity of their programs and the fact that sometimes they run correctly the first time. Proponents of the lax style speak disparagingly of "bondage-and-discipline" languages like Ada, and prefer the relative freedom of C.

Such taste is likely to change as a programmer changes. My first experience of programming (after plug-board computers) was in machine language, not even assembler language. Later, I relished the intricacies of SNOBOL, which is quite lax about typing. Algol was a real eye-opener, with its declared types and its control structures. I now prefer strong typing; to me, an elegant program is one that is readable the first time by a novice, not one that plays unexpected tricks. Strong typing helps me to build such programs. Still, I use C heavily because it is implemented so widely, and I often need to port my programs across machines.

ML is an elegant language that shows how to make functions first-class values and how to deal with type polymorphism and still be strongly typed. Type inference relieves the programmer of careful type declarations. Miranda extends these ideas with infinite lists and lazy evaluation. (There is also a lazy variant of ML with similar extensions.) Russell even allows some types to be manipulated in fairly simple ways. None of these languages truly allows types themselves to be first-class values. Such an extension would probably require runtime type checking or lose strong typing. (The exercises explore this concept.)

Type systems are an area of active research. Integrating dimensions into polymorphic languages like ML, for example, is being studied [Kennedy 94]. The SML variant of ML includes an experimental, higher-order extension of the module system, in which generic modules can be parameterized by other (possibly generic) modules.

Although I have intentionally avoided issues of syntax in this chapter, I would like to point out that syntactic design certainly affects the ease with which programmers can learn and use a language. Compare, for example, identical types in C and ML:

C	ML
`int z`	`z : int`
`int (*a)(char)`	`a : (char -> int) ref`
`int (*((*b)(int)))(char)`	`b : (int -> ((char -> int) ref))) ref`
`int (*c)(int (*)(char))`	`c : ((char -> int) ref -> int) ref`

Although the C type expressions are shorter, I find them difficult to generate and to understand.

EXERCISES

Review Exercises

3.1 What is the difference between the way Modula-2+ and Modula-3 handle type equivalence for derived types?

3.2 If two types are name-equivalent, are they necessarily structurally equivalent?

3.3 Would you consider `First` and `Second` in Figure 3.73 structurally equivalent? Why or why not?

Figure 3.73

```
type                                                      1
    First =                                               2
        record                                            3
                A : integer;                              4
                B : record                                5
                        B1, B2 : integer;                 6
                    end;                                   7
            end;                                           8
    Second =                                              9
        record                                            10
            A: record                                     11
                    A1, A2 : integer;                     12
                end;                                       13
            B : integer;                                  14
        end;                                              15
```

3.4 How can abstract data types be used to implement dimensions?

3.5 Why is instantiation of a generic module a compile-time operation, not a runtime operation?

3.6 What sort of type equivalence does ML use — name equivalence, structural equivalence, or something else?

Challenge Exercises

3.7   Enumerate the possible values of type TA in Figure 3.3 (page 66).

3.8   Given that First and Second are not structurally equivalent in exercise 3.3, suggest an algorithm for testing structural equivalence.

3.9   Suggest an algorithm for compile-time dimension checking. Is runtime dimension checking needed?

3.10 Explore adding dimensions to ML.

3.11 Write an accumulate procedure in ML that can be used to sum a list, as suggested on page 86.

3.12 Show a valid use of leftProjection, introduced in Figure 3.52 (page 102).

3.13 Program QuickSort in ML.

3.14 Show how **datatype** in ML could give me the effect of f1 : ((int **alt** bool) -> 'a) -> ('a * 'a), as suggested on page 95.

3.15 Use the dynamic type in an ML framework to declare a function BuildDeep such that BuildDeep 2 produces a function of dynamic type int -> (int -> int), BuildDeep 3 produces a function of dynamic type int -> (int -> (int -> int)), and so forth. The produced functions should return the sum of all their parameters.

3.16 Generalize types in ML so that types are true first-class values. That is, I should be able to build things of type type, or of type type -> int. Decide what the built-in functions on type type should be. Try to keep the language strongly typed.

3.17 Extend ML so that there is a type **expression**. Devise reasonable functions that use that type. These functions should have runtime (not just compile-time) significance.

3.18 What is the type (in the ML sense) of least in Figure 3.66 (page 110)?

3.19 Can Io constructs (see Chapter 2) be represented in ML?

3.20 Show two types in Russell that are type-equivalent, but are neither name-equivalent nor structurally equivalent.

3.21 Are all structurally equivalent types type-equivalent in Russell?

3.22 Russell prevents side effects in the presence of variables (**ref** types) by prohibiting functions from importing identifiers mapped to variables. Why is this rule important?

3.23 Russell also prohibits a block from exporting a value of a type declared locally in that block. Why is this rule important in Russell? Should ML also have such a rule? Can this rule be enforced at compile time?

Chapter 4

Functional Programming

Most of the programming languages you are familiar with (Pascal, Ada, C) are **imperative** languages. They emphasize a programming style in which programs execute commands sequentially, use variables to organize memory, and update variables with assignment statements. The result of a program thus comprises the contents of all permanent variables (such as files) at the end of execution.

Although imperative programming seems quite natural and matches the execution process of most computer hardware, it has been criticized as fundamentally flawed. For example, John Backus (the designer of FORTRAN) holds that almost all programming languages (from FORTRAN to Ada) exhibit a "von Neumann bottleneck" in which programs follow too closely the "fetch instruction/update memory" cycle of typical CPUs. These languages do not lend themselves to simultaneous execution of different parts of the program, because any command may depend on the changes to variables caused by previous commands. (An enormous amount of effort has gone into creating algorithms that allow compilers to discover automatically to what extent commands may be executed simultaneously.) Execution speed is therefore ultimately limited by the speed with which individual instructions can be executed. Another effect of imperative programming is that to know the state of a computation, one must know the values of all the variables. This is why compilers that provide a postexecution dump of the values of all variables (or, better yet, compilers that allow variables to be examined and changed during debugging) are so handy.

In contrast, **functional** programming languages have no variables, no assignment statements, and no iterative constructs. This design is based on the concept of mathematical functions, which are often defined by separation into various cases, each of which is separately defined by appealing (possibly recursively) to function applications. Figure 4.1 presents such a mathematical definition.

Figure 4.1

```
f(n) =                              1
    1 if n = 1                      2
    f(3*n+1) if n is odd, n ≠ 1     3
    f(n / 2) if n is even           4
```

In functional programming languages, such definitions are translated more or less directly into the syntax of the language. (The Miranda syntax is remarkably similar to this example.) The entire program is simply a function, which is itself defined in terms of other functions.

Even though there are no variables, there are identifiers bound to values, just as n is used in Figure 4.1. (When I use the term **variable**, I mean an identifier whose value can be changed by an assignment statement.) Identifiers generally acquire values through parameter binding. Variables are unnecessary in this style of programming because the result of one function is immediately passed as a parameter to another function. Because no variables are used, it is easy to define the effects (that is, the semantics) of a program. Often, functions are recursive. Functions have no side effects; they compute results without updating the values associated with variables. Functions are usually first-class values in functional programming languages. (First-class values are discussed in Chapter 3.)

The ML language, introduced in Chapter 3, is almost entirely functional. In that chapter, I concentrated on its type system, not on the way its lack of variables leads to a different programming style. This chapter presents examples in LISP, ML, and FP to give you a feeling for functional programming.

Functional programming is an area of current research. There is a biennial ACM Conference on LISP and Functional Programming.

1 ◆ LISP

LISP (List Processing language) was designed by John McCarthy at MIT in 1959. LISP actually represents a family of related languages, all sharing the common core of ideas first espoused in LISP 1.5. The most popular versions of LISP today are Scheme and Common LISP. Most dialects of LISP are not purely functional (variables are used sometimes, and certain functions do have side effects). I shall concentrate however on the functional flavor of programming in LISP.

The fundamental values manipulated by LISP are called **atoms**. An atom is either a number (integer or real) or a symbol that looks like a typical identifier (such as ABC or L10). Atoms can be structured into **S-expressions**, which are recursively defined as either

1. An atom, or
2. (S1.S2), where S1 and S2 are S-expressions.

Figure 4.2 shows some S-expressions.

Figure 4.2

```
100                                                                    1
(A.B)                                                                  2
((10.AB).(XYZ.SSS))                                                    3
```

All S-expressions that are not atoms have two components: the head (called, for historical reasons, the car), and the tail (called, for historical reasons, the cdr[1]). This definition leads to a simple runtime memory organization: numeric atoms are placed in one computer word, symbolic atoms are represented by a pointer to a symbol table entry, and S-expressions are represented by a pair of pointers to either atoms or subexpressions. Often, a box notation is used. The atom A is represented as follows:

(A.B) is represented as follows:

((A.B).(C.D)) is represented as follows:

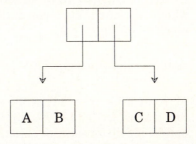

The predefined symbol nil is used to represent the pointer to nothing. S-expressions represent the class of simple binary trees.

---

[1] The term car stands for "contents of address register," and cdr stands for "contents of decrement register." These names refer to registers on the IBM 704 computer on which LISP was first implemented.

LISP provides a few predefined functions to assemble and disassemble S-expressions.

1. Car returns the head of a nonatomic S-expression. Thus car((A.B)) is A, car(((C.B).D)) is (C.B), and car(A) is undefined (because A is an atom). (These expressions are not syntactically correct LISP; I will introduce function syntax shortly.)

2. Cdr returns the tail of a nonatomic S-expression. Thus cdr((A.B)) is B, cdr(((C.B).D)) is D, and cdr(A) is undefined (because A is an atom).

3. Cons takes two S-expressions and builds a new S-expression composed of the two parameters. That is, cons(x,y) = (x.y) for any x and y (either atomic or not). Thus cons((A.B),C) = ((A.B).C). By definition, car(cons(x,y)) is x, and cdr(cons(x,y)) is y. Cons allocates space from the heap for the new cell that it needs.

Lists, the fundamental structured type in LISP, are a subset of the valid S-expressions. In particular,

1. The empty list, (), is represented by the atom nil.
2. A list with one element, (A), is equivalent to cons(A,nil). A list (A B) is equivalent to cons(A, cons(B,nil)). In general, the list (A B ... Z) is equivalent to cons(A, (B ... Z)). That is, a list is extended by using cons to add an element to its left end.

Lists that contain lists are allowed, and in fact are frequently used. For example, ((A)) is the list that contains one element, namely the list (A). ((A)) is created by first building (A), which is cons(A,nil). Then (A) is added to the empty list to make ((A)). So cons(cons(A,nil),nil) generates ((A)). Similarly, ((A B) () 11), which contains three elements, two of which are lists, is equal to the expression in Figure 4.3.

Figure 4.3   cons(cons(A,cons(B,nil)), cons(nil, cons(11,nil)))

The only difference is that the former expression is a literal (parsed and constructed by the LISP compiler/interpreter), and the latter is a combination of calls to runtime functions.

The Boolean values true and false are represented by the predefined atoms t and nil. Two fundamental predicates (that is, Boolean-returning functions) are eq and atom. Eq tests whether two atoms are the same (that is, equal). Atom tests whether a given S-expression is atomic.

1.1 Function Syntax

Programs as well as data are represented as lists. That is, LISP is **homoiconic:** Programs and data have the same representation. This property, rarely found in programming languages, allows a LISP program to create or modify other LISP functions. As you will see, it also allows the semantics of LISP to be defined in a particularly simple and concise manner. (Tcl, discussed in Chapter 9, is also homoiconic and enjoys the same benefits.)

To allow programs to be represented as lists, LISP function invocations aren't represented in the usual form of FunctionName(arg1, arg2, ...), but rather as (FunctionName arg1 arg2 ...). For example, the S-expression (10.20) can be built by evaluating (cons 10 20).

When a list is evaluated, the first element of the list is looked up (in the runtime symbol table) to find what function is to be executed. Except in special cases (forms such as **cond**), the remaining list elements are evaluated and passed to the function as actual parameters. The value computed by the body of the function is then returned as the value of the list.

1.2 Forms

Should the call (cons A B) mean to join together the atoms A and B, or should A and B be looked up in the symbol table in case they are formal parameters in the current context? LISP evaluates all actual parameters, so A and B are evaluated by looking them up in the symbol table. If I want A and B to be treated as atoms rather than identifiers, I need to **quote** them, that is, prevent their evaluation. The programmer can use **quote**, called as (**quote** arg), to prevent evaluation. **Quote** is called a **form**, not a function,[2] because it is understood as a special case by the LISP interpreter. If it were a function, its parameter would be evaluated, which is exactly what **quote** is designed to prevent. The code in Figure 4.4 builds the S-expression (A.B).

Figure 4.4

```
(cons (quote A) (quote B))
```

Since programmers often need to quote parameters, LISP allows an abbreviated form of **quote**: 'A means the same as (**quote** A), so (cons 'A 'B) will also build the S-expression of Figure 4.4.

To be effective, any programming language needs some form of conditional evaluation mechanism. LISP uses the **cond** form. (Some dialects

---

[2] So you see that sometimes form is more important than function.

of LISP also provide an **if** form.) **Cond** takes a sequence of one or more pairs (lists of two elements) as parameters. Each pair is considered in turn. If the first component of a pair evaluates to t, then the second component is evaluated and returned as the value of **cond** (and all other pairs are ignored). If the first component evaluates to nil (that is, false), then the second component is ignored, and the next pair is considered. If all pairs are considered, and all first components evaluate to nil, then **cond** returns nil as its value.

As an example, suppose I want to create a predicate that tests whether some list bound to identifier L contains two or more elements. Figure 4.5 shows the code.

Figure 4.5

```
(cond                                                          1
    ((atom L) nil)                                             2
    ((atom (cdr L)) nil)                                       3
    (t t)                                                      4
)                                                              5
```

First, line 2 tests if L is an atom. If it is, it is the empty list (equal to nil), which certainly doesn't have two or more elements. Next, line 3 tests if cdr(L) is an atom. Cdr gives the list that remains after stripping off its first element. If cdr(L) is an atom, then the list had only one element, and the predicate again returns false. In all other cases, the list must have had at least two elements, so the predicate returns true. In most cases, the last pair given to **cond** has t as its first component. Such a pair represents a kind of **else** clause, covering all cases not included in earlier pairs.

1.3 Programmer-Defined Functions

Functions are first-class values in LISP (as in most functional programming languages). In particular, they can be returned as the result of functions. Therefore, LISP must allow the programmer to construct a function directly without necessarily giving it a name. The function constructor in LISP therefore builds **anonymous functions**, that is, functions that are not yet bound to names. To define a function, the programmer must provide a list containing three things: the form **lambda**, a list of the formal parameters, and the body of the function in the form of an expression. The anonymous function in Figure 4.6 makes a list with one element, passed in as a parameter.

Figure 4.6

```
(lambda (x) (cons x nil))
```

(The ML equivalent is **fn** x => x :: nil.) The formal parameter of the function is x. Parameters are passed in value mode. An implementation is likely to use reference mode and avoid copying; reference mode is safe to use because there are no commands that can change the parameters' values. Thus the function call of Figure 4.7

Figure 4.7

```
((lambda (x) (cons x nil)) 10)
```

binds 10 to the formal parameter x, yielding (cons 10 nil), which is (10). If more than one parameter is provided, they are all evaluated and bound, in left-to-right order, to the formal parameters. The expression in Figure 4.8, for instance,

Figure 4.8

```
((lambda (x y) (cons y x)) 10 20)
```

yields (20.10). It is an error if too many or too few actual parameters are provided.

The anonymous function produced by the **lambda** form can be applied immediately (as I have been doing), passed as a parameter to a function, or bound to an identifier. Functions are bound to identifiers via the **def** form, which takes as parameters the function identifier and its definition (as a **lambda** form). Neither parameter should be quoted. Thus the expression in Figure 4.9

Figure 4.9

```
(def MakeList (lambda (x) (cons x nil)) )
```

defines the MakeList function, and (MakeList 'AA) = (AA).

1.4 Scope Rules

The same identifier can be used as a function name or as a formal parameter in one or more functions. LISP therefore needs a scope rule to say which declaration is to be associated with each use of a symbol. Early dialects of LISP (in particular, LISP 1.5) used dynamic scoping: As actual parameters are bound to formal parameters, they are placed at the front of an association list that acts as the runtime symbol table for formal parameters. The association list is searched from front to back, so the most recent association of a value to a formal parameter is always found. If a formal parameter identifier appears more than once, the nearest (that is, most recent) binding of it is used. The order of call, and not static nesting, determines which declaration of a symbol is used. Consider Figure 4.10.

Figure 4.10
```
(def f1 (lambda (x y) (f2 11)))          1
(def f2 (lambda (x) (cons x y)))         2
(f1 1 2)                                 3
```

When f1 is called, x is bound to 1, and y is bound to 2. Then f1 calls f2, which adds a new binding of 11 to x. Thus (cons x y) evaluates to (cons 11 2) = (11.2).

More recent dialects of LISP (including Common LISP and Scheme) use static scope rules, although Common LISP permits individual identifiers to be declared as dynamically scoped. Experience has shown that static scoping is much easier for the programmer to understand and is therefore less error-prone.

A program can also use the set function to change bindings in the association list, as in Figure 4.11.

Figure 4.11
```
(def f3 (lambda (x) (cons x (cons (set 'x 111) x))))     1
(f3 222)                                                 2
```

Formal parameter x is initially bound to 222 and becomes the first parameter to cons. Set binds 111 to x, and returns 111 as its value. The next appearance of x is now mapped to 111, and so LISP evaluates (cons 222 (cons 111 111)) = (222.(111.111)). If a symbol appears more than once in the association list, set updates its most recent binding. If a symbol isn't in the association list, it can't be bound using set.

LISP 1.5 has a more complicated scope rule. Each atom has a property list, which is a list (property name, value) pairs. An atom that has an APVAL property is evaluated to the associated value regardless of the contents of the association list. Function declarations are also stored in the property list under the EXPR property. If no EXPR property is present, the association list is searched, as shown in Figure 4.12.

Figure 4.12
```
(def f4 (lambda (x) (x 333 444) ))       1
(f4 'cons)                               2
```

When execution is in line 2, the body of the **lambda** form of line 1 is evaluated, and x's property list is searched for an EXPR entry. When none is found, the association list is tried. The binding of cons to x is found, so (cons 333 444) is evaluated.

The function get takes an atom and a property name and returns the value bound to that name on the atom's association list. If no binding is found, nil is returned.

1.5 Programming

Programming in LISP has a different flavor from programming in imperative languages. Recursion, rather than iteration, is emphasized. To perform a computation on a list, it is convenient to extract the first element of the list (using car), and then to recursively perform the computation on the remainder of the list.

To give you an appreciation of this style of programming, I will present a few examples. First, I will create an Append function that appends two lists to form one. For example, (Append '(1 2 3) '(4 5 6)) = (1 2 3 4 5 6). (The quote is needed to prevent (1 2 3) from being treated as a function call.) I construct Append by considering cases. If the first list (call it L1) is empty (that is, equal to nil), then the result is the second list (call it L2). Otherwise, I add the first element of L1 to the list consisting of the remainder of L1 appended to L2. I therefore obtain the program shown in Figure 4.13.

Figure 4.13

```
(def Append (lambda (A1 A2) -- append lists A1 and A2        1
    (cond                                                     2
        ((null A1) A2)                                        3
        (t (cons (car A1) (Append (cdr A1) A2))))             4
))                                                            5
```

In line 3, null is a function that returns t only if its argument is nil. The list returned by Append is a curious mixture of newly allocated storage (cons always returns a new cell) and storage belonging to A1 and A2. Neither actual parameter is modified. The returned list contains new cells for all of A1's elements, the last of which points to the first cell for A2. Figure 4.14 shows the result of calling (Append '(1 2 3) '(4 5 6)).

Figure 4.14 Appending lists

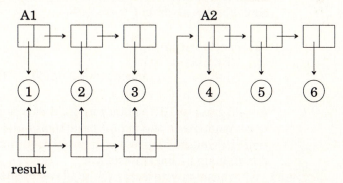

result

The Append function can be programmed very similarly in ML, as shown in Figure 4.15.

Figure 4.15

```
val rec Append =                                              1
    fn (nil, A2) => A2                                        2
     | (A1, A2) => (hd A1 :: Append (tl A1, A2));             3
```

The predeclared functions hd and tl are the same as LISP's car and cdr; the infix operator :: is the same as LISP's cons. Instead of using a conditional (ML has an **if** expression), I have chosen the more stylistic approach that uses patterns to distinguish cases. More sophisticated patterns allow me to avoid using hd and tl, as in Figure 4.16.

Figure 4.16

```
val rec Append =                                              1
    fn (nil, A2) => A2                                        2
     | (HA1 :: TA1, A2) => (HA1 :: Append (TA1, A2));         3
```

Next, I will build a LISP function that takes a list and returns its reversal. If the list is empty, the function returns the empty list; otherwise, the first element of the list will be the last element of the reversed list. I can make this element into a list (using MakeList defined earlier) then append it to the end of the reversal of the remainder of the list, arriving at the program shown in Figure 4.17.

Figure 4.17

```
(def Reverse (lambda (R) -- reverse list R               1
    (cond                                                2
        ((null R) R)                                     3
        (t (Append (Reverse (cdr R)) (MakeList (car R)))) 4
    )                                                    5
))                                                       6
```

The returned list is completely built out of new cons cells. The ML equivalent is given in Figure 4.18.

Figure 4.18

```
val rec Reverse =                                            1
    fn nil => nil                                           2
     | H :: T => Append(Reverse(T), [H]);                   3
```

As you can see, ML's ability to build formal parameters that correspond to components of the actual parameters and its syntax for list construction ([H] in line 3) give it a different feel from LISP, even though the underlying algorithm is identical.

Reverse only reverses the top-level elements of a list; if the elements are themselves lists, the lower-level lists aren't reversed. For example, (Reverse '(1 (2 3 4) 5))) = (5 (2 3 4) 1). I can define a related function, ReverseAll, that reverses all lists, even if they appear as elements of another list; thus, (ReverseAll '(1 (2 3 4) 5)) = (5 (4 3 2) 1). First,

I define the reversal of any atom (including `nil`) as equal to that atom itself. Now when I append the car of a list onto the end of the reversal of the remainder of the list, I make sure to reverse the car first; thus, I have the code shown in Figure 4.19.

Figure 4.19

```
(def ReverseAll (lambda (RA) -- reverse RA and sublists      1
    (cond                                                    2
        ((atom RA) RA)                                       3
        (t (Append                                           4
            (ReverseAll (cdr RA))                            5
            (MakeList (ReverseAll (car RA)) ))))             6
))                                                           7
```

This example cannot be directly translated into ML, because ML's type scheme requires that lists be homogeneous. A programmer can, however, introduce a new ML datatype for nonhomogeneous lists; this idea is pursued in Exercise 4.13.

Figure 4.20 takes a list and doubles it; that is, it generates a list in which every member of the original list appears twice.

Figure 4.20

```
(def Double (lambda (L)                                      1
    (cond                                                    2
        ((null L) nil)                                       3
        (t (cons (car L) (cons (car L)                       4
            (Double (cdr L)))))                              5
    )                                                        6
))                                                           7
```

Double can be generalized in the same way as Reverse; Exercises 4.6 and 4.7 explore several generalizations.

Figure 4.21 builds Mapcar, which is itself very useful for building other functions. Mapcar takes two parameters, a function and a list, and returns the list formed by applying that function to each member of the list.

Figure 4.21

```
(def Mapcar (lambda (F L)                                    1
    (cond                                                    2
        ((null L) nil)                                       3
        (t (cons (F (car L)) (Mapcar F (cdr L))))            4
    )                                                        5
))                                                           6
```

I can use MapCar to take a list L of integers and return a list of their squares, as in Figure 4.22.

Figure 4.22

```
(MapCar (lambda (x) (* x x)) L)
```

As a final example, I will demonstrate a function Subsets that takes a set of distinct atoms (represented as a list) and creates the set of all possible subsets of the original set. That is, (Subsets '(1 2 3)) = (nil (1) (2) (3) (1 2) (1 3) (2 3) (1 2 3)). Because the lists represent sets, the order of the elements is unimportant, and any permutation of the list elements will be acceptable. Thus, (Subsets '(1 2 3)) could also return (nil (3) (2) (1) (2 1) (3 1) (3 2) (3 2 1))).

I first need a recursive definition of subset construction. That is, given a list representing all subsets of $\{1, 2, \cdots, n\}$, how can I create a list representing all subsets of $\{1, 2, \cdots, n+1\}$? It helps to notice that $Subsets(\{1, 2, \cdots, n+1\})$ will contain exactly twice as many elements as $Subsets(\{1, 2, \cdots, n\})$. Moreover, the extended set will contain all the elements of the original set plus n new sets created by inserting the element $n+1$ into each of the elements of the original set. For example, (Subsets '(1 2)) = (nil (1) (2) (1 2)). Therefore (Subsets '(1 2 3)) =

```
(Append (Subsets '(1 2)) (Distribute (Subsets '(1 2)) 3 ))
```

where (Distribute (Subsets '(1 2)) 3) = ((3) (3 1) (3 2) (3 1 2)). Finally, (Subsets nil) equals the list containing all subsets of the empty set, which is (nil). I first define Distribute as shown in Figure 4.23.

Figure 4.23

```
(def Distribute (lambda (L E) -- put E in each elt of L      1
     (cond                                                   2
          ((null L) nil)                                     3
          (t (cons (cons E (car L))                          4
               (Distribute (cdr L) E))))                     5
))                                                           6
```

Distribute distributes element E through list L. If L is empty (line 3), there are no sets on the list to distribute E into, so Distribute returns nil. Otherwise (line 4), it takes the car of the list and conses E to it. It then joins the new list to the result of distributing E through the remainder of the list.

In Figure 4.24, I create an Extend function that extends a list L, which represents all subsets over n elements, to include element $n+1$, E. It does this by appending L to the list formed by distributing E through L.

Figure 4.24
```
(def Extend (lambda (L E) -- both L and L with E          1
        (Append L (Distribute L E))                      2
))                                                        3
```

Finally, I can define Subsets itself. The set of all subsets of the empty set (represented by nil) is the list containing only nil. For non-nil lists, I compute the list of all subsets of the cdr of the list, then extend it by adding in the car of the original list, obtaining the code in Figure 4.25.

Figure 4.25
```
(def Subsets (lambda (L) -- all subsets of L             1
        (cond                                            2
                ((null L) (MakeList nil))                3
                (t (Extend (Subsets (cdr L)) (car L))))  4
))                                                       5
```

1.6 Closures and Deep Binding

Because LISP functions are represented as lists, functions can be passed as parameters to other functions and returned as the result of functions. In Figure 4.12 (page 126), it is important that cons be quoted in the call to f4, since I don't want it evaluated until its parameters are available.

Now consider a more interesting function, sc (self-compose), that takes a function and returns a new function representing the given function composed with itself. (That is, the new function has the effect of the old function applied twice.) I could write sc as shown in Figure 4.26.

Figure 4.26
```
(def sc (lambda (F) (lambda (x) (F (F x)))))
```

This code isn't quite right, because a call such as (sc car) will try to evaluate the resulting **lambda** form prematurely. If I quote the **lambda** form to obtain the code of Figure 4.27,

Figure 4.27
```
(def sc (lambda (F) '(lambda (x) (F (F x)))))
```

things still aren't right, because now the binding of F will be lost; by the time the internal **lambda** form is evaluated, sc has already returned, and its formal parameter has lost its meaning. I want to retain the binding of F until it is time to evaluate the **lambda** form returned by sc. To do this, I use a variant of **quote** called **function** and create sc as in Figure 4.28.

Figure 4.28   `(def sc (lambda (F) (function (lambda (x) (F (F x)))))`

Function creates a closure in which the bindings in effect when the **lambda** form is created are retained with the **lambda** form. The closure preserves the binding of identifiers that are nonlocal to a routine until the routine is executed. In other words, it produces a deep binding.

The Scheme dialect of LISP makes this example somewhat easier to code; see Figure 4.29.

Figure 4.29
```
(define (sc F)                                          1
    (lambda (x) (F (F x))))                             2

((sc car) '((a b) c)) -- returns 'a                     3
```

Scheme uses **define** as a shorthand that combines **def** and **lambda**; the **lambda** in line 2 introduces deep binding by returning a closure.

In some ways building a closure is harder in LISP than in statically scoped languages in which procedures are not first-class values. In statically scoped languages in which procedures are not first-class values, scope rules guarantee that an identifier cannot be referenced as a nonlocal in a part of the program that is lexically outside the scope defining the identifier. For example, assume that routine P, which is nested in routine Q, is passed as a functional parameter. All calls to P (either directly or as a parameter) must be completed before Q is terminated. Implementers can employ a simple stack of activation records (each of which contains the local data for a particular routine activation). A closure is a pointer to the code for a routine and a pointer to the proper activation record.

Chapter 3 introduced the dangling-procedure problem, in which the nonlocal referencing environment of a procedure has been deallocated from the central stack before the procedure is invoked. LISP encounters the same problem. In sc, references to F will occur when the result of sc is invoked as a function, which is after sc itself has returned. Unless special care is taken, the binding of the formal parameter F is no longer in force at that point. Deep binding solves the dangling-procedure problem by retaining a pointer in the closure returned by sc that points to sc's referencing environment, which includes the binding for F. Consequently, sc's referencing environment must be retained until all such outstanding pointers are deallocated. The result is that the referencing environments are linked together not as a simple stack, but as a treelike structure, with a new branch formed whenever a closure is created. Initially, the new branch is the same as the current association list, but they diverge as soon as the caller returns, removing the bindings of its local parameters from the association list. Because cons cells and environment fragments have an indeterminate lifetime, most LISP implementations use garbage collection to reclaim free runtime store.

The alternative to deep binding is shallow binding, in which all non-local identifiers are resolved at the point of call. Under shallow binding, functions need never carry any bindings with them, because the only bindings that are used are those in effect when the function is actually evaluated. This simplification allows a simple stack of bindings to be used, but of course, functions such as sc must be implemented differently. One (rather ugly) way to define sc is to explicitly construct a function (using the list function, which makes a list out of its parameters) rather than to simply parameterize it. That is, I might code sc as in Figure 4.30.

Figure 4.30

```
(def sc (lambda (F)                                          1
        (list 'lambda '(x) (list F (list F 'x)))))           2
```

1.7 Identifier Lookup

Shallow and deep binding are also used (unfortunately, ambiguously) to denote two ways of implementing (as opposed to defining) identifier lookup in a dynamically scoped language such as early versions of LISP. I will call them shallow and deep search to avoid any confusion.

In block-structured languages with static scope rules, identifiers are translated to addresses (or offsets within an activation record) at compile time. In dynamically scoped languages like LISP, some runtime overhead to fetch the current binding (that is, value) of a symbol is to be expected, but this cost must be minimized to obtain reasonable performance. As you might expect, linear search through an association list every time an identifier is referenced is too inefficient to be practical.

A key insight is that an atom is actually represented as a pointer to its property list. It is possible to store the value associated with an atom in its property list, allowing fast access to the atom's value.

The question is, what happens when a given atom is re-bound; that is, the same identifier is re-bound as a formal parameter during application of a **lambda** form? A deep-search implementation places the original, or top-level, value of an atom in its property list. Re-bindings are pushed onto a runtime stack when an atom is re-bound. This stack must be searched when the current value of an atom is needed. (The first value found for that atom is the right one.) The name **deep search** is appropriate, since LISP must usually go deep into the stack to find out if an atom has been re-bound. The advantage of deep search is that creating and freeing new bindings is fairly efficient (and somewhat similar to pushing and popping an activation record in a conventional block-structured language).

Shallow search makes lookup faster by storing the most recent binding of an atom in its property list. Lookup is shallow indeed, but there is increased overhead in invoking and returning from functions. In particular, for each local identifier, the current value of that identifier (if there is one) must be saved on the runtime stack before the new binding is stored in the atom's property list. When a function returns, the last bindings pushed on the stack (if any) must be restored.

Deciding between deep and shallow search as an implementation technique therefore amounts to choosing whether to optimize identifier lookup or function invocation/return. The trend is toward shallow search, under the assumption that identifiers are referenced more often than functions are invoked and return. Tests show that in most cases shallow search does lead to faster execution.

As a final point, deep binding is compatible with shallow search. When a **function** form is evaluated, rather than copying the entire environment, the implementation copies only the bindings of selected nonlocal identifiers whose bindings it needs to preserve. This idea is similar to **import** statements found in imperative languages such as Modula-2. **Function** then creates a closure comprising the function body and the selected bindings. When a closure is invoked, the selected bindings are reinstated (almost like a second set of parameters), and then local bindings are created. Upon return, both local and deep bindings are removed.

1.8 The Kernel of a LISP Interpreter

It is possible to define a LISP interpreter in terms of a few primitive functions (car, cdr, cons, eq, atom, get, error, null), predefined identifiers (t, nil), forms (**cond**, **def**, **quote**), and metanotions of lambda binding and function application. An interpreter is a compact and exact specification of what any LISP program will compute. Few other languages can boast such a simple and elegant definition.

To simplify things, I will ignore fine points like deep binding, although deep binding can be handled without undue complexity. Whenever I invoke one of the primitive functions in the following functions, I assume that the result defined for that function is immediately computed, perhaps by a call to a library routine. Otherwise, the interpreter would encounter infinite recursion.

The interpreter is a function called Eval, shown in Figure 4.31.

Figure 4.31

```
(def Eval (lambda (List Env) -- evaluate List in Env         1
    (cond                                                    2
        ((null List) nil)                                    3
        ((atom List)                                         4
            (cond                                            5
                ((get List (quote APVAL))                    6
                    (get List (quote APVAL)))                7
                (t (Lookup List Env))))                      8
        ((eq (car List) (quote quote)) (car (cdr List)))     9
        ((eq (car List) (quote cond))                        10
            (EvalCond (cdr List) Env))                       11
        (t (Apply (car List)                                 12
            (EvalList (cdr List) Env) Env)))                 13
))                                                           14
```

Eval evaluates List in a given environment Env of identifier-value pairs.
Values of atoms are looked up in their property lists (lines 6 and 7) or
the environment Env (line 8). The forms **quote** (line 9) and **cond** (lines
10–11) are given special treatment. The eq function tests atoms for
equality. (We don't need to be concerned about what eq does with
nonatoms; distinguishing pointer equality, shallow equality, and deep
equality operations. These distinctions are discussed in Chapter 5.) All
other lists are evaluated (lines 12–13) by applying the car of the list (a
function) to a list of parameters evaluated in the current environment.
Apply is defined as in Figure 4.32.

Figure 4.32

```
(def Apply (lambda (Fct Parms Env) -- apply Fct to Parms     1
    (cond                                                    2
        ((atom Fct) (cond                                    3
            ((eq Fct (quote car)) (car (car Parms)))         4
            ((eq Fct (quote cdr)) (cdr (car Parms)))         5
            ((eq Fct (quote cons))                           6
                (cons (car Parms) (car (cdr Parms))))        7
            ((eq Fct (quote get))                            8
                (get (car Parms) (car (cdr Parms))))         9
            ((eq Fct (quote atom)) (atom (car Parms)))       10
            ((eq Fct (quote error)) (error (car Parms)))     11
            ((eq Fct (quote eq))                             12
                (eq (car Parms) (car (cdr Parms))))          13
            (t (cond                                         14
                ((get Fct (quote EXPR))                      15
                    (Apply (get Fct (quote EXPR))            16
                    Parms Env))                              17
                (t (Apply (Lookup Fct Env)                   18
                    Parms Env)))))                           19
        ) -- (atom Fct)                                      20
```

```
          ((eq (car Fct) (quote lambda))                     21
              (Eval (car (cdr (cdr Fct)))                     22
                    (Update (car (cdr Fct)) Parms Env)))      23
          (t (Apply (Eval Fct Env) Parms Env)))               24
))                                                            25
```

If Fct is an atom (line 3), Apply first checks for each primitive function. If the atom isn't one of these, Apply checks its property list (lines 15–17), and then its association list Env (lines 18–19). This step can lead to an infinite recursion (that is, an undefined result) if Fct is a symbol bound to itself. If Fct is nonatomic, Apply looks for a **lambda** form (line 21). If it sees one, it binds the actual parameters to the formal **lambda** parameters (using Update), and then evaluates the **lambda** body in the updated environment, which is discarded afterward. If a nonatomic form isn't a **lambda** form, Apply attempts to simplify Fct by evaluating it, and then applying the simplified function to the original parameters (line 24). The remaining procedures, shown in Figure 4.33, are straightforward.

Figure 4.33

```
(def EvalCond (lambda (Conds Env) -- evaluate cond       1
    (cond                                                  2
         ((null Conds) nil) -- could treat as error        3
         ((Eval (car (car Conds)) Env)                     4
             (Eval (car (cdr (car Conds))) Env))           5
         (t (EvalCond (cdr Conds) Env)))                   6
))                                                         7

(def EvalList (lambda (List Env) -- evaluate list         8
    (cond                                                  9
         ((null List) nil)                                10
         (t (cons (Eval (car List) Env)                   11
             (EvalList (cdr List) Env))))                  12
))                                                        13

(def Lookup (lambda (Id Env) -- lookup Id                14
    (cond                                                 15
         ((null Env) (error (quote UnboundVar)))          16
         ((eq Id (car (car Env))) (car (cdr (car Env))))  17
         (t (Lookup Id (cdr Env))))                       18
))                                                        19
```

```
(def Update (lambda (Formals Vals Env) -- bind parameters    20
    (cond                                                     21
        ((null Formals)                                       22
            (cond ((null Vals) Env)                           23
                (t (error (quote ArgCount))))))              24
        ((null Vals) (error (quote ArgCount)))               25
        (t (cons (cons (car Formals)                          26
            (cons (car Vals) nil))                            27
            (Update (cdr Formals) (cdr Vals) Env)))           28
))                                                            29
```

Many of the above functions assume that their parameters are syntactically well formed. For example, EvalCond (line 1) assumes Conds is a list of pairs. Similarly, most functions assume their parameters are lists, properly terminated by nil. A more careful interpreter would certainly check parameters (as does Update in lines 20–29).

The top level of many LISP implementations is an infinite loop:

```
(loop (Print (Eval (Read))))
```

The built-in Read function returns an expression typed in by the user, Eval derives a value from it, and Print displays that value. If the expression is a new function definition, it is treated as a top-level declaration and is added to the environment, so that later expressions can use it. Functions that are introduced within bodies of other functions are problematic, because if they modify the top-level environment, then function evaluation can have a side effect, which is not appropriate for a functional language. Scheme avoids this problem by forbidding function declarations except at the top level.

Any realistic LISP implementation would surely have more primitives than the above interpreter assumes. Arithmetic, debugging, and I/O functions are obvious omissions. Nevertheless, LISP has a remarkably small framework. To understand LISP one needs to understand lambda binding, function invocation, and a few primitive functions and forms (**cond**, for instance, is required). Everything else can be viewed as a library of useful predefined functions.

Consider how this situation contrasts with even so spartan a language as Pascal, which has a very much larger conceptual framework. Not surprisingly, semantic definitions for imperative languages like Pascal are a good deal more complex than for LISP. Chapter 10 discusses the formal semantics of imperative languages.

The Eval function is also known as a **metacircular interpreter**. Such an interpreter goes a long way toward formally defining the semantics of the language. If a question arises about the meaning of a

LISP construct, it can be answered by referring to the code of Eval. In a formal sense, however, metacircular interpreters only give one fixed point to the equation

```
Meaning(Program) = Meaning(Interpret(Program))
```

There are other fixed points (for example, that all programs loop forever) that aren't helpful in defining the semantics of a language. We will return to this subject in Chapter 10, which deals with the formal semantics of programming languages.

1.9 Run-time List Evaluation

Not only is Eval expressible in LISP; it is also provided as a predeclared function in every LISP implementation. Programmers can take advantage of the homoiconic nature of LISP to construct programs at runtime and then pass them as parameters to Eval.

For example, say I would like to write a function Interpret that accepts lists in the format of Figure 4.34.

Figure 4.34

```
'(MyAdd (MyAdd 1 5) (MyMult 2 3))
```

Here, MyAdd means "add the two parameters and then double the result," and MyMult means "multiply the two parameters and then subtract one from the result." The input to Interpret may be an arbitrarily nested list. One way to solve this puzzle is to program Interpret recursively. It would check to see if the car of its parameter was an atom, MyAdd, or MyMult, and then apply the appropriate arithmetic rule to the result of recursively interpreting the other parameters. But Figure 4.35 shows a much more straightforward, nonrecursive solution that takes advantage of Eval.

Figure 4.35

```
(def MyAdd (lambda (A B) (* (+ A B) 2)))
(def MyMult (lambda (A B) (- (* A B) 1)))
(def Interpret (lambda (L) (Eval L)))
(Interpret '(MyAdd (MyAdd 1 5) (MyMult 2 3))) -- result is 34
```

The list to be interpreted is treated not as data, but as program, and Eval is capable of executing programs.

1.10 Lazy Evaluation

Normally, a LISP evaluator operates by evaluating and binding actual parameters to formal parameters (first to last) and then evaluating function bodies. If an actual parameter involves a function call, that function is invoked as the parameter is evaluated. This strategy is known as **strict evaluation**. Given the functional nature of LISP programs, other evaluation strategies are possible.

One of the most interesting of these is **lazy evaluation**. As the name suggests, a lazy evaluator only evaluates an expression (typically, an actual parameter) if it is absolutely necessary. Evaluation is performed incrementally, so that only those parts of an expression that are needed are evaluated. For example, if only the car of an S-expression is needed, the cdr is not yet evaluated.

One form of lazy evaluation that is common even in imperative programming languages is short-circuit semantics for Boolean operators, as discussed in Chapter 1. In imperative languages, short-circuit evaluation can change the meaning of a program, because a subexpression could have a side effect (an assignment hidden in a function call, for example) that is avoided by not evaluating that subexpression. In functional languages, there are no side effects, so there is no danger that short-circuit evaluation will change the semantics. The order of evaluation of expressions (and subexpressions) is irrelevant. This freedom to evaluate in any order makes functional languages particularly fertile ground for generalizing the idea of short-circuit semantics. (The **cond** form requires care to make sure that the textually first successful branch is taken. Although the branches can be evaluated in any order, runtime errors encountered in evaluating conditions textually later than the first successful one need to be suppressed.)

An expression that is not yet evaluated is called a **suspension**. Suspensions are much like closures; they combine a function and a referencing environment in which to invoke that expression. They also include all the unevaluated parameters to that function. When a suspension is evaluated, it is replaced by the computed value, so that future reevaluations are not needed. Often, that computed value itself contains a suspension at the point that evaluation was no longer needed.

Lazy evaluation is of interest primarily because strict evaluation may evaluate more than is really needed. For example, if I want to compute which student scored the highest grade in an exam, I might evaluate (car (sort Students)). Strict evaluators will sort the entire list of students, then throw all but the first element away. A lazy evaluator will perform only as much of the sort as is needed to produce the car of the list, then stop (because there is no reference to the cdr of the sorted list). Now, sorting in order to find the maximum element is an inefficient approach to begin with, and we can't fault strict evaluators for inefficiency when the algorithm itself is so bad. However, lazy evaluation manages to salvage this inefficient (but very clear) approach and make it more efficient.

As a more detailed example, consider trees encoded as lists. For example, ((A B) (C D)) represents a binary tree with two binary subtrees. The frontier (or fringe) of a tree is the list of leaves of the tree (in left-to-right order). The frontier of this particular tree is (A B C D). I want to determine if two trees have the same frontier. An obvious approach is to first flatten each tree into its frontier, then compare the frontiers for equality. I might write the code in Figure 4.36.

Figure 4.36

```
(def SameFrontier (lambda (X Y)                      1
        (EqualList (Flatten X) (Flatten Y))))        2

(def EqualList (lambda (X Y)                          3
    (cond                                            4
        ((null X) (null Y))                          5
        ((null Y) nil)                               6
        ((eq (car X) (car Y))                        7
            (EqualList (cdr X) (cdr Y)))             8
        (t nil))                                     9
))                                                  10

(def Flatten (lambda (List)                         11
    (cond                                           12
        ((null List) nil)                           13
        ((atom List) (MakeList List))               14
        (t (Append (Flatten (car List))             15
            (Flatten (cdr List))))))                16
))                                                  17
```

Calls to SameFrontier (assuming a strict evaluation mechanism) will flatten both parameters before equality is ever considered. This computation will be particularly inefficient if the trees are large and their frontiers have only a small common prefix.

Lazy evaluation is more appropriate for such a problem. It follows an outermost-first evaluation scheme, postponing parameter evaluation until necessary. That is, in a nested invocation, such as that of Figure 4.37,

Figure 4.37

```
(foo (bar L) (baz (rag L)))
```

foo is invoked before bar or baz, and in fact they may never be invoked at all, if, for example, foo ignores its parameters. If foo needs to evaluate its second parameter, baz is invoked, but not rag, unless baz itself needs it. Furthermore, once a function has been invoked, the result it returns may not be completely computed. For example, the body of bar may indicate that it returns (cons 1 (frob L)). It will return a cons cell (allocated from the heap) with 1 in the car and a suspension in the cdr; the suspension indicates that a frob must be invoked on L in order to achieve a value. This suspension may never be activated.

The algorithm for lazy evaluation is as follows:

1. To evaluate a list, make a suspension out of it (combining the function name, the parameters, which are not to be evaluated yet, and the referencing environment).
2. To evaluate a suspension, make a suspension out of each of its parameters and invoke its function in its referencing environment.
3. To evaluate a cons invocation, create a new cons cell in the heap and initialize its car and cdr to the parameters, which are left as suspensions.
4. To evaluate a primitive Boolean function such as null or eq, evaluate the parameter(s) only as far as needed. Each primitive function has its own lazy evaluation method.

Let me trace how a lazy evaluator might evaluate

(SameFrontier '((A B) C) '(B C (A D))) .

The trace in Figure 4.38 shows the evaluation steps.

Figure 4.38

```
Goal = (SameFrontier S1='((A B) C) S2='(B C (A D)))          1
=[S body] (EqualList E1=(Flatten S1) E2=(Flatten S2))        2
=[E body] (cond ((null E1) .. ) .. ) .. )                    3
|     E1 = (Flatten F1=S1)                                   4
|     =[F body] (cond ((null S1) .. ) .. )                   5
|     [S1 is neither null nor an atom]                       6
|     = (Append A1=(Flatten (car F1))                        7
|            A2=(Flatten (cdr F1)))                          8
|     =[A body] (cond ((null A1) .. ) .. )                   9
|     |     A1 = (Flatten F2=(car F1))                       10
|     |     =[F body] (cond ((null F2) .. ) .. )             11
|     |     |     F2 = (car F1) = (car S1) = (car '((A B) C)) 12
|     |     |     = '(A B)                                    13
|     |     [F2 is neither null nor an atom]                 14
|     |     A1 = (Append A3=(Flatten (car F2))              15
|     |            A4=(Flatten (cdr F2)))                    16
|     |     =[A body] (cond ((null A3) .. ) .. )             17
```

```
|    |      |     A3 = (Flatten F3=(car F2))                         18
|    |      |     =[F body] (cond ((null F3) .. ) .. )              19
|    |      |      | F3 = (car F2) = (car '(A B)) = 'A              20
|    |      |     [F3 is not null, but it is an atom]               21
|    |      |     A3 = (MakeList F3) =[M body] (cons F3 nil)        22
|    |      |       = '(A)                                          23
|    |   [A3 is not null]                                           24
|    |   A1 = (cons (car A3) (Append (cdr A3) A4))                  25
|   [A1 is not null]                                                26
|   E1 = (cons (car A1) (Append (cdr A1) A2))                       27
[E1 is not null]                                                   28
Goal = (cond ((null E2) .. ) .. )                                  29
|    E2 = (Flatten F4=S2)                                           30
|    =[F body] (cond ((null F4) .. ) .. )                           31
|    [F4 is not null or an atom]                                    32
|    = (Append A5=(Flatten (car F4))                                33
|             A6=(Flatten (cdr F4)))                                34
|    =[A body] (cond ((null A5) .. ) .. )                           35
|    |    A5 = (Flatten F5=(car F4))                                36
|    |    =[F body] (cond ((null F5) .. ) .. )                       37
|    |     | F5 = (car F4) = (car S2)                               38
|    |     |  = (car '(B C (A D))) = 'B                             39
|    |    [F5 is not null, but it is an atom]                       40
|    |    A5 = (MakeList F5) =[M body] (cons 'B nil) = '(B)         41
|    [A5 is not null]                                               42
|    E2 = (cons (car A5) (Append (cdr A5) A6))                      43
[E2 is not null]                                                   44
Goal = (cond ((eq (car E1) (car E2)) .. ) .. )                     45
= (cond ((eq (car A1) (car A5)) .. ) .. )                          46
= (cond ((eq (car A3) 'B) .. ) .. )                                47
= (cond ((eq 'A 'B) .. ) .. )                                      48
= (cond (t nil))                                                   49
= nil -- frontiers are different                                   50
```

The notation is concise, but I hope not too clumsy. I show that a formal parameter is bound to an actual parameter by the notation Formal=Actual, as in S1='((A B) C) in line 1. The names of the formal parameters (here, S) start with the same letter as the name of the function (SameFrontier). I distinguish multiple parameters as well as new instances during recursive calls by numeric suffixes. Simplification steps are marked in various ways. In line 2, =[S body] means expanding a call by inserting the body of a function, in this case, SameFrontier. I have used the declaration of Append from Figure 4.13 (page 127) whenever [A body] is mentioned. The ellipsis (..) shows where evaluation of **cond** pauses in order to evaluate a subexpression. It only evaluates the subexpression to the point that it can answer the condition in question. For example, in line 9, it is necessary to discover if A1 is null. By line 25

A1 has been evaluated enough to answer the question, as reported in line 26. These subordinate evaluations are indented. Line 27 continues the evaluation of E1 started on line 4. It leaves the result in terms of A1 and A2, to be further evaluated in lines 46–48.

Lazy evaluation is more difficult (and costly) to implement than strict evaluation. The example shows that it has much of the flavor of coroutines (see Chapter 2), with control automatically shifting as needed among many computations in order to advance the computation.

An implementation of LISP might allow the programmer to select lazy evaluation when desired; any evaluation strategy will produce the same result so long as the program is written in "pure" LISP. (Some dialects include imperative facilities, which, as you have seen, can make the evaluation order significant.) Automatic determination of the preferable evaluation strategy is an open (and hard) problem.

Lazy evaluation is sometimes called "demand-driven evaluation" because evaluation is triggered by a demand for a value. We conventionally view a computation (very roughly) as first obtaining input values, then computing a result using them, and finally printing that result. Demand-driven evaluation reverses this view. Nothing happens until the evaluator sees a request to write a result. This request initiates computations, which solicit input values. If no demand for output is seen, nothing is computed.[3]

Lazy evaluation also has a declarative, nonprocedural flavor. (Chapter 8 discusses logic programming, which is declarative.) Although LISP is certainly procedural (both imperative and functional languages are in the larger category of procedural languages), lazy evaluation makes evaluation optional. That is, an expression is not a command, "Compute this!" but a suggestion as to how to obtain a value if it is needed.

Imperative languages also allow unnecessary computations to be suppressed. For example, optimizing compilers often eliminate "dead code." Since imperative languages are full of side effects, delaying major calculations for extended periods of time is quite difficult. Lazy evaluation is much more attractive in a functional programming-language environment.

---

[3] This is similar to a folk myth concerning the benchmarking of an optimizing FORTRAN compiler. The compiler was presented with a very complex program containing no write statements. It optimized the program by generating no code!

1.11 Speculative Evaluation

Another interesting evaluation strategy is **speculative evaluation**. As the name suggests, a speculative evaluator wants to evaluate as much as possible, as soon as possible. This evaluation strategy is best suited for multiprocessors or multicomputers that are able to perform many calculations concurrently. Present multicomputers have hundreds of processors; future machines may have hundreds of thousands or even millions.

A crucial problem in a multicomputer is finding a way to keep a reasonable fraction of the processors busy. Speculative evaluation seeks to evaluate independent subexpressions concurrently. For example, in an invocation of SameFrontier, a speculative evaluator could flatten both lists concurrently. Within a function, another source of potential concurrency lies in the evaluation of a **cond** form. Individual guards of a **cond** can be evaluated concurrently, as well as their associated bodies.

Care is required because of the evaluation ordering that is assumed in **cond**'s definition. Evaluation of a subexpression may lead to a runtime error (for example, taking the car of an atom), because a speculative evaluator will evaluate an expression that a strict evaluator would never examine. With care, faults can be suppressed until their effect on the overall result is known. Given this caveat, a **cond** form can be a rich source of concurrent evaluations.

Nonetheless, the cost of starting a processor and later receiving its result is often high. If the calculation started speculatively is too small, the overhead will overshadow any advantage provided by the concurrent evaluation. A speculative evaluator for LISP would probably evaluate primitive functions directly and reserve concurrent speculative evaluation for **lambda** forms. Such coarse-grain parallelism is discussed further in Chapter 7.

The ability to evaluate expressions in virtually any order makes speculative evaluation plausible for functional programming languages. In imperative languages, an elaborate analysis of what variables depend on what other variables is required even to consider any form of concurrent evaluation. Once again the von Neumann bottleneck rears its ugly head.

1.12 Strengths and Weaknesses of LISP

Functional programming is in many ways simpler and more elegant than conventional programming styles. Programmers do not need to keep track of potential side effects when a procedure is invoked, so programming is less error-prone. The lack of side effects allows implementations a rich variety of evaluation strategies.

LISP and its descendants have long been the dominant programming languages in artificial intelligence research. It has been widely used for expert systems, natural-language processing, knowledge representation, and vision modeling. Only recently has Prolog, discussed in Chapter 8, attracted a significant following in these areas. LISP is also the foundation of the widely used Emacs text editor. Much of LISP's success is due to its homoiconic nature: A program can construct a data structure that it then executes. The semantics of the core of LISP can be described in just a few pages of a metacircular interpreter.

LISP was the first language to have an extensive program development environment [Teitelman 81]. (Smalltalk, described in Chapter 5, was the second. Such environments are widely available now for Ada, Pascal, and C++.) Programs can be modified and extended by changing one function at a time and then seeing what happens. This facility allows elaborate programs to evolve and supports rapid prototyping, in which a working prototype is used to evaluate the capabilities of a program. Later, the program is fleshed out by completing its implementation and refining critical routines.

The most apparent weakness of the early dialects of LISP is their lack of program and data structures. In LISP 1.5, there are no type-declaration facilities (although some LISP dialects have adopted facilities for data typing). Certainly not everything fits LISP's recursive, list-oriented view of the world. For example, symbol tables are rarely implemented as lists.

Many LISP programmers view type checking as something that ought to be done after a program is developed. In effect, type checking screens a program for inconsistencies that may lead to runtime errors. In LISP, type checking amounts generally to checking for appropriate structures in S-expressions.

Most production LISP dialects (such as Interlisp, Franz LISP, Common LISP, and Scheme) have greatly extended the spartan facilities provided in LISP 1.5, leading to incompatibilities among LISP implementations. Indeed, it is rare to transport large LISP programs between different implementations. This failure inhibits the interchange of software tools and research developments.

It would appear that the corrupting influences of von Neumann programming are so pervasive that even functional languages like LISP can succumb. Most LISP implementations even have a prog feature that allows an imperative programming style! In addition, LISP has some decidedly nonfunctional features, such as the set function and property lists. In fact, it has been said that "LISP ... is not a functional language at all. [The] success of LISP set back the development of a properly functional style of programming by at least ten years." [Turner 85b]

2 ◆ FP

In comparison to typical block-structured languages, LISP 1.5 stands as a paragon of simplicity. (On the other hand, Common LISP is as big as Ada.) Nonetheless, Backus suggests that even simpler functional programming approaches may be desirable [Backus 78]. He thinks that LISP's parameter-binding and substitution rules are unnecessary and instead proposes a variable-free programming style limited to single-parameter functions. (A parameter may, however, be a sequence, and functions may be curried.) Further, LISP's ability to combine functions in any form (since functions are just S-expressions) is unnecessarily general. He compares this freedom to the unrestricted use of **goto** statements in low-level imperative languages. In contrast, Backus prefers a fixed set of higher-order functions that allow functions to be combined in various ways, analogous to the fixed set of control structures found in modern imperative languages. The result is the FP programming language.

2.1 Definition of an FP Environment

An FP environment comprises the following:

1. A set of objects. An object is either an atom or a sequence, $<x_1, \ldots, x_n>$, whose elements are objects, or $\perp$ ("bottom") representing "error," or "undefined." Included as atoms are ϕ, the empty sequence (roughly equivalent to nil in LISP), and T and F, representing true and false. Any sequence containing $\perp$ is equivalent to $\perp$. That is, the sequence constructor is bottom-preserving.

2. A set of functions (which are not objects) mapping objects into objects. Functions may be primitive (predefined), defined (represented by a name), or higher-order (a combination of functions and objects using a predefined higher-order function). All functions are bottom-preserving; f applied to $\perp$ always yields $\perp$.

3. An application operation that applies a function to an object, yielding an object. Function f applied to object x is denoted as f:x. Here, x isn't a variable name (there are no variables!), but rather a placeholder for an expression that will yield an object.

4. A set of higher-order functions used to combine existing functions and objects into new functions. Typical higher-order functions include those shown in Figure 4.39.

Figure 4.39

```
Composition                                    1
(f ∘ g):x ≡ f:(g:x)                            2
```

```
Construction                                                3
[f₁ , ... , fₙ ]:x ≡ <f₁:x, ... ,fₙ:x>                      4

Condition                                                   5
(p → f;g):x ≡                                               6
    if p:x = T then                                         7
        f:x                                                 8
    elsif p:x = F then                                      9
        g:x                                                10
    else                                                   11
        ⊥                                                  12
```

The conditional form handles nicely a problem that arises with bottom-preserving functions: One or the other branch of a conditional may be undefined (bottom) while the value of the conditional is itself well defined. If one tries to create a conditional function that takes a triple representing the Boolean value, the true-part value and the false-part value, then if any component is ⊥, so is the entire triple, forcing ⊥ as the result. Since conditional is a higher-order function, the evaluator doesn't apply the "**then** function" or "**else** function" until the conditional value has been evaluated and tested against T and F.

One of the advantages of restricting higher-order functions is that they form an algebra, which allows forms to be manipulated in well-defined ways. For example, Figure 4.40 is a theorem:

Figure 4.40

$$[f_1 , ... ,f_n] \circ g \equiv [f_1 \circ g, ... , f_n \circ g]$$

This theorem states that a composed function may be "distributed into" or "factored from" a list of functions. Such algebraic theorems can be viewed as the basis for automatic restructuring of FP programs, potentially allowing sophisticated optimizations.

5.   A set of definitions binding functions to identifiers. These identifiers serve merely as abbreviations and placeholders; there is no concept of redefinition or scoping.

2.2 Reduction Semantics

FP environments have a particularly simple semantics called **reduction semantics**. An FP program is composed of a number of functions applied to objects. The meaning of such a program is defined by repeatedly reducing the program by finding a function application and evaluating it. In some cases, function evaluation may be nonterminating. Such functions diverge and are considered undefined (that is, ⊥). There are only three kinds of valid functions: primitive functions, defined functions, and higher-order functions. Primitive functions are automatically evaluable. Defined functions are reduced by replacing their identifiers with their definitions. Higher-order functions are reduced by substituting their definitions. If a function does not belong to one of these three categories, it is invalid.

Reduction semantics have only a very weak form of identifier binding (defined names map to functions) and employ no changes to hidden states. There is clearly no way to cause side effects, so an evaluator can reduce a function in any order. In fact, early FP languages were called "Red" (reduction) languages.

3 ◆ PERSISTENCE IN FUNCTIONAL LANGUAGES

A value is **persistent** if it is retained after the program that created it has terminated. A database is a good example of persistent values. The conventional way to make values persistent is to write them out to a file. Chapter 3 discusses the type-safety considerations of such values.

If persistent values are to be incorporated into a programming language, we must be able to name such values and to be assured that once created, they do not change. Functional languages can incorporate persistent values in a natural way that avoids explicit input and output [Morrison 90].

Persistent values can be named by reference to a **persistence root**, which is something like the root of a file-system hierarchy. All such values are automatically saved after execution. If a value is structured, its components are also preserved; in particular, other values pointed to by a persistent value are also persistent. Using ML as an example, we might have the code shown in Figure 4.41.

Figure 4.41

```
let                                                          1
    val persist(MyRoot) a.b.c = 3;                           2
    val persist(MyRoot) d.e;                                 3
in                                                           4
    a.b.c + d.e                                              5
end;                                                         6
```

Here, the identifier a.b.c is introduced as persistent, under root MyRoot, and is given the (permanent) value 3. The identifier d.e is not given a value; instead, it gets its value from persistent storage, where it should already be defined.

Since functional languages have no side effects, persistent values are immutable, so there is no need to worry about getting consistent copies if two programs access the values at the same time: such values cannot change. It would be a runtime error to reintroduce the same identifier in a persistence hierarchy. The only modification allowed is inserting an object into (and perhaps removing an object from) the persistent store.

The possibility of lazy evaluation in functional programming languages make them even more attractive for persistent store. An incompletely evaluated value, that is, a suspension, can be saved in persistent store so long as the environment on which it depends is also treated as persistent. If later computation resolves, fully or partially, the suspension, it is safe to replace the stored suspension with the resolved value. Future evaluations, either by the same program or by other programs, will see effectively the same values.

One proposal for integrating persistence into a functional language is to build an imperative command outside the language (at the operating-system level, for example) [McNally 91]. The expression in Figure 4.42

Figure 4.42   **persist** ModuleA **requires** ModuleB, ModuleC

means that all identifiers exported from ModulaA are to be placed in persistent store. Both ModuleB and ModuleC must already be in persistent store; values in ModuleA may depend on them. If ModuleA is already in persistent store, the new copy replaces it, but any pointers to the identifiers of the previous ModuleA are still valid. The old ModuleA becomes collectable; that is, garbage collection routines may discard and reclaim the storage of any of its values that are no longer pointed to.

4 ◆ LIMITATIONS OF FUNCTIONAL LANGUAGES

The idea that variables are unnecessary is quite attractive. It is often sufficient either to bind values through parameter binding or as constants for the duration of a block. For example, in ML, the **let** construct allows an identifier to be bound to a meaning, but there is no assignment as such. There are situations, however, in which the inability to modify an existing value leads to awkward or inefficient programs [Arvind 89; Yuen 91].

The first problem involves initializing complex data structures, particularly two-dimensional arrays. For example, I might want an array A with the properties shown in Figure 4.43.

Figure 4.43

$$A[0,j] = A[i, 0] = 1 \ \forall \ 0 \leq i < n, \ 0 \leq j < n \qquad 1$$
$$A[i,j] = A[i, j-1] + A[i-1, j] + A[i-1, j-1] \qquad 2$$
$$\forall \ 0 < i < n, \ 0 < j < n \qquad 3$$

Short of embedding syntax for this elegant mathematical declaration into a programming language, the most straightforward way to accomplish this initialization is with an imperative program that iterates as in Figure 4.44.

Figure 4.44

```
variable                                                  1
    sum, row, col : integer;                              2
    A : array [0..n-1, 0..n-1] of integer;                3
begin                                                     4
    for sum := 0 to 2*n-2 do                              5
        for row := max(0,sum-n+1) to min(n-1,sum) do      6
            col := sum - row;                             7
            if row = 0 or col = 0 then                    8
                A[row, col] := 1                          9
            else                                          10
                A[row,col] := A[row, col-1] +             11
                        A[row-1, col] + A[row-1, col-1]   12
            end;                                          13
        end; -- for row                                   14
    end; -- for sum                                       15
end;                                                      16
```

In a functional language, initialization is usually performed by recursion, which returns the value that is to be associated with the identifier. But there is no obvious recursive method that works here, for several reasons. First, unlike lists, arrays are not generally built up by constructors acting on pieces. The entire array is built at once.[4] Second, the natural initialization order, which is by a diagonal wavefront, does not lend itself either to generating rows or columns independently and then combining them to make the array. Third, special-purpose predeclared array constructor functions can only handle simpler cases in which the value at each cell depends only on the cell's indices. For example, to build an array in which each cell has a value computed as the sum of its row and column, we could employ such a function and invoke it as MakeArray(1, n, 1, n, (**fn** row, col => row+col)). That approach fails here, because the value in a cell depends on other values within the array.

---

[4] APL, discussed in Chapter 9, allows arrays to be built piecemeal.

One solution to this problem that largely preserves **referential transparency**, that is, that references to an identifier should always produce the same results, is to separate allocation of data from initialization. After the array is built, a language could permit individual cells to be assigned values, but only once each. Accesses to values that have not been initialized would be erroneous. (In concurrent programming, discussed in Chapter 7, such accesses would block the thread that tries to access such a cell until the cell is initialized.) Unfortunately, this solution requires that the language have assignment and that there be runtime checks for violations of the single-assignment rule.

Initialized identifiers are not the only problem with functional languages. A different problem arises if I want to summarize information in counters. For example, I may have a function that returns values from 1 to 10, and I want to invoke the function a million times with different parameters. I want to know how often each of the possible return values appears. In an imperative language, it is quite easy to store such results in an array that is initially 0 everywhere and updated after each function invocation. In a functional language, there seems to be no alternative but to enter a new name scope after each function call, getting a new array that is initialized to the old one except for one position, where it is incremented. The only reasonable way to enter a million name scopes is by recursion, and even that seems problematic. A solution to the problem of summarizing information in a functional language is found in the guardians in Post (discussed in Chapter 6) and in multiparadigm languages like G-2.

Finally, functional languages sometimes lose nuances that are essential to efficiency. For example, the Quicksort algorithm can be expressed elegantly in Miranda (Chapter 3) as in Figure 4.45.

Figure 4.45

```
fun                                                          1
    QuickSort [] = []                                        2
    QuickSort (a :: rest) =                                  3
        QuickSort [ b | b <- rest; b <= a ] @               4
        [a] @                                                5
        QuickSort [ b | b <- rest; b > a];                  6
```

However, this representation misses some important details. First, it is inefficient to make two passes through the array to partition it into small and large elements. Second, stack space can be conserved by recursing on the smaller sublist, not always the first sublist (I assume the compiler is smart enough to replace the tail recursion with iteration). Third, Quicksort should sort elements in place; this implementation builds a new array. The first two details can be programmed in the functional model, although perhaps awkwardly. The other is too intricately associated with concepts of swapping values in memory locations.

5 ◆ LAMBDA CALCULUS

The mathematician Alonzo Church designed the lambda calculus in the 1930s as a way to express computation [Church 41]. LISP is a direct descendent of this formalism, and ML owes much of its nature to a restricted version called "typed lambda calculus." In one sense, lambda calculus is a set of rules for manipulating symbols; the symbols represent functions, parameters, and invocations. In another sense, lambda calculus is a programming language; it has given rise more or less directly to both LISP and ML.

The underlying ideas of lambda calculus are straightforward. Lambda calculus has only three kinds of terms: identifiers (such as x), abstractions, and applications. **Abstractions** represent functions of a single parameter. They follow the notation shown in Figure 4.46.

Figure 4.46

```
(λ x . (* x 2)) -- Lambda calculus                    1
(lambda (x) (* x 2)) -- LISP                          2
fn x => x * 2 -- ML                                   3
```

In general, an abstraction has the form $(\lambda x . T)$, where T is any term. **Applications** represent invoking a function with an actual parameter. A function F is invoked with actual parameter P by the notation (F P); both F and P are any terms. Parentheses may be dropped; the precedence rules stipulate that application and abstraction are grouped left to right and that application has a higher precedence than abstraction. Therefore, the terms in Figure 4.47 are equivalent.

Figure 4.47

```
(λ x . ((λ y . q) x) z) -- fully parenthesized        1
λ x . (λ y . q) x z -- minimally parenthesized        2
```

Another notational convenience is that curried functions may be rewritten without currying, as in Figure 4.48.

Figure 4.48

```
(λ x . (λ y . (λ z . T))) = (λ x y z . T)
```

Lambda calculus has a static scope rule. The abstraction $(\lambda x . T)$ introduces a new binding for the identifier x; the scope of this binding is the term T. In the language of lambda calculus, x is **bound** in $(\lambda x . T)$. An unbound identifier in a term is called **free** in that term. It is possible to define the concept of free identifiers in a recursive way: An identifier x is free in term T if (1) the term is just the identifier x; (2) the term is an application (F P), and x is free in F or in P; or (3) the term is an abstraction (λ y . T), and x is free in T, and x is not y. Figure 4.49 presents some examples.

Figure 4.49

```
(λ x . y) (λ y . z) -- y and z are free; x is bound          1
(λ x . y) (y z) -- y and z are free; x is bound             2
(λ y . (y z)) -- z is free; y is bound                      3
(λ x . (λ y . z)) -- z is free; x and y are bound           4
(λ x . (λ x . z)) -- z is free; x is bound                  5
```

The example in line 5 introduces two different bindings for x. This situation is analogous to an inner declaration that conflicts with an outer declaration. As you expect, the meaning of x within any term is based on the closest enclosing binding. The rules of lambda calculus, which you will see shortly, ensure that this interpretation is followed.

The heart of lambda calculus is the rule of Figure 4.50 that lets you simplify a term.

Figure 4.50

```
(λ x . T) P =β=> {P / x} T
```

This formula says that applying a function (λ x . T) to an actual parameter P yields the body T of the function, with all occurrences of the formal parameter x replaced by the actual parameter P. This simplification is called β **(beta) reduction**, and I denote it by the symbol =β=> . The notation {P / x} T can be read as "P instead of x in T". It is somewhat awkward to define this substitution operator precisely. First, x may have bound occurrences in T that should not be subject to substitution. These are like nested declarations of x, which hide the outer declaration that we are trying to bind to P. Second, P may have unbound instances of identifiers that are bound in T. These identifiers must remain unbound in the substitution. To achieve this goal, such identifiers need to be renamed in T before substitution takes place. Figure 4.51 shows some examples of substitution.

Figure 4.51

```
{a / b} b = a -- no renaming needed
{a / b} a = a -- no free instances of b
{a / b} (λ c . b) = (λ c . a) -- no renaming needed
{a / b} (λ b . b) = (λ z . z) -- b=>z; no free instances left
{a / b} ((λ b . b)(b c)) = (λ z . z)(a c) -- renamed bound b=>z
{(λ x . y) / x} (x y) = ((λ x . y) y)
```

The concept of renaming bound identifiers can be formalized; it is called α (**alpha) conversion** (see Figure 4.52).

Figure 4.52

$$(\lambda\ x\ .\ T)\ =\alpha=> \ (\lambda\ y\ .\ \{y\ /\ x\}\ T)$$

Be aware that α conversion requires that y not be free in T.

Figure 4.53 is a fairly complicated example that uses α-conversions and β-reductions.[5]

Figure 4.53

```
(λ a b c . (a c) (b c)) (λ a . a) (λ a . a) =α=>          1
(λ a b c . (a c) (b c)) (λ z . z) (λ y . y) =β=>          2
(λ b c . ((λ z . z) c) (b c)) (λ y . y) =β=>             3
(λ b c . c (b c)) (λ y . y) =β=>                         4
(λ c . c ((λ y . y) c)) =β=>                             5
(λ c . c c)                                              6
```

Line 2 renames bound identifiers in the second and third terms to remove confusion with identifiers in the first term. Line 3 applies β reduction to the first two terms. Line 4 applies β reduction to the inner application. This choice is analogous to evaluating the parameter to the outer application before invoking the function. In other words, it embodies strict evaluation and value-mode parameter passing; in lambda calculus, it is called **applicative-order** evaluation.

Instead, I could have applied β reduction to the outer application first. This embodies lazy evaluation and name-mode parameter passing; in lambda calculus, it is called **normal-order** evaluation. Under normal-order evaluation, I can reduce the same expression as shown in Figure 4.54.

Figure 4.54

```
(λ a b c . (a c) (b c)) (λ a . a) (λ a . a) =α=>          1
(λ a b c . (a c) (b c)) (λ z . z) (λ y . y) =β=>          2
(λ b c . ((λ z . z) c) (b c)) (λ y . y) =β=>             3
(λ c . ((λ z . z) c) ((λ y . y) c)) =β=>                4
(λ c . ((λ z . z) c) c)) =β=>                            5
(λ c . c c)                                              6
```

The final result is the same under both evaluation orders. A fundamental theorem of lambda calculus, due to Church and Rosser, is that it doesn't matter in what order reductions are applied. If you start with a particular term T and apply β reductions and α conversions, arriving at

---

[5] Modified from [Sethi 89].

terms S and R after two different lists of operations, then there is some ultimate result U such that both S and R derive U. All reduction sequences make progress toward the same ultimate result.

If reduction reaches a stage where no β reduction is possible, the result is in **normal form**. Line 6 in Figure 4.54 is in normal form. Surprisingly, not every term can be reduced to normal form; some reductions continue forever, as in Figure 4.55.

Figure 4.55

(λ x . (x x)) (λ x . (x x)) =α=>	1
(λ x . (x x)) (λ y . (y y)) =β=>	2
(λ y . (y y)) (λ y . (y y)) =α=>	3
(λ x . (x x)) (λ x . (x x)) =α=>	4

Line 4 is the same as line 1; the β conversion did not simplify matters at all.

Another example that I will use later is the term Y, defined as shown in Figure 4.56.

Figure 4.56

Y = (λ f . (λ x . f (x x)) (λ x . f (x x)))

This term has no free identifiers; such terms are called **combinators**. Figure 4.57 shows that Y has an interesting property.

Figure 4.57

Y g = (λ f . (λ x . f (x x)) (λ x . f (x x))) g =β=>	1
(λ x . g (x x)) (λ x . g (x x)) =β=>	2
g ((λ x . g (x x)) (λ x . g (x x))) =	3
g (Y g)	4

Line 4 is surprising; it comes from noticing the similarity between lines 2 and 3. If we continue this "reduction," we move from Y g to g (Y g) to g (g (Y g)) and so forth, expanding the result each time. Combinators like Y with the property that Y g = g (Y g) are called **fixed-point operators**. I will use Y later to define recursive functions.

A last simplification rule, shown in Figure 4.58, is called η **(eta) conversion**.

Figure 4.58

(λ x . F x) =η=> F

We can only apply η conversion when F has no free occurrences of x. Figure 4.59 shows several η conversions.

Figure 4.59

```
(λ a b  . (+ a b)) =                            1
(λ a . (λ b . (+ a b))) =                       2
(λ a . (λ b . (+ a) b))) =η=>                   3
(λ a . (+ a)) =η=>                              4
+                                               5
```

To make a programming language from the lambda calculus requires very little additional machinery. It is necessary to introduce predeclared identifiers, such as true and **if**, which are called "constants." The set of predeclared constants and their meanings distinguish one lambda calculus from another. The meanings of constants are expressed by reduction rules, such as

if false T F => F

Here, **if** is a curried function of three parameters. This lambda calculus can now be translated directly into ML:

Lambda calculus	ML
F P	F P
λ x . T	**fn** x => T
if B T F	**if** B **then** T **else** F
{A / x} T	**let val** x = A **in** T **end**

Recursive function definitions require the combinator Y defined in Figure 4.56 (page 155). Consider the ML declaration in Figure 4.60.

Figure 4.60

```
let val rec Parity = fn x =>                     1
        if x = 0 then 0                          2
        else if x = 1 then 1                     3
        else Parity (x - 2)                      4
    in                                           5
        Parity 3                                 6
end;                                             7
```

It is not hard to express the body of Parity as a lambda term B, as shown in Figure 4.61.

Figure 4.61

B = **if** (= x 0) 0 (**if** (= x 1) 1 (r (- x 2)))

The form of this lambda term bears a strong resemblance to LISP's parenthesized syntax. I have introduced some new constants, such as the nullary operators 0 and 1 (that is, classical constants), and the binary operators = and -.[6] The identifier r is free in this expression; I use it to refer to a recursive call to the function itself. I now define Parity as shown in Figure 4.62, using the fixed-point operator Y.

Figure 4.62

```
Parity = Y (λ r x . B)
```

To show that this definition makes sense, I need to perform some reductions; see Figure 4.63.

Figure 4.63

```
Parity = Y (λ r x . B) =                                        1
(λ r x . B) Y (λ r x . B) =                                     2
(λ r x . B) Parity =β=>                                         3
(λ x . if (= x 0) 0 (if (= x 1) 1 (Parity (- x 2))))           4
```

Line 1 represents the definition of Parity. Line 2 comes from the fixed-point nature of Y. Line 3 substitutes the definition of Parity back into the result. Line 4 performs a single β reduction, using the definition of B. Together, these lines show that Parity is in effect defined recursively.

The last step in turning lambda calculus into a programming language is to introduce the concept of types. The constant 0 is meant to be used differently from the constant **if**; the former is nullary, and the latter takes three parameters. In Figure 4.64, following the notation of ML, I can show the types of the constants introduced so far.

Figure 4.64

```
0: int
1: int
+: int*int -> int
-: int*int -> int
=: int*int -> bool
if: bool*'a*'a -> 'a
```

Complicated types may be parenthesized, but parentheses may be dropped. The precedence rules stipulate that * is grouped left-to-right and has high precedence, whereas -> is grouped right-to-left and has low precedence. The typed lambda calculus requires that abstractions include type information.

---

[6] The fact that I now have - means that I must have an integer type as well.

Figure 4.65   (λ x : t . T)

In Figure 4.65, t is some type indicator. Now it is possible to reject some malformed expressions that were acceptable, but meaningless, before, as shown in Figure 4.66.

Figure 4.66

```
λ x : int . x y                           1
if 1 (x y) (y x)                          2
if (= x y) 2 (= x z)                      3
```

Line 1 is unacceptable because x is used in the body of the application as a function, but has type int. Line 2 is invalid because 1 is not of type bool. Line 3 is rejected because both branches of the **if** must have the same type, but one is int and the other is bool. At this point, we have almost built the ML programming language. All that is lacking is some syntactic elegance (such as patterns), data types (lists are very useful for functional programming), and the many parts of ML that I have not discussed at all.

Lambda calculus is valuable for several reasons. First, it gives a purely mathematical, formal basis to the concept of programming, assigning a set of rules that determine the meaning of a program. This ability to mathematically define the semantics of a programming language is investigated in more detail in Chapter 10. Because all chains of reductions give rise to equivalent results, the semantics are not affected by the order of evaluation. Second, it introduces the concept of higher-order functions as a natural building block for programming. Lambda abstraction builds an anonymous function that can be applied or returned as the result of a function. Third, it gives rise to the functional style of programming, because it has no need for variables. The languages that are derived from lambda calculus, particularly LISP and ML, have been quite successful. Insofar as a purely functional subset of these languages is used, they lend themselves to lazy and speculative evaluation. ML takes the concept of typed lambda calculus and infers types in order to enforce strong typing.

EXERCISES

Review Exercises

4.1 Why is it natural for a language that has no variables to provide no iterative control constructs?

4.2 If a language treats functions as first-class values, does the language support higher-order functions?

4.3 In Figure 4.3 (page 122), I show that (cons (cons 'A (cons 'B nil)) (cons nil (cons 11 nil))) is the same as (('A 'B) () 11). What is the value of the following expression?

```
(cons (cons (cons 'A (cons 'B nil)) nil) (cons 11 nil))
```

4.4 In LISP, is parameter passing by value mode? If not, by what mode?

4.5 In Figure 4.25 (page 131), why introduce the function Extend?

4.6 Convert the Double function of Figure 4.20 (page 129) into ML.

4.7 Generalize the Double function of Figure 4.20 (page 129) so that it doubles recursively within sublists as well as at the top level.

4.8 Generalize the answer to problem 4.7 to make a Multiple function that accepts two parameters: a list L and a multiplier M, so that if M is 2, the effect is like Double, but higher and lower integer multipliers also work.

4.9 Under what circumstances does it make a difference in what order the parameters to a function are evaluated?

4.10 Reduce the following lambda expression to normal form.

$$(\lambda \; y \; . \; (\lambda \; z \; . \; x \; z \; (y \; z))) \; (\lambda \; a \; . \; (a \; b))$$

4.11 Reduce the lambda expressions given in Figure 4.67.

Figure 4.67

```
{a / b}(λ a . b)
{a / b}(λ b . a)
{a / b}(λ c . b)
{a / b}(λ b . c)
{a / b}(λ a . a)
{a / b}(λ b . b)
{a / b}(λ c . c)
```

Challenge Exercises

4.12 What does it mean for something to be a first-class value in a purely functional language?

4.13 As suggested in the text (page 129), show how to use an ML datatype to implement heterogeneous lists. You may assume that atoms are always integers or nil. Implement both Reverse and ReverseAll. If you use :: as a constructor for your list datatype, ML automatically overloads the [] syntax for you.

4.14 What sort of runtime storage organization is appropriate for ML? Restrict your answer to the purely functional part of ML.

4.15 On page 132, I claim that building a closure is easy in statically scoped languages in which procedures are not first-class values. Is it harder if procedures are first-class values?

4.16 Does LISP really need garbage collection? Wouldn't reference counts suffice?

4.17 On page 134, I suggest that the implementation copy only the bindings of selected nonlocal identifiers whose bindings it needs to preserve. How does it know which ones?

4.18 On page 136, I say that the updated environment is discarded after a **lambda** body is evaluated. But the example shows no explicit discard. Explain.

4.19 How must the LISP interpreter be enhanced to deal with deep binding?

4.20 The trace of lazy evaluation in Figure 4.38 (starting on page 141) happened not to need to return to a partially evaluated result. Trace the more interesting example

```
(SameFrontier '(A B C) '(A C D)),
```

which will need to do so.

4.21 In FP, the sequence constructor is bottom-preserving. Show how this requirement precludes lazy evaluation.

4.22 To introduce persistence into a functional language, I have used an imperative command. Is an imperative style necessary?

4.23 Use the combinator Y to build a lambda-calculus definition of integer multiplication that translates the ML program of Figure 4.68.

Figure 4.68

```
val rec Multiply = fn (x,y) =>                               1
    if x = 0 then 0 else Multiply(x-1,y) + y;               2
```

4.24 What is the type of Y in Figure 4.56 (page 155)?

4.25 Write a lambda term that grows longer after each β reduction.

Chapter 5

Object-Oriented Programming

In the imperative programming paradigm that has dominated the way programmers think about solutions to problems for the past twenty years or so, a program consists of one or more procedures that transfer control among themselves and manipulate one or more data items to solve a problem. Object-oriented programming (OOP) is a different paradigm based on Simula's classes. Many people like it because it allows code to be reused in an organized fashion.

Object-oriented programming is an area of current research. There is an annual ACM Conference on Object-Oriented Programming Systems, Languages, and Applications (OOPSLA).

1 ◆ DEFINITIONS

An **object-oriented** program consists of one or more **objects** that interact with one another to solve a problem. An object contains state information (data, represented by other objects) and operations (code). Objects interact by sending **messages** to each other. These messages are like procedure calls; the procedures are called **methods**. Every object is an instance of a **class**, which determines what data the object keeps as state information and what messages the object understands. The **protocol** of the class is the set of messages that its instances understand.

Objects in object-oriented programming correspond to variables and constants in structured programming. Classes in object-oriented programming correspond to types: Every object of a particular class has the same structure as every other object of that class.

Objects are a form of abstract data type, in that if two objects respond to the same messages in the same way, there is no way to distinguish them. Such objects may be freely interchanged. For example, I might have two Stack objects that respond to push and pop messages. One object might internally use an array, the other a linked list. The two stack objects are indistinguishable to their clients. I might even

163

have an array of stacks, some of whose components are implemented one way, while others are implemented the other way.

The term object-oriented has started to appear prominently in many advertisements, but people disagree about what object-oriented programming is and is not. The consensus seems to be that a programming language must support data encapsulation, inheritance, and overloading to be called an object-oriented programming language.

Data encapsulation dictates that an object A that wishes to examine or modify another object B may do so only in ways defined by B's protocol. In other words, the data associated with an object is hidden from public view. Only the operations an object supports are known to its clients. Data encapsulation makes it unlikely that changes in the implementation of an object or extensions to its protocol will cause failures in the code for unrelated objects. As long as the object's new protocol is a superset of its old one, code that relies on the old protocol will continue to work correctly.

Inheritance allows one class to share the properties of another. For example, Smalltalk includes the predefined class Magnitude, which defines several operations, including max (maximum). Any class that inherits from Magnitude, such as Integer, inherits this operation. The max operation for all subclasses of Magnitude is thus defined in one place, so any enhancements or corrections to the max operation become available automatically to all such classes. Inheritance is used in practice for two purposes: (1) to indicate that the new class specializes the old class, and (2) to allow the new class to use code from the old class. Inheritance makes the job of enhancement and maintenance much easier.

Overloading dictates that the code invoked to perform an operation must depend not only on the operation but on what sort of objects the operation is to manipulate. For example, the max operation provided by the Magnitude class is defined in terms of the > (greater than) operation. The > operation performed to obtain the larger of two integers and the > operation performed to obtain the larger of two real numbers are two different operations. Overloading ensures that the appropriate > operation is performed in each case. Overloading makes it possible to define an operation such as max in an abstract sense. So long as the parameters to the operation exhibit the appropriate behavior (in this case, they define >), the operation will succeed.

2 ◆ A SHORT EXAMPLE

The principal advantage claimed for object-oriented programming is that it promotes reuse of valuable code. If an abstract data type has been implemented as a class, then a related data type can be implemented as a subclass, automatically reusing the code that still applies (by inheriting it) and redefining those operations that differ (by overloading the old names with new implementations).

For example, consider the abstract type Collection, values of which are unordered groups of integers, where individual integers may appear more than once in a collection. Such an abstract data type would have several operations, such as the following:

```
insert(C : reference Collection;
      what : value integer)
present(C : reference Collection;
      what : value integer) : Boolean;
remove(C : reference Collection;
      what : value integer)
write(C : reference Collection)
```

The implementation of collections could use a linked list or an array. Let's not worry about what to do if there is an error, such as inserting when there is no more space, or removing an integer that is not in the collection; perhaps an exception mechanism (discussed in Chapter 2) could be used.

Collections sometimes have special requirements. I might want, for example, the related data type Set, which makes sure that an item is not inserted multiple times. Object-oriented programming lets me declare a class Set as a subclass of Collection, inheriting all the operations, but letting me reimplement the insert routine.

A different related data type is Queue, which is different in two ways. First, it must retain the order of inserted values. Second, the remove operation has a different form:

```
remove(Q : reference Queue) : integer;
```

I would define a class Queue as a subclass of Collection. Depending on the implementation of Collection, I may be able to reuse most of its code or very little. If I end up rewriting major amounts of code, I might decide to use the Queue-friendly code in Collection in order to save duplication of effort.

Finally, I may wish to introduce the type InstrumentedQueue, which has one additional operation:

```
report(I : reference InstrumentedQueue)
```

This operation writes the number of insertions and deletions that have been performed on the given queue. In order to reuse the statistics-gathering facility in other programs, I might implement it as a new class `Statistic` with operations `increment` and `report` (not to be confused with the `report` provided by `InstrumentedQueue`). Objects of class `InstrumentedQueue` would contain extra fields of type `Statistic` to hold the number of insertions and deletions.

The classes I have introduced form a tree, as shown in Figure 5.1.

Figure 5.1   Class hierarchy

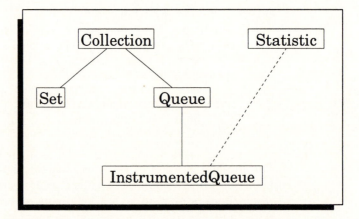

The solid lines indicate which classes are subclasses of others. The dashed line indicates that `InstrumentedQueue` has local fields of class `Statistic`.

A value of class `Collection` has only the operations from that class. It would not be appropriate to invoke a `report` operation on a `Collection` value. If the compiler can tell the class of any variable, then it can determine which operations are valid and which code to invoke. However, as you will see later, there is good reason to postpone binding the actual value with variables. I might want to invoke `report` on a variable and let it be decided at runtime which version of `report` is to be invoked, if any. The compiler might therefore need to generate code that decides at runtime which operations are valid and which code to invoke. We will see that object-oriented programming languages differ in the extent to which they allow such **deferred binding**.

I might want to generalize these classes to allow elements to be not just integers, but of any type, such as reals, records, and even other classes. In other words, I might want to build polymorphic classes.

This chapter starts with a brief look at Simula, the ancestor of all object-oriented programming languages, to introduce the concepts and the issues surrounding object-oriented programming. I then turn to Smalltalk, a good example of object-oriented programming, in which most binding is performed at runtime. Smalltalk uses dynamic typing, deferred binding of operations, and even deferred declaration of classes. Smalltalk is a "pure" language, in the sense that everything in the language follows the object-oriented paradigm. I also discuss C++, which is a hybrid language that adds support for object-oriented programming to C. It uses static typing, static binding of operations (by default), and static declaration of classes.

3 ◆ SIMULA

Object-oriented programming began when Simula introduced a novel concept: A record may contain a procedure field. Such records are called **classes**.[1] As an example, consider Figure 5.2.

Figure 5.2

```
class Stack;                                          1
    Size : 0..MaxStackSize := 0; -- initialized       2
    Data : array 0..MaxStackSize-1 of integer;        3

    procedure Push(readonly What : integer);          4
    begin                                             5
        Data[Size] := What;                           6
        Size := Size+1;                               7
    end; -- Push;                                     8

    procedure Pop() : integer;                        9
    begin                                            10
        Size := Size-1;                              11
        return Data[Size];                           12
    end -- Pop;                                      13

    procedure Empty() : Boolean;                     14
    begin                                            15
        return Size = 0;                             16
    end; -- Empty                                    17
end; -- Stack                                        18

variable                                             19
    S1, S2 : Stack;                                  20
```

---

[1] Simula's classes are the ancestors of Pascal's records and coroutines (Chapter 2), in addition to object-oriented programming.

```
begin                                                    21
    S2 := S1;                                            22
    S1.Push(34);                                         23
    if not S2.Empty() then S2.Pop() end;                 24
end;                                                     25
```

Classes are like types; variables may be declared of a class type, as in line 20. Each such declaration introduces a new instance of the class, that is, a new object. The object contains fields that are variables (that is, instance variables) and fields that are procedures (that is, methods). Object variables can be assigned (line 22); objects can be manipulated by their methods, which are named just like fields (lines 23 and 24). The three methods of Stack all have an implicit parameter: the stack object itself. Therefore, the call in line 23 implicitly acts on stack S1.

A problem with classes is that a binary operation, such as testing two stacks for equality, must be performed by either the first or the second object, taking the other object as a parameter, as shown in Figure 5.3.

Figure 5.3

```
class Stack;                                             1
    Size : 0..MaxStackSize := 0; -- initialized          2
    Data : array 0..MaxStackSize-1 of integer;           3

    procedure Equal(readonly Other : Stack) : Boolean;   4
    begin                                                5
        return Other.Size = Size and                     6
            Other.Data[0..Other.Size-1] =                7
                Data[0..Size-1] -- equality of slices    8
    end; -- Equal                                        9

    ... -- other procedures as before                    10
end; -- Stack                                            11

variable                                                 12
    S1, S2 : Stack;                                      13

begin                                                    14
    if S1.Equal(S2) then ...                             15
end;                                                     16
```

In lines 6–7, fields Size and Data of the implicitly passed Stack have simple names, but the variables of **Other**, which is explicitly passed, must be **qualified** by the object intended. (If needed, the pseudovariable Self may be used to name the implicit object explicitly.) Invoking the Equal method in line 15 shows how asymmetric the binary operation has become. The same problem appears in Smalltalk, but is solved in C++, as you will see below.

In this example, I have allowed the `Equal` method of one object to access the instance variables of another object of the same class. Object-oriented languages differ in how much access they permit to instance variables and how much the programmer can control that access. I will return to this issue when I discuss C++.

Simula allows new classes to inherit instance variables and methods of old classes. Subclasses raise the issues of assignment compatibility, overloading of procedures, and dynamic binding of procedures, all of which are discussed in detail below.

4 ◆ SMALLTALK

Smalltalk is the name of a family of programming languages developed at Xerox PARC (Palo Alto Research Center) as part of the Dynabook project. Dynabook was envisioned as the ultimate personal computer — small, portable, with excellent graphics and virtually unlimited memory and computing power. Smalltalk was designed as Dynabook's programming language.

Smalltalk has gone through a long evolution, including Smalltalk-72, Smalltalk-76, Smalltalk-78, and Smalltalk-80. Many individuals have contributed to the development of its variants, most notably Alan Kay, Daniel Ingalls, and Peter Deutsch. I will consider only Smalltalk-80, and whenever I say "Smalltalk," I mean Smalltalk-80. A standard Smalltalk reference is known as the Blue Book [Goldberg 83].

Smalltalk is remarkable in many ways. It has a very elaborate program development environment, with bit-mapped graphics and a variety of specially designed utilities for entering, browsing, saving, and debugging code. Even though syntactic forms exist for entering entire programs, they are seldom used. I will not discuss the program development environment at all. Instead, my examples will be in the "file-in" syntax used for bringing programs in from text files.

My primary interest is in the object-oriented programming model that Smalltalk presents. In Smalltalk, both data and program are represented as objects. Integers are objects, complex data structures are objects, all Smalltalk programs are encapsulated into objects. Objects interact through messages, which are requests for an object to perform some operation.

Messages are philosophically different from conventional procedure and function calls in that they request an operation rather than demanding it. An object may act on a message, it may pass the message to another object, or it may even ignore the message. Objects cannot directly access the contents of other objects. An object can send a message requesting information about another object's internal state, but it cannot force the information to be provided. Objects thus represent a very tightly controlled encapsulation of data and function.

Objects differ in their properties. Each object is an instance of some class. A class specifies the local data (called **instance variables**) and routines (called **methods**). Together, I will refer to instance variables and methods as **members**. Smalltalk classes are direct descendants of the classes of Simula.

4.1 Assignment and Messages

Assignment binds an object to an identifier, as in Figure 5.4,

Figure 5.4

```
count := 10
```

which binds the integer object 10 (that is, the particular instance of the class Integer that represents the number 10) to the identifier count. Count temporarily acquires type integer. Smalltalk has no type declarations for variables, but objects are typed by their class. Assignment statements are also expressions; they return the value of the right-hand side.

Literals are provided for some objects. These include numbers (integer or real), single characters (for example, $M or $a, where $ quotes a single character), strings (for example, 'hi there'), symbols (for example, #red, #left, where # quotes symbols), and heterogeneous arrays (for example, #(1 $a 'xyz')). Literals actually refer to unnamed objects of an appropriate class that are initialized to the appropriate values. Literals are no different from other objects — the protocol of their class defines the messages they will respond to.

Smalltalk predefines several objects, including nil (the only instance of class UndefinedObject), true (the only instance of class True), and false (the only instance of class False).

Expressions illustrate the way Smalltalk uses messages to define interobject communication. The expression 1+2 does not pass the values 1 and 2 to a + operator to produce a result. Instead, the message selector + and the parameter 2 are sent as a message to the integer object represented by the literal 1. An integer object responds to a + message by adding the parameter to its own value and returning a new object representing the correct sum. The message selector + can be used in composing messages to other object classes (for example, strings), so overloading of message selectors is trivially provided. Ordinary usage is inverted — data aren't sent to operators; rather operators (and parameters) are sent to data. This inversion emphasizes Smalltalk's view that an object is an active entity, interacting with other objects via messages.

Smalltalk recognizes three classes of message selector: unary, binary, and keyword. I will show unary and keyword selectors in **bold font** to make examples easier to read. A **unary** selector takes no parameters and appears after the object to which it is directed, as in x **sqrt** or theta **sin**.

Binary selectors look like ordinary operators; they are composed of one or two non-alphanumeric characters. A message with a binary selector takes a single parameter that follows the selector.

Keyword selectors allow one or more parameters to be included in a message. A keyword selector is an identifier suffixed with **:** . For example, the expression in Figure 5.5

Figure 5.5

```
anArray at: 3 put: 'xyz'
```

sends a message with two parameters to anArray (which happens to be an array, as indicated by its name). The **at:put:** message specifies an array update and is the standard way to access arrays (and symbol tables) in Smalltalk. To read an array value, the program sends an **at:** message, such as anArray **at:** 5. Unless parentheses are used, all keyword parameters are gathered into a single message.

In the absence of parentheses, if unary, binary, and keyword selectors are intermixed, unary selectors have the highest precedence, then binary selectors, and finally keyword selectors. Parsing proceeds strictly from left to right; there is no operator precedence. Figure 5.6, for instance,

Figure 5.6

```
anArray at: 2 + a * b abs squared
```

is interpreted as shown in Figure 5.7.

Figure 5.7

```
anArray at: ((2 + a) * ((b abs) squared))
```

An object that is sent a message is called the **receiver** of the message. The response to a message is an object. A receiver often returns itself (possibly after modifying its instance variables), but it may return a different object entirely.

4.2 Blocks

Smalltalk blocks represent a sequence of actions that are encapsulated into a single object. Blocks are used to implement control structures as well as functions. A block is a sequence of expressions, separated by periods and delimited by square brackets, as shown in Figure 5.8.

Figure 5.8

```
[index := index + 1.  anArray at: index put: 0]
```

When a block expression is encountered, the statements in the block aren't immediately executed. For example, the code in Figure 5.9

Figure 5.9

```
incr := [index := index + 1.  anArray at: index put: 0]
```

assigns the block to variable incr, but doesn't perform the addition or array update. The unary message selector **value** causes a block to be executed. Thus incr **value** will increment index and zero an element of anArray. In particular, [statement list] **value** directly executes the anonymous block. The value returned by a block when it is evaluated is the value returned by the last statement in the block.

Blocks are used in conditional and iterative constructs in an interesting manner. Consider an **if** statement, which is coded in Smalltalk, by sending two blocks (one for each branch) to a Boolean value, which selects the appropriate block and then executes it, as in Figure 5.10.

Figure 5.10

```
a < 0                                                          1
       ifTrue: [b := 0]                                        2
       ifFalse: [b := a sqrt]                                  3
```

Our usual model of conditional statements has been inverted. A Boolean value isn't passed to an **if** statement; rather the **if** statement is passed to the Boolean!

Repetitive execution is obtained by passing a loop body to an integer or to a Boolean block, as in Figure 5.11.

Figure 5.11

```
4 timesRepeat: [x := x sin]                                    1
[a < b] whileTrue: [b := b sqrt]                               2
```

The Boolean value a < b is enclosed in a block in line 2. The **whileTrue:** message is only understood by blocks, not by Booleans. The reason for this design is that the block can be reevaluated after each iteration, eventually resulting in False and terminating the loop. A Boolean value is immutable, so it is worthless for loop control.

Blocks can also take parameters and be used as functions. Block parameters are prefixed with : and are separated from the block body by |, as in Figure 5.12.

Figure 5.12

```
[:elem | elem sqrt]
```

Parameters can be supplied by using one or more **value:** keyword selectors, as in Figure 5.13.

Figure 5.13

```
[:elem | elem sqrt] value: 10 -- 10 sqrt
```

Anonymous blocks with parameters are handy for applying a function to an array of elements. The keyword selector **collect:** creates an array by applying a block to each element of an array, as in Figure 5.14.

Figure 5.14

```
#(1 2 3 4) collect: [:elem | elem sqrt]                            1
    -- (1 1.414 1.732 2)                                           2
```

4.3 Classes and Methods

Since all objects are instances of classes, the properties of an object are defined in its class definition. A class contains instance variables (each instance of the class contains an instance of each of these variables) and instance methods (each instance of the class responds to messages that invoke these methods). Instance variables have values that are private to a single object. Syntax rules require that instance variables begin with a lowercase letter. (Uppercase letters are only used for **shared variables**, visible globally, such as Object.)

Classes are themselves objects, and therefore are members (instances) of some other class. For example, Integer belongs to Integer class. Integer class is called a **metaclass**. All metaclasses belong to class Metaclass, which is the only instance of Metaclass class, which is itself an instance of Metaclass.

A new instance of a class is created by sending the message **new** to the corresponding class. Thus the code in Figure 5.15

Figure 5.15

```
anArray := Array new: 4
```

would create a new array object with 4 cells (each initialized to nil) and assign it to anArray.

Programming languages that support abstract data types (and a class is a glorified abstract data type) often allow the programmer to separate the description of a type (here, class) into a specification and implementation part. Smalltalk does not let the programmer separate specification from implementation cleanly, but it does provide much of what you would expect from abstract data types, particularly information hiding.

Figure 5.16 shows how to declare the abstract data type Stack.

Figure 5.16

```
Object subclass: #Stack                                        1
    instanceVariableNames: 'count elements'                    2
    classVariableNames: 'MaxDepth'                             3
    poolDictionaries: ''                                       4
    category: 'Example'                                        5
!                                                              6


!Stack class methodsFor: 'creation'!                          7
initialize -- sets default depth                              8
    MaxDepth := 100                                           9
!                                                             10
new -- builds a new stack of default depth                   11
    ^ super new init: MaxDepth                                12
!                                                             13
new: desiredDepth -- builds new stack of given depth         14
    ^ super new init: desiredDepth                           15
! !                                                           16


!Stack methodsFor: 'initialization'!                         17
init: depth                                                  18
    count := 0.                                              19
    elements := Array new: depth                             20
! !                                                          21


!Stack methodsFor: 'access'!                                 22
empty                                                        23
    ^ count = 0                                              24
!                                                            25
push: elem                                                   26
    count >= elements size                                   27
    ifTrue: [self error: 'Stack overflow']                  28
    ifFalse: [                                               29
        count := count + 1. elements at: count put: elem]   30
!                                                            31
pop |top|                                                    32
    self empty                                               33
    ifTrue: [self error: 'Stack is empty']                  34
    ifFalse: [                                                35
        top := elements at: count.                           36
        count := count - 1.                                  37
        ^ top                                                38
    ]                                                        39
! !                                                          40
```

The definition of a class first specifies its name (line 1), the names of the instance variables (line 2), and some other things (lines 3– 6). For the stack example, the instance variables are count and elements, the first an integer counting how many elements are in the stack, and the second an array holding the stack items. Since Smalltalk is dynamically typed, these declarations do not indicate any type.

Stack is a subclass of the class Object. You will see the implications of subclasses later; for now, it suffices that class Object will respond to a message of type **subclass:instanceVariableNames:...category:** and build a new class. The ! symbol in line 6 tells the Smalltalk interpreter to accept the previous expression(s) and evaluate them. In this case, evaluating the expression leads to the definition of a new class.

Methods are categorized for documentation sake; I have separated methods for creation (lines 7–16), initialization (lines 17–21), and access (lines 22–40). These names are arbitrary and have no meaning to Smalltalk itself.

Consider first the **init:** method (lines 18–20), which initializes the instance variables count and elements. This method takes a formal parameter called depth. To create the elements array (line 20), it sends a message to class Array using a keyword selector **new:** to define its extent. The **init:** method will (by default) return the stack object to which the message is sent.

The **empty** method (lines 23–24) tests count to determine if the stack is empty. The ^ symbol explicitly names the object to be returned by the message, superseding the default, which is to return the stack object itself.

The **push:** method (lines 26–30) first tests if elements is full. It does so by sending the **size** message to the elements array and comparing the result with the current count of elements. If the stack has overflowed, the method generates a diagnostic by directing a message with the **error:** keyword selector and a string parameter to itself. The destination of this message is specified by the pseudovariable self. (**Pseudovariables** are readonly variables with a Smalltalk-specific meaning.) As I will explain in detail later, all objects inherit the capability to respond to certain messages, including **error:**. The **push:** message to a stack object can therefore elicit an **error:** message to that same object.

Finally, **pop:** (lines 32–39) tests if the stack is empty by invoking the object's own **empty** method. If so, **pop:** issues an error message; otherwise, it modifies count and returns the popped element. This method shows how to declare variables such as top local to a method invocation.

It is the responsibility of each method that modifies instance variables to make sure that it leaves the object in a consistent state. For example, the **push:** method must adjust count as well as placing the new element in elements. In Chapter 7, you will see that the possibility of many simultaneous actions on the same object makes it harder to keep the internal state consistent.

You have probably noticed that some of these methods are declared as Stack methods, and others are Stack class methods. In general, most methods will be **instance methods** (here, Stack methods). Messages for these methods are sent to individual instances of the class. However, building a new instance pertains to the class, not to instances. Messages for such methods are sent to the class object itself and invoke **class methods**. For this reason, lines 7–16 are Stack class methods.

The **new** method not only creates a new instance but also sends it an **init:** message to cause it to initialize itself. Creation is accomplished by super **new**. The pseudovariable super has the same meaning as self, except that it ignores local redefinitions of inherited methods. I need super here because I am redefining **new**, and I want to make sure that I get the original meaning of **new** in lines 12 and 15.

Just as there are class methods, there are also **class variables**, which are shared by all instances of the class. Syntax rules require that class variables begin with an upper-case letter. In line 3, I declare a single class variable, MaxDepth. I use it only in initializing new stacks (line 12) to build an array of the required length. Although I only need a "class constant," Smalltalk does not provide either constants or readonly variables.

Class variables are conventionally initialized by a class method called **initialize** (lines 8– 9). **Initialize** is called only once, just after the single object corresponding to the class (such as Stack) is created.

A class can provide several alternative instance constructors. The example shows both **new** (lines 11–12), which creates a stack with a default maximum depth, and **new:** (lines 14–15), which takes a parameter specifying the maximum depth of the new instance. Overloading two selectors with the same name causes no problems so long as one is unary and the other is keyword.

4.4 Superclasses and Subclasses

There are two hierarchies of objects in Smalltalk. You have already seen one: the hierarchy of instances and classes. Every object is an instance of some class. Climbing up the hierarchy quickly leads to a cycle of Metaclass and Metaclass class. The other, richer, hierarchy is built from the subclass and superclass relations. Climbing up this hierarchy leads to Object, which has no superclass. The Stack class of the previous example is a direct subclass of Object.

Each new class is defined as a subclass of some existing class. A **subclass** inherits all the members of its immediate **superclass** as well as those of its indirect superclasses. You have already seen that instances of class Stack inherit the methods **error:** and **new** from Stack's superclass Object. A subclass may declare its own members and may introduce methods that override those inherited from its superclass. When a reference to a message or a variable appears in an object, it is resolved (if possible) in that object. Failing this, the object's superclass is considered, then the superclass of the superclass, up to class `Object`. If no definition is found, a runtime error occurs.

Subclasses are used to extend or refine the protocol of an existing class. In Figure 5.17, I define a subclass of `Stack` called `IntegerStack`. `IntegerStack`s will limit stack elements to integers and will provide a new operation +, which adds corresponding elements of two stacks, yielding a new stack, similar to vector addition.

I will add two additional methods, **pos:**, which returns the stack element at a particular position, and **currentDepth**, which returns the current depth of the stack. I need **pos:** and **currentDepth** because + can directly access only its own stack, not the stack passed to it as a parameter. (The same asymmetry of access plagues Simula, as discussed earlier.) I want these new methods to be private to the class; they are to be used only by +, not by the clients of the class. Unfortunately, Smalltalk does not provide a way to prevent such misuse. Still, I have placed comments on lines 35 and 38 to indicate my intent.

Figure 5.17

```
Stack subclass: #IntegerStack                               1
     instanceVariableNames: ''                              2
     classVariableNames: ''                                 3
     poolDictionaries: ''                                   4
     category: 'Example'                                    5
!                                                           6

!IntegerStack methodsFor: 'access'!                         7

push: elem                                                  8
     count >= elements size                                 9
     ifTrue: [self error: 'Stack overflow']                10
     ifFalse: [                                             11
          elem class = Integer                              12
          ifTrue: [                                         13
               count := count + 1.                          14
               elements at: count put: elem                 15
          ]                                                 16
          ifFalse: [self error: 'Can only push integers.'] 17
     ]                                                      18
!                                                           19
```

```
    + aStack |answer i|                                    20
        (self currentDepth) = (aStack currentDepth)        21
        ifFalse: [self error:                              22
            'Incompatible stacks for addition']            23
        ifTrue:  [                                         24
            answer := IntegerStack init: (elements size).  25
            i := 1.                                        26
            self currentDepth timesRepeat: [               27
                answer push:                               28
                    (elements at: i) + (aStack pos: i).    29
                i := i + 1                                  30
            ].                                             31
          ^ answer                                         32
        ]                                                  33
    ! !                                                    34

    pos: i -- a private method                             35
        ^ elements at: i                                   36
    !                                                      37

    currentDepth -- a private method                       38
        ^ count                                            39
    !                                                      40
```

In line 12, the **push:** method checks that the class of the element about
to be pushed is, in fact, Integer. All objects answer the message **class**
with the class of which they are an instance. They inherit this ability
from Object.

The class hierarchy based on the subclass relation is quite extensive.
Figure 5.18 shows a part of the hierarchy.

Figure 5.18

```
Object                                      1
|    BlockContext                           2
|    Boolean                                3
|    |    True                              4
|    |    False                             5
|    Collection                             6
|    |    Set                               7
|    |    |    Dictionary                   8
|    |    |    |    SystemDictionary        9
|    |    |    |    IdentityDictionary      10
|    |    MappedCollection                  11
|    |    Bag                               12
```

```
|    |      SequenceableCollection              13
|    |    | OrderedCollection                   14
|    |    |    | SortedCollection               15
|    |    | Interval                            16
|    |    | ArrayedCollection                   17
|    |    |    | CompiledMethod                 18
|    |    |    | ByteArray                      19
|    |    |    | String                         20
|    |    |    |    | Symbol                     21
|    |    |    | Array                          22
|    |    | LinkedList                          23
|    |    |    | Semaphore                      24
|  Magnitude                                    25
|    |    LookupKey                             26
|    |    Number                                27
|    |    | Integer                             28
|    |    | Float                               29
|    |  Date                                    30
|    |  Time                                    31
|    |  Character                               32
|  UndefinedObject                              33
```

This hierarchy shows how different data types are related. For example, an Integer is a kind of Number, but it has some extra methods (such as **even**, + , and **printOn:base:**) and some overriding methods (such as =). A Number is a kind of Magnitude, but it has its own extra methods (such as **squared** and **abs**, which are actually defined in terms of methods of the subclasses). A Magnitude is a sort of Object, but it has some extra methods (such as <=). Finally, an Object has no superclass, and provides methods for all other classes (such as **new** and **error:**).

4.5 Implementation of Smalltalk

Smalltalk is designed to be portable. Ironically, Smalltalk has only recently become widely available because of proprietary restrictions. Over 97 percent of the Smalltalk package, including editors, compilers, and debuggers, is written in Smalltalk. Smalltalk executes under a virtual machine that requires 6–12 KB of code. Creating a Smalltalk virtual machine for a new target machine takes about one staff-year.

The Smalltalk virtual machine consists of a storage manager, an interpreter, and a collection of primitive methods. The storage manager creates and frees all objects (it uses garbage collection), and provides access to fields of objects. The manager also makes it possible to determine the class of any object. Methods are compiled into an intermediate form called "bytecode" (since each operation is represented in a single byte). The interpreter executes bytecode to evaluate expressions and methods. Primitive methods, such as I/O, arithmetic operations, and array indexing, are implemented directly in machine language for fast execution.

To understand how Smalltalk is implemented, you must understand how objects, classes and messages/methods are implemented. Objects are represented uniformly; they contain a header field (indicating the size of the object), a class (realized as a pointer to the corresponding class), and the instance variables of the object. If an object is of a primitive type, the object contains bit patterns defining the value of the object to the interpreter. Instance variables in a programmer-defined object are represented by pointers to the objects that the instance variables represent. The only exception to this rule is the primitive class Small-Integer, which is limited to the range from −16384 to 16383. Smalltalk provides other integer classes, admitting values as large as 2^{524288}. All objects are required to have an even address. An odd address is an immediate representation of a SmallInteger, encoded as the integer value concatenated with a low-order 1.

This representation of objects influences how operations are implemented. In particular, consider assignment (that is, copying) of objects. Since most objects are accessed through a pointer, does a := b mean "copy b" or does it mean "copy a pointer to b"? Smalltalk understands := to mean pointer copying; it is very fast. However, the class Object includes two copy methods: **shallowCopy** and **deepCopy**. **shallowCopy** creates a new object, but pointers in the new object reference the same objects as the pointers in the old object. If b is assigned a shallow copy of variable a, and b contains an instance variable s that is a stack, then both a and b will share the same stack. A message to the stack that causes it to be changed (for example, **pop**) will be reflected in both a and b. One the other hand, if a message to b causes its s to be assigned a different stack, this assignment won't affect a's instance variable s.

In contrast, **deepCopy** creates new copies of all instance variables in an object. If b is assigned to variable a by deep copy, then a change to b's instance variables never affects a's instance variables. Deep copying an object causes all its instance variables to be deep copied, which can lead to infinite loops in cyclic structures.

These distinctions also apply to equality testing. Smalltalk uses pointer equality; it is possible to program shallow and deep equality operations as well. Franz LISP provides all these operations, which can lead to confusion.

Classes are themselves objects, so they fit the same format as all other objects. For example, the class Stack is an object (of class Stack class). The instance variables of a class are the variables that define the properties of a class. Classes contain pointers to the superclass, class variables, and strings representing the name of the class and its variables (for display purposes). They also include "method dictionaries," which are hash tables that allow rapid access to methods. All messages are given a unique message code by the Smalltalk compiler. This message code is searched for in the method dictionaries of first the instance and then the class to determine if a corresponding method exists. If it does, the dictionary contains a pointer to the bytecode (or primitive method) used to implement the method.

Messages are implemented in much the same way as ordinary procedure calls. The main difference is that the method to which a message is addressed is determined by the receiver of the message rather than by the sender. To transmit a message to an object, the sender pushes the object and the message's parameters (if any) onto the central stack. It then saves its own state (such as the program counter) and passes control to the appropriate bytecode, determined by the search described above. Space is allocated to accommodate the parameters as well as temporary variables for the method. A link to the caller (to allow return) is saved. A link is also created to the object containing the method that handles the message; this link allows access to instance (and indirectly) class variables, as well as class variables of superclasses. This device is very similar to the static chain used to implement imperative languages.

A given method always knows at compile time in which class or superclass a given variable is defined. As a result, all variables can be addressed at a known offset relative to some object (either the object handling the message or some superclass). Method execution is comparatively fast, since variable names don't need to be resolved at runtime. Once a method is finished, it uses a saved link to return to the caller and returns a pointer to the object computed by the method.

Bytecode is quite compact and reasonably efficient to execute. The main cost is that all computation is done with messages, and all messages must be resolved at runtime to determine the method that will handle the message. Consider Figure 5.19.

Figure 5.19   a := b + c

This program translates to the following bytecode sequence:

1. Push the address of b (the receiver of the message) onto the central stack.
2. Push the address of c (the parameter) onto the stack.
3. Construct a message with the message code for + . Search for that code in b's instance dictionary, then its class dictionary, then superclass dictionaries in turn. Send the message to the method that is found.

4.   Pop the result off the stack and store it as a.

In an ordinary compiler, this program translates to two or three instructions if b and c are simple integers. Smalltalk doesn't know until runtime what b and c are. In the case of SmallIntegers, things aren't too bad. The addresses of b and c encode their class membership, and a primitive method can be invoked. Nonetheless, substantially more than two or three instructions have been executed.

For all classes other than SmallInteger, a dictionary must be consulted to determine the method that will handle the message. For example, + might be used to concatenate strings or add stacks. The advantage of a using a primitive method is that the overhead of creating local space and linking to the method's object are avoided; the operation is performed directly on the objects on the central stack, and the resulting object replaces them.

4.6 Subtle Features

Blocks are implemented by closures. Even though a block may be executed in an environment quite different from its defining environment, it can still access its nonlocal variables correctly. Thus Smalltalk uses deep binding. Smalltalk manages to avoid the pitfall of accessing deallocated regions of a stack by using a garbage collector instead of a stack (with its explicit release) to manage object store. The anonymous method in Figure 5.20 prints 4.

Figure 5.20

```
|innerBlock outerBlock aVariable|                              1
    outerBlock := [ :aVariable |                               2
        innerBlock := [                                        3
            aVariable write -- write aVariable                 4
        ]                                                      5
] .                                                            6
    outerBlock value: 4 .                                      7
    aVariable := 6 . -- Try to confuse the issue              8
    innerBlock value -- writes 4                               9
!                                                             10
```

Smalltalk methods are perfectly capable of coercing their parameters; only by looking at the documentation (or the implementation) can a programmer be sure what types are accepted by a method and whether the method will coerce types.

Even more surprising is the **become:** method provided by Object (and therefore available in all classes unless overridden). It is used as in Figure 5.21.

Figure 5.21   anObject **become:** anotherObject

After this message, all references to anObject and anotherObject are interchanged. Conventionally, anotherObject had no references before, so it now acquires references. This facility can be used to build abstract data types that change their implementation at some point. That is, in response to some message, an object may execute the code in Figure 5.22.

Figure 5.22   self **become:** newObject

From that point on, all references to the old object are rerouted to the new object, which could be of a different class entirely.

In many ways tree-structured inheritance rules are too restrictive. For example, I might have a class DisplayItem that represents items that can be graphically displayed on a screen. Objects of this class would respond to messages like **rotate:** or **highlight**. Another useful class might be InventoryItem, which represents items that I might inventory. Objects of this class would respond to messages like **report-Backlog** or **nameSupplier**. It would be nice to allow some objects to be both DisplayItems and InventoryItems (for example, a bumper or aircraft wing). This can only be done in Smalltalk 1.0 by making Display-Item a subclass of InventoryItem or vice versa. Neither alternative is attractive, because not all objects of one class necessarily belong to the other. (For example, I might be able to display a Saturn V rocket, but I probably won't have it in my inventory.)

A means of achieving **multiple inheritance**, in which a class is a direct subclass of more than one superclass, was introduced in Smalltalk 2.0. It is complicated to use (none of the built-in Smalltalk classes uses it), because there can be name conflicts among the multiple ancestral lines. Smalltalk 2.0 notices such conflicts at runtime and declares a conflict error. Since all classes are subclasses of Object, a class that inherits multiply sees Object along two different ancestry lines. The programmer needs to indicate whether such multiply defined ancestors are to be treated as a single ancestor or whether both are wanted. In the latter case, every invocation of a multiply defined method or access to a multiply defined instance variable must be qualified to indicate which ancestor is meant. In Eiffel, the programmer may rename inherited identifiers to avoid such name conflicts. Circular inheritance is always disallowed.

5 ◆ C++

C++ was developed at AT&T by Bjarne Stroustrup, who wanted to write event-driven simulations for which Simula would have been ideal but would also have been too inefficient. The original version of the language was developed in 1980; at that time it was known as "C with Classes" and lacked a number of its present features. The name C++ was coined by Rick Mascitti in 1983 as a pun on the C operator ++ , which increments its operand. C++ is explicitly intended as the successor to C. (The same pun has been used to name [incr Tcl], an object-oriented enhancement to Tcl.) C++ was implemented for some time as a preprocessor that generated C. Full compilers are now available. C++ has an ANSI standard and a standard reference, the ARM [Ellis 90], which also includes some of the design rationale. Of particular interest is Meyers' book [Meyers 92], which explains how to use some of the language features and also why C++ does things the way it does.

5.1 The Consequences of Static Binding

Most of the differences between C++ and Smalltalk can be explained by the fact that C++ is designed to be an efficient, compiled language. It performs as much binding as possible statically, not dynamically. Unlike Smalltalk, C++ is a statically typed programming language. Every identifier in a C++ program has a type associated with it by a declaration. That type can be either an ordinary C type or a class.

One consequence of static typing is that C++ does not allow classes to be introduced at runtime, unlike Smalltalk, in which introducing a class is a runtime operation accomplished by an appropriate invocation to the superclass. For this reason, the class hierarchy based on the subclass relation is less extensive than in Smalltalk. It is common for C++ programs to build many top-level classes, whereas in Smalltalk, all classes are subclasses, directly or indirectly, of the class Object.

Another consequence of static typing is that classes are not themselves objects. C++ programs have no hierarchy of instances and classes. In this regard, C++ displays less uniformity (in the sense introduced in Chapter 1) than Smalltalk. On the other hand, the result is perhaps easier to comprehend. C++ has no need to introduce metaclasses.

A third consequence of static typing is that polymorphism in C++ is much more limited than in Smalltalk. It is not possible to build heterogeneous stacks, for example, except by the awkward trick of declaring the elements to be members of a statically declared choice type (in C++, called a "union") or by circumventing type checking by casting of pointers. However, C++ follows Ada's lead in providing generic classes.

(Ada's generic modules are discussed in Chapter 3). I will show later
how to implement a generic Stack class.

In order to generate efficient code, C++ tries as far as possible to bind
method invocations to methods at compile time. Every variable has a
known type (that is, its class), so the compiler can determine exactly
which method is intended by any invocation. If a subclass introduces an
overriding method or instance-variable declaration, then variables of
that subclass use the new method or instance variable. The programmer may still access the hidden identifiers by qualifying accesses by the
name of the superclass.

C++ must deal with variables declared to be of one class and assigned a value of a subclass. In particular, any pointer variable may be
assigned a pointer to an object of its declared class C or any direct or indirect subclass S.[2] The compiler cannot tell whether this variable will be
pointing to an object of its declared class C; it may be dynamically assigned an object of subclass S. Therefore, the compiler cannot tell for
certain which method to use if S overrides a method of its superclass C.
C++ solves this problem by distinguishing static and dynamic binding of
methods.

By default, all binding is static. In order to force the compiler to generate the more expensive code necessary to defer binding until runtime,
the programmer must declare that the method in the superclass S is **virtual**. Objects of class S (and its subclasses) contain not only fields for
the instance variables, but also pointers to the code for all virtual
methods.

It is also possible for the programmer to specify dynamic binding for
a particular method and not have C implement that method at all. Such
a method is called **pure virtual**. In this case, subclasses of C are expected to provide the method; it is erroneous to invoke a method that is
not provided by an object or one of its superclasses. For example, class
Complex could be a subclass of Magnitude, which could define a max operation. In Smalltalk, if you send a max message to a Complex object, the
inherited version of max will be automatically invoked; all binding is dynamic. This method might in turn invoke the > method, which is also
provided by Magnitude. However, Magnitude's version of > is not meant
to be invoked; it is meant to be overridden by a method introduced in
subclasses like Complex. Magnitude's > method just generates an error
message. In C++, the > method would be declared as a pure virtual
method of Magnitude, and Complex would be obliged to provide it.

---

[2] Simula has exactly the same problem and uses the same solution. However, in
Simula, all variables of object type are actually pointers to objects; in C++, a variable may
either have a stack-based value or point to a heap-based value.

If the programmer knows that a particular pointer (declared to be pointing to a value of class C) in fact references a value of subclass S, a method specific to S may be invoked by fully qualifying it with the subclass name. This qualification leads to a runtime check to make sure the value is in fact of class S.

5.2 Sample Classes

I will rely on examples to describe C++. The syntax of C++ is compatible with the syntax of C; the examples use correct C++ syntax. The first example shows how to introduce complex numbers in C++, even though the standard C++ library already includes an implementation of complex numbers.

I first declare a new class Complex and make it a subclass of Magnitude, which I will not show here. A Complex object contains two floating-point numbers, one to hold the real part of the number and one to hold the imaginary part. In Smalltalk, a program creates a new class dynamically by sending a message to its intended superclass, in this case Magnitude. In C++, the programmer creates a new class statically by declaring it, as in Figure 5.23.

Figure 5.23

```
class Complex : Magnitude {                          1
    double realPart;                                 2
    double imaginaryPart;                            3
};                                                   4
```

The braces { and } take the role of **begin** and **end**. The class Complex is declared in line 1 to be a subclass of Magnitude. Top-level classes omit the colon and the name of the superclass. Complex contains two instance variables, realPart and imaginaryPart, both declared to be of type double. Instance variables are called "data members" in C++, and the methods are called "member functions." I will continue to follow Smalltalk nomenclature for consistency.

The first operation I will declare is to create and initialize a complex number. The Smalltalk class inherits a method called **new** from its superclass for this purpose. The C++ compiler provides a default new function that is passed a hidden parameter that specifies the amount of space to be allocated from the heap; an explicit allocator function can be provided if the programmer desires. Complex variables can also be allocated from the central stack in the normal manner without recourse to the new function, as in Figure 5.24.

Figure 5.24

```
Complex *pz = new Complex; // allocated from the heap     1
Complex z; // allocated from the central stack            2
```

The comment delimiter in C++ is `//` . The `*` in line 1 declares pz as a pointer type, pointing to objects of type `Complex`. The proper version of new is specified by adding the class name.

I will rely on the defaults provided to allocate `Complex` objects; however, I must provide a way to initialize such objects. In Smalltalk, I would establish a **real:imaginary:** method to set the values of a Complex object. C++ allows the program to provide an initializer (also called a "constructor") and a finalizer (also called a "destructor") for each class. The **initializer** is called each time an object of the class is created (either explicitly or implicitly, as when a parameter is passed by value), and the **finalizer** is called whenever an instance of the class goes out of scope or is explicitly freed. Initializers can be used to establish values of instance variables; finalizers can be used to free storage pointed to by instance variables. Both are good for gathering statistics.

A reasonable declaration of `Complex`, including some procedure headers that I will need later, is given in Figure 5.25.

Figure 5.25

```
class Complex {                                            1
private: // the following are generally hidden             2
      double realPart;                                     3
      double imaginaryPart;                                4
public: // the following are generally visible             5
      Complex(); // initializer                            6
      Complex(double,double); // another initializer       7
      ~Complex(); // finalizer                             8
      Complex operator << (ostream); // write              9
      int operator > (Complex); // compare                10
};                                                        11
```

Lines 6–10 introduce methods. C++ does not use a keyword **procedure**; the presence of the parentheses for the parameter lists indicates that procedures are being declared. The fact that the procedures in lines 6–7 have the same name as the class is understood to mean that they are initializers. The compiler resolves the overloaded initializer identifier by noting the number of parameters and their types. The name of the finalizer is the name of the class preceded by a tilde `~` , as in line 8. Initializers and finalizers do not explicitly produce a result, so they are not given types. The operators `<<` , used for output, and `>` , used for numeric comparison, are overloaded as well (lines 9–10). The ostream type in line 9 is a class used for output and declared in a standard library. Comparison returns an integer, because C++ does not distinguish Booleans from integers. The operator procedures do not require two parameters, because a Complex value is understood to be presented as the left-hand operand.

So far, the example has only included the method headers, that is, the specification of the methods. The implementation of each procedure (declarations of local variables and the body) may be separated from the specification to promote modularity. C++ also allows the implementation to be presented immediately after the method specification (within the scope of the **class** declaration). Immediate placement informs the compiler that the programmer intends calls on such methods to be compiled with inline code. It is usually better programming practice to separate the implementations from their specifications, perhaps in a separate file. Figure 5.26 presents separate implementations of the initializers specified in Figure 5.25:

Figure 5.26

```
Complex::Complex()                                             1
{                                                              2
    realPart = 0;                                              3
    imaginaryPart = 0;                                         4
};                                                             5

Complex::Complex(double real, double imaginary)               6
{                                                              7
    realPart = real;                                          8
    imaginaryPart = imaginary;                                9
};                                                             10

// sample usage in a declaration                              11
Complex z1 = Complex(5.0, 7.0);                               12
Complex z2; // will be initialized by Complex::Complex()     13
```

In lines 1 and 6, the procedure names are qualified by the class name. C++ uses :: instead of . to indicate qualification. In lines 3, 4, 8, and 9, instance variables are named without any qualification; they refer to the variables in the instance for which the procedure is invoked.

The next operation (Figure 5.27) prints complex values; the specification is in line 9 of Figure 5.25.

Figure 5.27

```
Complex Complex::operator << (ostream output)        1
{                                                    2
    output << realPart;                              3
    if (imaginaryPart >= 0) {                        4
        output << '+';                               5
        (output << imaginaryPart) << "i";            6
    }                                                7
    return *this;                                    8
};                                                   9

main() { // sample usage                             10
    z1 << cout; // cout is the standard output stream 11
}                                                    12
```

The way I have defined the Complex operator << (line 1) requires that it output complex values as shown in line 11, instead of the more stylistic cout << z. There is a way to define the operator that avoids this reversal, but it is more complicated; I will show it later. Line 6 shows that the << operator for doubles returns the stream; the stream is then given another << message with a string parameter. Clearly, << is highly overloaded.

A Smalltalk > method for Complex must have access to the instance variables of both operands. That is, the object receiving the > message must be able to inspect the instance variables of the parameter. But Smalltalk objects never export instance variables. The IntegerStack example in Figure 5.17 (page 177) shows how to wrestle with this problem; I needed to define private selector methods. Alternatively, I could have introduced a **magnitude** unary operator. Neither solution is particularly elegant.

C++ addresses this concern by allowing the programmer to relax the walls of separation between objects. Members can be declared public, protected, or private. By default, instance variables are private. The procedures shown in Figure 5.25 (page 187) are declared public. The following chart shows what accesses are permitted for each level of security.

	Same	Friend	Subclass	Client
Smalltalk instance variables	n	—	y	n
Smalltalk methods	y	—	y	y
C++ public members	y	y	y	y
C++ protected members	y	y	y	n
C++ private members	y	y	n	n

Each entry shows whether a member of an object O of class C is exported to various contexts. "Same" means other objects of the same class C. C++ allows such contexts access to instance variables; Smalltalk does not. Therefore, the > operator in C++ has permission to access the instance variables of its parameter. "Friends" are procedures or classes that class C declares to be its friends. Friends are permitted to refer to all members of instances of C. More restrictively, a method M may declare procedures and classes to be its friends; those friends are permitted to invoke M even though M may be hidden to others. "Subclass" refers to code within subclasses of C. Subclasses have access to all members except for private ones in C++. "Clients" are instances of classes unrelated to C.

The design of C++ makes it easier to deal with binary operations that take two instances of the same class than in Smalltalk. All instance variables of one instance are visible to the other. For example, the implementation of > (the specification is in line 10 of Figure 5.25 on page 187) can inspect the instance variables of its formal parameter right (see Figure 5.28).

Figure 5.28

```
int Complex::operator > (Complex right)              1
{                                                    2
    double leftmag, rightmag;                        3
    leftmag = (realPart * realPart) +                4
        (imaginaryPart * imaginaryPart);             5
    leftmag = (right.realPart * right.realPart) +    6
        (right.imaginaryPart * right.imaginaryPart); 7
    return leftmag > rightmag;                       8
}                                                    9
```

C++ lets subclasses further restrict the visibility of identifiers by explicitly redeclaring all inherited public and protected identifiers protected or private. (Subclasses do not inherit private identifiers.)

Other security arrangements are possible. In Oberon-2, instance variables may be exported read-write, exported readonly, or not exported at all [Reiser 92]. Oberon-2 does not distinguish between exports to other classes and inheritance by subclasses.

Polymorphism in C++ is achieved by generic classes. A generic Stack class that can be instantiated (at compile time) to become a class of any given type, including a stack of stacks, can be written as in Figure 5.29.

Figure 5.29

```
#define MAXSIZE 10                                             1

template <class BaseType> class Stack {                        2
private:                                                       3
    BaseType elements[MAXSIZE];                                4
    int count;                                                 5
public:                                                        6
    Stack() { // initializer                                   7
        count = 0;                                             8
    }                                                          9
    void Push(BaseType element) {                             10
        elements[count] = element;                            11
        count = count + 1;                                    12
    }                                                         13
    BaseType Pop() {                                          14
        count = count - 1;                                    15
        return(elements[count]);                              16
    }                                                         17
    int Empty() {                                             18
        return(count == 0);                                   19
    }                                                         20
    friend ostream                                            21
        operator << (ostream output, Stack<BaseType> S) {     22
        int index;                                            23
        output << "[";                                        24
        for (index = 0; index < S.count; index++) {           25
            output << S.elements[index];                      26
            if (index+1 == S.count) break;                    27
            output << ",";                                    28
        }                                                     29
        output << "]";                                        30
        return(output);                                       31
    } // <<                                                   32
}; // Stack                                                   33
```

```
main(){ // sample usage                                     34
    Stack<int> myIntStack;                                  35
    Stack<float> myFloatStack;                              36
    Stack<Stack<int> > myRecursiveStack;                    37
    myIntStack.Push(4);                                     38
    myIntStack.Push(8);                                     39
    cout << myIntStack; // [4,8]                            40
    myFloatStack.Push(4.2);                                 41
    cout << myFloatStack; // [4.2]                          42
    myRecursiveStack.Push(myIntStack);                      43
    cout << myRecursiveStack; // [[4,8]]                    44
}                                                           45
```

The definition in line 1 effectively declares MAXSIZE a constant with value 10. The **template** declaration in line 2 indicates that Stack is parameterized by a type (literally, by a class). I have ignored all error conditions in the methods for simplicity's sake. The declarations in lines 35–37 show how to supply parameters to the generic class; a generic class must have all parameters bound in order to declare a variable. The compiler compiles a specific class separately for each instantiation of the generic class. In this example, three specific classes are compiled. Line 37 shows that it is possible to declare stacks of stacks of integer. (The extra space between the > characters is needed to prevent the parser from misinterpreting them as the single >> operator.) The header for the overloaded operator << (lines 21–32) is unusual; it is declared to be a friend of ostream, so that the stream output routines have access to the contents of the stack. The stack itself is passed as a parameter, so that the output statements of lines 40, 42, and 44 can be written with cout on the left, as is proper style in C++, not the right, as I have been doing previously.

6 ◆ FINAL COMMENTS

At first glance, object-oriented languages are just a fancy way of presenting abstract data types. You could argue that they don't present a new paradigm of programming, but rather a structuring principle that languages of any sort might employ. However, I would counter that Smalltalk and C++ have developed the concept of abstract data type into a new form of programming.

First, object-oriented programming provides a new view of types. The type of an object is the protocol it accepts. Two objects are type-compatible if they respond to the same set of messages. This view is highly abstract, because it doesn't say the objects have the same form, only that they are functionally interchangeable. There is no straightforward way to check type compatibility.

Second, the nature of instantiation distinguishes a class from an abstract data type exported from a module. Each instance is independent, with its own data and procedures, although all instances may share common class variables. Data types exported from a module may be instantiated, but the exporting module itself cannot be. A module is much more of a static, compile-time, passive entity. A class is more dynamic, with more runtime and active qualities.

Third, the hierarchy of subclasses leads to a style of programming known as **programming by classification**. The abstract data types are organized into a tree, with the most abstract at the root and the most specified at the leaves. Incremental modifications to a program are accomplished by introducing new subclasses of existing classes. Each new class automatically acquires much of what it needs by reference to its superclass. Methods are automatically overloaded. Programming by classification is an important tool for achieving reuse of valuable code, and this tool goes well beyond the reuse that comes from modularization into abstract data types.

Smalltalk is attractive in many ways. It provides a highly interactive and integrated programming environment that uses the latest in computer technology (in short, a graphical user interface). Its object-oriented style provides an interesting inversion of our usual view of programming. Objects are preeminent, uniform, and autonomous. They cooperate by passing messages, but no object controls any other. Objects are fairly robust, since the worst thing a program can do is send one a message it can't handle. In this case, the object doesn't fail, but rather ignores the message and issues an error.

Smalltalk is not without its problems, both real and perceived. It has only recently become generally available for small machines. Smalltalk may have been too quick to abandon concepts common in imperative programming languages. For example, it makes no provision for named constants; you must create a variable and then be careful not to change it. This shortcoming could easily be overcome without injustice to the design of the language. Similarly, it would be nice to introduce some type checking (even if dynamically checked) by allowing variables to have a type (that is, a class) specifier. Programs would be easier to read and less error-prone. It might also make manipulation of variables more efficient, particularly for primitive types. As a small step in this direction, Smalltalk suggests that identifiers like `anInteger` or `aStack` be used conventionally for variables whose class is meant to be fixed. Of course, an identifier named `anInteger` need not actually map to an integer under Smalltalk's rules. Finally, Smalltalk provides no control over whether identifiers are exported (instance variables aren't, methods are) or inherited (all are). A finer level of control, such as that provided by C++, could improve the safety of programs.

C++ fixes some of these problems. First, types and methods are bound at compile time. Numeric values and code blocks are not objects at all. There is no need to understand expressions as evaluated by messages sent to objects. The result is that C++ programs execute quite efficiently, because they usually avoid Smalltalk's dynamic method binding, use ordinary procedure invocation, and use inline code to accomplish arithmetic. Second, members can be individually controlled with regard to export and inheritability. The concept of friends allows identifiers to be exported only to instances of particular classes.

However, C++ suffers from its ancestry; C is notorious for being error-prone (the operators for equality and assignment are easily confused, for example), syntactically obscure (complicated types are hard for humans to parse), and unsafe (loopholes allow all type checking to be circumvented).

Other object-oriented languages have been designed, of course. Best known perhaps is Eiffel [Meyer 92]. Nor is C the only language that has been extended to give it an object orientation. Other good examples include CLOS (the Common LISP Object System) and [incr Tcl]. Some people believe that Ada 95 will be the most widespread object-oriented programming language in a few years. Even object-oriented COBOL has been considered [Clement 92].

EXERCISES

Review Exercises

5.1   What are the consequences in C++ of static typing?

5.2   Does an object in Smalltalk require its own private stack? In C++?

5.3   Write a class in Smalltalk and/or in C for rational numbers, that is, numbers that can be represented by an integer numerator and denominator. Instance variables should include both the numerator and the denominator. Your implementation should always reduce fractions to their lowest terms. You must overload all arithmetic and conditional operators.

5.4   Consider an array of stacks, some of whose components are implemented one way, while others are implemented the other way. Is this a homogeneous array?

5.5   How would you implement the array of stacks mentioned in Problem 5.4 in C++?

Challenge Exercises

5.6   Simula classes contain procedures. Unlike ordinary procedures, procedures inside classes may not declare **own** variables, that is, variables whose values are retained from one invocation to the next. If you want to add such a feature, what would you like it to mean?

5.7   In Smalltalk, not everything is an object. Name three programming-language entities that are not objects. Could Smalltalk be modified so that they are objects?

5.8   Show how the `timesRepeat:` method in Figure 5.11 (page 172) could be coded.

5.9   In line 12 of Figure 5.17 (page 177), show how an element of a different class could masquerade as an `Integer` and bypass the type check.

5.10 `True` and `False` are subclasses of `Boolean`. Each has only one instance (`true` and `false`, respectively). First, how can class `True` prevent other instances from being created? Second, why not use the simpler organization in which `Boolean` has two instances? Hint: Consider the code for `ifTrue:ifFalse:`.

5.11 Build a method for `Block` that accepts a **for:from:to:** message to implement **for** loops. Don't use **whileTrue:**.

5.12 Build a subclass of `Block` that accepts a **for:in:** message to implement CLU-style iterators.

5.13 Defend Smalltalk's design decision that error messages are to be generated by objects via messages to themselves, and that the **error:** method is to be inherited from `Object`.

5.14 Why should `Magnitude` define methods like `>` but give them error-generating code? In other words, what is the point of introducing pure virtual methods?

5.15 In Smalltalk, a new class is constructed at runtime by sending a message to its superclass. In C++, classes are constructed at compile time by declaration. Show how the Smalltalk method is more powerful.

5.16 Enumerate what is missing in Smalltalk and in C++ for building abstract data types.

5.17 What is the effect of a C++ class declaring that it is its own friend?

5.18 C is not block-structured. In particular, one cannot introduce a type within a name scope. What complexities would be introduced if C++ were based on a block-structured language, and classes could be introduced in a name scope?

5.19 Is a class a first-class value, a second-class value, or neither, in Smalltalk and in C++?

5.20 In C++, say there is a class A with a protected instance variable varA. Subclasses B and C inherit this variable. May instances of B and C access each other's copy of varA?

5.21 In Figure 5.29 (page 192), I went to considerable trouble to allow output statements to place cout on the left of the << operator. Why was this so important for this example?

Chapter 6

Dataflow

There is some evidence that the next big wave of change to wash over programming languages will be concurrency. Both architectures and languages for concurrency have been around for some time. In this chapter, I will discuss the dataflow architectural concept and the languages that have been designed to conform to it. Dataflow is one way to achieve concurrency, particularly at the fine-grain level: It finds multiple operations that can be undertaken concurrently within the evaluation of a single expression. Ideas from dataflow have found their way into parallelizing compilers for more conventional architectures, as well. The ideas here in some ways prepare for Chapter 7, which deals with concurrent programming languages that work at a coarser level of granularity.

Sequential execution is an essential characteristic of the von Neumann computer architecture, in which programs and data are stored in a central memory. The concepts embodied by classical architecture have not been directly applicable to the domain of parallel computation. Most programming languages have evolved from von Neumann languages, designed specifically for the von Neumann architecture, so programmers have been conditioned to analyze problems and write programs in sequential fashion.

The dataflow approach was first suggested by Karp and Miller [Karp 66] as an alternative to the von Neumann architectural and linguistic concepts. Consider computation of the series of statements in Figure 6.1.

Figure 6.1

```
A := B*C + D/F;                                    1
G := H**2 + A;                                     2
```

A data-dependency graph called a **dataflow graph** represents the ordering of evaluation imposed by data dependencies. It encodes the fact that an expression can't be evaluated before its operands are evaluated. The dataflow graph for Figure 6.1 appears in Figure 6.2.

197

Figure 6.2   Dataflow graph

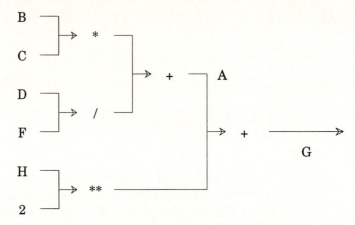

This graph represents a partial order on the evaluation sequence. In contrast, a typical von Neumann language will create a totally ordered instruction sequence to evaluate these statements, but such an order loses a significant amount of potential concurrency. If more than one set of operands is available, more than one expression should be evaluated concurrently.

In a dataflow computer, a program isn't represented by a linear instruction sequence, but by a dataflow graph. Moreover, no single thread of control moves from instruction to instruction demanding data, operating on it, and producing new data. Rather, data flows to instructions, causing evaluation to occur as soon as all operands are available. Data is sent along the arcs of the dataflow graph in the form of **tokens**, which are created by computational nodes and placed on output arcs. They are removed from the arcs when they are accessed as input by other computational nodes. Concurrent execution is a natural result of the fact that many tokens can be on the dataflow graph at any time; the only constraint on evaluation order is the presence of tokens on arcs in the graph.

Most computational nodes in a dataflow graph compute arithmetic results. However, some sort of conditional structure is necessary. Loops are accommodated in dataflow graphs by introducing nodes called **valves** that control the flow of tokens within the graph. Two kinds of valves are commonly built: distributors and selectors. A distributor takes an input token and a Boolean control token. It distributes the input token to one of two output arcs (labeled T and F), as shown graphically in Figure 6.3.

Figure 6.3 Distributor
node

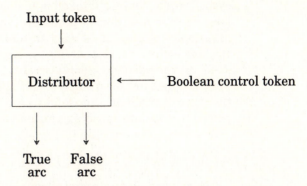

A selector uses a Boolean control token to accept one of two input tokens and passes the selected token onto its output arc, as shown in Figure 6.4.

Figure 6.4 Selector
node

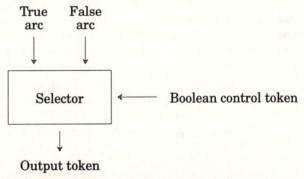

Viewing a computation as a dataflow graph leads directly to a functional view of programming. Dataflow graphs do not include the notion of variables, since there are no named memory cells holding values. Computation does not produce side effects. Functional programming languages lend themselves to various evaluation orders. Dataflow evaluators are typically speculative evaluators, since they are data-driven. Computations are triggered not by a demand for values or data, but rather by their availability.

However, there are some important differences between dataflow and functional programming. First, dataflow graphs have no simple concept of a function that returns a value. One could surround part of a dataflow graph with a boundary and call it a function, where all inbound arcs to the region would be the parameters and all outgoing arcs would be the results. Such an organization could lead to recursively defined dataflow graphs. Second, as you saw in Chapter 4, functional programming languages rely heavily on recursion, because they do not support iteration. However, dataflow manages to support recursion by building cyclic graphs; an initial token may be placed inside a cycle in order to allow the first iteration to proceed. Third, the values placed on arcs are all simple values. It is easy to understand integers, reals, and even Boolean values moving along the arcs, but values of structured types such as records and arrays might take more underlying machinery. Pointer types are most likely out of the question. Most important, function types, which are so useful in functional programming, are not supported by the dataflow graph formalism.

1 ◆ DATAFLOW COMPUTERS

There are two classes of dataflow architectures. The first class is called "static," since such architectures do not support reentrant dataflow code (that is, code that is used simultaneously in multiple places in the dataflow graph) and recursion. The simple dataflow computer model introduced above is static, as is the machine proposed by Dennis [Dennis 77].

The second class is called "dynamic." Such machines support simultaneous multiple incarnations of an activity, recursion, and loop unfolding. In a dynamic dataflow architecture, an arc may carry multiple tokens, and care is taken to ensure that activities fire only upon receipt of matching tokens along their input arcs. Tokens are labeled to distinguish values arising in different contexts or from different incarnations of an activity. Two tokens match only if their activity labels match. For example, I might wish to perform the computation specified by a dataflow graph on each element of a vector of 1000 values. With a dynamic dataflow architecture, I can place 1000 tokens on the input arc. Tokens are labeled to insure that values produced during the computation can be ascribed to the appropriate input value.

The dynamic architecture outlined below is essentially that of the classical Manchester Dataflow Computer [Gurd 85]. Modern dynamic dataflow architectures may look different. Tokens are labeled, but I leave out the specific details of how the labels are generated or used, except that labels are matched to identify matching tokens.

The architecture is schematically depicted in Figure 6.5. The machine operates as a circular pipeline divided into four sections. The processing unit receives packets containing operands and an instruction. The instruction is executed on the accompanying operands, and the result tokens (after appropriate labeling) are placed back on the bus to be sent to the I/O switch. The I/O Switch is included in the pipeline to serve as an I/O port. The matching unit consists of associative token storage. When a token arrives at the matching unit, the storage is searched for any tokens with the same label and destination. If matches are discovered, these tokens are read out of the store, and a packet is formed of all these tokens to be sent on to the program store. The destination field of a token carries the address in the program store of the instruction to which the token is directed.

Figure 6.5 Dataflow architecture

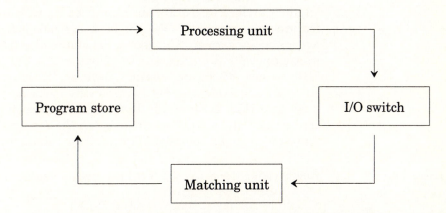

If no match for the arriving token is found in the matching store, the token is written into storage and held in abeyance for matching tokens expected to arrive in the future. For unary operators, no matching is needed, and the token can bypass the matching unit and proceed directly to the program store. It is estimated that 55–70 percent of all tokens are able to bypass the matching section.

When a packet of tokens reaches the program store, the instruction to which the tokens are directed is accessed, and a packet is formed of the tokens and the instruction. This instruction is an opcode, the operands being already available in the packet. Opcodes are elementary operations like addition and multiplication. The program store effectively holds the dataflow graph. Instructions are vertices, and the arcs are represented by link fields associated with each instruction to indicate the successor nodes in the dataflow graph. The packet consisting of the operands, the opcode, and successor information is then sent to the processing unit, and the operation of the machine continues as described.

2 ◆ VAL

Val is a dataflow language developed at MIT by J. Dennis and others [McGraw 82]. This language was originally designed for the static dataflow architecture of Dennis, so it does not support dynamic dataflow features like recursion. Val has been meticulously defined both by an axiomatic [Ackerman 80] and a denotational [Gehani 80] semantics (these concepts are discussed in Chapter 10.) Val is functional in nature, so side effects are absent. However, Val is strongly typed (using structural equivalence) and intentionally looks more like conventional languages than LISP or FP does. In fact, it looks much like ML (described in Chapter 3). For example, the Val function in Figure 6.6 computes the mean and standard deviation for parameters X, Y, and Z.

Figure 6.6

```
function stats(X, Y, Z: real) : real, real;          1
    let                                              2
        Mean : real := (X+Y+Z)/3;                    3
        SD : real := sqrt((X – Mean)**2 +            4
            (Y – Mean)**2 + (Z – Mean)**2)/3;        5
    in                                               6
        Mean, SD                                     7
    end                                              8
end                                                  9
```

In Val, functions return tuples of values. This syntax simplifies composition of functions, as the values returned by one function can be immediately used as parameters to a calling function.

Val has the usual scalar types (integer, real, Boolean, and character) as well as arrays, records, and choice types. Arrays are all flexible, with only the index type declared. A variety of array operations such as concatenation, extension, and contraction are provided. During array construction, all elements of an array may be specified simultaneously, allowing all the evaluations of array entries to proceed concurrently. Record construction is patterned after array construction to promote concurrency. Val defines error values, discussed in Chapter 2, so that the result of all computations is well defined, no matter what the evaluation order.

Val appears to have an assignment statement, but this appearance is misleading; like ML, identifiers can be bound in a block to values, but the binding cannot be changed within that block. Such bindings get confusing when an iterative loop is employed, since the program may need to update values between iterations. Val views each iteration as creating a new name-value binding, with values from the previous iteration included in the computation of the new loop values.

Structured values are viewed as single values, so array and record components can never be individually modified. If you want to change an array element, you must create a new array differing from the original in only one element.

Val provides implicit concurrency. Operations that can execute independently are evident (once the dataflow graph is built by the compiler) without needing any explicit notation. Val achieves implicit concurrency by using functional language features, and makes use of the fact that evaluation of a function or expression has no side effects. If two operations do not depend on the outcomes of each other, they can execute simultaneously. A source of side effects in conventional languages is **aliasing**, whereby the same memory cell can be referenced by more than one name. Reference-mode parameters, pointers, and overlays can create aliases. All aliasing is forbidden in Val. The fact that Val relies on implicit concurrency is justified on the grounds that concurrency can be at a very low level (at the level, say, of individual arithmetical operations), and it is unreasonable to expect the programmer to specify concurrency details at this level.

In addition to implicit concurrency, Val provides explicit concurrency in the **forall** expression, which concurrently evaluates an expression for all values in a range or structure. The width of parallelism is specified as a control identifier that assumes all values in a given range. In addition to specifying the control identifier and introducing a new name scope, loops also specify how to merge the values from all the parallel streams into one result. There are two ways to generate results: **construct**, which allows each parallel execution path to generate a value that becomes an element of an array of results, and **accumulate**, in which values from all the result streams are merged into one result using one of a fixed set of associative binary operators like + . (The operation specified by **accumulate** can be computed by an implicit balanced binary tree, allowing the merged value to be produced in logarithmic time.) Figure 6.7 clarifies these notions.

Figure 6.7

```
forall i in [1, 100] do                               1
    left: real      := point[i].x_low;                2
    bottom: real    := point[i].y_low;                3
    right: real     := point[i].x_high;               4
    top: real       := point[i].y_high;               5
    area: real      := (right-left) * (top-bottom);   6
    okay: Boolean   := acceptable(area);              7
    abort: Boolean  := erroneous(area);               8
```

```
        accumulate + if okay then area else 0.0 end;          9
        accumulate or abort;                                  10
        construct if okay then area else 0.0 end;             11
  end                                                         12
```

In this program, the **forall** produces 100 concurrent streams of execution. Their results are merged using **accumulate** + to add all acceptable areas (line 9), **accumulate or** to determine if abort was true in any of the streams (line 10), and **construct** to create an array of elements calculated by a formula (line 11). The entire **forall** expression returns a 3-tuple comprising those three results.

The **for** expression implements loops that cannot execute in parallel because values produced in one iteration must be used in the next. The decision concerning whether to continue loop iteration occurs within the loop body as a conditional expression, as in Figure 6.8.

Figure 6.8

```
for                                                           1
    a: real := 0.0;                                           2
    b: real := 1.0;                                           3
do                                                            4
    let                                                       5
        c: real, done: Boolean := Compute(a, b);              6
    in                                                        7
        if done then                                          8
            c                                                 9
        else                                                 10
            iter                                              11
                a := NewA(a, b);                              12
                b := NewB(a, b);                              13
            end                                               14
        end                                                  15
    end                                                       16
end                                                           17
```

The identifiers a and b (lines 2 and 3) are loop parameters. During the first iteration of the loop, the parameters have values 0.0 and 1.0. The Compute invocation (line 6) returns two values, which are bound to c and done. If **iter** is selected (lines 11–14), a new iteration is begun. New values for a and b are evaluated for the next iteration. The binding in line 13 uses the old value of a on the right-hand side. When done is true, the expression returns the value bound to c (line 9).

A choice type is built as shown in Figure 6.9.

Figure 6.9
```
type list =                                                       1
    choice [                                                      2
            empty : void;                                         3
            nonempty : record [item : real; rest : list]         4
    ]                                                             5
```

Void (line 3) is a predeclared type with no values. This example defines
list as an ordinary linked list, but with an interesting difference — it is
recursively defined without using pointers. Val disallows pointers because of aliasing issues. A list is therefore a recursive data structure
rather than a sequence of individual elements linked with pointers.

A value of a choice type is created by using a **make** constructor (Figure 6.10).

Figure 6.10
```
make list[empty : nil]
```

To guarantee type compatibility, the contents of a **choice** can only be accessed via **tagcase**, as in Figure 6.11.

Figure 6.11
```
function IsEmpty(L : list) : Boolean;                             1
    tagcase L of                                                 2
            when tag empty => true                               3
            when nonempty => false                               4
    end                                                          5
end                                                              6
```

Val also has conditional expressions.

Because Val lacks side effects and provides error values, it is an ideal
candidate for speculative evaluation. In some places, however, Val inhibits speculative evaluation to reduce unneeded computations. In particular, in **if**, **tagcase** and **for** expressions, computations are not
initiated until the controlling expression is computed and tested. Val
uses a lazy evaluator for these constructs. In contrast, components of
ordinary expressions are assumed to be data-driven, implying a speculative evaluator. Parameters to functions are always fully evaluated before the function is invoked.

Evaluation order in Val is primarily dictated by efficiency and simplicity concerns, allowing lazy, speculative, and strict evaluation to coex-
ist. An interesting problem arises if a computation fails to return any
value (even an error value), because it diverges (that is, loops forever).
A lazy evaluator avoids a diverging subcomputation if its result isn't
needed. A speculative evaluator tries to compute everything, and unnecessary diverging subcomputations proceed concurrently with other
computations. A conventional evaluator does not proceed beyond the

diverging subcomputation. Thus, Val's evaluation rules can affect the results computed by otherwise equivalent constructs. For example, an **if** expression can't be replaced by a call to an equivalent function, because **if** evaluates only some of its components, while a function evaluates all its parameters.

Val programs obey many of the laws of FP (Chapter 4), so many of the FP theorems can be used to transform (and optimize) Val programs. Val differs from FP in the way it handles error values, which can invalidate certain FP theorems. FP functions are bottom-preserving, and $\perp$ represents "error." Val, on the other hand, allows error values to be detected, and further computation can repair or ignore the error and produce an ordinary value. For example, I might like to establish that in Val line 1 of Figure 6.12 is equivalent to line 2.

Figure 6.12

```
H(if p(...) then F(...) else G(...) end)                    1
if p(...) then H(F(...)) else H(G(...)) end                2
```

That is, that I can distribute a call of H into both arms of a conditional. This theorem is true in bottom-preserving FP environments, but it isn't true in Val, because H(error_value) need not be error_value.

3 ◆ SISAL

Val was one of the first serious attempts to produce a production-quality dataflow language. A descendent of Val called Sisal was created to exploit the capabilities of dynamic dataflow computers [McGraw 83]. A Sisal compiler exists, with code generators for Vax, Crays, HEP multiprocessors, and the Manchester dataflow computer.

The most obvious advantage of Sisal over Val is its support of recursion. Recursive functions are useful and natural, especially in functional languages. Val's rejection of recursion was a reflection of the design of early static dataflow machines. Sisal also supports streams, which are needed for ordinary sequential I/O and as a means of composing functions.

Sisal programs can be decomposed into distinct compilation units that explicitly import and export functions. Sisal also extends Val's iterative and parallel (**forall**) loop forms. They can return arrays or streams. Parallel loops can also define explicit inner and outer products, making array manipulation cleaner and potentially more efficient.

4 ◆ POST

Chinya V. Ravishankar developed Post as a Ph.D. thesis starting in 1981 [Ravishankar 89]. Post introduces several novel ideas. First, it lets the programmer determine the level of speculation in evaluation. As I mentioned earlier, speculative evaluation can lead to nontermination under certain circumstances, but strictly lazy evaluation reduces parallelism. A second novel concept is **polychronous data structures** that are partly **synchronous** (must be available before used) and partly **asynchronous** (parts can be used when ready). Third, Post provides communication between computational activities in order to terminate speculative computation that may turn out to be unnecessary. Communication between computations is not natural in purely functional programming languages. Much of their semantic elegance derives from their lack of side effects, so computations scheduled in parallel must not depend on each other's results. Further, a purely functional language permits only deterministic computations and prohibits history-sensitivity.

Post was never fully implemented, but a prototype compiler was built. It first builds a dataflow graph from the program and then converts that graph into instructions for a dynamic dataflow machine. Post needs a dataflow machine (never implemented) that has a few special features, such as a "hold" node for implementing lazy evaluation and a "terminate store" to help find and remove terminated tokens.

4.1 Data Types

Values can be either primitive (`integer`, `real`, `Boolean`, `char`) or structured. Structured values are constructed using the abstractions **stream** and **tuple**. Both are sequences of values, but a tuple may be heterogeneous and is of fixed length, while a stream is homogeneous and of unbounded length. All operators and functions are automatically overloaded to apply to streams; they create streams of results of pointwise application. Nested structures are allowed; an element of a stream may itself be a stream.

After a finite set of values, streams continue with an infinite number of **eos** (end of stream) values. The **eos** value may be used as an operand in arithmetic, logical, and comparison operations. It acts as an identity with arithmetic and logical operations. With comparison operations, **eos** may be made to behave either as the minimal or maximal element by using different comparison operations. Post has two predeclared functions that generate streams of values: (1) `stream(a,b)` generates a stream of integers ranging from a to b, followed by an infinite number of **eos** values; and (2) `const(a)` generates an infinite stream of integers with value a.

Values are implemented by the target dataflow architecture as tokens containing a name (identifying the arc in the dataflow graph), a value (typically, a real number), and a label. The label is unexpectedly complicated, containing fields describing scope, index, and program-defined information. Each of these three fields is a stack containing information pertaining to different dynamic scopes in the program. The scope field identifies those dynamic scopes. The index field distinguishes elements of a stream. The program-defined field permits the programmer to tag values so that computations tagged in a particular way can be terminated; this facility allows Post to manage speculative computation, as described below.

4.2 Programs

A program consists of a name, a parameter list (used as a pattern), and a target expression. The pattern is matched against input data and serves to bind formal parameters to values in the input. The target expression generates a value that is returned by the program. The target expression may introduce a new name scope, with type definitions and identifier declarations. Post is statically scoped. Figure 6.13 shows a simple program.

Figure 6.13

```
function AddNumbers{a,b,c};                    1
    type a, b, c : int                         2
    in a+b+c                                   3
end;                                           4
```

The structure is much like a classical procedure declaration, with formal parameters (the pattern {a,b,c} in line 1), type declarations for the formal parameters (line 2), and a body (line 3).

The type declarations are separated from the pattern for clarity, because the pattern can become complex. For example, {x,y,z,}* is a pattern that repeats the template {x,y,z} indefinitely, matching three more values of the input stream each time. On the other hand, {x,{y,}*,z} is a 3-tuple with a stream as the second component. Figure 6.14 uses a pattern that matches a stream.

Figure 6.14

```
function AddPairs{x,y,}*;                       1
    type x, y : int                            2
    in x+y                                      3
end;                                           4
```

This program outputs a stream consisting of the sums of adjacent values in the input stream; the order of the output stream matches the order of the input stream. If the input stream consists of an odd number of elements, y in the final instance of the template matches an **eos** token, which is an identity for arithmetic operations.

4.3 Synchrony Control

By using connectors other than a comma, the programmer may specify the degree of synchrony required in pattern matching. The comma indicates completely asynchronous matching; the actual parameters may be accessed independently of each other. If the pattern uses only ˆ , matching is synchronous: all elements must be present before any element is made available to the target expression.[1] If the pattern uses only ˜ , matching is sequential: the ith element of the matched data structure is available only after all previous elements have arrived (even if they have not been accessed). Any or all of these combinators may occur within a pattern. If several of them occur, access is polychronous; precedence rules indicate how to group subpatterns in the absence of parentheses.

In Figure 6.14, I could change the input pattern to {xˆy,}*, forcing pairwise synchronization of input elements. The program would compute the same results, because + requires both operands before proceeding.

Sequential patterns are used for loops, as shown in the Figure 6.15.

Figure 6.15

```
function Largest{x˜}* init 0;                                          1
      type x : int                                                    2
      in if Largest > x then Largest else x end                       3
end;                                                                  4
```

This program finds the largest value in a stream of integers. It terminates when the last instance of the target expression terminates; the value generated in this last instance is returned as the value of the program. The program name is used to name the current value, initialized to 0 in line 1 and compared with the next value in line 3. The dataflow graph corresponding to this program has a cycle holding an initial token with value 0. Conditional expressions, like the one in line 3, are evaluated speculatively. The result from the branch that is not needed is

---

[1] The concept of synchronization in concurrent programming languages is related; it is discussed in Chapter 7.

discarded after evaluation is complete.[2]

An alternative syntax for conditionals is shown in Figure 6.16.

Figure 6.16

```
function OddSquares{x,}*;                          1
    type x : int                                  2
    in [(x mod 2) ≠ 0] x*x                        3
end;
```

Line 3 evaluates to x*x only if the condition in square brackets is true, that is, when x is odd. For other instances, the expression evaluates to nil. All nil values are removed from the resulting stream before it is returned.

4.4 Guardians

Guardians implement shared data. They look like procedures and act like variables. In a sense, they are like objects in an object-oriented programming language (discussed in Chapter 5). Assignment to the guardian invokes the procedure with the given value as an actual parameter. The procedure computes a stored value, which can differ from the value of the actual parameter. When the program accesses the guardian's value, it gets a copy of the current stored value. Such access is lazy, in the sense that it occurs only after all nonguardian values used in the expression have arrived. The guardian only has one instance, which prevents simultaneous computations from attempting simultaneous assignment. For example, consider the program of Figure 6.17.

Figure 6.17

```
function LargestFactor{x,}*;                       1
    type x : int                                  2
    guardian Largest{v} init 0;                   3
        type v : int                              4
        in if Largest < v then v else Largest end 5
    end -- Largest                                6
    in Largest := if (N mod x) = 0 then x end     7
end; -- LargestFactor                             8

LargestFactor(stream(2,99));                       9
```

This program finds the largest factor of N (a nonlocal variable) smaller than 100. Even though a new instance of LargestFactor is created for each element of the input stream, there is only one instance of its local

---

[2] If conditionals were evaluated lazily, the programmer could hoist both branches out of the conditional to force them to be evaluated speculatively.

guardian, Largest (lines 3–6). Each element of the input stream is
tested by an instance of line 7; the result is assigned into the guardian.
The conditional expression in line 7 evaluates to nil if the Boolean is
false; nil values are filtered out and are not passed to the guardian.
Each assignment invokes Largest's target expression (line 5). This
expression computes a new value for the guardian, namely, the largest
value so far assigned to it. The value of a program containing guardians
is a tuple of the guardians' final values; in this case, there is only one
guardian, so a single value is returned.

Because guardians may have different values if they are evaluated at
different times, it is necessary to permit lazy evaluation of actual parameters that are expressions involving guardians. Post allows parameters to be passed in value mode (the default) or lazy value mode.

4.5 Speculative Computation

Speculative computation can be terminated by a combination of program-defined labels and an explicit **terminate** statement. Any expression may be labeled, and the value resulting from that expression
carries the label until it exits the scope in which the label is declared.
An individual value may carry many labels, since it may be composed of
many components, each of which may acquire multiple labels in different computations. Figure 6.18 is an example of labeling.

Figure 6.18

```
function ReportEvens{x,}*;                                    1
        type x : int;                                         2
        label Even;                                           3
        function AddLabel{y};                                 4
            type y : int                                      5
            in                                                6
                if (y mod 2) = 0 then                         7
                        tag y with Even                       8
                else                                          9
                        y                                    10
                end;                                         11
        end; -- AddLabel                                     12
        in [ AddLabel(x) haslabel Even ] x;                  13
end; -- ReportEvens                                          14
```

This program returns only the even elements of the input stream. Add-
Label labels its parameter if the parameter is even (line 8). The body of
ReportEvens in line 12 checks to see if its parameter, passed through
AddLabel, is labeled. If so, the parameter is returned; otherwise, the
value nil is returned (and then removed from the resulting stream).

If the program chooses to delete all tokens that have a particular label, any computation they are involved in is thereby terminated. Figure 6.19 demonstrates termination.

Figure 6.19

```
function SomeFactor{x,}*;                              1
    type x : int;                                     2
    guardian Factor{y};                               3
        type y : int                                  4
        in terminate y                                5
    end; -- Factor                                    6
    in Factor := if (N mod x)=0 then x end;           7
end; -- SomeFactor                                    8

SomeFactor(stream(2,99));                             9
```

The program returns the first factor of N assigned to the guardian Factor; it may return different values for different runs. For each input value, line 7 reports a factor, if any, to the guardian. The guardian Factor executes a **terminate** statement and returns the value y (line 5). The **terminate** statement does not specify a label in this case; all computation in the current scope (which is implicitly given a scope label) is canceled. There is also a syntax (not shown in this example) for specifying a program-defined label to control termination.

5 ◆ FINAL COMMENTS

Val and Sisal look, at first glance, like ordinary imperative languages. What makes them dataflow languages is that they are functional, so that speculative evaluation is possible, and they provide for explicitly concurrent loop executions.

Post was developed in reaction to this imperative appearance. It tries to give the programmer a feeling of labeled tokens being routed on arcs. The **terminate** statement only makes sense in such a context, for example. Although Post is a worthy attempt to mirror dataflow architectures better than Val or Sisal, the result is not particularly readable. Lack of clarity, in the sense introduced in Chapter 1, is its major weakness.

In a sense, all these languages are failures, because dataflow computing never became popular. Very few dataflow computers were ever built, and interest in this field has mostly subsided. Still, it is instructive to see how architectural design and programming language design influence each other. Not only did dataflow architecture lead to new languages, but those languages dictated enhancements to the architecture (such as multiple-field label stacks on tokens). A similar interplay is now taking place between architecture and languages as massively parallel and distributed computers are becoming available. That is the subject of Chapter 7.

Dataflow has had some successes. Optimizing compilers for vector machines build dataflow graphs in order to schedule computations effectively. The graphs indicate what dependencies constrain the order of evaluation.

From one point of view, you could say that dataflow has been quite successful and is widely used. Spreadsheets incorporate a form of data-driven computation to update values that depend on other values that may have changed. The internal representation of a spreadsheet is very like a dataflow graph. Strangely, the languages used in spreadsheet programming are quite different from any of the languages described here. First, they are not linear; that is, they are not organized as a text with a start, an ordered set of commands, and an end. Instead, each cell of a spreadsheet (typically, a two-dimensional grid of cells) is separately "programmed." For a cell acting as a leaf in the dataflow graph, the program indicates the value of that cell. For a cell acting as a computation node, the program indicates how to recompute the value of that cell based on the values of other cells. These other cells can be named explicitly, but accumulation operators such as summation and averaging can also specify a set of cells (generally, a contiguous one-dimensional subset). This organization is reminiscent of declarative programming (the subject of Chapter 8), in which there is no necessary order to the pieces that together make up a program.

A second difference in spreadsheet programming is that the user can often control to what extent computation is speculative. This control is specified as the number of times to reevaluate each computational cell when one of its inputs changes. Zero means do not update; an infinite value means to reevaluate until values do not change. In other words, the binding of evaluation strategies, which is usually done at language-design time, and only occasionally at compile time, can be deferred until runtime.

EXERCISES

Review Exercises

6.1   Draw a dataflow graph for the code of Figure 6.20.

Figure 6.20

```
(A + B) * (A + B + C)
```

6.2   Draw a dataflow graph for the code of Figure 6.21.

Figure 6.21

```
A := 0;                                    1
while A < 10 do                            2
      A := A + 3;                          3
end;                                       4
```

6.3   How do nondataflow languages allow the programmer to specify evaluation strategy?

Challenge Exercises

6.4   Draw a dataflow graph for the code of Figure 6.22.

Figure 6.22

```
procedure Orbit(A : integer) : integer;       1
begin                                          2
    if A = 1 then                              3
        return 1;                              4
    elsif even(A) then                         5
        return Orbit(A/2);                     6
    else                                       7
        return Orbit(3*A+1);                   8
    end;                                       9
end;                                          10
```

6.5   In Figure 6.15 (page 209), which version of > is meant on line 3? That is, does **eos** act as the minimal or maximal element?

6.6   In Figure 6.18 (page 211), what would be the effect of changing line 13 as follows?

```
in [ AddLabel(x) haslabel Even] AddLabel(x)
```

6.7 Modify Figure 6.19 (page 212) so that speculative computation is not terminated, but the first factor found is still returned.

6.8 In spreadsheets, how can reevaluating more than once have a different effect from evaluating only once?

Chapter 7

Concurrent Programming

Architectural advances of recent years, coupled with the growing availability of networked computers, have led to a new style of computing, called **concurrent programming**, that allows multiple computations to occur simultaneously in cooperation with each other. Many people distinguish two classes of concurrent programming: **Distributed programming** refers to computations that do not share a common memory, and **parallel programming** refers to computations that share a common memory. This distinction is not always helpful, since it is possible to implement a distributed computation on a shared-memory computer, and to implement a parallel computation on a distributed-memory computer. It is up to the compiler and operating system to implement on the underlying architecture whatever concurrency style the programming language promotes. Terminology is less standard in the area of concurrent programming than elsewhere, so I will be somewhat arbitrary, but consistent, in my nomenclature.

A **thread** is a sequential computation that may interact with other simultaneous computations. A program that depends on a particular thread reaching some point in computation before another thread continues must make that dependency explicit; it is erroneous to assume anything about relative speeds of execution. The reason for this rule is that the language does not usually have much control over execution speeds. Individual threads may be implemented by time-sharing a single CPU, and the scheduler may be outside the control of the language (in the operating system). If threads are on different CPUs, the CPUs may have different speeds or may have other work that renders them slow in an unpredictable way. The communication expense for cooperation among threads may be unpredictable. Threads might be dynamically migrated from one CPU to another to improve performance, but with a temporary delay.

The connection between programming languages and operating systems is especially close in the area of concurrent programming. First, threads are sometimes supported by the underlying operating system, so the language implementation needs to make use of those facilities, and the language designer may choose to present or to omit features, depending on the operating system and what it can do. For example, a thread can be modeled by a Unix process. Generally, Unix processes cannot share memory. However, some versions of Unix, such as Solaris, offer threads within a single address space; these threads do share memory. Second, operating systems themselves are often multithreaded; the language design issues in this chapter are often identical with operating-system design issues.

1 ◆ STARTING MULTIPLE THREADS

Syntax for starting multiple computations tends to be straightforward. In Modula (I mean original Modula [Wirth 77], not Modula-2), a thread is started by invoking a procedurelike object; when the "procedure" returns, the thread disappears. Meanwhile, the computation that started the thread continues executing. The new thread may itself create other threads by invoking them. Figure 7.1 shows a program that merge-sorts an array by recursively creating threads.

Figure 7.1

```
type                                                            1
    DataArray = array whatever of integer;                      2

thread MergeSort(                                               3
    reference Tangled : DataArray;                             4
    value LowIndex, HighIndex : integer);                      5
variable                                                       6
    MidPoint : integer := (LowIndex + HighIndex) div 2;        7
begin                                                          8
    if LowIndex + 1 < HighIndex then -- worth sorting          9
        MergeSort(Tangled, LowIndex, MidPoint);               10
        MergeSort(Tangled, MidPoint+1, HighIndex);            11
        Merge(Tangled, 1, MidPoint, MidPoint+1,               12
            HighIndex);                                       13
    end; -- worth sorting                                     14
end; -- MergeSort                                             15
```

MergeSort is declared in line 3 as a **thread**, not a **procedure**. All invocations of MergeSort, including the recursive ones on lines 10 and 11, create new threads running instances of MergeSort that work independently of the main program. Unfortunately, MergeSort fails to wait for its children to finish and rushes ahead to line 12, merging the two halves of the array before they are properly sorted. You will soon see mechanisms for synchronization that will let me fix this bug.

Each thread gets its own stack. Variables declared locally to a thread are like local variables in a procedure; each thread gets its own local variables. Likewise, any procedures called from a thread (such as `Merge`, called in line 12) get new activation records on the thread's stack. However, variables that are outside the scope of the thread are shared among all threads in which they are visible by normal scope rules. That is, the static chain in a thread's stack eventually points outside of the private stack of the thread into shared stack. (Sometimes this arrangement is called a **cactus stack**, since the stacks resemble the branches on a saguaro or cholla cactus.)

Some languages let threads be started by a **cobegin** statement. All the statements within the **cobegin** are started as separate threads. This construct includes an implicit synchronization step: The **cobegin** does not complete until each of its children has completed. I could fix the `MergeSort` program by surrounding lines 10 and 11 with **cobegin** and making `MergeSort` an ordinary procedure.

Some languages, like Modula-3, present a fairly low-level view of threads. A thread is started by a call to a `fork` procedure, which returns a thread identifier that can be used later for synchronization. Fork takes a procedure parameter that tells it what the thread should do.[1] Usually, programming languages restrict the parameter to `fork` to be a global procedure, so that cactus stacks are not needed.

Other languages, like Ada, present a much higher-level view of threads. Each thread runs in a module, exporting procedures that may be called by other threads and importing types, procedures, and shared variables. If a block contains a thread declaration, the thread is started when its declaration is elaborated. The block does not complete until all threads started in it have finished.

2 ⬩ COOPERATION BY MEANS OF SHARED VARIABLES

The `MergeSort` example shows that threads sometimes need to wait for each other. We say that a waiting thread is **blocked**. Generally, there are two reasons why threads need to block. First, they may be using variables that are shared with other threads, and they need to take turns. Taking turns is often called **mutual exclusion**, because while one thread is executing instructions that deal with the shared variables, all other threads must be excluded from such instructions. Second, they may need to wait for some operation to complete in some other thread before they may reasonably do their own work. We can explain the

---

[1] In Modula-3, the parameter is an object of a particular class that provides a method called `apply`.

MergeSort example by either reason. First, the variables in the Tangled array are shared between parents and children. Second, it makes no sense to merge the two halves of Tangled until they have been sorted.

2.1 Join

The simplest form of synchronization is to block until another thread completes. Such blocking is achieved by the **join** statement, which specifies which thread is to be awaited. The thread that invokes **join** is blocked until that thread has completed. Some languages, such as Modula-3, make **join** an expression that evaluates to the value returned by the thread at the time it terminates. **Cobegin** implicitly invokes **join** at the end of the compound statement for each thread started by that statement.

2.2 Semaphores

The heart of most synchronization methods is the **semaphore**. Its implementation (often hidden from the programmer) is shown in Figure 7.2.

Figure 7.2

```
type                                                        1
    Semaphore =                                             2
        record -- fields initialized as shown               3
                Value : integer := 1;                       4
                Waiters : queue of thread := empty;         5
        end;                                                6
```

Semaphores have two operations, which are invoked by statements. (The operations can be presented as procedure calls instead.) I call the first **down** (sometimes people call it **P**, **wait**, or **acquire**). The second operation is **up** (also called **V**, **signal**, or **release**):

* **down** S decrements S.Value (line 4). It then blocks the caller, saving its identity in S.Waiters, if Value is now negative.
* **up** S increments S.Value. It unblocks the first waiting thread in S.Waiters if Value is now nonpositive.

Both these operations are **indivisible**, that is, they complete in a thread instantaneously so far as other threads are concerned. Therefore, only one thread at a time can either **up** or **down** a particular semaphore at a time.

Semaphores can be used to implement mutual exclusion. All regions that use the same shared variables are associated with a particular semaphore, initialized with Value = 1. A thread that wishes to enter a region **down**s the associated semaphore. It has now achieved mutual exclusion by acquiring an exclusive lock. When the thread exits the region, it **up**s the same semaphore, releasing the lock. The first thread to try to enter its region succeeds. Another thread that tries to enter while the first is still in its region will be blocked. When the first thread leaves the region, the second thread is unblocked. Value is always either 0 or 1 (if only two threads are competing). For this reason, semaphores used for mutual exclusion are often called **binary semaphores**.

Besides mutual exclusion, semaphores can also help achieve more complex synchronization. If thread T needs to wait until thread S accomplishes some goal, they can share a semaphore initialized with Value = 0. When S accomplishes its goal, it **up**s the semaphore. When T reaches the place where it must wait, it **down**s the same semaphore. No matter which one reaches the semaphore call first, T will not proceed until S has accomplished its goal.

2.3 Mutexes

Some languages, such as Modula-3, predeclare a **mutex** type that is implemented by binary semaphores. The **lock** statement surrounds any statements that must exclude other threads, as shown in Figure 7.3.

Figure 7.3

```
variable                             1
    A, B : integer;                  2
    AMutex, BMutex : mutex;          3

procedure Modify();                  4
begin                                5
    lock AMutex do                   6
        A := A + 1;                  7
    end;                             8
    lock BMutex do                   9
        B := B + 1;                  10
    end;                             11
    lock AMutex, BMutex do           12
        A := A + B;                  13
        B := A;                      14
    end;                             15
end; -- Modify                       16
```

Variable A is protected by mutex AMutex, and B is protected by BMutex. The **lock** statement (as in line 6) is equivalent to a **down** operation at the start and an **up** operation at the end. Several threads may simultaneously execute in Modify. However, a thread executing line 7 prevents any other thread from executing any of lines 7, 13, and 14. It is possible for one thread to be at line 7 and another at line 10. I lock lines 7 and 10 because on many machines, incrementing requires several instructions, and if two threads execute those instructions at about the same time, the variable might get incremented only once instead of twice. I lock lines 13 and 14 together to make sure that no thread can intervene after line 13 and before line 14 to modify A. The multiple lock in line 12 first locks AMutex, then BMutex. The order is important to prevent deadlocks, as I will describe later.

2.4 Conditional Critical Regions

The Edison language has a way to program synchronization that is more expressive than mutexes but less error-prone than bare semaphores [Brinch Hansen 80]. As I mentioned before, synchronization in general is the desire to block an action until a particular condition becomes true.

A standard example that displays the need for synchronization is the **bounded buffer**, which is an array that is filled by producer threads and emptied by consumer threads. All producers and consumers must mutually exclude each other while they are inspecting and modifying the variables that make up the bounded buffer. In addition, when the buffer is full, producers should block instead of **busy waiting**, which is repeatedly testing to see if the buffer has room. Likewise, when the buffer is empty, consumers should block. Figure 7.4 shows how to code this application with conditional critical regions.

Figure 7.4

```
constant                                                  1
    Size = 10; -- capacity of the buffer                  2
type                                                      3
    Datum = ... -- contents of the buffer                 4
variable                                                  5
    Buffer : array 0..Size-1 of Datum;                    6
    InCount, OutCount : integer := 0;                     7

procedure PutBuffer(value What : Datum);                  8
begin                                                     9
    region Buffer, InCount, OutCount                      10
    await InCount - OutCount < Size do                    11
        Buffer[InCount mod Size] := What;                 12
        InCount := InCount + 1;                           13
    end; -- region                                        14
end -- PutBuffer;                                         15
```

```
procedure GetBuffer(result Answer : Datum);                16
begin                                                      17
    region Buffer, InCount, OutCount                       18
    await InCount - OutCount > 0 do                        19
        Answer := Buffer[OutCount mod Size];               20
        OutCount := OutCount + 1;                          21
    end; -- region                                         22
end GetBuffer;                                             23
```

The **region** statements starting in lines 10 and 18 are like **lock** statements, except that they name variables to be protected, not mutexes, and they have an **await** component. The compiler can check that shared variables are only accessed within **region** statements, and it can invent appropriate mutexes. The awaited condition is checked while the corresponding mutexes are held. If the condition is false, the mutexes are released and the thread is blocked (on an implicit semaphore). Whenever a thread exits from a region, all threads in conflicting regions (those that use some of the same shared variables) that are blocked for conditions are unblocked, regain their mutexes, and test their conditions again. This repeated rechecking of conditions can be a major performance problem.

2.5 Monitors

One objection to using conditional critical regions is the cost of checking conditions, which must occur whenever a thread leaves a region. A second objection is that code that modifies shared data may be scattered throughout a program. The **monitor** construct, found in Modula and Mesa, was invented to address both issues [Hoare 74; Lampson 80]. It acts both as a data-abstraction device (providing modularity) and a synchronization device.

Monitors introduce a new name scope that contains shared data and the procedures that are allowed to access the data. Procedures exported from the monitor are mutually exclusive; that is, only one thread may execute an exported procedure from a particular monitor at a time.

The most straightforward use of monitors is to package all routines that use a set of shared data (represented by a collection of variables) into a single monitor. All accesses to those variables will be forced to use exported procedures, because the variables themselves are hidden from the outside world. For example, I can implement a shared counter that records the number of times some interesting event has happened, as in Figure 7.5.

Figure 7.5

```
monitor Counter;                                              1
    export RaiseCount, ReadCount;                             2
    variable Count : integer := 0;                            3

    procedure RaiseCount();                                   4
    begin                                                     5
        Count := Count + 1;                                   6
    end; -- RaiseCount;                                       7

    procedure ReadCount() : integer;                          8
    begin                                                     9
        return Count                                         10
    end; -- ReadCount;                                       11

end; -- Counter                                              12
```

One way to picture the monitor is shown in Figure 7.5, which shows the monitor as a floor plan of a building. When a thread tries to invoke an exported procedure, it enters through the entrance queue, where it is blocked until the exported procedure is free of any thread. Door 1 is unlocked only if there is no thread in the main room. Door 2 is always unlocked; when it is opened to let a thread out, door 1 is unlocked.

Figure 7.6   A simple monitor

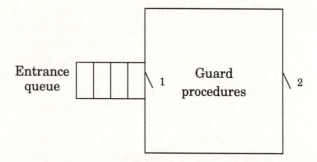

It is not hard to implement this kind of monitor using only binary semaphores. Since the programmer does not need to remember the **up** and **down** operations, monitors are easier and safer to use than bare semaphores. In addition, all the code that can affect shared variables is packaged in one place, so it is easier to check that the variables are properly used.

In order to program a bounded buffer, I also need a way to have threads wait if conditions are not right. Instead of Boolean expressions, monitors introduce the predeclared condition data type. The operations on conditions are **wait**, **signal**, and **broadcast**. Using condition variables is more clumsy than programming Boolean expressions in conditional critical regions, because the programmer must remember which variable is associated with each situation and must also remember to signal the conditions when the time is right. A bounded buffer can be programmed as in Figure 7.7.

Figure 7.7

```
monitor BoundedBuffer;                                          1

    export GetBuffer, PutBuffer;                                2

    constant                                                    3
        Size = 10; -- capacity of the buffer                    4
    type                                                        5
        Datum = ... -- contents of the buffer                   6
    variable                                                    7
        Buffer : array 0:Size-1 of Datum;                       8
        InCount, OutCount : integer := 0;                       9
        NotEmpty, NotFull : condition;                          10

    procedure PutBuffer(value What : Datum);                    11
    begin                                                       12
        if InCount - OutCount = Size then                       13
            wait NotFull;                                       14
        end;                                                    15
        Buffer[InCount mod Size] := What;                       16
        InCount := InCount + 1;                                 17
        signal NotEmpty ;                                       18
    end; -- PutBuffer;                                          19

    procedure GetBuffer(result Answer : Datum);                 20
    begin                                                       21
        if InCount - OutCount = 0 then                          22
            wait NotEmpty;                                       23
        end;                                                    24
        Answer := Buffer[OutCount mod Size];                    25
        OutCount := OutCount + 1;                               26
        signal NotFull ;                                        27
    end; -- GetBuffer;                                          28
end; -- BoundedBuffer;                                          29
```

The situations in which the buffer is not full or not empty are indicated by the condition variables NotFull and NotEmpty. Consumers call Get-Buffer (line 20), which checks to see if the buffer is empty. If so, it waits on NotEmpty (line 23). This operation releases mutual exclusion and blocks the thread. It will remain blocked until some other thread **sig-nal**s NotEmpty. Producers do exactly that in line 18. **Signal** has no ef-fect on a condition for which no thread is waiting, unlike **up** on a semaphore. The consumer can be sure when it arrives at line 25 that the buffer is not empty, because either it was not empty when the consumer called `GetBuffer`, and this routine excludes any other threads from the monitor, or it was empty, but some producer has signaled `NotEmpty`, and the consumer has been awakened and regained exclusion.

This discussion raises some troubling questions. Exactly when does the blocked consumer continue? If immediately, then there may be two threads in the monitor at once, and mutual exclusion is ruined. If later, then by the time the consumer continues, some other consumer may already have taken the last datum, and the assumption on line 25 that the buffer is not empty is wrong. If several consumers are waiting at the same time, which one or ones are unblocked by a signal?

The definitions of monitors in the literature disagree on the answers to these questions.

Figure 7.8 Monitors with conditions

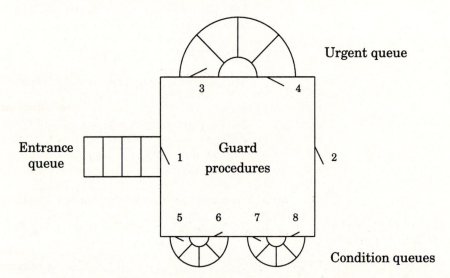

Figure 7.8 expands Figure 7.6 (page 224) to show the effect of conditions. Every condition has a condition queue (shown on the bottom of the monitor), and there is one urgent queue (shown at the top of the monitor). All queues are ordered first in, first out. Threads that are blocked are placed in these queues according to the following rules:

1. New threads wait in the entrance queue. A new thread may enter through door 1 if no thread is currently in the central region.
2. If a thread leaves the central region through door 2 (the exit), one thread is allowed in through door 4 (from the urgent queue) if there is one waiting there. If not, one thread is allowed through door 1 (from the entrance queue) if there is one waiting there.
3. A thread that executes **wait** enters the door to the appropriate condition queue (for example, 5 or 7).

4. When a thread executes **signal**, the signaled condition queue is inspected. If some thread is waiting in that queue, the signaler enters the urgent queue (door 3), and one waiter is allowed into the central region (door 6 or 8). If no thread is waiting in that queue, the signaler proceeds without leaving the central region. The signal is ignored.

These rules assure that a waiting consumer is unblocked immediately when a producer signals NotEmpty and that the producer is blocked in the urgent queue until the consumer has taken the datum.

Programmers have noticed that **signal** is almost always the last operation performed in an exported procedure. You can see this behavior in my producer-consumer code (lines 18 and 27). The rules will often make the signaler wait in the urgent queue and then return to the central region (acquiring exclusion) just to get out of the monitor altogether (releasing exclusion). These extra waits ands locks are inefficient. If **signal** is not the last operation, the signaler can't assume that the situation of shared variables is unchanged across **signal**. While it was in the urgent queue, the thread that was unblocked is likely to have modified the variables. The result is that **signal** is error-prone. For these reasons, some languages require that **signal** must be the last operation of an exported procedure and must cause the signaling thread to leave the monitor. Then the implementation doesn't need an urgent queue, and signalers never make invalid assumptions about shared data. However, this restriction makes monitors less expressive. (Such monitors are strictly less powerful in a theoretical sense.)

A related suggestion is to use **broadcast** instead of **signal**. **Broadcast** releases all the members of the given condition queue. Since they can't all be allowed into the central region at once, most are placed in the urgent queue. A released thread can no longer assume that the condition it has awaited is still met by the time it resumes. Programs written with **broadcast** usually replace the **if** statement in lines 13 and 22 of Figure 7.7 with a **while** loop to retest the condition after **wait** returns.

Proper use of monitors follows the guideline that no thread should take too long in the central region. It shouldn't take too long for a thread that is waiting in the entrance queue to get into the monitor and access the shared variables. Any lengthy operation should relax exclusion by entering a condition queue or by doing its work outside the monitor. A fascinating violation of this guideline arises if the thread in an exported procedure makes a call on a procedure exported by another monitor. Under the rules, this thread is still considered to be in the first monitor, preventing any other thread from entering. However, it may take a long time before it returns because it may be forced to wait in the second monitor in a condition queue. (By the guideline, it shouldn't have to wait very long in either the entrance queue or the urgent queue.) This delay in returning violates the guideline with respect to the first monitor. The situation can even lead to deadlock if the condition it awaits in the second monitor can be signaled only by a thread that is currently waiting patiently to enter the first monitor.

Several solutions have been proposed to this **nested-monitor** problem [Haddon 77]:

1.   Disallow nested monitor calls.
2.   Warn the programmer, but allow the bad situation to develop. That is, nested monitor calls maintain exclusion on the old monitor while in the new one.
3.   Release exclusion on the old monitor and enforce it only on the new one. When the thread is ready to return, it must wait in the urgent queue of the first monitor until it can once again achieve exclusive use of the central region.
4.   Let the programmer decide whether the nested call should maintain exclusion in the old monitor or not. By default, method 2 is used. The programmer can say **duckout** to release exclusion while still in the monitor and **duckin** to achieve exclusion again. These calls can bracket a nested call to simulate method 3.

Although monitors represent an important advance over raw semaphores, they do have significant problems. Monitors have been criticized for not providing any control over how the queues are ordered. The policy of treating queues in first-in, first-out order is not always appropriate. For example, several threads simultaneously in the urgent queue are like nested interrupts, which are usually released in first-in, last-out (stack) order. Similarly, different waiters in a condition queue may have different priorities, which could be taken into account in selecting an order. Some people prefer a more general mechanism for inspecting and reordering the various queues.

Monitors also display unexpected complexity with respect to nested calls. It is not easy to describe the semantics of **wait** and **signal** without resorting to pictures like Figure 7.8. Complexity is also introduced by the artificial use of condition variables. The programmer is more likely to understand the underlying condition (like InCount − OutCount > 0) than to represent that condition properly by judicious use of NotEmpty, including **signal** at the appropriate places.

Another objection to monitors comes from their data-abstraction ability. If I have several bounded buffers to implement, I would be tempted to build only one monitor and to have the PutBuffer and GetBuffer procedures take a parameter that describes which buffer is to be manipulated. This solution has two drawbacks. One is that the buffer has an existence outside the monitor and so might be inadvertently modified by a nonmonitor procedure. Ada addresses this limitation by providing for variables to be exported from modules in an opaque fashion, so that they cannot be manipulated outside the module. The other drawback is that using only one monitor is too conservative. Every manipulation of one buffer now excludes operations on all other buffers, because mutual exclusion is governed by which monitor is entered, not by which data structure is accessed. What we want is a monitor class that can be instantiated once for each separate buffer.

Mesa addresses the problem of overconservatism in two different ways. A monitor instance can be constructed dynamically for each buffer. However, there is a large space and time penalty for building monitor instances. Instead, the programmer may place the data (the buffer) in a monitored record, which is passed as a parameter to every exported procedure. The monitor declaration indicates that it uses a mutex in that record instead of its own mutex for mutual exclusion among threads executing exported procedures. For example, the bounded buffer in Mesa might be programmed as shown in Figure 7.9.

Figure 7.9

```
constant                                                     1
    Size = 10; -- capacity of the buffer                     2
type                                                         3
    Datum = ... -- contents of a buffer                      4
    BufferType :                                             5
        monitored record                                     6
            Buffer : array 0:Size-1 of Datum;                7
            InCount, OutCount : integer := 0;                8
            NotEmpty, NotFull : condition;                   9
        end;                                                10
    BufferPtrType : pointer to BufferType;                  11

monitor BoundedBuffer;                                      12
    locks BufferPtr^ using BufferPtr : BufferPtrType;       13
    export GetBuffer, PutBuffer;                            14

    procedure PutBuffer(                                    15
        value What : Datum;                                16
        value BufferPtr : BufferPtrType);                  17
    begin                                                  18
        if BufferPtr^.InCount-BufferPtr^.OutCount = Size   19
        then                                               20
            wait BufferPtr^.NotFull;                       21
        end;                                               22
        BufferPtr^.Buffer[BufferPtr^.InCount mod Size]     23
            := What;                                       24
        BufferPtr^.InCount := BufferPtr^.InCount + 1;      25
        signal BufferPtr^.NotEmpty ;                       26
    end; -- PutBuffer;                                     27
```

```
      procedure GetBuffer                                     28
          (result Answer : Datum;                            29
          value BufferPtr : BufferPtrType);                  30
      begin                                                   31
          if BufferPtr^.InCount - BufferPtr^.OutCount = 0    32
          then                                                33
              wait BufferPtr^.NotEmpty;                      34
          end;                                                35
          Answer := BufferPtr^.Buffer                        36
              [BufferPtr^.OutCount mod Size];                37
          BufferPtr^.OutCount := BufferPtr^.OutCount + 1;    38
          signal BufferPtr^.NotFull ;                        39
      end; -- GetBuffer;                                      40
  end; -- BoundedBuffer;                                      41
```

The buffer type (lines 5–10) implicitly contains a mutex. BoundedBuffer is written as a monitor, which means it implicitly acquires and releases that mutex on entrance and exit from exported procedures and when waiting for conditions. The monitor specifies that it locks BufferPtr^, which must be a parameter to every exported procedure. Unfortunately, if an exported procedure modifies its parameter BufferPtr, chaos can ensue, since the wrong mutex will then be accessed.

Modula-3 goes farther in solving the problem of overconservatism in monitors. It gives up on monitors entirely, providing only the building blocks out of which the programmer can build the necessary structures. That is, Modula-3 has conditions and mutexes as ordinary data types. The **wait** statement specifies both a condition and a mutex. As the thread begins to wait, it releases the mutex. When the thread is awakened by either **signal** or **broadcast**, it regains the mutex. Exported procedures and condition variables may be packaged into modules (to make monitors), data structures (so that each bounded buffer is independently exclusive), or classes (to allow monitors to be instantiated any number of times).

A serious objection to monitors is related to the guideline that exclusion should not be in force for very long. The problem is that shared data might be needed for a very long time. This is exactly the situation in the **readers-writers problem**, in which some threads (the readers) need to read shared data, and others (the writers) need to write those data. Writers must exclude readers and all other writers. Readers must exclude only writers. Reading and writing are time-consuming operations, but they always finish eventually. If we export Read and Write from the monitor, two readers cannot execute at the same time, which is too restrictive. Therefore, Read must not be a monitor procedure; it must be external to the monitor. Proper use of Read would call the exported procedures StartRead and EndRead around calls to Read, but there is no assurance that a programmer will follow these rules. Monitors can therefore fail to protect shared data adequately.

2.6 Crowd Monitors

Crowd monitors are a nice extension to monitors that address this last problem [Horn 77]. Crowd monitors distinguish exclusive procedures from ordinary procedures within the monitor. Only exclusive procedures are mutually exclusive. Ordinary procedures may be invoked only by activities that have permission to do so; this permission is dynamically granted and revoked by exclusive procedures. A skeleton of the crowd-monitor solution to the readers-writers problem appears in Figure 7.10.

Figure 7.10

```
crowd monitor ReadWrite;                                          1

    export StartRead, EndRead, Read, StartWrite,                  2
        EndWrite, Write;                                          3

    variable                                                      4
        Readers : crowd Read;                                     5
        Writers : crowd Read, Write;                              6

    exclusive procedure StartRead();                              7
        ... -- block the caller until reading is safe             8
        enter Readers;                                            9
        ...                                                      10

    exclusive procedure EndRead();                               11
        ...                                                      12
        leave Readers;                                           13
        ... -- bookkeeping, maybe signal a waiting writer        14

    exclusive procedure StartWrite();                            15
        ... -- block the caller until writing is safe            16
        enter Writers;                                           17
        ...                                                      18

    exclusive procedure EndWrite();                              19
        ...                                                      20
        leave Writers;                                           21
        ... -- bookkeeping, maybe signal waiter                  22

    procedure Read(...);                                         23
        ... -- actually read from the shared data                24
```

```
    procedure Write(...);                                  25
    ... -- actually modify the shared data                 26

end; -- ReadWrite                                          27
```

In lines 5 and 6, I declare two crowds called Readers and Writers. Threads can dynamically enter and leave these crowds. Any member of Readers may access the Read procedure (lines 23–24), and any member of Writers may access both the Read and the Write procedure (lines 25–26). Threads initially belong to no crowds. The exclusive procedures decide when it is appropriate for a thread to enter or leave a crowd. They may use conditions to wait for the right situation. When the exclusive procedure decides to let a reader proceed, it executes **enter** for the Readers crowd (line 9). Similarly, a guard can let a writer enter the Writers crowd (line 17). Although any thread may call Read and Write, because they are exported from the monitor, a runtime check prevents threads from calling them if the threads are not in appropriate crowds. A member only of Readers may not call Write, but, a member of Writers may call either Read or Write, since both are specified in the definition of Writers (line 6).

2.7 Event Counts and Sequencers

Mutual exclusion is not always desirable because it limits concurrency. It is also unnecessary in some cases on physically distributed computers. In fact, if one hasn't yet implemented mutual exclusion, the method discussed here can be used to build semaphores to provide mutual exclusion, too [Reed 79]. Those semaphores will even allow simultaneous **down** operations on several semaphores.

The first type needed is the **event count**. An event count is implemented as a nondecreasing integer variable. It keeps a count of the number of events of interest to the program, such as the number of times a variable has been modified. Event counts have three operations:

1. **advance** E is used to signal the occurrence of events associated with event count E. It has the effect of incrementing E indivisibly.
2. **read** E is an expression that evaluates to the value of the event count E. If **read** returns some number n, then at least n **advance** operations must have happened. By the time this number is evaluated, the event count may have been advanced again a number of times.
3. **await** E **reaches** v waits for the event count E to have the value v. It blocks the calling thread until at least v **advance** operations have occurred. It is acceptable if more than v **advance** operations have

occurred when the thread is finally unblocked. This overshoot could result from very frequent **advance** operations.

These definitions allow both **await** and **read** to be concurrent with **advance**, since the programmer won't care if **read** gives a somewhat stale value or if **await** waits a trifle too long.

Figure 7.11 shows how to encode the bounded buffer using event counts. For the time being, I assume that there is only one producer and one consumer.

Figure 7.11

```
-- other declarations as before                           1
variable InEvents, OutEvents : eventcount := 0;           2

procedure PutBuffer(value What : Datum);                  3
begin                                                     4
    await OutEvents reaches InCount - Size;               5
    Buffer[InCount mod Size] := What;                     6
    advance InEvents;                                     7
    InCount := InCount + 1;                               8
end ; -- PutBuffer;                                       9

procedure GetBuffer(result Answer : Datum);              10
begin                                                    11
    await InEvents reaches OutCount;                     12
    Answer := Buffer[OutCount mod Size];                 13
    advance OutEvents;                                   14
    OutCount := OutCount + 1;                            15
end; -- GetBuffer;                                       16
```

There is no need to worry that the consumer and producer will simultaneously access the same cell in Buffer. The producer will wait until the consumer has taken the value from any cell before **await** in line 5 will allow it to proceed to refill it. Similarly, the consumer knows that when it accesses a cell of Buffer, the producer must have placed data there, or the **await** in line 12 would not have unblocked. Even if both **advance** operations (lines 7 and 14) happen at the same time, there is no problem, because they deal with different event counts. The bounded buffer may be used simultaneously by both threads because it guarantees that the very same datum will never be touched by both at once. I could have omitted InCount and OutCount, replacing them with **read** InEvents and **read** OutEvents, respectively, but since they are used for indices into Buffer, and **read** can return a stale value, I used separate variables to make sure the right index was always computed.

The second data type for synchronization is the **sequencer**, which assigns an arbitrary order to unordered events. A sequencer is implemented as a nondecreasing integer variable, and has only one operation: **ticket**.

- **ticket** S is an expression that first evaluates to the current value of the sequencer S and then increments S. This operation is indivisible.

Now I can implement a bounded buffer in which there are many producers. For simplicity, I will still have only one consumer. As before, consumption and production need not exclude each other. Multiple producers will take turns to make sure that they don't write into the same cell in Buffer. The new producer program is given in Figure 7.12.

Figure 7.12

```
variable ProducerTurn : sequencer := 0;                            1

procedure PutBuffer(value What : Datum);                           2
variable SequenceNumber : integer;                                 3
begin                                                              4
    SequenceNumber := ticket ProducerTurn;                         5
    await InEvents reaches SequenceNumber;                         6
        -- wait for turn                                           7
    await OutEvents reaches SequenceNumber - Size;                 8
        -- wait for Buffer                                         9
    Buffer[SequenceNumber mod Size] := What;                      10
    advance InEvents;                                             11
end ; -- PutBuffer;                                               12
```

Each producer must await its turn to produce. The **ticket** operator in line 5 orders active producers. There will be no wait in line 6 unless another producer has just grabbed an earlier ticket and has not yet arrived at line 11. The **await** in line 8 makes sure that the cell in Buffer that is about to be overwritten has been consumed. The **advance** in line 11 tells waiting consumers that this cell in Buffer may be consumed, and it tells waiting producers that this thread has finished its turn.

The **await** in line 6 might seem unnecessary. It's there to make sure that producers write cells of Buffer in order, so that consumers may assume that when InCount is advanced in line 11, the next cell of Buffer has new data. Unfortunately, one effect of this imposed sequential behavior on producers is that separate cells of Buffer cannot be written simultaneously. If the cells are large, producers may exclude each other for a long time.

2.8 Barriers

Some computations occur in phases, and threads that finish one phase must wait until all have finished until any may proceed to the next phase. The **barrier** type provides the necessary synchronization. It has one operation:

- **meet** B causes the thread to block on barrier B until all threads have executed a **meet** statement on B.

An example of barrier synchronization is a bottom-up version of Merge-Sort, shown in Figure 7.13.

Figure 7.13

```
constant UpperBound = ... -- size of array              1
type DataArray = array 0..UpperBound of integer;       2
variable                                                3
    Tangled : DataArray;                                4
    MergeBarrier : barrier UpperBound div 2;            5

thread MergeSort(Start : integer);                      6
variable Width : integer;                               7
begin                                                   8
    Width := 1;                                         9
    while Width < UpperBound+1 do -- a phase           10
        -- Sort Tangled[Start .. Start+2*Width-1]      11
        if Start mod Width = 0 -- participate          12
            Merge(Tangled, Start, Start+Width-1,       13
                  Start+Width, Start+2*Width-1);       14
        end;                                           15
        meet MergeBarrier; -- ends phase              16
        Width := 2 * Width; -- preparation for next phase 17
    end;                                               18
end; -- MergeSort                                      19

begin -- main                                          20
    for Start := 0 to UpperBound step 2 do            21
        MergeSort(Start); -- creates a thread         22
    end;                                               23
end; -- main                                           24
```

If UpperBound (line 1) is, say, 9, then line 22 starts five threads, each working on a different two-element section of Tangled. Each thread enters the first phase, sorting its own two-element section. Lines 13 and 14 sort that section, assuming that the two subsections are already sorted. Each thread waits for the phase to complete (line 16) before starting the next. MergeBarrier is declared in line 5 with a capacity equal to the number of threads. Threads that **meet** at the barrier wait until the full capacity of the barrier is reached. Only half the threads active in one phase need to participate in the next phase; they select themselves in line 12. Those that become inactive still participate in the barrier in future phases in order to permit the active ones to make progress.

Two-thread barriers can be implemented by shared variables and busy waiting or by two semaphores. Multithread barriers can be built by various combinations of two-thread barriers; there are also other ways to build them. In most implementations, when the barrier is first initialized, it needs to know exactly which threads will participate.

Some researchers have suggested that **meet** be split into two operations [Gupta 89]. The first, **arrive**, indicates that the thread has finished the previous phase. The second, **depart**, indicates that the thread is about to start the next phase. Between **arrive** and **depart**, the thread need not block if it has useful work to do. Threads are blocked at **depart** until all threads have **arrive**d. This suggestion can increase the effective parallelism of a program if there is significant work that can be done between phases. In the MergeSort example, I could place **arrive** at line 16 and **depart** after line 17. Separating **arrive** from **depart**, however, can lead to programming errors in which the operations fail to balance. I am tempted to place **depart** after line 11, but then threads would **depart** before **arrive**ing.

2.9 Performance Issues

Concurrent programs may fail not only because they contain programming errors that lead to incorrect results, but also because they make no progress due to blocking. They may also run more slowly than necessary because of poor programming.

I have already mentioned that **signal** usually occurs as the last operation in a monitor's exported procedure. In Modula-3, where the exported procedure must explicitly acquire a mutex, it is advisable to release the mutex before **signal**ing. Otherwise, the awakened thread will try to acquire the mutex and immediately block again. The same problem occurs with **broadcast**, but now many threads will try to acquire the mutex, and only one will succeed. It may be preferable (although clumsier) to use **signal** and to have each awakened thread **signal** the next one.

Starvation is a form of unfairness in which a thread fails to make progress, even though other threads are executing, because of scheduling decisions. Although starvation can be the fault of the thread scheduler, it is more often a programming error. For example, a poorly programmed solution to the readers-writers problem will block writers so long as there are any readers. New readers can come and go, but so long as there are any readers, all writers starve. The solution to starvation is to prevent new threads from acquiring mutexes until old threads have completed. In the readers-writers case, new readers can be kept out if any writers are waiting.

Deadlock occurs when a group of threads is blocked waiting for resources (such as mutexes) held by other members of the group. For example, the code of Figure 7.14 will deadlock.

Figure 7.14

```
variable                                          1
    Mutex1, Mutex2 : mutex;                        2
    BarrierA : barrier;                            3

procedure ThreadA();                               4
begin                                              5
    lock Mutex1 do                                 6
        lock Mutex2 do                             7
            -- anything                            8
        end;                                       9
    end;                                          10
end; -- ThreadA                                   11

procedure ThreadB();                              12
begin                                             13
    lock Mutex2 do                                14
        lock Mutex1 do                            15
            -- anything                           16
        end;                                      17
    end;                                          18
end; -- ThreadB                                   19
```

ThreadA might reach line 7 just as ThreadB reaches line 15. Each will then try to lock a mutex held by the other. Neither can make any progress.

The standard and simplest way to avoid deadlock is always to acquire resources in the same order. If ThreadB would first lock Mutex1 and then Mutex2, then there is no schedule that will lead to deadlock between these threads. For this reason, languages that provide conditional critical regions implicitly sort the necessary mutexes and acquire them in a standard order. Of course, nested conditional critical regions can still deadlock.

Another way to deal with deadlock is to provide a way for **wait** statements to be interrupted. Modula-3 provides a version of **wait** that will unblock if an exception is raised in the thread. This exception can be raised by another thread by the **alert** statement. The **alert** statement also sets a flag in the alerted thread that it can inspect in case it is busy with a long computation and is not waiting on a condition.

3 ◆ TRANSACTIONS: ARGUS

The concept of acquiring exclusion over data structures is often extended to deal gracefully with failure. This behavior is especially important for programs that modify large shared databases. A **transaction** is a set of operations undertaken by a thread. Transactions have two important properties. First, these operations are indivisible when taken as a whole. From the point of view of other threads, either they have not started or they have all finished. Second, the transaction is **recoverable**; that is, it can either **commit**, in which case all modifications to shared data take effect, or it can **abort**, in which case none of its modifications takes effect. Because transactions are indivisible, threads cannot see modifications performed by other transactions that are still in progress.

For example, in an airline reservation database, a customer may wish to exchange a seat on a given flight for a seat on another flight. The program might give up the first seat and then reserve the second. If the second plane is full, it is necessary to get back the initial seat, which may already have been allocated to another passenger. If both actions (releasing the first seat and reserving the second) are part of a transaction, then the program can just abort when it fails to reserve the second seat. The first seat will still be reserved by the original customer.

Transactions can be nested. In order to increase concurrency, programs might want to start several threads as children of an initial thread. Each can enter its own subtransaction. If any child thread fails, its own data modifications are recovered, but the parent transaction can still proceed. Unrelated transactions do not see any data modifications until and unless the top-level transaction commits.

Argus provides programming-language support for nested transactions [Liskov 83a]. The statements comprising a transaction are the body of a **transaction** statement. Of course, a procedure may be called from inside a transaction, and the procedure may be recursive, so the lexical nature of transaction entry does not limit the number of transactions. If the transaction statements finish execution, the transaction commits. The statement **abort** causes the current transaction to fail.

Data that are shared among threads must be built out of recoverable types. Argus provides recoverable versions of primitive types, such as integers and arrays. Read and write locks are implicitly acquired when recoverable variables are accessed. (These locks are typically held until the transaction completes.) If a lock cannot be granted immediately because of conflicting locks held by other threads, the accessing thread is blocked. Deadlock is automatically detected and handled by aborting one or more transactions. It is also possible for a program to explicitly acquire a read or write lock and to avoid blocking if the lock is not currently grantable. Structured types can be made recoverable by providing access procedures that use mutual exclusion and ensure that exclusion is only released when the structure's value is internally consistent.

These facilities can be used to build, for example, a bounded buffer of integers for which GetBuffer does not necessarily get the oldest remaining data [Weihl 90], as in Figure 7.15.

Figure 7.15

```
module BoundedBuffer;                                    1

    export GetBuffer, PutBuffer;                         2

    type                                                 3
        Entry = recoverable -- choice type               4
                Valid : integer;                         5
                Invalid : void;                          6
            end;                                          7
    variable                                             8
        Buffer : array of Entry -- flexible;             9

    procedure PutBuffer(value What : integer);          10
    begin                                               11
        region Buffer do -- get exclusion               12
            Append(Buffer,                              13
                MakeRecoverable(Entry, Valid, What));   14
        end;                                            15
    end; -- PutBuffer;                                  16

    procedure GetBuffer(result Answer : integer);       17
    variable Item : Entry;                              18
    begin                                               19
        region Buffer do -- get exclusion               20
            loop -- iterate until success               21
                for Item in Buffer do                   22
                    tagcase Item of                     23
                        when writeable Valid(Answer)    24
                            => ChangeRecoverable         25
                                (Item, Invalid);         26
                            return;                      27
                            -- releases exclusion        28
                        end; -- writeable               29
                    end; -- tagcase                     30
                end; -- for Item                        31
```

```
                duckout; -- release exclusion        32
                sleep();                              33
                duckin; -- regain exclusion          34
            end; -- iterate until success            35
        end; -- mutual exclusion                     36
    end; -- GetBuffer;                               37

end; -- BoundedBuffer;                               38
```

Enqueued integers are kept in the flexible array Buffer (line 9). Both PutBuffer and GetBuffer acquire mutual exclusion over the array by using **region** statements. Each item in the array is a recoverable object, which is a choice type (lines 4–7). PutBuffer (lines 10–16) puts a new recoverable entry in Buffer with the appropriate initial value. I use Append to add to the end of a flexible array and MakeRecoverable to generate a new recoverable item with an initial value. GetBuffer searches the array for an item on which it can acquire a write lock and which is valid. I use a **for** loop (lines 22–31) to scan through the flexible array. The **tagcase** statement (lines 23–30) checks both the variant (I am interested only in Valid items) and whether a write lock can be achieved. For those items where the variant is wrong or a write lock cannot be achieved, the single branch of **tagcase** is not selected. For the first item where the variant is correct and the write lock can be achieved, GetBuffer stores the value in Answer (line 24), changes the value to Invalid (Lines 25–26), and returns, releasing exclusion. If it fails to find such an item, it releases exclusion, waits a while, then tries again (lines 32–34). Any value returned by GetBuffer is guaranteed to have been placed there by a transaction that is visible to the current one (that is, one that has committed or is an ancestor of the current one) and not to have been removed by any active or committed transaction. Invalid initial elements of the buffer can be removed by a separate thread that repeatedly enters a top-level transaction and removes elements that are writeable and invalid.

This example shows a few drawbacks to the way Argus deals with recoverable types. Given the Argus facilities, it appears that the algorithm shown is the most efficient that can be achieved. However, GetQueue is inefficient, because it needs to glance at all initial buffer entries, even if they are in use by other transactions. It uses busy waiting in case it cannot find anything at the moment. Programmers have no control over when commit and abort actually make their changes, so it is possible for a consumer to get several items produced by the same producer out of order. Attempts to enhance the language by adding transaction identifiers and explicit finalization code to be executed upon commit or abort can relieve these shortcomings, but at the expense of far more complicated programs [Weihl 90].

4 ◆ COOPERATION BY PROCEDURE CALL

So far, I have described ways in which threads that cooperate through shared variables can synchronize access to those variables. A different sort of cooperation is achieved by procedure calls. When one thread (the **client**) calls another (the **server**), information can be passed in both directions through parameters. Generally, parameters are restricted to value and result modes. A single thread can act as a client with respect to some calls and a server with respect to others.

4.1 Rendezvous

In Ada, SR, and Concurrent C, procedure calls between threads are handled by a mechanism called a **rendezvous**, which is an explicit way for the server to accept procedure calls from another thread. A thread executes within a module. This module exports **entries**, which are the procedurelike identifiers that may be invoked by other threads. The declaration of an entry includes a declaration of its formal parameters.

A server accepts a call from a client by an **accept** statement, which names the entry and the formal parameters. The **accept** statement blocks until some client invokes this procedure. At that time, the actuals provided by the client are bound to the formals, and the server executes the body of the **accept**. The **accept** statement may be nested in a **select** statement, which may enable several rendezvous, based on values of current variables and even on the values of the actual parameters presented.

A client invokes a rendezvous by a syntax that looks like procedure call. The client blocks until the server executes a matching **accept** statement and either completes the body of that **accept** or explicitly releases the client. Figure 7.16 shows a bounded buffer (in Ada syntax).

Figure 7.16

```
task BoundedBuffer is                                          1
    entry GetBuffer(Answer : out Datum);                       2
    entry PutBuffer(What : in Datum);                          3
end;                                                           4

task body BoundedBuffer is                                     5
    Size := constant 10; -- capacity of the buffer             6
    type Datum is ... -- contents of the buffer                7
    Buffer : array (0..Size-1) of Datum;                       8
    InCount, OutCount : integer := 0;                          9
    entry GetBuffer(Answer : out Datum);                       10
    entry PutBuffer(What : in Datum);                          11
```

```
        begin -- body of BoundedBuffer                    12
            loop -- each iteration accepts one call       13
                select                                    14
                    when InCount - OutCount > 0 =>        15
                        accept GetBuffer(Answer) do       16
                            Answer :=                     17
                                Buffer[OutCount mod Size];  18
                            return;                       19
                            OutCount := OutCount + 1;     20
                        end; -- accept                    21
            or                                            22
                    when InCount - OutCount < Size =>     23
                        accept PutBuffer(What) do         24
                            return;                       25
                            Buffer[InCount mod Size] := What; 26
                            InCount := InCount + 1;       27
                        end; -- accept                    28
                end; -- select                            29
            end; -- loop                                  30
        end; -- BoundedBuffer                             31
```

BoundedBuffer is a **task**, that is, a module that contains a thread. Ada separates the specification (lines 1–4) from the implementation (lines 5–31). This module would be declared in the same block as a producer and a consumer module. The **entry** declarations in lines 2–3 (repeated in lines 10–11) provide procedurelike headers that clients of this module may call.

Each of the alternatives in the **select** statement (lines 14–29) is headed by a Boolean guard. When BoundedBuffer executes the **select** command, the guards are evaluated. Those that evaluate to true dictate which branches are open. BoundedBuffer is then blocked until a client invokes a procedure **accept**ed by one of the open branches. If more than one client has already invoked such a procedure, then **select** is nondeterministic; one branch is arbitrarily chosen. It is up to the implementation to attempt to be fair, that is, not to always prefer one branch over another.

The **accept** statements (lines 16–21 and 24–28) introduce new name scopes in which the formal parameters are defined. A client remains blocked until the rendezvous is finished or the server executes **return** (lines 19 and 25). I have placed the **return** statements as early as possible to allow the client to proceed with its own activities.

There is no danger that InCount and OutCount will be simultaneously accessed by several threads, because they are not shared variables. Only BoundedBuffer itself can access them. By the same token, it is not possible for two rendezvous to be active simultaneously.

Therefore, rendezvous have less parallelism than can be obtained by, for instance, event counts.

Figure 7.17 Rendezvous

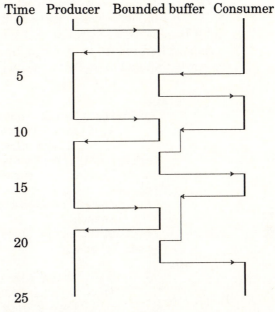

Figure 7.17 shows how the rendezvous code might execute. Time starts at the top and progresses downward. Solid vertical lines indicate execution; spaces indicate waiting. The producer invokes PutBuffer at time 1 and gets a response at time 3. Between those times, the producer and the bounded buffer are in rendezvous. The consumer invokes GetBuffer at time 5 and gets a response at time 7. The producer makes its second call at time 9. This call is still in progress when the consumer calls Get-Buffer at time 10. The consumer is blocked until the producer's rendezvous finishes at time 10. The consumer calls the bounded buffer again at time 16. The buffer is empty, so its call is not accepted. The consumer is blocked until the following rendezvous between the producer and bounded buffer finishes.

I have written BoundedBuffer as an unterminated loop. Ada terminates all remaining threads in a name scope if all are blocked in calls, **accept**, or **select** statements. Therefore, when the producer thread finishes, the consumer will be allowed to consume all the remaining entries from the bounded buffer. Then the consumer will block on a call to Get-Buffer, and BoundedBuffer will block in the **select** statement. Both will be terminated.

SR and Concurrent C add extra features to Ada's rendezvous to affect the scheduler's decision about which branch of **select** to prefer if several are open and have incoming calls. Each branch can be given a numeric priority. (Ada has the concept of static task priority, but not dynamic branch priority.) If there are several waiting calls on a particular **accept**, they may be sorted based on the values of the actual parameters. (In Ada, calls are processed strictly in first-come, first-served order.) To show these features, in Figure 7.18 I have rewritten the **select** loop from Figure 7.16 to prefer producers to consumers unless the buffer is nearly full, and to prefer low values of data to high values.

Figure 7.18

```
select                                                      1
    priority -- high number is better                       2
        if Size - (InCount - OutCount) < 2                  3
            then 1 else 0                                   4
    accept GetBuffer(Answer)                                5
    when InCount - OutCount > 0                             6
    do                                                      7
        Answer := Buffer[OutCount mod Size];                8
        return;                                             9
        OutCount := OutCount + 1;                          10
    end; -- accept                                         11
or                                                         12
    priority -- high number is better                     13
        if Size - (InCount - OutCount) < 2                14
            then 0 else 1                                 15
    accept PutBuffer(What)                                16
    when InCount - OutCount < Size                        17
    sortedby (-What) -- prefer low values                 18
    do                                                    19
        return;                                           20
        Buffer[InCount mod Size] := What;                 21
        InCount := InCount + 1;                            22
    end; -- accept                                        23
end; -- select                                            24
```

The **priority** clauses (lines 2–4, 13–15) decide which branch to prefer if several are open. In this case, the second branch has higher priority unless the buffer is nearly full. I have placed the **when** guard (lines 6, 17) after the **accept** clause so that the guard can take advantage of the formal parameters introduced by **accept**, even though this example doesn't do so. (SR uses this order.) The **sortedby** clause (line 18) reorders multiple calls to PutBuffer based on the formal parameter What.

4.2 Remote Procedure Call (RPC)

If threads do not share variables (for example, if they are running on different machines connected by a network), the only way they can cooperate is by procedure call or messages. Rendezvous is one way of accepting procedure calls. The only calls that are handled are those that match open **accept** statements. **Remote procedure call** (RPC) means an invocation that is handled not by **accept** statements, but by an ordinary exported procedure. Such calls can cross compilation units, processes, computers, and even programs that are written at different times in different languages.

The model of computation for remote procedure calls is somewhat different from what I have been discussing so far. Each address space may have multiple threads, which may share variables in that address space, subject to any scope rules the language imposes. Threads in separate address spaces do not share variables.

A thread may invoke an exported procedure inside another address space by a remote procedure call. There are two equivalent ways to picture the effect of such a call. You can imagine the thread migrating temporarily to the address space of the server, performing the call there, and then returning to the client's address space. Address spaces thus share information by sending their threads to visit other address spaces, bringing and returning data in their parameters. Alternatively, you can imagine the calling thread sending a message to the server and then blocking. A new service thread starts in the server address space for the purpose of handling the call. When it finishes, it sends results back to the blocked client thread, causing the client to awaken. The service thread then terminates. The first view is simpler. The underlying implementation is likely to use something closer to the second view.

In the DP (Distributed Processes) language of Brinch Hansen [Brinch Hansen 78], each address space starts with one thread, which starts running the main program of that address space. That thread cannot create new threads, but it may wait for conditions (using an **await** statement). Remote procedure calls are blocked until no thread is active in the server. A thread is considered inactive if it has terminated or if it is blocked waiting for a condition. It is active, however, if it is in the middle of a remote procedure call to some other address space. Therefore, the programmer does not need to be afraid that variables will suddenly have different values after a remote procedure call returns; such a call is indivisible. An **await** relaxes exclusion, though, allowing a client thread to visit. Therefore, data can change during **await**, but **await** checks a Boolean condition that can prevent it from unblocking until the situation is appropriate.

Figure 7.19 is an implementation of a bounded buffer in DP.

Figure 7.19

```
-- declarations as in Figure 7.4 (page 222).              1

procedure PutBuffer(value What : Datum);                  2
begin                                                     3
    await InCount - OutCount < Size do                    4
        Buffer[InCount mod Size] := What;                 5
        InCount := InCount + 1;                           6
    end; -- region                                        7
end -- PutBuffer;                                         8

procedure GetBuffer(result Answer : Datum);               9
begin                                                     10
    await InCount - OutCount < Size do                    11
        Answer := Buffer[OutCount mod Size];              12
        OutCount := OutCount + 1;                         13
    end; -- region                                        14
end GetBuffer;                                            15
```

This code is remarkably similar to Figure 7.4 (page 222). The only difference is that there is no need to lock any mutexes, since the thread executing either PutBuffer or GetBuffer is guaranteed exclusion in any case.

Languages like C that do not have remote procedure call built in can take advantage of a **stub compiler**, which takes a specification of the exported procedures and builds suitable code for both the client and the server [Nelson 81]. One widely available stub compiler is Sun RPC, a remote-procedure-call library designed by Sun Microsystems, Inc.[2] This library includes procedures for both the client (*c*) and server (*s*) for establishing a connection between them (*c* and *s*), sending a remote procedure call (*c*), receiving a remote procedure call (*s*), sending a response (*s*), and receiving the response (*c*). Parameters are transmitted in both directions in a machine-independent data format called "External Data Representation" (XDR); the client and server must call conversion routines to package and unpackage parameters to and from this format.

Many experimental languages have been designed to offer RPC directly, without explicit recourse to library packages. They all offer some mechanism for establishing a connection between a client and server, typically involving search through some name space (so the client can find a server) and connecting to some interface (to make sure the client and the server agree on what calls are valid). They might provide synchronization methods based on any of the methods I have described earlier to control access to variables that are accessed by multiple threads

---

[2] 2550 Garcia Avenue, Mountain View, California, 94043

in the same address space. They often include automatic transmission of structured parameters. Argus even allows the parameters to contain pointer types. The runtime routines expand such values for transmission by traversing all the pointers. Argus also supports remote invocation of CLU iterators and lets the invoked procedure raise exceptions.

The compiler sees to it that remote procedure calls are packaged into messages in the client and unpackaged in the server by using a stub compiler. It also tries to ensure that RPC is type-secure, that is, that the procedure header in the server matches the call that the client is making. One mechanism for type security is to represent the type of the procedure (that is, its name and the types and modes of its parameters) as a string and then to derive a hash value from that string [Scott 88]. These hash values can be compiled; they need not be computed at runtime. The hash value is sent in each call message from client to server. The server checks that the hash value is correct; if not, there is a type error. A related idea is to represent each type as a tree, derive a polynomial from the tree, and evaluate the polynomial at a special point to produce a hash value [Katzenelson 92].

4.3 Remote Evaluation (REV)

Remote procedure call only works if the server exports the procedure that the client needs. But clients are often written long after the server, and they may have needs that were not foreseen in the server. Some clients may need the server to run specialized procedures that most clients would not be interested in but which could run far more efficiently on the server than on a client, because the client would need to repeatedly invoke server routines remotely.

Remote evaluation (REV) is a technique that allows clients to send not only parameters, but also procedures, to the server [Stamos 90]. The procedures may refer to other procedures exported by the server. For example, a mail-delivery server might export a procedure DeliverMail. A client that wants to send a hundred identical messages could use RPC, invoking DeliverMail a hundred times, each time passing the message. Alternatively, it could use REV, sending a small procedure to the server that invokes DeliverMail a hundred times. The REV method is likely to be far more efficient. It also frees the mail-server designer of worries that the set of procedures exported by the server is not exactly right for every client.

A programming-language implementation of REV must be able to determine whether the server exports enough operations to support an REV request; if not, it must decide how much code actually needs to be sent. At one extreme, the procedure that is to be evaluated is itself exported by the server. In that case, the client needs to send only the parameters and receive the results; REV becomes RPC. At the other extreme, not only does the server not export the procedure, but several other procedures that it calls in turn are also not exported. The client must bundle and send enough procedures to ensure that the server will be able to complete the REV request. Any nonlocal variables needed by those procedures must also be bundled, and they must be returned by the server to update the values in the client.

The client can bundle the procedures needed by an REV request either at compile time or runtime. Compile-time bundling is more efficient but more restrictive. To make a compile-time bundle, the compiler must know what procedures are exported by the server, and it must traverse the invocation graph of the invoked procedure to discover all the procedures that must be included. To make a runtime bundle, the compiler must prepare the invocation graph and keep it until runtime. When an REV request is encountered, the client must query the server to discover its list of exported procedures and traverse the invocation graph.

REV requests may be nested. A procedure that is sent from a client to a server may contain another REV request to some other server. Compile-time bundling is unlikely to work for nested requests, because the contents of the nested bundle depend on the invocation graph in the server, which is not necessarily available to the compiler of the client.

REV requests that pass procedures as parameters cause a special problem. Compile-time bundling might refuse to deal with such parameters unless their binding is known at compile time.

REV can cause a major security headache. The server must be protected against misbehaving procedures that are sent to it. Authentication protocols can be used to restrict clients to those on an approved list. Running the procedure in a separate thread on the server under some sort of time slicing can protect the server against wasting all its time on a nonterminating computation. Giving that separate thread readonly access to server variables can protect the server against data corruption, but it restricts REV to operations that do not need to modify server data. Interpreting the REV request in the server instead of running it can allow the server to refuse potentially dangerous operations.

REV can be made implicit in every call and divorced from language design. The language runtime support can choose on every RPC whether to implement the request by sending a message for RPC, sending a bundle for REV, or requesting a bundle from the server for local evaluation. This decision can be based on statistics gathered during execution in an attempt to balance communication and computational resources among machines [Herrin 93]. The contents of the bundle need not include more than the procedure mentioned in the RPC; there is no need either at compile time or runtime to deal with invocation graphs.

Any procedure that cannot be resolved locally can certainly be resolved remotely.

5 ◆ COOPERATION BY MESSAGES

Although a procedure-call syntax makes concurrent programming look superficially like sequential programming, not all cooperation is easily shoehorned into the procedure-call model. First, a single query might generate multiple results spread over time. If the query is represented as a procedure call, then the results must either be result parameters, which means the client is blocked until the last result is ready, or the results are independent calls in the other direction, which confuses the issue of which thread is client and which is server. Second, some cooperation is unidirectional; there is no need to block the client until the server receives, acts on, and responds to a call. Third, some computations are best viewed as interactions among peers, where no simple client-server hierarchy applies. Fourth, some computations require multicast of the same data to groups of address spaces. It is wasteful to program multicast as multiple procedure calls. Fifth, it might be necessary to reply to requests in a different order from the order in which they arrive.

For these reasons, some experimental languages provide more primitive message-passing notions instead of or in addition to RPC. Often, message passing is provided as a library package to be used within some other language such as C. Operating-system support is needed to make the individual operations efficient. The following table indicates some of the facilities that can be provided as simple language extensions or in library packages.

Operation	Parameters	Results
`connect`	partner	connection
`group`	set of partners	connection
`send`	connection, data	
`receive`	connection	data
`reply`	data	
`forward`	connection	

This list is neither complete (library packages often provide many more routines) nor required (many library packages have no `group` or `forward` operations, for example). Still, it provides a reasonable set of functions for message passing.

The connect operation builds a connection, that is, a channel across which communication takes place; thus, individual send operations need not specify which process is to receive the message. Such a specification is given only once. It might be as simple as a process identifier or as complex as giving a process name or other characteristics to be looked up in a database. The group operation builds a connection that leads to multiple recipients. This facility is helpful for multicast.

The send operation might be designed to block the sender until the message can be copied to a safe place, until the message is sent, until the destination machine(s) receives it, until the destination thread(s) receives it, or until a response arrives back to the sender from the destination thread(s). Semantics that do not wait for the destination machine are usually called **asynchronous**, and those that wait for a response are called **synchronous**. There is a wide spectrum of synchronicity, so these terms are not very precise. The data that are sent can be treated just as an array of characters, or they may have associated type information.

The receive operation is used to accept incoming messages. It may be **selective**; that is, it might only accept messages that arrive on a set of connections or messages that match some pattern. It might reorder messages based on their contents. It might block until such a message arrives; it may have a timeout period, after which it fails if no message arrives; or it may just enable a receive but allow the thread to continue executing other statements.

The reply operation sends data back to the originator of the most recent message. In some languages, such as SR and Hermes, the program can specify which message is being responded to, so replies need not follow the order of receives. Packages that provide reply often have a single operation that combines send and receive. The client uses send/receive and the server uses receive followed by reply.

The forward operation redirects the most recent incoming message (or a specified message) to a different destination. The recipient can then reply directly to the original sender. This facility is called **delegation**.

5.1 CSP

CSP (Communicating Sequential Processes) is a proposal made by C. A. R. Hoare for message passing between threads that do not share variables [Hoare 78]. It is the framework upon which Occam was developed [May 83]. Communication is accomplished by **send** and **receive** statements. Although the **send** statement looks like a procedure invocation, in fact it is a pattern specification, much like Prolog (discussed in Chapter 8). The pattern is built out of an identifier and actual parameters. It is matched against a pattern in a **receive** statement in the destination thread. Variables in the **receive** pattern are like formal parameters; they acquire the values of the actual parameters in the matching **send** pattern. Patterns match if the pattern name and the number of parameters are the same and all formal parameter patterns match the actual parameter patterns. Matching is even used for the assignment statements, as in the examples shown in Figure 7.20.

Figure 7.20

```
left := 3;                                                    1
right := 4;                                                   2
x := cons(left, right); -- assigns pattern "cons(3,4)"        3
form(right) := form(right+1); -- right := right+1             4
factor(cons(left,right)) := factor(cons(5,6));               5
       -- left := 5; right := 6                               6
right = imply(); -- pattern with no parameters               7
muckle(left) := mickle(left+1); -- match error               8
```

Variables can hold pattern values, as in line 3. Here, cons is not a procedure call, just a pattern constructor. Line 4 shows that matching the actual to the formal is like an ordinary assignment. Line 5 shows that matching works recursively. Patterns need not have parameters (line 7). If the pattern name disagrees, match fails (line 8). In each of these cases (except the last), a **receive** in one thread with the pattern on the left-hand side would match a **send** in another thread with the pattern on the right-hand side.

CSP's control structures include Ada's nondeterministic **select** and also a nondeterministic **while**, which iterates open branches until no branch is open. Guards can be Boolean expressions, but they may also have as a final condition a **send** or **receive** statement. If the guard has such a statement, it is called an **output guard** or an **input guard**. For implementation reasons, original CSP did not allow output guards. It is hard, but not impossible, for an implementation to pair communicating threads when several have both **send** and **receive** guards open. Pairing is easier under the restriction that a guarded **send** or **receive** can only be matched with an absolute (unguarded) **receive** or **send**; some implementations of CSP make that restriction and allow output guards.

Figure 7.21 shows how a bounded buffer can be implemented in CSP, using both input and output guards.

Figure 7.21

```
type                                                          1
       Datum = ... -- contents of the buffer                  2
```

```
    thread BoundedBuffer;                                         3
    constant                                                      4
        Size = 10; -- capacity of the buffer                      5
    variable                                                      6
        Buffer : array 0..Size-1 of Datum;                        7
        InCount, OutCount : integer := 0;                         8

    begin                                                         9
        while -- each iteration handles one interaction          10
            when InCount - OutCount > 0 and                      11
                receive PutBuffer(Buffer[InCount mod Size])      12
                from Producer =>                                 13
                    InCount := InCount + 1;                      14
            when InCount - OutCount < Size and                   15
                send TakeBuffer(Buffer[OutCount mod Size])       16
                to Consumer =>                                   17
                    OutCount := OutCount + 1;                    18
        end; -- while                                            19
    end; -- thread Buffer                                        20

    thread Producer;                                             21
    begin                                                        22
        loop                                                     23
            Value := ...; -- generate value                     24
            send PutBuffer(Value) to BoundedBuffer;             25
        end; -- loop                                             26
    end; -- Producer                                             27

    thread Consumer;                                             28
    begin                                                        29
        loop                                                     30
            receive TakeBuffer(Value) from BoundedBuffer;       31
            ...; -- use value                                   32
        end; -- loop                                            33
    end; -- Consumer                                             34
```

The Producer thread (lines 21–27) repeatedly generates a value and **send**s it to the BoundedBuffer thread inside a PutBuffer pattern. This **send** blocks Producer if BoundedBuffer is not able to accept the match immediately, either because it is occupied with something else or because there is no matching **receive** currently open. The Consumer thread (lines 28–34) repeatedly **receive**s a value from BoundedBuffer with a TakeBuffer pattern. This **receive** can block Consumer if BoundedBuffer does not have a matching **send** currently open. BoundedBuffer spends all its time in a nondeterministic **while** loop (lines 10–19) with two branches, one to accept data from Producer (lines 11–14), and the other to feed data to Consumer (lines 15–18). Each branch is guarded to make sure that the buffer situation allows it to be selected. The first guard is an input guard, and the second is an output guard. If the buffer is neither full nor empty, both guards will be open, and whichever of Producer and Consumer is ready first will match its respective **receive** or **send** statement. If both are ready, then the scheduler will select one in an arbitrary, but in the long run fair, way. The `while` will always have at least one branch open, so it will never terminate.

5.2 Lynx

Lynx is an experimental language implemented at the University of Wisconsin and at the University of Rochester [Scott 84, 86]. Address spaces and modules in Lynx reflect the structure of a multicomputer, that is, a distributed-memory machine. Each outermost module represents an address space. As in DP, each address space begins executing a single thread. That thread can create new threads locally and arrange for threads to be created in response to messages from other processes. Threads in the same address space do not execute simultaneously; a thread continues to execute until it blocks, yielding control to some other thread. It is not an error for all threads to be blocked waiting for a message to be sent or received.

Lynx is quite helpful for programming long-running processes (called **server processes**) that provide assistance to ephemeral processes (called **client processes**). Typically, server processes are programmed to build a separate thread for each client process to keep track of the ongoing conversation between server and client processes. That thread may subdivide into new threads if appropriate. Lexical scope rules determine what variables are visible to any thread; the runtime organization uses a cactus stack.

Lynx provides two-way communication **links** as first-class values. A link represents a two-way channel between address spaces. The program dynamically binds links to address spaces and entries. Links can be used for reconfigurable, type-checked connections between very loosely coupled processes that are designed in isolation and compiled and loaded at disparate times.

A link variable accesses one end of a link, much as a pointer accesses an object in Pascal. The only link constant is `nolink`. Built-in functions allow new links to be created (both ends start by being bound to the creator's address space) and old ones to be destroyed. Neither end of a destroyed link is usable.

Objects of any data type can be sent in messages. If a message includes link variables or structures containing link variables, then the link ends referenced by those variables are moved to the receiving address space. This method could be called "destructive value" mode, since the value is transmitted, but becomes inaccessible at the sender. Link variables in the sender that refer to those ends become dangling references; a runtime error results from any attempt to use them.

Message transmission looks like RPC from the client's point of view. The client dispatches a request and waits for a reply from the server. From the server's point of view, messages may be received by rendezvous, using an **accept** statement, or by thread creation, in which a new service thread is built to execute a procedure when a message arrives.

Servers decide dynamically which approach to use for each link. They arrange to receive requests by thread creation through the **bind** statement, which binds a link to an exported procedure (I will call it an "entry"). This arrangement is cancelled by **unbind**. A link may be simultaneously bound to more than one entry and may even be used in **accept** statements. These provisions make it possible for threads to multiplex independent conversations on the same link. If a client invokes an entry via a link that is not currently bound to that entry, the invocation blocks until the server either binds the link to that entry, enters a rendezvous for that entry, or destroys the link.

When all threads in an address space are blocked, the runtime support package attempts to receive a message on any link that is bound or is the subject of an outstanding **accept**. Since messages are like RPC, they specify the exported procedure that they are attempting to invoke. The name of the procedure is matched against those of the active **accept**s and the bound links to decide whether to resume a blocked thread or create a new one. Bindings or **accept**s that cause ambiguity are runtime errors.

Lynx provides type-secure RPC in the fashion described earlier on page 247. Its exception-handling mechanism permits recovery from errors that arise in the course of message passing, and allows one thread to interrupt another.

Figure 7.22 shows how a bounded buffer can be programmed in Lynx.

Figure 7.22

```
constant                                                          1
    Size = 10; -- capacity of the buffer                          2
type                                                              3
    Datum = ... -- contents of the buffer                         4
variable                                                          5
    Buffer : array 0..Size-1 of Datum;                            6
    InCount, OutCount : integer := 0;                             7
    ParentLink, ProducerLink, ConsumerLink : link;                8
entry                                                             9
    Initialize(value link, link); -- for rendezvous             10
    PutBuffer, GetBuffer; -- full header and bodies below        11
```

```
procedure PutBuffer(value What : Datum);                              12
begin                                                                13
    Buffer[InCount mod Size] := What;                                14
    InCount := InCount + 1;                                          15
    if InCount - OutCount = 1 then -- no longer empty               16
        bind ConsumerLink to GetBuffer;                             17
    end;                                                            18
    if InCount - OutCount = Size then -- now full                   19
        unbind ProducerLink from PutBuffer;                         20
    end;                                                            21
end -- PutBuffer;                                                   22

procedure GetBuffer(result Answer : Datum);                          23
begin                                                                24
    Answer := Buffer[OutCount mod Size];                            25
    OutCount := OutCount + 1;                                        26
    if InCount - OutCount = 0 then -- now empty                     27
        unbind ConsumerLink from GetBuffer;                         28
    end;                                                            29
    if InCount - OutCount = Size-1 then -- no longer full           30
        bind ProducerLink to PutBuffer;                             31
    end;                                                            32
end; -- GetBuffer                                                   33

begin -- main                                                       34
    accept Initialize(ProducerLink, ConsumerLink)                   35
        on ParentLink;                                              36
    bind ProducerLink to PutBuffer;                                 37
end; -- main                                                        38
```

The program defines three entries (lines 9–11); one is for rendezvous, and the others are handled by thread creation. This program begins with one thread that executes **accept** (lines 35–36) to get values for the links to the producer and consumer. It gets these values in a startup message from its parent, to which it is connected by ParentLink. I ignore how ParentLink gets initialized. Then the program **bind**s ProducerLink (line 37) to its entry PutBuffer. It makes no sense to bind ConsumerLink yet, because there is nothing yet to consume. Then the main thread terminates. Incoming RPC will create new threads as needed. Both PutBuffer and GetBuffer arrange for **bind**ing and **unbind**ing entries when the buffer gets full, empty, or no longer full or empty (lines 16–21 and 27–32). PutBuffer and GetBuffer themselves do not need to block if the buffer is not ready for them, because the pattern of bindings and the nonpreemptive scheduler assure that they cannot be called unless the state of the buffer permits them to proceed.

5.3 Linda

Like CSP, Linda also uses patterns instead of procedure calls in its messages [Gelernter 85]. Unlike CSP, the **send** statement does not indicate the thread to which data are to be sent, nor does **receive** indicate from which thread the data are coming. Instead, **send** places the data in a global data pool that can be accessed by any thread, and **receive** takes data from that pool. It is up to the implementation to organize data so that threads running on multiple machines can find data in the global pool. Typically, implementations will hash on the pattern name[3] and store each bucket redundantly on $n^{1/2}$ out of n machines. The **receive** pattern can include parameters that are variables (like actual parameters in result mode, to be bound to values during matching), constants (to selectively receive by restricting what data match this pattern), and don't-cares. **Receive** blocks the caller until matching data appears in the pool, and then it indivisibly removes the matching data from the pool. There is also a **read** statement with the same semantics as **receive** except that the data are not removed from the pool.

A Linda implementation of the bounded buffer would be identical to the CSP one in Figure 7.21 (page 251), except that the **send** and **receive** statements would not indicate which thread was the intended partner. Multiple producers and consumers could use the same code. However, such a bounded buffer thread would be illogical in Linda, since the data pool itself is an unbounded buffer. Even if the bounded buffer is full, the producer would still be able to repeatedly **send** the PutBuffer pattern. It would be more straightforward for the producer to just **send** a BufferData pattern and for the consumer to **receive** that pattern. A truly bounded buffer can actually be implemented in Linda; see the exercises for details.

The advantage of the Linda approach is that programs need not consider the destination and synchronization aspects of each message that is passed. If a particular destination thread is important, that can be coded into the pattern, of course, but many applications will not need such explicit control.

One set of applications to which Linda is well suited involves problems whose solutions create subproblems. All problems are placed in a "problem heap" as they are generated. The heap is stored in the global pool. Each thread repeatedly extracts a problem (using **receive**) and solves it, putting any new subproblems back on the heap (using **send**).

---

[3] What I call the pattern name would actually be the first element of a tuple in Linda, but I find CSP nomenclature a bit easier to understand.

This situation is much like a bounded buffer, but there is no concept of order connecting the elements of the buffer.

Linda is generally implemented as a library package added to some other language, such as C. A more type-safe design called Lucinda, which combines Linda with Russell, has also been devised [Butcher 91].

5.4 SR

The SR language was developed over a period of ten years by Gregory Andrews at the University of Arizona [Andrews 88]. It contains features for both distributed- and shared-memory concurrency.

SR modules are separately compiled. A module specification and its body may be compiled separately. At runtime, modules are dynamically instantiated and given initial actual parameters. By default, a new module shares the address space of its creator, but it can be placed on any machine (physical or virtual) instead.

Ordinary modules may import declaration modules. Each declaration module may import other declaration modules and introduce constants, types, variables, entries, and procedures. These may appear in any order, so dynamic-sized arrays are easy to build. Declaration modules also have initialization code. The declaration modules are instantiated (at most once each) and initialized at runtime in whatever order is dictated by the partial order of imports. One copy is created dynamically per address space the first time it is needed, so that threads in each space have access to the declarations. Global variables imported from declaration modules should be treated as readonly; modifying a global variable only affects the copy in the current address space.

SR contains a wide variety of synchronization and communication methods. It provides synchronization by semaphores (implemented as a module type with entries for **up** and **down**), and communication by rendezvous, RPC, and messages. The client may choose whether to use synchronous or asynchronous calls, that is, RPC or messages. The server may choose to receive messages by thread creation or by rendezvous. It may inspect how many calls are outstanding on any entry. The rendezvous **accept** statement[4] includes both a synchronization (**when**) clause and a scheduling (**sortedby**) clause, both of which may depend on the formal parameters of the call. Both a **reply** and a **forward** statement are included.

Destinations for calls can be represented by pointers to modules, which can even reference modules across machine boundaries. The

---

[4] I am changing the keywords, as usual, for the sake of consistency.

declaration for module pointers includes which module type they may reference. Every module instance has a pseudovariable self that points to itself. Calls and replies may pass module pointers, so communication paths may vary dynamically. In addition, threads may invoke an entry imported from a declaration module. Any module instance that imports that declaration module may receive such an invocation.

In addition to initialization code, a module can be contain a **thread** declaration, much as in Modula. The compiler converts that declaration to an anonymous entry with no parameters; the act of instantiating the module implicitly sends a message to that entry, which creates the new thread. A module may also contain finalization code, which is invoked in any instance when the instance is terminated. All instances are terminated when deadlock occurs, as in Ada.

5.5 Object-Oriented Programming

The object-oriented paradigm (see Chapter 5) lends itself nicely to distributed-memory machines, because each object may reside entirely within a single memory, and interaction between that object and the rest of the computation is entirely mediated by messages. There are several object-oriented languages for concurrent programming. For example, DC++ is a version of C++ with threads [Carr 93], Distributed Eiffel [Gunaseelan 92] and Eiffel Linda [Jellinghaus 90] extend the object-oriented Eiffel language, and CST (Concurrent Smalltalk) extends Smalltalk [Dally 89]. You can read a survey of these languages and others in [M. Nelson 91].

To show you a concrete example, I will focus on the ALBA language [Hernández 93], another example of an object-oriented concurrent programming language. ALBA is strongly typed and is in many ways a typical object-oriented language; that is, it provides classes and inheritance. What sets it apart is its recognition that it executes in a distributed environment. Unfortunately, the ALBA document is incomplete, so I have added further specifications of my own that the authors may not agree with.

There are no class variables, because different instances of a class are likely to be in different memories. Instance variables, of course, exist. Any number of threads may simultaneously execute methods in an object unless the object is an instance of a **serialized class**, which allows only one thread at a time. It is unclear whether serialized ALBA objects accept new threads when the existing thread is blocked waiting for a call or when the existing thread is in the middle of invoking a method in some other object.

Objects may be created at any time; their identity is stored in an instance variable of their creator, so that the creator can send them messages. This identity can be passed to other objects in a parameter in order to allow them to invoke methods in the newly created object. Each object has a pseudovariable `creator` that points to the creator and `self` that points to itself.

When an object is created, the programmer has some control over where it will be placed initially. The ALBA implementation does not dynamically move objects once they are created, but techniques for such migration are well understood [Artsy 89]. The class declaration may restrict its instances to a subset of the machines, and the instance-creation request may further restrict the positioning. For this purpose, ALBA has a data type for sets of machine identifiers.

As in Ada, Lynx, and SR, ALBA objects can accept incoming messages by rendezvous. Alternatively, an invocation of a method may be handled by thread creation.

During execution of a method, two more pseudovariables are defined: `sender` and `reply`. Typically, they are identical, pointing to the object that invoked the method. However, ALBA provides for delegation. A method may be invoked with an explicit "reply-to" specification, which will be copied to the recipient's `reply` pseudovariable.

Figure 7.23 shows an ALBA implementation of merge sort.

Figure 7.23

```
type                                                              1
    DataArray = array whatever of integer;                        2

class MergeSort;                                                  3

method Done -- for rendezvous                                     4
    (Sorted : DataArray; LowIndex, HighIndex : Integer);         5

method Sort -- thread-creating                                    6
    (Tangled : DataArray; LowIndex, HighIndex : integer);        7
variable                                                          8
    MidPoint : integer := (LowIndex + HighIndex) div 2;          9
    LeftChild, RightChild : MergeSort;                           10
    Responses : integer := 0;                                    11
begin -- method Sort                                             12
    if LowIndex + 1 < HighIndex then -- worth sorting            13
    MidPoint : integer := (LowIndex + HighIndex) div 2;          14
        create LeftChild;                                        15
        create RightChild;                                       16
        send LeftChild.Sort(Tangled, 1, MidPoint);               17
        send RightChild.Sort                                     18
            (Tangled, MidPoint+1, HighIndex);                    19
```

```
        while Responses < 2 do                              20
            accept Done(Sorted, LowIndex, HighIndex)        21
            from {LeftChild, RightChild}                    22
            do                                              23
                Tangled[LowIndex .. HighIndex] :=           24
                    Sorted[LowIndex ..  HighIndex];         25
                Responses := Responses + 1;                 26
            end; -- accept                                  27
        end -- while                                        28
        Merge(Tangled, 1, MidPoint, MidPoint+1,             29
            HighIndex);                                     30
    end; -- worth sorting                                   31
    send creator.Done(Tangled, 1, HighIndex);              32
    destroy(self);                                          33
end; -- method Sort                                         34

end; -- class MergeSort                                     35
```

A client that wishes to sort an array creates an instance of MergeSort (I will call it the "worker") and invokes the thread-creating Sort method (lines 6–34). Because objects do not share memory, all parameters to Sort are passed in value mode. The worker creates left and right child instances (lines 15–16); they are declared in line 10. The worker then invokes the Sort method in the children on the appropriate regions of the array (lines 17–19). These calls are marked **send** to indicate that the call is asynchronous; that is, the caller need not wait for a response. Asynchronous calls are only allowed on methods that do not return values. When the children are finished, they will invoke the Done method in their creator, the worker. The worker accepts these invocations in a rendezvous (lines 21–27), placing the result that comes with the invocation back into a slice of the local array (lines 24–25). When it has received both responses, the worker merges the two halves of the array (lines 29–30). It then tells its own creator that it is done (line 32), providing the sorted array as a parameter. This invocation of Done is asynchronous, but it does not create a new thread, because it is accepted in a rendezvous by the creator. The worker then destroys its instance (line 33), including all threads that may currently be active. Its purpose has been accomplished.

ALBA supports multicast by letting a program asynchronously invoke a non-value-returning method on any subset of the existing instances of a class. The destination of an invocation can be an instance (the usual case), a set of instances, or a class (all existing instances are sent the message). Rendezvous can be selective by restricting attention to messages from a given instance, a set of instances, or a class. In line

22, I have restricted attention to the two children, although such a restriction is not necessary.

5.6 Data-Parallel Programming

Scientific applications often require similar computations across very large data sets, which may represent a connected physical entity. For example, a weather simulator might advance time in small increments while keeping track of wind patterns, cloud cover, precipitation, sunlight-induced wind currents, and so forth over a large geographical area represented as interconnected records, each covering a few square miles. Such applications often strain the computational ability of any single computer, so they are programmed on shared-memory or distributed-memory computers. Each computer is given a region of the data and computes as independently as possible of the other computers. When necessary, computers exchange information with others that deal with neighboring data. This style of computing is called **data-parallel** computing with **coarse-grain parallelism**. That is, the machines work in parallel on different parts of the data, and they only coordinate their activities on occasion.

Several languages have been implemented specifically to deal with coarse-grain parallelism. Some, like PVM [Sunderam 89], are implemented as library packages to be invoked from any conventional language for passing messages. Charm is a more complex language that extends C with dynamically creatable threads that inhabit modules [Kalé 90]. Global variables can be accessed only by a runtime procedure because they may be stored anywhere. The threads communicate both by messages (much like method invocations in object-oriented programming) and through serialized modules that accumulate data, creating such results as sums and averages.

The Canopy language is more complex yet. It is implemented as a library package to be used by ordinary C programs. Unlike PVM and Charm, it imposes a distinctively data-parallel view on the programmer.

Data in Canopy are represented as records stored on a grid of sites. Grids are dynamically constructed by calls to a runtime routine. Definition routines are provided for many standard topologies, such as three-dimensional meshes, and the programmer may define any desired topology by using a more primitive routine. A computation may use several different grids, although using more than one is unusual. Each site in a grid has coordinates and is connected to its neighbors by links. Data records are associated with each site and each link.

The runtime support software arranges for sites to be located on physical machines. Typically, there are far more sites than machines; a typical problem may have a million sites running on a hundred machines. The programmer has no control over the mapping of sites to machines, and there is no way for a program to discover that mapping. Each machine has a complete copy of all code and global data and has space to allocate site-local data.

Computation proceeds in phases. Each phase is initiated by a distinguished site called the controller, which executes the control program. Before the first phase, the controller establishes the grids, site sets, mappings between grids, and record fields (local variables) that will be used. It then calls CompleteDefinitions to activate these definitions. For each phase, the control program may initialize global variables by broadcasting a copy to all sites (actually, to all machines). Individual sites should treat such global data as readonly. The controller then invokes a procedure on each site in a grid or subset of a grid by calling DoTask. Each such site gets its own thread to execute that procedure simultaneously with all other sites. (Actually, the implementation has each machine cycle through all the sites that reside on that machine, but the programmer doesn't need to know that.) When all sites have finished, the control program resumes to begin the next phase.

The controller passes information to the sites and receives information back from them via parameters of DoTask. These parameters are arranged in triples, which represent the parameter-passing mode, the address of the parameter, and its length. (A true compiler, instead of a library package for C, would not use addresses and would not need to be told the lengths.) The modes available are value, procedure (that is, passing a procedure), and accumulate, which combines results from all the sites and presents them to the controller. The accumulation techniques include summation, maximum, and minimum, and the programmer may provide other accumulation techniques. The parameter-passing mode is presented as a pointer to a record that includes a routine that combines two values. This routine, which should be commutative and associative, is repeatedly invoked as sites terminate. (The implementation invokes it on the site's own machine until it has exhausted all its sites, and then repeatedly on the controller's machine until all machines have reported values.)

During a phase, each thread has access not only to its own local variables (those in the records associated with its site) and the local variables of its adjacent links, but all local variables in every site and link. Canopy provides library routines that fetch and store the values of these variables. Fetches return a pointer, which either points to the data itself, if it is on the same machine, or to a temporary copy, if it is not. Therefore, threads should treat fetched data as readonly.

Sites can be described in various ways for the purpose of fetching and storing. The pseudovariable home is the thread's own site. Site variables point to sites. Their values can be computed based on a path from home or any other site, or based on absolute site coordinates.

Synchronization is sometimes needed among threads to prevent conflicts over local variables. For example, the sites may be arranged in a two-dimensional grid, and each site may need read access to local variables owned by adjacent sites. Canopy provides several alternative synchronization methods. First, the controller can choose to start only a subset of the sites during each phase. For example, the sites in the two-dimensional grid may be "colored" red or black as on a checkerboard. The controller can start only black sites during one phase, and then red sites in the next. Then each thread is assured that its neighbors are not active when it is. Second, the sites in a grid can be given priorities. A thread may call a synchronize routine specifying any site. This routine will block until that site has finished the current phase if it is of higher priority than the thread's own site. So the controller can start all the sites in the two-dimensional grid, but assign black sites higher priority than red sites. Each site will synchronize with its neighbors before fetching their local variables. The effect is that black sites will execute first, then red sites, but if the amount of computation varies across sites, some black sites may still be executing when red sites elsewhere are already in progress or even finished. Thus this technique allows greater parallelism than the first one. Since it is so useful, Canopy provides a synchronized version of the fetch routine that combines it with synchronize.

Good programming practice in Canopy suggests that a thread should only update local variables on its home site, and that if it updates a local variable, it should never read the same variable from another site that is currently active. This second rule is achieved by using synchronized fetch for such variables, but the faster ordinary fetch for variables that are not modified locally.

Canopy programmers must be careful with global variables of the underlying language, C. They can be used for readonly initialized data, but only if the value is broadcast by the controller before the phase starts. If a site writes into a global variable, the change is observable only by those sites that happen to be on the same machine. A thread that uses a global variable for communication between procedures runs the risk of having the variable overwritten by another site when the local machine chooses to suspend that thread to achieve synchronization or to batch cross-machine communication.

6 ◆ FINAL COMMENTS

Concurrent programming has been studied for at least twenty years, but it has been steadily gaining popularity. One reason is that high-performance computers have turned increasingly to parallelism as a way of achieving a high rate of computation. Another is that workstation clusters are increasingly common in research environments. The former trend has led to increased interest in threads that cooperate by shared variables; the latter makes message passing attractive. Operating systems are being designed that make shared variables meaningful across memories and that make message passing fast within a single memory, so the correspondence between physical architecture and programming language approach is not straightforward.

Languages that provide some modest extensions to successful sequential languages, such as ML, C++, or even FORTRAN, might be more successful in the long run than specialty languages, because they already have widespread use and are perhaps easier to learn than completely new languages. Concurrent C, Concurrent Pascal, and HPF (High Performance FORTRAN) extend standard imperative languages; CST (Concurrent Smalltalk), DC++, and Distributed Eiffel extend object-oriented languages.

High-level operations can go a long way toward efficient use of the underlying architecture without introducing concurrency explicitly into the language. For example, FORTRAN 90 specifies vector and matrix operations that a subroutine library may implement quite efficiently in a concurrent fashion. As another example, speculative evaluation in functional programming languages, as discussed in Chapter 4, can take advantage of implicit concurrency.

EXERCISES

Review Exercises

7.1   What is the usual initial value for the Value field in a semaphore?

7.2   Show a code fragment that, if executed by two threads, can leave the value of x either 0 or 14, depending on the order in which the two threads interleave their execution. Don't use any synchronization.

7.3   Show how to use each of the following methods to restrict a code fragment C so that it can only be executed by one thread at a time: semaphores, mutexes, conditional critical regions.

7.4   Make a deadlock situation with only one thread, using each of the following methods: semaphores, mutexes, conditional critical regions.

7.5   What will be the effect in a CSP program if I misspell a pattern in an input guard?

Challenge Exercises

7.6   On page 224, I say that arguments to fork are usually restricted to global procedures so that cactus stacks do not need to be built. What is the connection between using global procedures and cactus stacks?

7.7   Does Ada require cactus stacks?

7.8   What will be the effect of a semaphore whose Value field is initialized to 2 if it is used for mutual exclusion?

7.9   What would be the use of a semaphore whose Value field is initialized to –2 with two dummy threads initially enqueued on its Waiters field?

7.10 Show how to implement conditional critical regions using semaphores. You will need an indivisible **updown** statement that **up**s one semaphore and **down**s another, and **upall** which performs **up** until there are no more threads blocked on the semaphore.

7.11 Show how to implement a capacity-2 barrier using two semaphores. You may use different code for the two threads involved. Implement not only **meet**, but also **arrive** and **depart**.

7.12 Show how to build a multiple-producer, multiple-consumer bounded buffer using event counts and sequencers.

7.13 Figure 7.9 (page 229) shows a Mesa solution to the bounded buffers problem. It assumes that **signal** only awakens one waiter. Actually, Mesa provides only **broadcast**, not **signal**. Fix the code.

7.14 Show how to build semaphores with event counts and sequencers. The **up** and **down** operations should not require mutual exclusion.

7.15 I suggest on page 247 representing the type of a procedure as a string in order to implement type-secure RPC. What sort of type equivalence does this method represent?

7.16 What are the ramifications of using REV in an environment where each address space has several threads?

7.17 The CSP implementation of a bounded buffer Figure 7.21 (page 251) uses both input and output guards. Can bounded buffers be implemented without output guards? Without input guards? Without either?

7.18 On page 256, I suggest that a proper Linda implementation of the bounded buffer (one that does not use an intermediate thread to hold the data and is truly bounded) is possible. Show how. Hint: Use antidata to indicate an available slot in the buffer.

7.19 Languages like Lynx, ALBA, and SR allow servers to handle messages either by rendezvous or by thread creation. Would it make sense to allow a single entry to be handled both ways?

Chapter 8

Logic Programming

Although LISP has long been the language of choice for artificial intelligence (AI) research, other languages are increasingly common for some branches of AI. C and C++ have become quite popular. Some AI programs are meant to reason about the world, given some initial knowledge. Knowledge can be represented in property lists of LISP atoms, but it can also be stored as a set of rules and facts. One form of reasoning is to try to derive new facts or to prove or disprove conjectures from the current set of facts. Programs that follow this approach are called "inference engines."

In this chapter, I will present several languages intended for knowledge representation and inference engines. These logic languages tend to be **declarative**. Programs state goals and rules to achieve goals, but do not explicitly invoke those rules in order to achieve the goals. In contrast, both imperative and functional languages tend to be **procedural**; that is, programs are organized around control structures such as iteration and procedure invocation.

1 ◆ PROLOG

Prolog is a declarative programming language designed in 1972 by Philippe Roussel and Alain Colmerauer of the University of Aix-Marseille and Robert Kowalski at the University of Edinburgh. Prolog programs are related to computations in a formal logic. A programmer first provides a **database** of facts and rules of inference. Programs are formulated as assertions involving facts in the database. Programs are executed by proving or disproving a particular assertion.

267

1.1 Terms, Predicates, and Queries

Elementary values in Prolog are called **terms**. Terms are either constants (numbers like 43 and identifiers like parsley, starting with a lowercase letter), variables (identifiers like X, starting with an uppercase letter), or structures (identifiers starting with a lowercase letter, followed by parameters that are themselves terms, such as tasty(parsley)). The identifier that heads a structure (like tasty) is called a **functor**, based on its similarity in appearance to a function name. Figure 8.1 shows a sample term.

Figure 8.1

```
near(house, X, 22, distance(Y))
```

There are two constants (22 and house), two variables (X and Y), one unary functor (distance), one 4-ary functor (near), and two structures (distance(Y) and the whole term). This term has no inherent meaning; a program could use it to mean that house is within 22 miles of some object X, and that the actual distance is Y miles.

Programs are built out of facts, rules, and queries, which are all based on predicates. A **predicate** has the same form as a structure: a name in lowercase followed by parameters, which must be terms. Predicates represent a fact (actual or to be proven) relating the values of their parameters. I will often call the predicate name itself a predicate when there is no chance for confusion.

Although structures and predicates have parameters and otherwise look like function calls, this appearance is deceiving. Structures are used as patterns, and predicates are used to define rules and facts and to pose queries. Only in their role as queries are predicates at all like function calls.

A database is constructed out of facts and rules. To build a simple family-relation database, I will start with constants representing people: tom, dick, harry, jane, judy, and mary. I describe relationships among these people with binary predicates: fatherOf, motherOf, parentOf, grandparentOf, and siblingOf.

One of the hardest problems in reading Prolog programs is figuring out what predicates are supposed to mean. The predicate motherOf(mary,judy) could be taken to mean that Judy is the mother of Mary or that Mary is the mother of Judy; the proper interpretation is up to the programmer. I follow the convention that the first parameters represent the traditional inputs, and the last parameters represent outputs, although Prolog does not make this distinction. I therefore understand motherOf(mary,judy) to mean that the mother of Mary is Judy. The predicate motherOf(mary,judy) may be true, but motherOf(mary,tom) is very likely to be false.

My Prolog program begins by stating facts that define fundamental relations among the terms. **Facts** are predicates that are assumed true, such as those in Figure 8.2.

Figure 8.2

```
fatherOf(tom,dick) . /* read: "father of tom is dick" */    1
fatherOf(dick,harry) .                                       2
fatherOf(jane,harry) .                                       3
motherOf(tom,judy) .                                         4
motherOf(dick,mary) .                                        5
motherOf(jane,mary) .                                        6
```

The period is used to terminate facts and rules, which are allowed to cross line boundaries.

Given this database of facts, I can form queries. A **query** is a request to prove or disprove an assertion built of predicates. Interactive Prolog implementations expect that anything the user types in is a query. To input facts, the user must type a pseudoquery that causes Prolog to load the user's file of facts. My examples just show facts and queries together; I distinguish queries by prefixing them with the question symbol ?- , which is the usual prompt in an interactive Prolog session. Prolog will determine if the queried predicate is true or false and will reply Yes or No. Figure 8.3 shows an interactive example of queries (all examples in this chapter are in syntactically correct Prolog).

Figure 8.3

```
in:   ?- fatherOf(dick,harry) .                              1
out:  Yes                                                    2

in:   ?- fatherOf(harry,tom) .                               3
out:  No                                                     4
```

Any predicate that Prolog cannot prove true is assumed to be false. In logic, this rule is known as the **closed-world assumption**. When Prolog says No, it means "not as far as can be proven."

Queries can include variables, which are distinguished from constants by their initial capital letter. A variable that appears in a query acts like an unknown in an equation. Prolog tries to find an assignment to the variable that will make the predicate true. The assignment is then reported as the result of the query. In a sense, variables in queries are like result parameters, and the rest of the parameters are like value parameters. Consider Figure 8.4.

Figure 8.4

```
in:   ?- fatherOf(X,harry) .                            1
out:  X = dick ;                                        2
      X = jane ;                                        3
      No                                                4
```

Line 1 presents a query with one variable, X, and one constant, harry. It asks for matches in the database to the given predicate name (fatherOf) that match the constant second parameter (harry); the first parameter is to be returned in the variable X. This query has two solutions. Prolog first presents the first (line 2). The user may request another solution by typing ; (at the end of line 2). When there are no more solutions, Prolog prints No. In the examples that follow, I omit the final No.

Variables may be placed in any number of parameters, as shown in Figure 8.5.

Figure 8.5

```
in:   ?- fatherOf(jane,X) .                             1
out:  X = harry                                         2

in:   ?- motherOf(X,Y) .                                3
out:  X = tom, Y = judy;                                4
      X = dick, Y = mary;                               5
      X = jane, Y = mary                                6
```

A complex query is built from multiple predicates joined by , , which represents logical **and**. Each predicate is then called a **conjunct**. Consider Figure 8.6.

Figure 8.6

```
in:   ?- fatherOf(jane,X) , motherOf(jane,Y) .          1
out:  X = harry, Y = mary                               2

in:   ?- fatherOf(tom,X) , fatherOf(X,harry)  .         3
out:  X = dick                                          4
```

The query in line 1 asks for both parents of jane; the query in line 3 asks for the person who is both the father of tom and the son of harry. If a variable appears more than once in a query, as X does in line 3, it must be replaced by the same solution in all its occurrences.

What makes Prolog particularly interesting as a programming language is that it allows us to write **rules** that define one predicate in terms of other predicates. A rule is of the form shown in Figure 8.7.

Figure 8.7

```
predicate1(param,param, ...) :-                                   1
       predicate2(param,param, ...) , ... ,                      2
       predicateN(param,param, ...) .                            3
```

The predicate on the left is called the **head** of the rule; the predicates on the right form its **body**. A rule states that if the predicates in the body can all be proved (they have a simultaneous solution), then the head is true. You can read :- as **if**. Continuing Figure 8.2 (page 269), typical rules might include those of Figure 8.8.

Figure 8.8

```
/* grandmotherOf(X,GM) means the grandmother of X is GM */  1
grandmotherOf(X,GM) :- motherOf(M,GM) , motherOf(X,M) .     2
grandmotherOf(X,GM) :- motherOf(F,GM) , fatherOf(X,F) .     3

/* siblingOf(X,Y) means a sibling of X is Y */              4
siblingOf(X,Y) :- motherOf(X,M) , fatherOf(X,F) ,          5
       motherOf(Y,M) , fatherOf(Y,F) , not(X = Y) .        6
```

There are two ways in which GM can be a grandmother of X, so there are two alternative rules (lines 2–3). However, there is only one way for X and Y to be siblings, although it is fairly complicated (lines 5–6). This rule introduces variables M and F just to force X and Y to have the same parents.

Given these rules, I can pose the queries in Figure 8.9.

Figure 8.9

```
in:   ?- grandmotherOf(tom,X) .                             1
out:  X = mary                                              2

in:   ?- siblingOf(X,Y) .                                   3
out:  X = dick, Y = jane;                                   4
      X = jane, Y = dick                                    5
```

The query in line 3 generates two results because siblingOf is symmetric.

These examples begin to demonstrate the power of Prolog. The programmer states facts and rules, but queries don't specify which facts and rules to apply. This is why Prolog is called declarative.

Prolog attempts to satisfy a query by satisfying (that is, finding a way to prove) each conjunct of the query. Rules are applied as necessary by substituting the body of a rule for its head. This process isn't at all trivial, because more than one rule may apply to the same predicate. Each rule is tried in turn, which may lead to **backtracking**, in which alternative possibilities are tried (recursively) if a particular possibility fails. The way Prolog selects goals and subgoals during backtracking distinguish it from a more abstract language, LP (for logic programming), which selects goals and subgoals nondeterministically.

To demonstrate Prolog backtracking, I will return to the query grandmotherOf(tom,X). The database is consulted to find either facts or rules with a grandmotherOf predicate as the head. (A fact is a rule with the given predicate as the head and true as the body.) The order of facts and rules is significant in Prolog (but not in LP); they are scanned from first to last. This ordering can affect the speed of a query and even determine if it will terminate, as you will see soon. In this case, no facts match, but two rules define grandmother. The first applicable rule is

```
grandmotherOf(X,GM) :- motherOf(M,GM) , motherOf(X,M) .
```

It is applicable because its head matches the query: they both use the binary predicate grandmotherOf. To avoid confusion, Prolog renames any variables in the rule that appear in the query. Since X appears in both, it is renamed in the rule, perhaps to Y. Prolog then binds the rule's Y (which is like a formal parameter) to the query's tom (which is like an actual parameter), and the rule's GM (a formal) to the query's X (an actual). The rule effectively becomes

```
grandmotherOf(tom,X) :- motherOf(M,X) , motherOf(tom,M) .
```

This matching, renaming, and binding is called **unification**.

There is a new subgoal: to prove

```
motherOf(M,X) , motherOf(tom,M) .
```

The only applicable rules are facts involving motherOf. These facts are unified in turn with the first conjunct, motherOf(M,X). Each unification binds M and X (in both conjuncts). For each unification, the second conjunct, which is now fully bound, is matched against existing facts. No match succeeds, so Prolog backtracks to the point where the first grandmotherOf rule was selected and tries the second rule instead. Unifying the query and the second grandmotherOf rule gives rise to the new subgoal

```
motherOf(F,X) , fatherOf(tom,F) .
```

This subgoal can be satisfied with F = dick and GM = mary. If the second rule had failed, the entire query would have failed, since no other rules apply.

The backtrack tree of Figure 8.10 shows these steps in more detail.

Figure 8.10

```
goal: grandmotherOf(tom,X)                                        1
    rule: motherOf(M,X), motherOf(tom,M)                          2
        fact: motherOf(tom,judy) [M = tom, X = judy]              3
            goal: motherOf(tom,tom)                               4
            fail                                                   5
        fact: motherOf(dick,mary) [M = dick, X = mary]            6
            goal: motherOf(tom,dick)                              7
            fail                                                   8
        fact: motherOf(jane,mary) [M = jane, X = mary             9
            goal: motherOf(tom,jane)                             10
            fail                                                  11
        fail                                                      12
    rule: motherOf(F,X), fatherOf(tom,F)                         13
        fact: motherOf(tom,judy) [F = tom, X = judy]             14
            goal: fatherOf(tom,tom)                              15
            fail                                                  16
        fact: motherOf(dick,mary) [F = dick, X = mary]           17
            goal: fatherOf(tom,dick)                             18
            succeed                                               19
        succeed; F = dick, X = mary                              20
    succeed; X = mary                                            21
```

I have bound all identifiers based on the unification steps so far. For example, in lines 2 and 13 I have changed GM to X.

The Prolog unification algorithm can be fooled by having it unify a variable with a term containing that same variable, as in Figure 8.11.

Figure 8.11

```
strange(X) :- X = strange(X) .                                    1

in:  ?- strange(Y) .                                              2
```

The variable Y in the query is unified with X in the rule in line 1, leading to Y = strange(Y). The = constraint causes Y to be unified with strange(Y), which represents a result, but one that cannot be displayed in a finite space. Prolog will try to print the nonsense result, which begins strange(strange(. It turns out to be relatively difficult to solve this "occur-check" problem and prevent such mistaken unification, so most Prolog implementations don't try. They do, however, handle the easier situation encountered in Figure 8.12.

Figure 8.12

```
yellow(green(X)) :- X=puce .                                          1

in:   ?- yellow(X) .                                                  2
out:  X = green(puce) .                                              3
```

The query lin line 2 matches the actual parameter X with the formal parameter green(X). Since one X is actual and the other formal, Prolog does not confuse them.

The backtracking algorithm can also be represented by a box model [Byrd 80]. Each predicate is represented as a box with two inputs and two outputs, as shown in Figure 8.13.

Figure 8.13 Box model of a predicate

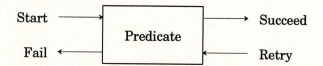

The first invocation of a predicate enters from the left. If the predicate is satisfied, control continues out to the right. If a different solution is required, control reenters from the right. If there are no (more) solutions, control exits to the left.

The logical **and** of two predicates is formed by joining them together, as in Figure 8.14.

Figure 8.14 Logical **and** of two predicates

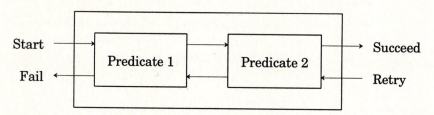

The logical **or** of two predicates is formed by a different combination, shown in Figure 8.15.

Figure 8.15 Logical **or** of two predicates

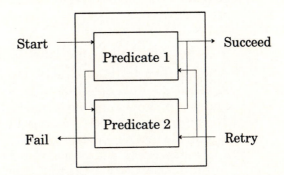

When control returns from the right in a retry attempt, it goes to whichever of the two predicates provided the most recent success.

The query grandmotherOf(tom,X) can be represented in Figure 8.16 in a box model:

Figure 8.16

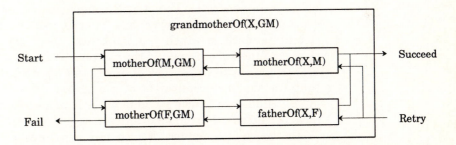

The box model shows execution paths and what happens when a goal succeeds or fails. It doesn't show variable substitutions, however.

Backtracking examines the backtrack tree by depth-first search, that is, in a top-down order. The order of alternatives tried when more than one rule or fact can be applied can have a startling effect on the speed at which a query is satisfied (or found to be unsatisfiable). Assume that an evaluator must go through n levels of rules and facts to provide a solution for a query, and that at each level, it must choose between two alternatives. If the right decision is made at each point, the evaluator will operate in $O(n)$ time, because only n decisions are made. However, if the wrong decision is made at each point, it is possible that $O(2^n)$ time will be required, because there are that many different settings for the decisions. As a result, Prolog programmers tend to sort rules and introduce other aids I will present shortly to help the evaluator make the decisions. For example, the rules for grandmotherOf in Figure 8.8 (page 271) can be improved by reordering the bodies, as shown in the exercises. Nonetheless, except in the case of recursive rules (in which an infinite expansion of rules can occur), the issue is one of speed, not correctness.

1.2 Separating Logic and Control

A well-known textbook on data structures by Niklaus Wirth is titled *Algorithms + Data Structures = Programs* [Wirth 76]. This equation defines the programming model implicit in modern procedural languages. The programming task is essentially to design data structures and the algorithms that manipulate them.

An interesting alternative view is presented by Robert Kowalski in "Algorithms = Logic + Control" [Kowalski 79]. This article proposes a declarative programming view. The programmer first specifies the logic of an algorithm. This component specifies what the result of the algorithm is to be. Then the control component is defined; it specifies how an evaluator may proceed to actually produce an answer. The logic component is essential because it defines what the programmer wants the program to generate. The control component may be optional, since it controls how fast an answer may be obtained. This represents a two-tiered approach in which you think first about getting the correct answer, and then about making the computation sufficiently fast.

Prolog supports this view of programming; its facts and rules are essentially the logic component of a program. The control component is largely hidden in Prolog's evaluator, although certain Prolog commands have been devised to aid an evaluator, as you will see shortly.

In theory, a language that cleanly separates logic and control has great advantages over conventional languages, which thoroughly intermix the definition of what is wanted and how to compute it. The logic component is the essential part of the program and often suffices to produce an answer. The control component allows efficiency issues to be addressed. It may be complex and detailed but can be ignored by most users of the program.

1.3 Axiomatic Data Types

One advantage of languages that support abstract data types is that the specification of an abstract data type can be separated from its implementation details. Prolog carries this idea further still: you can specify an abstract data type by axioms without any implementation at all. The axioms define the properties of the abstract data type, which is all the programmer really cares about. Of course, the evaluator must find some way to actually realize the operations of an abstract data type, but since Prolog is declarative, this isn't the programmer's concern!

I will show you how to define lists, a fundamental data structure of LISP, as seen in Chapter 5, based on terms, predicates, facts, and rules.

I define the set of valid lists by indicating when cons generates a list, as in Figure 8.17.

Figure 8.17

```
isList(nil) .                                              1
isList(cons(_, T)) :- isList(T) .                          2
```

Line 1 indicates that nil is a valid list, and line 2 shows that cons is a binary functor that builds new lists if the second parameter is a list. Because the body of this rule does not refer to the first parameter, I use the don't-care variable _ . If _ is used more than once in a rule or fact, each occurrence represents a different don't-care variable. If you want the same value to be forced in two different positions, you must use an explicit variable name. Line 2 shows that predicates can take parameters that are arbitrary terms, including structures. Although you may be tempted to treat cons(_,T) as a procedure call, it is only a structure. When it appears nested in the head of a rule, it is treated as a pattern to be matched to a query.

Predicates specifying the car and cdr functors are easy, as shown in Figure 8.18.

Figure 8.18

```
/* car(X,Y) means the car of X is Y */                     1
car(cons(H,T),H) :- isList(T) .                            2

/* cdr(X,Y) means the cdr of X is Y */                     3
cdr(cons(H,T),T) :- isList(T) .                            4
```

Once again, the functor cons is used in the head of rules as a pattern. Using these definitions, I can pose queries like those in Figure 8.19.

Figure 8.19

```
in:   ?- car(cons(2,cons(3,nil)),X) .                      1
out:  X = 2                                                2

in:   ?- car(cons(a,b),X) .                                3
out:  No                                                   4

in:   ?- car(cons(X,nil),2) .                              5
out:  X = 2                                                6

in:   ?- car(cons(a,X),a) .                                7
out:  X = nil;                                             8
      X = cons(_1, nil);                                   9
      X = cons(_2, cons(_1, nil));                         10
      ...                                                  11
```

The first query (line 1) asks for the car of a particular valid list. The second (line 3) asks for the car of an invalid list. It fails because the rules only allow car to be applied to valid lists. The third query (line 5) inverts the question by asking what has to be consed to a list to obtain a car of 2. The fourth query (line 7) requests lists whose car is a. There are infinitely many answers. Prolog invents internal temporary names for unbound results, which I display as _1, _2, and so on (lines 9–10). I call such names **don't-care results**.

In this example, both car and cdr can be used to form queries. However, cons cannot be used that way; there are no rules with heads matching cons. In other words, cons is a functor, whereas car and cdr are predicate names.

Stacks are frequently used to illustrate abstract data types, so let me present an axiomatic definition of stacks in Figure 8.20.

Figure 8.20

```
isStack(nil) .                                      1
isStack(push(_,S)) :- isStack(S) .                  2
top(push(Elem,S),Elem) :- isStack(S) .             3
pop(push(_,S),S) :-  isStack(S) .                   4

in:   isStack(push(a,push(b,nil))) .                5
out:  Yes                                           6

in:   pop(push(a,push(b,nil)),X) .                  7
out:  X = push(b, nil)                              8
```

I have used push as a functor, whereas top and pop are predicates. I leave making pop a functor as an exercise. The Prolog definition of stacks is similar to that of lists, which shouldn't be surprising, since lists are often used to implement stacks in conventional languages. The stacks defined above are heterogeneous. The exercises explore restricting stacks to hold only integers.

These examples show that Prolog can deal fairly directly with algebraic specification of data types, a field pioneered by Guttag [Guttag 77]. In the notation of algebraic specification, an integer stack looks like this:

Figure 8.21

```
type IntegerStack                                   1

operations                                          2
    create: → IntegerStack                          3
    push: IntegerStack × integer → IntegerStack     4
    pop: IntegerStack → IntegerStack                5
    top: IntegerStack → integer                     6
```

```
axioms                                               7
    top(create) = error                              8
    top(push(S,I)) = I                               9
    pop(create) = error                              10
    pop(push(S,I)) = S                               11
```

Operations are first defined by naming their input and output types. In procedural languages, the operations are analogous to the specification part of an abstract data type. In Prolog, which has no need to distinguish input from output, the operations can be predicates or functors. Operations that result in `IntegerStacks` are called **constructors**; here, `create`, `push`, and `pop` are all constructors. Actually, `pop` is a special kind of constructor because it reduces the amount of information; such constructors are called **destructors**. Operations that do not result in the abstract data type are called **inspectors**; here, `top` is the only inspector. The axioms are simplification rules. It is not always easy to see what axioms are needed; a rule of thumb is that an axiom is needed for all combinations of inspectors and non-destructive constructors (lines 8 and 9) and all combinations of destructors and non-destructive constructors (lines 10 and 11). In Prolog, axioms are expressed as rules, which means that inspectors (`top`) and destructors (`pop`) will be predicates, whereas non-destructive constructors (`push`) will be functors.

An algebraic specification could in general be satisfied by many different models. The axioms equate such elements as `create` and `pop(push(create,4))`, which some models would keep distinct. If only those elements that the axioms equate are considered equal, the resulting algebra is called an **initial algebra**. If all elements are equated that cannot be distinguished by inspectors, the resulting algebra is called a **final algebra**. In the case of stacks, these two algebras are the same. In an algebraic specification of arrays, however, the order in which elements are assigned values does not affect what an inspector returns, so the final algebra is more appropriate than the initial algebra, which would distinguish arrays with the same elements that happen to have acquired the elements in a different order.

1.4 List Processing

Because lists are such a familiar and flexible data structure, Prolog provides a notation for the structures that represent lists. Predefining lists also makes their manipulation more efficient. Predefined arithmetic operators are provided for much the same reason. In Prolog, lists are delimited by brackets. The empty list is `[]`, and `[[a,b],[c,d,e]]` is a list containing two sublists (with 2 and 3 elements respectively). The notation `[H | T]` is used to represent any list with car `H` and cdr `T`, as in Figure 8.22.

Figure 8.22

```
p([1,2,3,4]) .                                              1

in:  ?- p([X|Y]) .                                          2
out: X = 1, Y = [2,3,4]                                     3

in:  ?- p([_,_,X|Y]) .                                      4
out: X = 3, Y = [4]                                         5
```

Using this notation, Figure 8.23 defines the list operation append in a manner analogous to its definition in LISP (actually, append is often pre-defined).

Figure 8.23

```
/* append(A,B,C) means C is the list formed by              1
     appending element B to the end of list A */            2
append([],[],[]) .                                          3
append([],[H|T],[H|T]) .                                    4
append([X|L1],L2,[X|L3]) :- append(L1,L2,L3) .              5

in:  ?- append([1,2],[3,4],S) .                             6
out: S =  [1,2,3,4]                                         7
```

The correspondence to the LISP definition of append is almost exact, except that no explicit control structure is given. Instead, rules that characterize append are defined; they allow Prolog to recognize (or build) correctly appended lists. A LISP-like approach to list manipulation can be used to structure Prolog rules. Thus I could define a list-membership predicate memberOf (again, it is often predefined) as shown in Figure 8.24.

Figure 8.24

```
/* memberOf(X,L) means X is a member of list L */           1
memberOf(X,[X|_]) .                                         2
memberOf(X,[_|Y]) :- memberOf(X,Y) .                        3

in:  ?- memberOf(4,[1,2,3]) .                               4
out: No                                                     5
in:  ?- memberOf(4,[1,4,3]) .                               6
out: Yes                                                    7
```

This definition is strongly reminiscent of LISP's tail recursion. However, Prolog's declarative nature allows definitions that are quite foreign to LISP's procedural nature. Consider the alternative definition of memberOf in Figure 8.25.

Figure 8.25   `memberOf(X,L) :- append(_,[X|_],L) .`

This definition says that X is a member of L exactly if there exists some
list that can be appended to a list beginning with X to form list L.

Although both definitions of memberOf are correct, the first one will
probably be more efficiently executed, because it is somewhat more procedural in flavor. In fact, Prolog definitions are often structured specifically to guide an evaluator toward a more efficient evaluation of a query.
Sorting is a good example. The simplest abstract definition of a sort is a
permutation of elements that puts the elements in nondecreasing (or
nonincreasing) order. This definition has a direct Prolog analogue,
shown in Figure 8.26.

Figure 8.26

```
naiveSort(L1,L2) :- permutation(L1,L2) , inOrder(L2) .          1

permutation([],[]) .                                           2
permutation(L,[H|T]) :- append(V,[H|U],L) ,                    3
     append(V,U,W) , permutation(W,T) .                        4

inOrder([]) .                                                  5
inOrder([_]) .                                                 6
inOrder([A,B|T]) :- A =< B , inOrder([B|T]) .                  7
```

Since a list with n distinct elements has $n!$ permutations, the above definition may well lead to long and tedious searches in an effort to find a
sorting of a list. An alternative is to define inOrder in a manner that
leads to a more efficient evaluation sequence. For example, using the
infamous bubble sort (shame on me!) as inspiration, I create the alternative definition in Figure 8.27.

Figure 8.27

```
bubbleSort(L,L) :- inOrder(L) .                                1
bubbleSort(L1,L2) :- append(X,[A,B|Y],L1), A > B ,             2
     append(X,[B,A|Y],T), bubbleSort(T,L2) .                   3

inOrder([]) .                                                  4
inOrder([_]) .                                                 5
inOrder([A,B|T]) :- A =< B , inOrder([B|T]) .                  6
```

Actually, a trace of execution of bubbleSort will show that it always
looks for and then swaps the first out-of-order pair in the list. There are
$O(n^2)$ swaps, each of which requires $O(n)$ effort to discover by searching
from the start of the list. The result is an $O(n^3)$ algorithm, which is
worse than the $O(n^2)$ expected for bubble sort.

1.5 Difference Lists

List processing can be expensive. The append operation must step to the end of the first parameter in a recursive fashion before it can begin to construct the result. Prolog programmers have invented a programming trick called a **difference list** to alleviate this problem [Sterling 94]. Each list is represented in two pieces, which I will call listextra and extra. The actual list is listextra with extra removed from the end. What extra information to place at the end of a list is arbitrary and is based on convenience. For example, the list [a,b] can be represented in many ways, including [a,b] [] and [a,b,c,d] [c,d]. In general, I can represent the list as [a,b | Extra] [Extra] and not specify what Extra might be. The append routine can now be written as a single, nonrecursive rule, as in Figure 8.28.

Figure 8.28

```
append(diff(A,B), diff(B,C), diff(A,C)) .                        1

in:   ?- append(diff([1,2|X],X), diff([3,4|Y],Y),               2
              diff(ListExtra,Extra)) .                          3
out:  X = [3,4|_1],                                            4
      Y = _1,                                                  5
      ListExtra = [1,2,3,4|_1],                               6
      Extra = _1                                              7
```

The append predicate defined in line 1 takes three parameters, each of which is a pattern representing a list in difference-list form. Figure 8.28 shows how line 1 represents appending two lists by explicitly showing A, B, and C. Lines 2–3 use this definition to append [1,2] and [3,4]. Each of these lists is represented with a variable (X and Y) to represent the extra parts. Lines 4–5 show how these variables get bound during match. The result is represented by (ListExtra,Extra), which (according to lines 6–7) is [1,2,3,4|_1] _1. So long as I am willing to use difference-list form, I have not needed to perform any recursion.

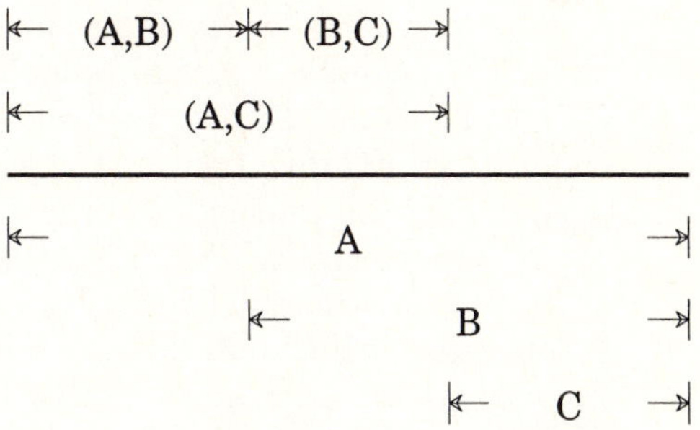

Figure 8.29 Difference
lists

1.6 Arithmetic

In Prolog, the infix equality predicate = can be used for two purposes.
In $\alpha = \beta$, if α and β are both constants, literals, structures, or bound variables, then the predicate succeeds or fails depending on whether or not the two operands are identical. Thus 1 = 1 is true, [1,2] = [] is false, and X = 2 is true if X has been bound to 2. This is the natural interpretation of the equality operator.

However, if α or β (or both) are unbound variables, then $\alpha = \beta$ succeeds and binds them together. So the same symbol acts both as an equality operator and as an assignment operator. Actually, the symbol introduces a constraint. Figure 8.30 illustrates this point.

Figure 8.30

```
set(A,B) :- A=B .                          1

in:   ?- set(1,2) .                        2
out:  No                                   3

in:   ?- set(X,2) .                        4
out:  X = 2                                5

in:   ?- set(3,X) .                        6
out:  X = 3                                7

in:   ?- set(Y,Z) .                        8
out:  Y = _1, Z = _1                       9
```

For free (unbound) variables, = constrains the value of the variable, and this binds it, as shown in lines 4 and 6. These values hold only for the duration of the search for solutions, not afterward. Line 9 shows that Y and Z have been bound together, both to the same don't-care result.

For programmers accustomed to procedural programming, using = to bind variables is familiar, but in Prolog a few pitfalls await the unwary. For example, you will probably be surprised that the query (1+1) = 2 results in No. In fact, in Prolog 1+1 doesn't equal 2, because 1+1 is taken as an abbreviation for the structure +(1,1). This structure isn't the same as the integer 2, so the negative response is justified. Prolog doesn't automatically evaluate arithmetic expressions.

To force arithmetic expressions to be evaluated, Prolog provides the **is** operator, which effects assignment. It first evaluates its second operand as an arithmetic expression (it must not have any unbound variables), then tests for equality, and (if necessary) binds the free variable in the first operand. However, **is** will not invert expressions to bind free variables. Consider Figure 8.31.

Figure 8.31

```
in:   ?- 1 is 2*2-3 .                                          1
out:  Yes                                                      2

in:   ?- X is 2*2 .                                            3
out:  X = 4                                                    4

in:   ?- 4 is X*3-7 .                                          5
out:  Unbound variable in arithmetic expression.              6
```

As lines 5–6 show, Prolog avoids the complexity of solving arbitrary equations. (Metafont can solve linear equations, and mathematics languages like Mathematica, discussed in Chapter 9, can handle a wide variety of equations.) Unfortunately, this restriction violates the symmetry between inputs and outputs found in other Prolog constructs.

1.7 Termination Issues

If free variables in queries may be bound only to a finite set of values, a Prolog evaluator should be able to prove or disprove any query. However, Prolog allows recursive definitions (such as the ones I showed earlier for lists and stacks) that imply infinite domains, as well as primitive objects (such as integers) with infinite domains. Not all queries will necessarily terminate. Prolog specifies that the order in which rules and facts are specified determines the order in which an evaluator attempts to apply them in proofs. Bad orders can sometimes lead to an infinite recursion. Suppose that I define the isList predicate as in Figure 8.32.

Figure 8.32

```
isList(cons(H,T)) :- isList(T) .                              1
isList(nil) .                                                 2
```

A query like `isList(nil)` works fine, but `isList(X)` runs into a real snag. The top-down evaluator will set `X = cons(H,T)` and try to prove `isList(T)`. To do this, it will set `T = cons(H',T')`[1] and try to prove `isList(T')`, and so forth. Eventually, the evaluator runs out of stack space. Putting the fact `isList(nil)` before the rule solves the problem.

Other problems may arise because of an inadequate set of rules. For example, I might provide a definition for odd integers and ask if any odd integer is equal to 2, as in Figure 8.33.

Figure 8.33

```
in:   odd(1) .                                                    1
      odd(N) :- odd(M), N is M + 2 .                              2
      ?- odd(2) .                                                 3
out:  [does not terminate]                                        4
```

The evaluator never finishes the query in line 3. It keeps generating odd numbers (1, 3, ...) to match `M` in line 2, but none of them satisfies 2 **is** `M + 2`. It doesn't know that after considering 1, all succeeding odd numbers will be greater than 2 and hence not equal to 2. The query is false, but Prolog has no mechanism to prove it!

1.8 Resolution Proof Techniques

Prolog is designed to be amenable to a particular class of automatic proof techniques termed "resolution techniques." **Resolution** is a general inference rule shown in Figure 8.34.

Figure 8.34

if	$A_1 \wedge \cdots \wedge A_n \Rightarrow B_1 \vee \cdots \vee B_m \vee C$	1
and	$D_1 \wedge \cdots \wedge D_p \wedge C \Rightarrow E_1 \vee \cdots \vee E_q$	2

then $A_1 \wedge \cdots \wedge A_n \wedge D_1 \wedge \cdots \wedge D_p \Rightarrow B_1 \vee \cdots \vee B_m \vee E_1 \vee \cdots \vee E_q$ 3

That is, if a term C appears on the right-hand side of one implication and on the left-hand side of a second implication, it can be removed, and the two rules can be joined. If C contains any free (that is, unbound) variables, these must be unified (that is, matched). This resolution operation doesn't appear to lead to any great simplification. Fortunately, Prolog limits the form of rules of inference to "Horn clauses," which are those that have only one term on the right-hand side of an implication (the head of a rule) and only '$\wedge$' as a connective. That is, Prolog rules of the form

---

[1] All variable names in a rule are local to that rule; hence, recursive applications cause no naming conflicts.

```
A or B :- X, ... .
```

aren't allowed. For Prolog, the resolution rule takes the form shown in Figure 8.35.

Figure 8.35

if	$A_1 \wedge \cdots \wedge A_n \Rightarrow C$	1
and	$D_1 \wedge \cdots \wedge D_p \wedge C \Rightarrow E$	2
then	$A_1 \wedge \cdots \wedge A_n \wedge D_1 \wedge \cdots \wedge D_p \Rightarrow E$	3

This rule is the basis of the substitution technique employed earlier in top-down evaluation. Still, this substitution appears to make things more, rather than less complex. However, a Prolog fact F can be viewed as an implication of the form `true` $\Rightarrow$ F. When a fact is resolved, resolution in effect replaces a term with `true`, and since `true` $\wedge X \equiv X$, this substitution does lead to a simplification.

Resolution is interesting in that it doesn't actually try to prove a query directly from known facts and rules. If

$$A_1 \wedge \cdots \wedge A_n \Rightarrow B$$

then

$$A_1 \wedge \cdots \wedge A_n \wedge \neg B \Rightarrow \mathsf{false} \ .$$

That is, if B is implied from known rules and facts, then $\neg B$ must lead to a contradiction. If a resolution theorem-prover is asked to prove B, it introduces $\neg B$ by introducing the implication $B \Rightarrow \mathsf{false}$. It then manipulates implications by resolution, trying to establish the implication `true` $\Rightarrow$ `false`.

Resolution theorem-provers use this unintuitive approach because resolution is "refutation complete"; that is, if a set of rules and facts are contradictory (that is, inconsistent), then resolution will always be able to conclude that `true` $\Rightarrow$ `false`. It doesn't guarantee that an evaluator will not pursue useless paths of unbounded length. Rather it says that if a finite resolution path exists, a smart enough evaluator will find it.

1.9 Control Aspects

So far I have emphasized the logic component of Prolog. The language also contains features that exercise control over the evaluation process. Such features in general compromise the otherwise declarative nature of Prolog. (Prolog also contains I/O, testing, and debugging features that are not purely declarative.)

The most frequently used control operator is **cut** (represented by ! in Prolog syntax). **Cut** terminates backtracking within a rule. (**Cut** is similar to **fence** in SNOBOL, described in Chapter 9. SNOBOL patterns use a backtrack mechanism that is very similar to the one Prolog uses.) In particular, if **cut** is encountered, all alternatives prior to **cut** in the rule are frozen, as shown in the box model in Figure 8.36.

Figure 8.36 Cut
operator

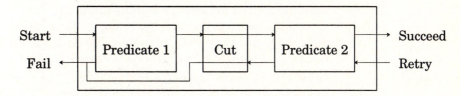

Prolog will not try alternative matches to earlier conjuncts of the rule's body. In fact, it will not try alternative rules to the rule that contains **cut**. Consider Figure 8.37.

Figure 8.37

```
even(X) :- X=2 , X>0, !, X < 0 .                                    1
even(X) :- X=10 .                                                   2

in:  even(E) .                                                      3
out: No                                                             4
```

The query in line 3 matches the rule in line 1. The first conjunct binds X to 2, the second succeeds, but the last conjunct fails. The **cut** prevents not only a reevaluation of the first conjuncts (which wouldn't find anything new in any case) but also any attempt to use the rule of line 2, which would succeed. Without the **cut** operation, Prolog would report that X = 10.

Cut can be useful in cases where once one rule is found to match, it is unnecessary to try other rules. For example, recall the list membership predicate, memberOf, shown in Figure 8.38.

Figure 8.38

```
memberOf(X,[X|_]) .                                                1
memberOf(X,[_|Y]) :- memberOf(X,Y) .                               2
```

Since an element may appear in a list more than once, if a goal containing a successful memberOf conjunct later fails, Prolog might try to resatisfy it by looking for an alternative match to memberOf. In general this search will be futile, since once an item is known to be in a list, backtracking can't establish anything new. Thus, we have Figure 8.39.

Figure 8.39

```
memberOf(X,[X|_]) :- ! .                              1
memberOf(X,[_|Y]) :- memberOf(X,Y) .                  2
```

This code implements our observation that once membership is established, further backtracking should be avoided. Unfortunately, **cut** changes the meaning of the memberOf rule. If the program uses this rule not to verify that X is a member of some list L but to find a list L with X as a member, **cut** will force X to be the first element in L, which prevents other perfectly good lists from being formed.

Another control operator in Prolog is **fail**, which always fails; that is, it can never be proven true. (Again, SNOBOL has an analogous **fail** pattern.) A program may use **fail** to state that a goal can't be established. For example, given a predicate male(X), I might create the rule in Figure 8.40.

Figure 8.40

```
grandmotherOf(X,GM) :- male(GM) , fail .
```

This rule states that if GM is male, then GM can't be anyone's grandmother. Interestingly, this rule doesn't achieve its intended purpose. The problem is that backtracking takes effect, saying (in effect) that if this rule doesn't work, maybe some other rule will. To avoid backtracking, **cut** must added, as in Figure 8.41.

Figure 8.41

```
grandmotherOf(GM,X) :- male(GM) , ! , fail .
```

Cut is often used in conjunction with **fail** when backtracking is to be suppressed. Another use for **fail** is to create a sort of **while** loop, as in Figure 8.42.

Figure 8.42

```
while(X) :- cond(X) , body(X) , fail .                1
cond(X) :- memberOf(X, [1,2,3,7]) .                   2
body(X) :- write(X) , write(' ') .                    3

in:  while(_) .                                        4
out: 1 2 3 7                                            5
     No                                                 6
```

Other more complex Prolog operators exist. For example, **assert** and **retract** can be used to add or remove facts and rules from the database while evaluation is in progress. These operators can be used to allow a program to learn, but since they have the flavor of self-modifying code, they are potentially very dangerous.

1.10 An Example of Control Programming

To illustrate some of the subtleties of programming in Prolog, I will consider the canonical (mis-)example of recursive programming, factorial. The obvious definition appears in Figure 8.43.

Figure 8.43

```
fact(N,F) :- N >= 0, N =< 1 , F = 1 .                        1
fact(N,F) :- N > 1 , M is N-1 , fact(M,G) , F is N*G .       2
```

This definition, though correct, is not entirely satisfactory. The problem is that fact can be used in a surprisingly large number of ways, depending on what values are bound (that is, input parameters) and what values are to be computed (that is, output parameters). Possible combinations that should be handled are the following:

1. Both N and F are bound: Fact should succeed or fail depending on whether or not N! = F.
2. N is bound, but F is free: F should be correctly computed. Attempts to resatisfy fact to obtain a different value for F should fail (since N! is unique for bound N).
3. F is bound, but N is free: If an integer N exists such that N! = F, it should be computed; else fact should fail. Attempts to resatisfy fact to obtain a different value for N should fail, except when F=1.
4. Both N and F are free: The initial solution fact(1,1) should be found. Attempts to resatisfy fact to obtain different values for N and F should succeed, producing monotonically increasing (N,F) pairs.

The program in Figure 8.43 works when N is bound, but not when it is free. This isn't too surprising, since the definition I chose is the one used in languages that assume that N must be bound. The problem is that my definition gives no clue as to how to choose a value for N when it is free. I can take a step toward a better solution by dealing with the simpler case in which N is bound.[2] The predeclared predicates bound and free (in some implementations nonvar and var) can be used to determine whether a parameter is bound or not. That is, bound(X) is true whenever X is bound (even temporarily, by resolution during backtrack) to a value. Consider Figure 8.44.

---

[2] This solution was provided by Bill Pugh.

Figure 8.44

```
fact(0,1) .                                                      1
fact(N,F) :- bound(N) , N > 0 , M is N-1 ,                       2
    fact(M, G) , F is N*G .                                      3
fact(N,F) :- free(N) , bound(F) , fact(M,G) , N is M+1 ,         4
   F2 is N*G , F =< F2 , ! , F = F2 .                            5
fact(N,F) :-  free(N) , free(F) , fact(M,G) , N is M+1 ,         6
     F is N*G .                                                  7
```

The rule in line 1 defines the base case for factorial. The rule in line 2 covers the case where N is bound and greater than 0. **Cut** is used to prohibit backtracking, since N! is single-valued. The rule in line 3 covers the case where N is bound and greater than 1. It recursively computes or verifies N!. The case in which N is free but F is bound is more interesting. The rule in lines 4–5 covers this case. It computes factorial pairs (using the rule in lines 6–7) until the factorial value is ≥ the bound value of F. At this point it cuts the backtracking. If the computed factorial value F2 is equal to F, it succeeds, and N is correctly bound. Otherwise it fails, indicating that F isn't a factorial value. Finally, the general case in which both N and F are free is considered in lines 1 and 6–7. Prolog first matches the base case of fact(0,0), then generates the next solution, fact(1,1), from it, using the rule in lines 6–7. Successive solutions are obtained by building upon the most recently discovered factorial pair.

1.11 Negation

If a query cannot be satisfied by any binding of its free variables, Prolog considers it false. Prolog has a built-in higher-order predicate not that tests for unsatisfiability. (It is higher-order in that it takes a predicate, not a term, as its parameter.) Consider Figure 8.45.

Figure 8.45

```
motherOf(nora, fatima) .                                         1

in:   ?- not(motherOf(nora, jaleh)) .                            2
out:  Yes                                                        3

in:   ?- not(motherOf(nora, fatima)) .                           4
out:  No                                                         5
```

Line 1 introduces a new fact. Line 2 tests to see if a particular fact is unknown. Because it is, the response is Yes. Line 4 tests to see if a known fact is unknown; it elicits No.

Under the closed-world assumption that facts that cannot be proved are false, the facts and rules known to the program constitute the entire world; no new facts or rules from "outside" will be added that might render a previously unprovable conclusion true. The closed-world assumption is an example of **nonmonotonic reasoning**, which is a property of a logic in which adding information (in the form of facts and rules) can reduce the number of conclusions that can be proved.

It is only safe to use not with all parameters bound. Otherwise, unexpected results may occur, as in Figure 8.46.

Figure 8.46

```
motherOf(nora, fatima) .                                               1

in:   ?- not(motherOf(X,jaleh)) .                                      2
out:  X=_1                                                             3

in:   ?- not(motherOf(_,jaleh)) .                                      4
out:  Yes                                                              5

in:   ?- not(motherOf(X, fatima)) .                                    6
out:  No                                                               7

in:   ?- not(motherOf(nora, Y)) .                                      8
out:  No                                                               9

in:   ?- not(motherOf(X, fatima)), X=jaleh .                           10
out:  No                                                               11

in:   ?- X=jaleh, not(motherOf(X,fatima)) .                            12
out:  X=jaleh                                                          13
```

In line 2, since no facts match motherOf(X,jaleh), any substitution for X serves to satisfy its negation. Prolog returns a don't-care result. Line 4 asks the same query, without expecting a binding; it replaces the free variable X with the don't-care pattern _ . The result, Yes, shows that any substitution works. The next two queries produce surprising results. Lines 6 and 8 present queries where the free variable could be set to a known constant to make the query fail (X could be nora in line 5, and Y could be fatima in line 7); all other settings allow the query to succeed. If Prolog implemented **constructive negation**, it would be able to report X ≠ nora in line 7 and Y ≠ fatima in line 9. But most implementations of Prolog do not provide constructive negation. Prolog can't even represent the answers by a single don't-care result, such as Y=_1, because at least one value is *not* part of the answer. Instead, Prolog gives up and fails. Line 10 tries to suggest a reasonable result: X = jaleh. However, Prolog binds variables from left to right in a query, and X is unbound within the not predicate. Line 12 succeeds in binding X by reordering the query. In short, unbound variables inside not only give the expected result if either all bindings succeed (as in line 2) or no bindings succeed. Intermediate possibilities just lead to failure.

A different problem is shown by Figure 8.47.

Figure 8.47

```
blue(sky) .                                                    1

in:  not(not(blue(X)) .                                        2
out: X = _1                                                    3
```

The query in line 2 begins by unifying blue(X) with blue(sky), binding X to sky. This unification succeeds. The first not therefore fails, causing the binding of X to be lost. The second not therefore succeeds, but X has no binding, so it is presented as a don't-care result.

Negation in rules can also lead to anomalies, as shown in the rule in Figure 8.48.

Figure 8.48

```
wise(X) :- not(wise(X)) .
```

This rule appears to be a conundrum. A person is wise if that person is not wise. In symbolic logic, there is a solution to this puzzle: everyone is wise. The derivation in Figure 8.49 demonstrates this result.

Figure 8.49

```
¬ wise(X) => wise(X)                                          1
¬ ¬ wise(X) ∨ wise(X)                                         2
wise(X) ∨ wise(X)                                             3
wise(X)                                                       4
```

However, Prolog enters an unterminated loop when a query such as wise(murali) is presented. In general, there is no completely accurate way to handle logical negation, and most Prolog implementations don't do very well with it.

1.12 Other Evaluation Orders

Prolog programmers must sort rules to avoid infinite loops. They must also sort the conjuncts within rules for the sake of efficiency. The naiveSort example in Figure 8.26 (page 281) would fail to terminate if line 1 were written as in Figure 8.50.

Figure 8.50

```
naiveSort(L1,L2) :- inOrder(L2) , permutation(L1,L2) .
```

The Prolog interpreter builds more and more fanciful values of L2 that have nothing at all to do with L1 and fails on each one. Prolog programmers learn to build rules so that the first conjunct generates potential solutions, and the remaining conjuncts test them for acceptability. If the generator builds too many unacceptable results, the rule will be very inefficient.

The fact that rule and conjunct order is so crucial to efficiency detracts from the declarative nature of Prolog. It would be nice if the rules merely stated the desired result, and if the implementation were able to dynamically sort the rules and conjuncts to generate the result efficiently.

One proposal for a different evaluation strategy is found in Specint [Darlington 90]. A static version of the idea, called "sideways information passing," appears in Datalog. The idea is to reorder the conjuncts as they are satisfied, so that attention is directed to the first conjunct that has not yet been satisfied. As each conjunct is satisfied, it is rotated to the *end* of the list of conjuncts; it may be retested (and resatisfied) later if other conjuncts fail in the meantime. The programmer can supply hints for each predicate that suggest what parameters will satisfy that predicate. Predefined predicates have their own hints. For example, Figure 8.51 gives a slightly different version of naiveSort.

Figure 8.51

```
naiveSort(L1,L2) :- permutation(L1,L2) , inOrder(L2) .          1

permutation(X,Y) :- X = Y                                       2
permutation(X|Z,Y) :- delete(X,Y,T) , permutation(Z,T)         3

inOrder([]) .                                                   4
inOrder([_]) .                                                  5
inOrder([A,B|T]) :- A =< B , inOrder([B|T]) .                  6
```

To evaluate naiveSort([1,3,2],result), the evaluator first tries to satisfy the first conjunct of line 1. This conjunct brings it to line 2 to find an acceptable permutation Y of X = [1,3,2]. By default, permutation will first try the empty list for Y. It fails, because it satisfies neither line 2 nor line 3. However, the equality test of line 2 has a default hint: set Y to X. Now permutation(X,Y) is satisfied, so the Specint evaluator moves to the inOrder conjunct of line 1, bringing it to line 6. In line 6, A is 1, B is 3, and T is [2]. The first conjunct succeeds, and inOrder is called recursively on [3,2]. In the recursive call of line 6, A is 3, B is 2, and T is []. The first conjunct fails. The hint for satisfying =< is to interchange the two values. Now line 6 succeeds (after a brief further recursion), and the new values are backed up to the first instance of line 6. Now A is 1, B is 2, and T is [3]. This instance rechecks the first conjunct. It was previously satisfied, but values have changed. Luckily, the new values still satisfy this conjunct. Evaluation returns to line 1. Now L2 is [1,2,3], and the second conjunct is satisfied. The first conjunct is rechecked. After several instantiations of line 3, this check is satisfied.

Specint ends up with something like insertion sort, using quadratic time, instead of Prolog's exponential-time evaluation.

Standard Prolog evaluation starts at the goal and moves to subgoals; this approach is called **top-down evaluation**. Another evaluation order that has been proposed is **bottom-up** evaluation. In its pure form, bottom-up evaluation would mean starting with facts and deriving consequences, both direct and indirect. But this sort of undirected evaluation is unlikely to tend toward the desired goal. Luckily, bottom-up evaluation can be implemented in a more directed fashion. Given a query, some preprocessing based on the top-down tree can lead to insight concerning a reasonable ordering of the conjuncts in the bodies of rules. This insight is based on sideways information passing, which determines what information is passed in variables between the conjuncts. The result is a transformed program that can be executed bottom-up. The bottom-up approach leads to certain simplifications. In particular, the unification algorithm is not needed if every variable that appears in the head of the rule also appears in its body. This restriction does not seem unreasonable. Avoiding unification can be essential in some domains. In particular, strings can be introduced into Prolog with matching rules that match "abcd" to A + B, matching any initial substring to A and the rest to B. Unification is intractable in this setting.

1.13 Constraint-Logic Programming (CLP)

A small extension to Prolog's evaluation mechanism simplifies programs like factorial in Figure 8.44 (page 290). This extension, called constraint-logic programming, or CLP, lets identifiers have a **constrained** status, which lies between bound and free [Fruhwirth 92]. CLP(R) is Prolog with constraints expressed with respect to real numbers.

A conjunct in CLP(R) such as X < 5 is merely checked if X is bound, but if X is free or constrained, this conjunct introduces a constraint on X. If the new constraint, in combination with previous constraints, makes a variable unsatisfiable, the evaluator must backtrack. The power of this idea can be seen in Figure 8.52.

Figure 8.52

```
in:   Nice(X, Y) :- X = 6 , Y < 5 .                        1
      ?- Nice(A,B) .                                        2
out:  A = 6, B < 5                                          3

in:   ?- Nice(A,B) , B > 7 .                                4
out:  No                                                    5
```

Line 2 is only satisfied by a restricted set of values; the output shows the applicable constraints. When I add a conflicting constraint in line 4, no results can be found. Figure 8.53 is a factorial predicate.

Figure 8.53

```
fact(N,F) :- N <= 1 , F = 1 .                                           1
fact(N,F) :- N >  1 , M = N-1 , fact(M,G) , F = N*G .                   2
```

Line 2 does not use the **is** predicate, because my intent is to introduce a constraint, not to perform arithmetic. The query fact(X,Y) elicits the following solutions:

```
X ≤ 1, Y = 1
X = Y, 1 < Y ≤ 2.
2 < X ≤ 3, Y = X*(X-1)
3 < X ≤ 4, Y = X*(X-1)*(X-2)
4 < X ≤ 5, Y = X*(X-1)*(X-2)*(X-3)
...
```

If we add the constraint that all numbers are integers, not arbitrary reals, then these values reduce to exact solutions. Figure 8.54 computes Fibonacci numbers.

Figure 8.54

```
fib(0,1).                                                               1
fib(1,1).                                                               2
fib(N, X1 + X2) :- N > 1 , fib(N - 1, X1) , fib(N - 2, X2) .            3
```

This program works correctly no matter whether the parameters are free or bound. Figure 8.55 shows how to multiply two complex numbers.

Figure 8.55

```
complexMultiply(c(R1, I1), c(R2, I2), c(R3, I3)) :-                     1
    R3 = R1 * R2 - I1 * I2 ,                                            2
    I3 = R1 * I2 + R2 * I1 .                                            3
```

The functor c is used as a pattern. We can give CLP(R) queries about complexMultiply, as in Figure 8.56.

Figure 8.56

```
in:  ?- complexMultiply(X, c(2,2), c(0,4))                             1
out: X = c(1,1)                                                        2

in:  ?- complexMultiply(X, Y, c(0,0))                                  3
out: X = c(A,B), Y = c(C,D), A*C = B*D, A*D = -B*C                     4
```

There are rare occasions when a term someFunctor(3 + 4) is meant to be different from the term someFunctor(4 + 3). CLP(R) allows the programmer to prevent evaluation of the + operator in such cases by means of a quoting mechanism.

As a final example of constraint-logic programming, consider the program of Figure 8.57, which finds the circuits that can be built from two available resistors in series and a single voltage source so that the drop in voltage across the second resistor is between 14.5 and 16.25 volts [Jaffar 92]:

Figure 8.57

```
/* available resistors */                                    1
    Resistor(10) .                                           2
    Resistor(14) .                                           3
    Resistor(27) .                                           4
    Resistor(60) .                                           5
    Resistor(100) .                                          6
/* available voltage sources */                              7
    Voltage(10) .                                            8
    Voltage(20) .                                            9
/* electrical law */                                         10
    Ohm(Voltage, Amperage, Resistance) :-                    11
        Voltage = Amperage * Resistance .                    12
/* query about our circuit */                                13
?- 14.5 < V2, V2 < 16.25 , /* voltage constraints */         14
    Resistor(R1) , Resistor(R2), /* choice of resistors */   15
    Voltage(V) , /* choice of voltages */                    16
    Ohm(V1,A1,R1) , Ohm(V2,A2,R2), /* electrical laws */     17
    A1 = A2, V = V1 + V2 . /* series circuit */              18
```

An evaluator might choose to solve linear constraints before nonlinear ones in order to achieve the three solutions.

1.14 Metaprogramming

Chapter 4 shows how a LISP interpreter may be written in LISP. Prolog provides a similar ability. As with LISP, the trick is to make the language homoiconic, that is, to be able to treat programs as data. Programs are just sets of rules (a fact is a rule with a body of true). The body of a rule is a comma-separated list of predicates. In addition to the bracket-delimited lists shown earlier, Prolog also accepts simple comma-separated lists.[3] The head of a rule is also a predicate, and the :- separator can be treated as an infix binary predicate.

---

[3] Comma-separated lists are the underlying concept. The list a,b,c is equivalent to a,(b,c). The bracketed list [H | T] is syntactic sugar for the predicate .(H,T), where the dot is a binary cons functor.

So a program is a set of predicates, and Prolog provides a way to inspect, introduce, and delete the predicates that currently make up the program, that is, to treat the program as data. The clause predicate is used for inspecting rules, as in Figure 8.58.

Figure 8.58

```
grandmotherOf(X,GM) :- motherOf(M,GM) , motherOf(X,M) .      1
grandmotherOf(X,GM) :- motherOf(F,GM) , fatherOf(X,F) .      2

in:   ?- clause(grandmotherOf(A,B),Y).                       3
out:  A = _1,                                                4
      B = _2,                                                5
      Y = motherOf(_3 _2), motherOf(_1, _3);                 6

      A = _1,                                                7
      B = _2,                                                8
      Y = motherOf(_3, _2), fatherOf(_1, _3)                 9

motherOf(janos,hette) .                                     10

in:   ?- clause(MotherOf(X,Y),Z) .                          11
out:  X = janos,                                            12
      Y = hette,                                            13
      Z = true                                              14
```

Lines 1–2 reintroduce the grandmotherOf predicate that I used before. Line 3 asks for all rules that have a left-hand side matching grandmotherOf(A,B). This line treats grandmotherOf(A,B) as a structure, not a predicate. Prolog finds the two results shown, which are expressed in terms of don't-care results. The result Y treats motherOf as a functor, not a predicate name. This ability to interchange the treatment of structures and predicates is essential in making Prolog homoiconic, because structures are data, whereas predicates are program. Facts, such as the one shown in line 10, are also discovered by clause; the second parameter to clause matches true for facts.

The clause predicate can be used to build an evaluation predicate eval, as in Figure 8.59.

Figure 8.59

```
eval(true).                                                 1
eval((A,B)) :- eval(A), eval(B).                            2
eval(A) :- clause(A,B), eval(B).                            3
```

This set of rules defines standard Prolog evaluation order. Line 1 is the base case. Line 2 indicates how to evaluate a list of conjuncts. (The parenthesized list notation (A,B) matches any list with at least two elements; the first matches A, and the rest match B. This alternative list notation is not interchangeable with [A | B]; it is a historical relic.) Line 3 shows how to evaluate a single conjunct that happens to match the left-hand side of some rule or fact. (Some implementations of Prolog have a more generous implementation of clause; for these, I would need to introduce **cut** at the start of the body of line 2.)

The fact that you can write your own evaluator means that you can override the standard interpretation of conjuncts. Building new evaluators is called **metaprogramming**. The ordinary Prolog evaluator remains available to metaprograms as the call predicate. The exercises pursue these ideas.

So far, I have concentrated on the static aspect of Prolog, which treats rules as an unchangeable set of givens. Prolog also allows rules to be introduced and deleted during the execution of queries by using assert and retract, as in Figure 8.60.

Figure 8.60

```
allow(X) :- assert(person(zul)) ,                            1
      assert(person(Y) :- Y=kealoha), person(X).             2
deny(X) :- retract(person(X)).                               3

in:   ?- person(X) .                                         4
out:  No                                                     5

in:   allow(fred) .                                          6
out:  No                                                     7

in:   ?- person(X) .                                         8
out:  X = zul;                                               9
      X = kealoha                                            10

in:   ?- deny(beruria) .                                     11
out:  No                                                     12

in:   ?- person(X) .                                         13
out:  X = zul;                                               14
      X = kealoha                                            15

in:   ?- deny(zul) .                                         16
out:  Yes                                                    17

in:   ?- person(X) .                                         18
out:  X = kealoha                                            19

in:   ?- deny(kealoha) .                                     20
out:  No                                                     21
```

```
in:   ?- retract(person(X) :- Y) .                    22
out:  X = _1,                                         23
      Y = _1 = kealoha                                24

in:   ?- person(X) .                                  25
out:  No                                              26
```

Lines 1–3 introduce rules that, when evaluated, cause facts and rules to be introduced and deleted. Lines 4–5 show that at the start, nobody is known to be a person. The query in line 6 fails, but it still manages to execute two assert conjuncts, which introduce new rules. It is valid to introduce duplicate rules; Prolog does not automatically check for or remove duplicates. Lines 8–10 prove that new rules have been introduced. Evaluating the deny predicate in line 11 tries to retract a rule that is not present; it fails. However, deny(zul) (line 16) succeeds and does retract a rule. Line 20 tries to retract the fact person(kealoha). However, this predicate does not correspond to any fact, even though it is currently derivable that kealoha is a person. The way to remove that derivation is by retracting the rule. Line 22 retracts the first rule whose head is person(X). There is only one such rule, and retract succeeds in removing it.

All asserted facts and rules are added to the top-level environment. In fact, Prolog rules do not follow scope; there is only one environment. A program can simulate dynamic scope for rules, however, by introducing new rules in the first conjunct of a body and retracting those rules in the last conjunct. The programmer must make sure that the rules are retracted in case the intervening conjuncts fail. Also, the programmer must be careful not to introduce rules with heads that already exist in the environment; such introduced rules will be added to, not replace, existing rules, and retraction might accidentally remove more rules than are intended.

2 ◆ GÖDEL

Gödel, developed by P. M. Hill, is intended to be the successor of Prolog [Hill 94]. It borrows much of Prolog's form, but attempts to address many of the problems and deficiencies of Prolog. It provides modules to make the language suitable for large projects, has a strong type system, permits enhanced logical forms, and has more consistent search-pruning operators. Gödel also directly supports integers, floats, rational numbers, strings, lists, and sets.

2.1 Program Structure

A program in Gödel consists of at least one module. Each module is divided into several parts, most of which are optional.

- **module** names the module. Modules can also be declared **closed** (which means the implementation is not provided, and may well be in a different language), **export** (all definitions are exported to other modules), or **local** (all definitions are private).
- **import** lists the modules whose declarations are imported.
- **base** declares types.
- **constructor** declares type constructors.
- **constant** declares constants.
- **function** lists functions and declares their type. (These are like functors in Prolog.)
- **predicate** lists predicates and defines their type.
- **delay** lists conditions for controlling evaluation of predicates.
- **proposition** lists propositions.
- Finally, there is a list of rules.

For example, the module in Figure 8.61 calculates factorials.

Figure 8.61

```
module Factorial.                                      1
import Integers.                                       2
predicate Fact : Integer * Integer.                    3

Fact(0,1).                                             4
Fact(1,1).                                             5
Fact(n,f) <- n > 1 & Fact(n-1,g) & f = g * n.          6
```

The module is named Factorial and imports types, functions, and predicates from the (library) module Integers. It has one predicate, Fact, which has two integer parameters. Three rules define Fact (lines 4–6). The program is executed by supplying a query, as in Figure 8.62.

Figure 8.62

```
in:   <- Fact(4,x).                                    1
out:  x = 24                                           2
```

2.2 Types

Figure 8.63 illustrates construction of programmer-defined types.

Figure 8.63

```
module M1.                                              1
base Day, ListOfDay.                                    2
constant                                                3
      Nil : ListOfDay;                                  4
      Monday, Tuesday, Wednesday, Thursday, Friday,     5
            Saturday, Sunday : Day.                     6
function Cons : Day * ListOfDay -> ListOfDay.           7
predicate Append : ListOfDay * ListOfDay * ListOfDay.   8

/* Append(a,b,c) means list a appended to list b;       9
      results in list c. */                            10
Append(Nil,x,x).                                        11
Append(Cons(u,x),y,Cons(u,z)) <- Append(x,y,z).        12
```

Day and ListOfDay (line 2) are the only types of this program. Cons (line 7) is not a pattern symbol, as it would be in Prolog, but rather a function. Every constant, function, proposition, and predicate of the language must be declared, but variable types are inferred, as in ML. Constructors can be used in type declarations. They may be applied to the ground types defined in the **base** clause to create new types. This process can be recursively applied to make an infinite number of types. I can improve this module by making the concept of list polymorphic, as in Figure 8.64.

Figure 8.64

```
module M2.                                              1
base Day, Person.                                       2
constructor List/1.                                     3
constant                                                4
      Nil : List('a);                                   5
      Monday, Tuesday, Wednesday, Thursday, Friday,     6
            Saturday, Sunday : Day;                      7
      Fred, Barney, Wilma, Betty : Person.              8
function Cons : 'a * List('a) -> List('a).              9
predicate Append : List('a) * List('a) * List('a).     10

Append(Nil,x,x).                                        11
Append(Cons(u,x),y,Cons(u,z)) <- Append(x,y,z).        12
```

The constructor List (line 3) is followed by an integer indicating its arity. The identifier 'a in lines 5, 9, and 10 is a type identifier. The types for this program are Day, Person, List(Day), List(Person), List(List(Day)), and so forth.

LISP-like lists form such a common structure in declarative programming that Gödel, like Prolog, predeclares the List constructor, the Cons function, and the Nil constant. The constructors for lists are the

same as in Prolog; the list Cons(Fred,Cons(Bill,x)) can be written as
[Fred, Bill | x].

2.3 Logic Programming

Unlike Prolog programs, Gödel programs are not limited to Horn
clauses. The following quantifiers and connectives are allowed.

Symbol	Meaning
&	conjunction (**and**)
\\/	disjunction (**or**)
~	negation (**not**)
<-	implication
->	right implication
<->	equivalence
all	universal quantifier
some	existential quantifier

The quantifiers have two parameters, a list of variables and the body, as
in Figure 8.65.

Figure 8.65

```
module Inclusion.                                              1
import Lists.                                                  2
predicate IncludedIn : List(a) * List(a)                      3
     -- IncludedIn(a,b) means list a is included in list b.  4

IncludedIn(x,y) <- all [z] (MemberOf(z,y) <- MemberOf(z,x)). 5
     -- MemberOf(a,b) means element a is a member of list b. 6
```

The rule in line 5 indicates that list x is included in list y if all members
of x are also members of y. This example also illustrates some of the use
of modules. The predicate MemberOf (used in line 5) is declared in the
imported module Lists.

Queries are quite simple to write. For example, assume that a module has been declared with the classic family relationship predicates and
facts FatherOf, MotherOf, ParentOf, AncestorOf, and so forth. Then the
query "Does everyone who has a mother also have a father?" can be
written, as in Figure 8.66.

Figure 8.66   `<- all [x]`   1
                 `(some [z] FatherOf(x,z) <- some [y] MotherOf(x,y))).`   2

In practice, **some** is seldom used, because Gödel provides _ as a don't-care pattern. The above query can be written more simply as in Figure 8.67.

Figure 8.67   `<- all [x] (FatherOf(x,_) <- MotherOf(x,_))`

The quantifier **some** may also be used in queries to restrict the display of results to the variables of interest to the user. For example, the query in Figure 8.68

Figure 8.68   `<- some [y] (ParentOf(x,y) & ParentOf(y,Jane)).`

will display the value to which x is bound, but not y. The same query can be written using the colon notation (: is read "such that"), as in Figure 8.69.

Figure 8.69   `<- x : ParentOf(x,y) & ParentOf(y,Jane).`

2.4 Conditionals

Gödel allows the use of conditional statements primarily as a concession to computational efficiency. The structure **if** condition **then** formula is logically equivalent to condition -> formula. The semantics of conditionals differ procedurally from implications, however. Unlike implications, the evaluation of a conditional waits until the condition has no free variables.

If the condition and the formula share local variables, the form in Figure 8.70 is used.

Figure 8.70   **if some** `[r1, ..., rn]` condition **then** formula

This form is equivalent to that in Figure 8.71.

Figure 8.71   `(some [r1, ..., rn] (condition & formula)) \/`   1
                 `~ some [r1, ..., rn] condition.`   2

The **if** construct is defined similarly, but oddly enough, the rule for resolving the dangling-**else** problem is contrary to standard convention.

The module for defining LISP-like association lists in Figure 8.72 illustrates conditionals.

Figure 8.72

```
module AssocList.                                             1
import Strings.                                               2
base PairType.                                                3
function Pair : Integer * String -> PairType.                4
predicate Lookup : Integer * String * List(PairType)         5
        * List(PairType).                                     6

Lookup(key, value, assoc_list, new_assoc_list) <-            7
    if some [v]                                              8
        MemberOf(Pair(key,v), assoc_list)                    9
    then                                                     10
        value = v &                                          11
        new_assoc_list = assoc_list                          12
    else                                                     13
        new_assoc_list = [Pair(key,value) | assoc_list].     14
```

2.5 Control

Logic programming in its pure form allows the parameters of predicates to be arbitrarily bound or unbound. As you saw in Prolog, it is often difficult (and unnecessary) to write rules that cover all cases. Gödel uses something like Prolog's bound predicate, but it enhances it with a control structure that delays evaluation of predicates until certain conditions are met. Predicates in a conjunction can be processed like coroutines. For example, the definition of Permutation in Figure 8.73 might be placed in the Lists module.

Figure 8.73

```
predicate Permutation : List(a) * List(a).                   1
    -- Permutation(a,b) means list a is                      2
    -- a permutation of list b                               3
delay Permutation(x,y) until bound(x) \/ bound(y).           4

Permutation([],[]).                                          5
Permutation([x|y],[u|v]) <-                                  6
    Delete(u,[x|y],z) & Permutation(z,v).                    7
    -- Delete(a,b,c) means deleting element a                8
    -- from list b gives list c                              9
```

The **delay** construct in line 4 causes Permutation to pause until one of its parameters is bound. If it is invoked with both parameters unbound and no other predicates can be explored to bind one of the parameters, as in Figure 8.74, Permutation will fail. (This behavior is nonmonotonic.)

Figure 8.74

```
in:  <- Permutation(x,y).                           1
out: No                                             2

in:  <- Permutation(x,y) & x = [1,2].               3
out: x = [1,2], y = [1,2];                          4
     x = [1,2], y = [2,1]                           5
```

In line 1, neither parameter is bound, so the query fails. In line 3, evaluation of Permutation delays until the second conjunct is evaluated. That conjunct binds x to a value, so now Permutation may be invoked.

In order to build a sort program similar to naiveSort in Figure 8.26 (page 281), I will introduce in Figure 8.75 a Sorted predicate for the Lists module.

Figure 8.75

```
predicate Sorted : List(integer).                   1
delay                                               2
     Sorted([]) until true;                         3
     Sorted([_]) until true;                        4
     Sorted([x,[y|_]) until bound(x) & bound(y).    5

Sorted([]).                                         6
Sorted([_]).                                        7
Sorted([x,y|z]) <- x =< y & Sorted([y|z]).          8
```

The **delay** construct in line 2 takes multiple patterns, each of which may be treated differently. If Sorted is invoked with a list of length 0 or 1, it will not delay, even if the list element is not bound (lines 3–4). For more complex lists, Sorted will be delayed until the first two elements of the list are both bound. I can now use Sorted and Permutation to define a Sort module, as in Figure 8.76.

Figure 8.76

```
module Sort.                                        1
import Lists. -- brings in Sorted and Permutation   2
predicate SlowSort : List(Integer) * List(Integer). 3

SlowSort(x,y) <- Sorted(y) & Permutation(x, y).     4
     -- SlowSort(a,b) means list a is sorted to produce b.  5
```

SlowSort works if either x or y (or both) is bound. If y is bound, Sorted will not be delayed. If Sorted succeeds, Permutation will either verify that x is a permutation of y if x is bound or find all values of x that are permutations of y. If y is not bound and x is, then Sorted(y) will delay, and Permutation will instantiate y to a permutation of x. The entire permutation need not be produced before Sorted continues; only the first two elements of the permutation are necessary. Perhaps these elements are enough to show that y is not sorted, and this permutation may be abandoned. If the first two elements of y are in order, Sorted makes a recursive call, which may again be delayed. At this point, Permutation will continue producing more elements of the permutation. If Sorted fails at any point, Permutation will backtrack to an alternative permutation. In effect, **delay** gives Gödel lazy evaluation, which makes SlowSort much faster than Prolog's equivalent naiveSort in Figure 8.26 (page 281). It is still a very poor sorting method, however.

The **delay** construct also helps the programmer to guarantee termination. Consider the definition of Delete in Figure 8.77, which is needed to define Permutation in Figure 8.73 (page 304).

Figure 8.77

```
-- Delete(a,b,c) means deleting element a          1
-- from list b gives list c                        2
predicate Delete : a * List(a) * List(a).          3
delay Delete(_,y,z) until bound(y) \/ bound(z).    4

Delete(x,[x|y],y).                                 5
Delete(x,[y|z],[y|w]) <- Delete(x,z,w).            6
```

Without the **delay** in line 4, the query Permutation(x, [1, 2, 3]) would first produce the answer x = [1, 2, 3] and then go into an infinite loop. With the **delay** present, the six possible permutations are produced, and then Permutation fails.

Gödel also allows the programmer to prune the backtrack search tree in a fashion similar to Prolog's **cut**, but in a more consistent fashion. The simplest version of pruning is **bar commit**. **Bar commit** works like conjunction but with the added meaning that only one solution will be found for the formula in its scope (to its left); all branches arising from other statements for the same predicate are pruned. The order of statement evaluation is not specified, so **bar commit** lacks the sequential property of **cut**. For example, a Partition predicate to be used in Quicksort is shown in Figure 8.78.

Figure 8.78

```
-- Partition(a,b,c,d) means list a partitioned about      1
-- element b results in lists c and d.                    2
predicate Partition : List(Integer) * Integer *           3
    List(Integer) * List(Integer)                         4
delay                                                     5
    Partition([],_,_,_) until true;                       6
    Partition([u|_],y,_,_) until bound(u) & bound(y).     7

Partition([],y,[],[]) <- bar.                             8
Partition([x|xs],y,[x|ls],rs) <- x =< y bar              9
    Partition(xs,y,ls,rs).                               10
Partition([x|xs],y,ls,[x|rs]) <- x > y bar              11
    Partition(xs,y,ls,rs).                               12
```

In this case, I use **bar commit** (I denote it just by **bar** in lines 8–11) because the statements in the definition of Partition (lines 8–12) are mutually exclusive, so it prunes useless computation. It is possible to use **bar commit** to prune answers as well.

Gödel also provides **singleton commit**. A formula enclosed in curly brackets { and } will only produce one answer. For example, the query {Permutation([1,2,3], x)} will produce only one of the permutations instead of all six.

The **delay** construct can prevent premature **bar commit**s that could lead to unexpected failures. Figure 8.79 shows how to code the Delete predicate differently.

Figure 8.79

```
-- Delete(a,b,c) means deleting element a                 1
-- from list b gives list c                               2
predicate Delete : Integer * List(Integer) * List(Integer).  3
delay Delete(x,[u|_],_) until bound(x) & bound(u).        4

Delete(x,[x|y],y) <- bar .                                5
Delete(x,[y|z],[y|w]) <- x ~= y bar Delete(x,z,w).        6
```

If the program did not delay Delete until x was bound, the query Delete(x, [1, 2, 3], y) & x = 2 could commit with x bound to 1, by line 5. Then x = 2 would fail, causing the entire query to fail, because the **bar** in line 6 prevents backtracking for another binding to x.

3 ✦ FINAL COMMENTS

In some ways, Prolog is a hybrid of three ideas: LISP data structures, recursive pattern matching as in SNOBOL, and resolution theorem-proving. As a programming language, Prolog lacks mechanisms for structuring programs and has no type facilities. It is hard to read Prolog programs, because the order of parameters in predicates is not always obvious. This is a problem in other languages, but it seems especially severe in Prolog. For all its shortcomings, Prolog is widely used, especially in Europe, for artificial intelligence rule-based programs. It has been successfully used in such applications as genetic sequence analysis, circuit design, and stock-market analysis.

Enhancements of Prolog to give it an understanding of constraints and to organize search differently reduce the difficulty of writing clear and efficient programs. Various constraint-based extensions to Prolog have been developed, including CLP(Σ^*), which understands regular expressions [Walinsky 89], and versions that deal with strings in general [Rajasekar 94].

Concurrent logic programming is an active research topic. All the conjuncts in the body of a rule can be evaluated simultaneously, with bindings of common variables communicated as they arise between otherwise independent evaluators. This technique is called **and**-parallelism. Similarly, multiple rules whose heads match a goal can be evaluated simultaneously; this technique is called **or**-parallelism. Research topics include the ramifications of using shared and distributed memory, how to manage bindings for variables, how much parallelism can be discovered by the compiler in ordinary Prolog programs, and how the programmer can assist that task in extensions to Prolog. One such extension, called Guarded Horn Clauses, allows guard predicates, much like the guards in Ada's **select** statement (discussed in Chapter 7), to restrict the rules that are to be considered during concurrent evaluation. Much of the literature on concurrent logic programming has been surveyed by Shapiro [Shapiro 89].

Gödel manages to blend Prolog with strong typing, some type polymorphism, and modularization, while increasing the range of logical operators. It also provides lazy evaluation, which makes some naive programs far more efficient. However, it is a much more complex language; one of Prolog's advantages is its relative simplicity.

There are other languages specifically intended for knowledge-based reasoning. In particular, OPS5 shares with Prolog and Gödel the concept of rules, facts, and queries [Brownston 86]. It is based on an inference engine, which repeatedly (1) determines which rules match existing facts, (2) selects one of those rules based on some strategy, and then (3) applies the actions specified in the selected rule, usually adding to or altering the set of facts. Step 1 can be extremely costly, but step 3 can propagate changes to a data structure to make step 1 reasonably efficient.

EXERCISES

Review Exercises

8.1 Figure 8.10 (page 273) shows the backtrack tree for the query grandmotherOf(tom,X). Show the backtrack tree with the rules for grandmotherOf in Figure 8.8 (page 271) reordered as in Figure 8.80.

Figure 8.80
```
grandmotherOf(X,GM) :- motherOf(X,M) , motherOf(M,GM) . 1
grandmotherOf(X,GM) :- fatherOf(X,F) , motherOf(F,GM) . 2
```

8.2 What is the result of the query in Figure 8.81?

Figure 8.81
```
in:   ?- append([1,2],X,[1,2,3,4]) .
```

8.3 Modify the eval rules in Figure 8.59 (page 297) so that bodies are interpreted from right to left, that is, with the last conjunct first.

8.4 Design a functor faction with two parameters (the numerator and denominator) and predicate lessThan that takes two fractions and is satisfied if the first fraction is less than the second. The lessThan predicate does not need to be defined for unbound parameters.

Challenge Exercises

8.5 Does Prolog have static or dynamic scope rules for formal parameters?

8.6 Are predicates in Prolog first-, second-, or third-class values? How about predicate names, functors, and terms?

8.7 Show how to build a stack containing {1,2,3} and to verify that it is a stack, using the definitions of Figure 8.20 (page 278).

8.8   In Figure 8.20 (page 278), I defined nonhomogeneous stacks. Show
how the existence of a built-in `integer` predicate allows you to define integer stacks.

8.9   In Figure 8.20 (page 278), pop is a predicate name. Rewrite this
example so that pop is a functor.

8.10   In Figure 8.26 (page 281), how many solutions are there to `naive-
Sort([11,2,11],S)`?

8.11   In Figure 8.26 (page 281), how many solutions are there to
`naiveSort(S,[1,2])`?

8.12   As an alternative to `naiveSort` and `bubbleSort`, encode
`insertionSort` in Prolog. Make sure your program works cor-
rectly in all four cases of `insertionSort`(α,β), whether α or β is a
constant or a variable.

8.13   In Figure 8.33 (page 285), modify the definition of odd so that
`odd(2)` evaluates to No instead of leading to an infinite computation.

8.14   In Chapter 2, a CLU program is shown for generating all binary
trees with n nodes. Write a Prolog program that accomplishes the
same task.

8.15   Prolog's **cut** operator is not quite the same as SNOBOL's **fence**,
which only freezes alternatives selected within the current body,
but does not prohibit the evaluator from trying other rules whose
heads match. How can we achieve SNOBOL semantics in Prolog?

8.16   Modify the `eval` rules in Figure 8.59 (page 297) so that `eval` takes
an additional parameter, which matches a tree that shows the subgoals that succeed leading to each result.

8.17   What is the complexity of `SlowSort` in Figure 8.76 (page 305) when
x is bound and y is free?

8.18   Write `SlowSort` from Figure 8.76 (page 305) using CLU iterators to
achieve the lazy evaluation needed.

Chapter 9

Aggregates

This chapter deals with language features for dealing with **aggregates**, which are data that are structured according to some commonly useful organization, such as strings, arrays, and databases. Although many programming languages provide general-purpose facilities to structure data (such as records) and organize routines that manipulate the data (such as abstract data types), some structures are so important that languages deal with them specifically in order to make it easier to write clear and efficient programs. In this chapter, I concentrate on strings, arrays, databases, and mathematical formulas.

1 ◆ STRINGS

Most languages provide some facility for dealing with strings, that is, connected groups of characters. Some languages, however, specialize in string processing. This chapter will look at both elementary string operations and more complex control and data structures introduced in specialized string-processing languages.

1.1 Literals and Simple Operations

String literals are usually enclosed in double quotes ("). Some syntax is often provided to include unusual characters in string literals. For example, the C language allows an escape character to precede special forms, such as \r for a carriage return, \t for a tab, \" for a double quote, and \023 for the character whose internal representation is octal 23. One nice escape sequence that doesn't exist in any language I know of skips to the next nonwhite text without including the white space in the string. I use \c to represent this special form, as in Figure 9.1.

Figure 9.1

```
StringVar := "this is a very long string that \c        1
             I place on several lines, but it represents \c    2
             a string without line breaks or gaps."       3
```

Operations on strings are provided either by predefined procedures or by operators in the language. The simplest operations on strings, such as copying, equality testing, and lexical comparison, are often provided as overloaded meanings of := , = , and < . Another simple operation is concatenation, often represented by the overloaded operator + . (SNOBOL represents concatenation by an empty space operator, which is quite confusing, particularly since the same invisible operator also represents pattern matching!) In addition, a few languages, such as ABC, provide operators for string repetition ("ho" * 3 is "hohoho"), string length, and arcane operations such as finding the minimum character in a string.

Languages usually provide ways to convert other data types to strings. This facility is particularly important for output, which is often a long string computed from values of various types. Conversions to string are usually separate functions for each type to be converted, but C has a single function sprintf that can convert and concatenate any combination of basic types according to a format string, as in Figure 9.2.

Figure 9.2

```
IntVar := 23;                                          1
sprintf(ResultString,                                  2
    "Give me %d number%s between %5g and 10%c.",        3
    IntVar, if IntVar = 1 then "" else "s" end,        4
    4.5, '0'");                                         5
```

The format string in line 3 is copied to ResultString, but certain escapes prefixed by % cause later actual parameters to be converted and inserted into the string. The formats are specified by %d for integer, %s for string, %g for float, and %c for character. Formats can include width specifiers, as shown by %5g. This code places in ResultString the value

```
"Give me 23 numbers between  4.5 and 100."
```

A related and even simpler method is provided by Sal in the form of **edited strings** [Sturgill 89]. Figure 9.3 is the edited string equivalent of Figure 9.2.

Figure 9.3

```
IntVar := 23;                                        1
ResultString :=                                      2
    'Give me {IntVar} number\c                       3
    {if IntVar = 1 then "" else "s" end} \c          4
    between {4.5:5} and 10{'0'}.'                     5
```

Expressions in braces are evaluated at runtime and formatted as appropriate to their type and according to any width specification given. Edited strings use a different set of delimiters from ordinary strings as a way to warn the compiler to inspect them for included expressions, which the compiler interprets to generate code. This code is executed when the edited string is first evaluated; the result is an ordinary string that is not reevaluated later. Edited strings are more type-secure than the sprintf function, because there is no way to accidentally request that a value of some type be treated as a different type.

Languages often provide either a special syntax or a function call to extract substrings of a subject string based on position and length, as in Figure 9.4.

Figure 9.4

```
substr("A sample", 3, 4)
```

This string evaluates to "samp", starting at the third position of "A sample" and continuing for 4 characters.

It is also common to provide for character or substring search. Search can be designed to return a Boolean to indicate success, the position of the character or substring if found (0 otherwise), or a pointer to the character or substring if found (nil otherwise), as in Figure 9.5.

Figure 9.5

```
CharSearch("sample string", 's')                     1
StringSearch("Target string", "get")                 2
```

The search in line 1 could return true, 1, or a pointer to the entire string. The search in line 2 could return true, 4, or a pointer to the substring "get string". There might also be variants to conduct the search from right to left.

Slightly more complex than searching for characters is extracting data from a string while converting types; see Figure 9.6.

Figure 9.6

```
MyString := "4 and 4 make 8 in base 10"              1
sscanf(MyString, "%d and %d make %g.", First, Second, 2
    Third); -- First := 4, Second := 4, Third := 8.0  3
```

Here the formats are used not to convert from numeric data to string data, but the reverse, to convert parts of the string into numeric data. The occurrences of %d in line 2 cause the substring "4" to be converted to the integer 4; the %g format converts "8" to the real 8.0.

Another way to extract data from a string is to split it into fields based on some character. Several languages (for example, ABC, Perl, and Sal) provide a split procedure that takes a string and a set of characters considered to be field separators and a string array (passed by result) into which the given string is to be separated, as in Figure 9.7.

Figure 9.7

```
split("Veni, vidi, vici", ",", ResultArray)
```

This call would assign "Veni" into ResultArray[0], " vidi" into ResultArray[1] (with the initial space), and " vici" into ResultArray[2].

1.2 Representation

Usually, programmers don't need to worry about how a language implementation represents strings. However, the representation can affect both the speed of computation and the way the program must manipulate strings. For example, C defines strings as consecutive characters terminated by a null (binary zero) character. This representation makes it slow to concatenate a string to the end of another (the implementation must find the end of the second string by a linear method) and does not allow nulls to be contained within strings. It encourages a programming style in which a variable points into the string and advances character by character until the terminating null is seen.

Alternative representations have some advantages. If the length of the string is encoded, perhaps in the first few bytes, then concatenation becomes faster, and strings may contain null characters. If strings are declared with a compile-time length, many operations become faster, and the compiler can keep track of the length of intermediate strings in complex expressions. However, some operations produce results whose length cannot be predicted. For example, a substring operation might take a variable length parameter. Therefore, languages in which strings are explicitly declared usually declare the maximum length that the string value might attain. This information determines storage requirements but does not dictate the length of particular values put into storage.

One attractive proposal is to omit a string-length code at the start of the storage area for a string, use a terminating null, but use the last byte of the storage area to indicate the distance back to the terminating null [Bron 89]. If the string just fits in the storage area, so that the terminating null is in the last place, the null looks like the number 0, indicating zero distance to the terminating null. This representation makes it a bit harder for programs to build new strings directly, but a reasonable library of string-building operations can circumvent this problem, and programs may still scan through strings by using explicit pointers.

1.3 Pattern Matching

Sal, Awk, and Perl provide a match operator ˜ that compares a target string to a regular expression. The result is Boolean, indicating success. A **regular expression** is a string, where most characters match themselves, but some characters and character combinations have special meanings. The following table lists some of these special meanings; Perl has an even richer set.

Regular expression	Matches
.	any character
\<	start of word
\>	end of word
\s	white space
\d	a digit (like [0-9])
\w	a word
^	the beginning of the target string
$	the end of the target string
[abc...]	any character in the set; ranges like: [3-7A-P]
[^abc...]	any character not in the set
r1 | r2	either r1 or r2 (alternation)
r*	zero or more r's
r+	one or more r's
r?	zero or one r's
r{3,5}	match 3, 4, or 5 r's
(r)	match r, call it a group
\2	string matched by the second group

Some of these expressions, like . and '\s , match (and "use up") a single character. Others, like \< and ^ , do not use up any characters. For example, the \< expression matches the beginning of an alphanumeric region of the string; it is used to signal the start of a word. Grouping a subpattern allows you to refer to it later. Groups are numbered according to the left-to-right order of their opening parentheses. Figure 9.8 shows some examples of regular expressions.

Figure 9.8

```
"literal" -- matches "literal"                                      1
"l*iteral" -- matches "iteral", "literal", "lllliteral" ...        2
"(l|b)(i|o)b\2" -- matches "libi", "lobo", "bibi", "bobo"          3
"[lb][io]b" -- matches "lib", "lob", "bib", "bob"                  4
```

The match operator can return the start and length of the matched sub-string via predeclared global variables or make them available through functions to be called after the match. If several matches are possible, one match is chosen. The usual rule is that * extends its match as far as possible and that the alternatives indicated by | are tried in the order given. In Perl, the search can be made insensitive to the case of the subject string, it can be made to start either at the beginning of the string or where the previous search left off, and it can be set not to extend the match as far as possible.

Slightly more sophisticated than matching a pattern is replacing the matched substring with new contents. The new contents can depend on parts of the matched patterns. Those parts are typically parenthesized groups, numbered in the order of their opening parentheses, as in Figure 9.9.

Figure 9.9

```
MyString := "here is a nice sample";                               1
Substitute(MyString, "(i(s) )", "wa\2");                           2
```

The Substitute procedure in line 2 assigns "here was a nice sample" to MyString. The '\2' in line 2 fills in what the second group, (s), matched, namely, "s". Some languages provide sequences that can be placed in the third parameter of Substitute to indicate the part of the target string before the match, the entire matched part, and the part after the match, as in Figure 9.10.

Figure 9.10

```
MyString := "I think, therefore I am";                             1
Substitute(MyString, ",", " that \'\&\',");                        2
```

The expression \'\&\' in line 2 indicates the entire string, built up of the parts before, during, and after the match. The substitution changes MyString to "I think that I think, therefore I am, therefore I am".

1.4 Associative Arrays

Languages dealing with strings often provide a data type known as an **associative array**, which is indexed by strings instead of by integers or other scalar types. Associative arrays are usually implemented by hash tables. In some languages, like Sal and SNOBOL, the declaration of such an array indicates how large to make the hash table. If more elements are stored than the hash table size, access will become progressively slower but will still work. Other languages, like Perl, use extensible hashing and do not require any size declaration. ABC uses binary trees instead of hashing, so that a program can iterate through the array in key order. Other languages can only iterate in an implementation-dependent order.

Associative arrays are quite helpful in database applications. For example, to check for duplicates in a database with one field, say, Student-Name, I could use the Boolean associative array Present of Figure 9.11.

Figure 9.11

```
variable                                                        1
    Present : array string of Boolean;                          2
    ThisEntry : string;                                         3

loop                                                            4
    ThisEntry := GetNextEntryOfDatabase();                      5
    if ThisEntry = "" then break end; -- exit loop              6
    if defined Present[ThisEntry] then -- found duplicate       7
        write("{ThisEntry} is a duplicate.");                   8
    end;                                                        9
    Present[ThisEntry] := true;                                10
end;                                                           11
```

In line 7, the **defined** operator indicates whether a value has been defined for the particular index value given; it returns a Boolean. The assignment in line 10 could just as easily use false; what counts is that some value is placed in Present[ThisEntry].

Associative arrays often come with a control structure for iterating over all index values that have been defined. Figure 9.12 continues the previous example.

Figure 9.12

```
for Entry in Present do                                         1
    write(Entry);                                               2
end;                                                            3
```

1.5 Substrings as First-Class Values

Allowing substrings to be first-class values of a predeclared substring type has several advantages [Hansen 92]. Substring values can record not only their contents but also the identity of their base string. Dynamic allocation of space for substrings can be handled by the language at runtime.

Each value of the substring type contains a base string (perhaps implemented as a pointer) and the left and right positions in that string that delimit the substring. As with Icon, I understand positions to be between characters of the string.

The primitive operations on substrings can be simple and few. Here is a reasonable set of primitive operations:

- start(x). Returns a substring with the same base as x, with both left and right set to left of x.
- base(x). Returns a substring with the same base as x, left set before the first character of x, and right set to after the last character of x.
- next(x). Returns a substring with the same base as x, left set to right of x, and right set one character after left if possible. Otherwise, right is set to the same position as left.
- prev(x). Returns a substring with the same base as x, right set to left of x, and left set one character before right if possible. Otherwise, left is set to the same position as right.
- extent(x,y). If x and y have different base strings, returns an empty substring of the empty base "". Otherwise, returns a substring with right set to the right of y and left set to either left of x or right of y, whichever is earlier in the base.
- x = y. The base strings of the two substrings are compared character by character between their left and right positions. The result is true if and only if the lengths are identical and the selected characters match exactly.
- x + y. Returns a substring containing a new base string that is the concatenation of the substrings x and y, and left and right at the beginning and end of that new base string.
- x := y. The old value of x is discarded; x acquires the same value as y, including the base string and the left and right positions.

Given these primitive operations, I can write a function that takes a substring representing a word terminated by blanks and returns a substring representing the next word, as in Figure 9.13 [Hansen 92].

| **Figure 9.13** | ```
function NextWord(value aWord : substring) : substring;
begin
    loop -- skip to end of word
        aWord := next(aWord);
        if aWord ≠ " " then break end;
    end;
    while next(aWord) ≠ "" and next(aWord) ≠ " " do
        aWord := extent(aWord, next(aWord));
    end;
    return aWord;
end; -- NextWord
``` | 1<br>2<br>3<br>4<br>5<br>6<br>7<br>8<br>9<br>10<br>11 |

The primitive substring operations can be used to build slightly more sophisticated operations, such as rest, which returns all but the first character of its substring parameter, and last, which returns just the last character of its substring parameter. They can also be used to build Icon's matching procedures.

1.6 SNOBOL

SNOBOL was developed by Ralph E. Griswold and others at Bell Telephone Laboratories around 1965 [Griswold 71]. It has a strange syntax, partially because it was developed before Algol-like syntax became popular. Spaces act as both the concatenation and the match operators. The only statement form includes pattern match, replacement, and success and failure **goto**s. To avoid confusion, I translate all the SNOBOL examples into an Ada-like syntax, using **match** and **replace** operators. SNOBOL uses dynamic typing and dynamic scope rules; its primitive data types are strings, integers, and reals. The structured types include patterns (distinct from strings), nonhomogeneous arrays, and associative arrays.

Variables are not declared; all conceivable strings (even the empty string) name variables. Initially, all variables have the value "". In a sense, therefore, all string values point to other strings, as in Figure 9.14.

| **Figure 9.14** | ```
somewhere := "over";
over := "the";
the := "rainbow";
write(somewhere^^); -- writes "rainbow"
``` | 1<br>2<br>3<br>4 |

SNOBOL is homoiconic, after a fashion. A program is a string, and it is possible at runtime to compile a string and to branch to a label in it. However, this facility is much less attractive than LISP's equal treatment of program and data structure. SNOBOL has not been heavily used for artificial intelligence programming.

SNOBOL patterns are like regular expressions, but more powerful. They are structured values built recursively. The simplest patterns are string literals and string-valued expressions, which match themselves. More complex patterns are formed by sequencing (somewhat like **and**), alternation (somewhat like **or**), and by invoking pattern-returning pre-declared functions. Patterns are matched by a backtracking algorithm, trying earlier alternatives first. Backtracking in pattern matching is very similar to backtracking in logic programs (see Chapter 8). Consider Figure 9.15.

Figure 9.15

```
aString := "The boy stood on the burning deck, \c        1
          Eating peanuts by the peck.";                   2
aPattern := ("ing" | "the") & " " & ("deck" | "peck");    3
aString match aPattern;                                   4
```

The pattern in line 3 includes alternation, represented by | , and sequencing, represented by & . The | operator indicates that if the pattern on its left fails to match, the pattern on its right should be tried. The & operator indicates that if the pattern on its left succeeds, the pattern on its right should then be matched at the position following the match of the pattern on the left. If the pattern on the right fails, the pattern on the left is retried. Line 4 would succeed, matching "ing deck". If forced to backtrack, it would match "the peck".

The predeclared pattern-returning functions are as follows:

Pattern	Matches
len(4)	any string of 4 characters
tab(5)	to position 5 of the string
rtab(6)	to position 6 from the end of the string
pos(7)	succeeds if at position 7; matches empty string
rpos(7)	succeeds if at position 7 from right; matches empty string
any("abc")	any character in the set
notany("abc")	any character not in the set
span("abc")	until a character not in the set
break("abc")	until a character in the set
rem	the remainder of the string
arb	0 chars, on reevaluation any 1 char, then 2, and so on
bal	like arb, but not matching unbalanced parentheses

Special patterns control backtracking. The pattern **fence** succeeds, but backtracking refuses to reevaluate it. It is equivalent to Prolog's **cut** operator, except that it does not prevent alternatives elsewhere in the pattern from being tried. The **succeed** pattern succeeds the first time and all succeeding times; consider Figure 9.16.

Figure 9.16
```
"a string" match (succeed & "p")
```

This match will never terminate, because **succeed** will continue to retry, even though "p" keeps failing. A related pattern is **fail**, which fails each time it is attempted. It is used to force subsequent matches of the previous part of the pattern, usually for the side effects that matching can produce. Finally, **abort** causes the match attempt to terminate entirely with failure.

SNOBOL programmers often employ patterns for their side effects. The matched substring may be replaced by a new string, as in Figure 9.17.

Figure 9.17
```
far := "away";                                                          1
far match "y" replace "ke";                                             2
```

Line 2 will assign "awake" into far. The part of the string matched by a subpattern can be immediately assigned into a variable, as in Figure 9.18.

Figure 9.18
```
there := "dream";                                                       1
pat := (len(3) =: bluebird);                                            2
there match pat;                                                        3
```

The pattern has a side effect, to assign into variable bluebird the results of matching the subpattern len(3). The **match** in line 3 will succeed and will assign "dre" to bluebird. I have used =: to denote the **immediate assignment** operator. The side effect of assignment takes place as soon as the immediate assignment operator is encountered during pattern matching. I can use immediate assignment to construct a pattern that will match any doubled string, as in Figure 9.19.

Figure 9.19
```
pat := pos(0) & (arb =: firstpart) & (delay firstpart) &               1
    rpos(0);                                                            2
"abab" match pat; -- succeeds                                           3
```

The four components of the pattern in line 1 are sequenced together. The pos(0) and rpos(0) components force the rest of the pattern to apply to the entire subject string. The predefined pattern arb matches any length string, starting with the empty string. Whatever it matches is immediately assigned to firstpart. The pattern then looks for firstpart itself, that is, a repetition of the first part. The unary **delay** operator forces lazy evaluation of its argument. Otherwise, the value of firstpart at the time the pattern is constructed would be embedded in the pattern instead of its value at the time the pattern is evaluated during matching. When the pattern is applied in line 2, arb first matches "", so **delay** firstpart also matches "". But rpos(0) fails, so matching backs up. The pattern **delay** firstpart fails to find an alternative, but arb finds the alternative "a". This time, **delay** firstpart fails. The next alternative for arb is "ab", and this time the entire match succeeds.

In addition to immediate assignment, SNOBOL also provides **conditional assignment**, placing the value of a matched substring in a variable only if the match completely succeeds. Conditional assignment tends to be more efficient than immediate assignment, since it can avoid multiple assignments as the pattern match backtracks, but it can't be used in the double-word example. Finally, the **position assignment** operator @ assigns the position in the subject string (that is, a number such as 6) to a variable during matching.

Programmers often use immediate and conditional assignment to assign values to the pseudovariable output. Every assignment to output causes the value to be output from the program. Similarly, every evaluation of input reads in a value from the program.

SNOBOL allows an arbitrary procedure call to be inserted in a pattern. The value returned by the procedure is treated as part of the pattern being matched. (String values are coerced to patterns for this purpose.) Usually, such a call is prefixed by the **delay** operator to postpone the evaluation of the actual parameters and the invocation of the procedure until match time. If the procedure fails, then that part of the pattern match fails, and backtracking takes over. Information resulting from the match so far can be passed to the procedure via immediate assignment to global variables or to local variables passed as actual parameters.

1.7 Icon

Icon was developed by Ralph E. Griswold, one of the developers of SNOBOL, in the late 1970s as a result of his dissatisfaction with how SNOBOL's patterns fit into the language [Griswold 80]. It retains the virtues of SNOBOL's pattern matching without a pattern data type. It is an expression-oriented language, with each evaluation resulting in either a value (counted as a success) or failure. Instead of using Boolean values, conditionals base their actions on the success or failure of evaluating their conditions.

The first novel idea in Icon is the **scan** statement. (I call it a statement, even though all constructs in Icon are actually expressions, because it is usually not used for its value.) This statement introduces a name scope that creates a new binding for two predeclared variables, subject and pos, which specify the current string being matched and the current position within the string. Consider Figure 9.20 (I take liberties with actual Icon syntax to keep my examples consistent).

Figure 9.20

```
scan "peristalsis" using                                   1
     write("[" + move(4) + "]")                            2
end;                                                       3
```

This program prints "[peri]". The **scan** in line 1 maps subject to "peristalsis" and sets pos initially to 1. The body of **scan** is in line 2; it implicitly uses both subject and pos (modifying the latter). The predeclared procedure move causes the position to be incremented, if subject is long enough, and if it succeeds, it returns the substring of subject over which it has advanced. The + operator is string concatenation. After the body, both subject and pos revert to whatever values they had before. Figure 9.21 shows a more complex nested example.

Figure 9.21

```
scan MyString using                                        1
     loop -- each iteration deals with one word            2
          scan tab(upto(" ")) using                        3
               if upto("-") then -- word has a hyphen      4
                    write(subject);                        5
               end;                                        6
          end; -- scan tab(upto(" "))                      7
          move(1); -- past " "                             8
     end; -- loop                                          9
end; -- scan MyString                                      10
```

This program prints out all space-delimited words in MyString that contain a hyphen. The outer **scan** (lines 1–10) contains a loop that repeatedly advances pos to a space, scans the intervening word (lines 3–7), and then moves past the space (line 8). The predefined function upto (lines 3 and 4) returns the position of the first occurrence of any character in its actual parameter. If there is no such occurrence, it fails, and this failure is tested by a conditional (line 4). The function tab (line 3) moves pos to the value of its actual parameter and returns the substring of subject that it has moved over (in either direction). The expression in line 3 is interpreted in the outer scope; that is, it moves the cursor in MyString, and the move in line 8 moves the cursor again. The inner scope, lines 4–6, has its own subject and pos. Even if it modified pos (it doesn't), that modification would not be seen by the outer scope.

The pattern-returning functions of SNOBOL are replaced in Icon by a small set of predeclared matching procedures, which return either positions or matched strings if they succeed, and which can have the side effect of modifying pos. These are the procedures:

Procedure	Returns	Side effect
tab(n)	string between pos and n	pos := n
move(n)	string between pos and pos + n	pos := pos + n
upto(s)	position of next character in s	none
many(s)	position after 0, 1, ... characters in s	none
any(s)	pos + 1 if current character in s	none
find(s)	position before first occurrence of s	none
match(s)	position after s starting at pos	none
bal()	position of end of balanced string starting at pos	none

The first procedures, tab and move, are the only ones that modify pos. Instead of numbering character positions, Icon indexes strings between characters, starting with 1 before the first character of a string. This convention makes it unnecessary to say such things as "up to and including position 4." Each intercharacter position has an alternative index, which is 0 at the end of the string and increasingly negative toward the front of the string. So tab(0) moves to the end of the string, and tab(-3) moves before the character 3 before the end. If tab or move would exceed the limits of the string, they fail and have no side effect.

The remaining procedures examine subject and return a position that can be given to tab or move. For example, to move past "ThisString", I could write the expression in Figure 9.22.

Figure 9.22   tab(match("ThisString"))

Icon lets the programmer introduce new matching procedures. The currently active pos and subject are automatically inherited by procedures, since Icon uses dynamic scope rules. Procedures may directly modify pos, or they may indirectly modify it by invoking other matching procedures, such as the predefined ones. Usually, though, they are designed only to return a position, and the invoker may then use tab to modify pos. Figure 9.23 shows a procedure `MatchDouble` that looks for the given string twice in succession:

Figure 9.23

```
procedure MatchDouble(Given) : integer;          1
    return match(Given + Given);                 2
end;                                             3
```

The **return** statement in line 2 returns failure if its expression fails. A programmer may also explicitly return failure by a **fail** statement.

The second novel idea in Icon is that each expression is, either implicitly or explicitly, an iterator in the CLU sense, as discussed in Chapter 2. Backtracking can require that an expression be reevaluated, and it may produce a different result the next time.

Some matching procedures, such as `match` and `pos`, fail if reevaluated. The reason is that if the first success is not good enough for whatever invoked it, it wasn't the fault of the procedure, which has no better result to offer. Other matching procedures try to find additional answers if reevaluated. For example, `upto("a")` applied to "banana" at position 1 will first return 2, and on successive evaluations will return 4, 6, and then failure. Likewise, `find` and `bal` locate matches further and further from the original position.

Backtracking causes the previous value of pos to be restored before reevaluation. Reevaluation of a procedure invocation first tries new answers from the procedure without changing the actual parameter and then tries reevaluating the actual parameter. For example, `tab(upto("a"))` applied to "banana" can be reevaluated after it has succeeded in moving pos to 2. Since `tab` fails on reevaluation, its parameter `upto("a")` is reevaluated. This reevaluation is in the context before `tab` had advanced pos; that is, pos is first restored to 1. Now `upto("a")` returns 4, so `tab` will set pos to 4.

The real novelty comes from the fact that the programmer can explicitly build iterator expressions without using predefined matching procedures. Such expressions can be built with the **alternation** operator | . For example, 4 | 3 is an iterator expression with values 4, 3, then failure. Iterator expressions can be used anywhere an expression is expected, such as an actual parameter. When first evaluated, `tab(4 | 3)` moves pos to 4. If it is reevaluated, it moves pos to 3 instead. Further evaluations lead to failure.

The sequence operator & also builds iterator expressions, as in Figure 9.24.

Figure 9.24
```
scan "malarky" using                                              1
    write(tab(upto("a")) & match("ark")); -- outputs 7           2
end;                                                              3
```

In line 2, upto("a") returns 2, tab advances pos to 2, and match("ark") fails. The sequence operator causes tab to reevaluate, which fails, causing upto("a") to reevaluate, returning 4. Now tab advances pos to 4, and match("ark") succeeds, returning 7. The result of the sequence operator is its second operand, so write outputs 7. If the sequence operator were replaced by ; , match("ark") would fail once, and write would not be called at all.

Iterator expressions are useful in many surprising contexts, such as in conditional and iterative statements; consider Figure 9.25.

Figure 9.25
```
if (ThisVar | ThatVar) = (5 | 2 | 10) then ...                   1
while LowBound < (ThisVar & ThatVar) do ...                      2
```

In line 1, if ThisVar = 4 and ThatVar = 5, reevaluation stops after the second alternative of the first clause and the first alternative of the second clause; ThatVar is not compared against 2 and 10. Line 2 shows a nice shorthand for LowBound < ThisVar **and** LowBound < ThatVar.

Backtrack can be invoked directly by an **every** statement, as in Figure 9.26.

Figure 9.26
```
scan "malarky" using                                              1
    every place := upto("a") do                                  2
        write(place); -- 2, 4                                    3
    end;                                                          4
end;                                                              5
```

This program outputs both 2 and 4. The **every** statement in lines 2–4 reevaluates place := upto("a") until it fails; for each successful evaluation, line 3 is executed.

Iterator procedures look just like any other procedure, except that they use **yield** to return a value. Figure 9.27 converts the MatchDouble procedure of Figure 9.23 (page 325) to an iterator that will return the position after any double instance of its parameter.

```
Figure 9.27        procedure MatchDouble(Given : string) : integer;        1
                       variable place : integer;                           2
                       every place := find(Given + Given) do               3
                           yield place + 2*length(Given)                   4
                       end;                                                5
                   end;                                                    6

                   -- sample use                                           7
                   scan "committee meets three times" using                8
                       variable here : integer;                            9
                       every here := MatchDouble("e") do                   10
                           write(here); -- 10, 14, 22                      11
                       end;                                                12
                   end;                                                    13
```

Iterator procedures can be used to parse using a BNF grammar. For example, the grammar of balanced parentheses is shown in Figure 9.28.

```
Figure 9.28        Bal ::= ε | "(" Bal ")" Bal
```

An iterator procedure that finds longer and longer balanced parenthesis strings appears in Figure 9.29.

```
Figure 9.29        procedure Bal() : integer;                             1
                       every                                              2
                               match("") | (                             3
                                   tab(match("(")) & tab(Bal()) &        4
                                   tab(match(")")) & tab(Bal())          5
                               )                                         6
                       do                                               7
                           yield pos;                                   8
                       end;                                             9
                   end;                                                10

                   -- sample use                                        11
                   scan "()(())(" using                                 12
                       variable here : integer;                         13
                       every here := Bal() do                           14
                           write(here); -- 1, 3, 7                       15
                       end;                                             16
                   end;                                                 17
```

1.8 Homoiconic Use of Strings: Tcl

Several syntax rules in Tcl interact to make it homoiconic. Lists are represented as strings; the individual elements are delimited by white space. Every string names a variable. The R-value of a variable is denoted by $ before the string that represents the variable. (This rule makes Tcl programs error-prone, because it is so easy to forget the $.) Strings need not be delimited by quotes unless they have embedded spaces. There are quotes ({ and }) that prevent any evaluation within a string, quotes (") that allow evaluation, and quotes ([and]) that force the string to be evaluated. Evaluating a string means treating it as a series of commands delimited by end-of-line characters or semicolons. Each command is the name of a procedure (many are predeclared; I will show them in **bold monospace**) followed by parameters. The whole program is a string to be evaluated. Figure 9.30 shows a simple Tcl example.

Figure 9.30

```
set a 4 -- a := 4                              1
set b [expr $a + 5] -- b := 9                  2
while {$b > 0} {                               3
     puts "b is now $b"                        4
     set b [expr $b - 2]                        5
}                                              6
```

This program prints b is now 9 and then four more similar outputs. Line 1 is the assignment statement. It takes the name, not the R-value, of the variable to be assigned. Line 2 shows the quotes that force evaluation: [and] . The **expr** command evaluates any number of parameters as an arithmetic expression. It returns the value of that expression. Line 3 introduces the quotes that prevent evaluation: { and } . The **while** command takes two unevaluated strings, the first representing a conditional and the second representing the body of the loop. It repeatedly invokes **expr** on the first parameter, and if the result is true, it evaluates the second parameter, thereby executing the body. The body contains end-of-line characters, allowing the parser to separate it into individual statements. Line 4 shows the last kind of quotes, which can build a string containing spaces, but which do not prevent evaluation of such constructs as $b.

To see how Tcl is homoiconic, consider Figure 9.31, a less readable version of the same program.

Figure 9.31

```
set a 4 -- a := 4                                           1
set rhs {expr $a +} -- rhs := "expr $a +"                  2
set rhs [append rhs 5] -- rhs := "expr $a + 5"             3
set b [eval $rhs] -- b := 9                                4
set cond {$b > 0} -- cond := "$b > 0"                      5
set body {                                                 6
    puts "b is now $b"                                     7
    set b [expr $b - 2]                                    8
}                                                          9
while $cond $body                                         10
```

The condition and the body of the **while** loop in line 10 are the result of previous computations. Even commands can be computed, as in Figure 9.32.

Figure 9.32

```
set a ile -- a := "ile"                                    1
wh$a {$b > 0} {set b [expr $b - 2]}                        2
```

Line 2 is actually a **while** command, because the first word evaluates to while.

2 ♦ ARRAYS: APL

Arrays are especially important in mathematical computation. One of the principal advances in FORTRAN 90 over earlier versions of FORTRAN is its ability to manipulate arrays without dealing with the individual array elements. However, the best example of an array language is not FORTRAN, but APL. The APL language was invented by Kenneth E. Iverson in the early 1960s and has had a small but devoted following ever since. It could be considered a single-minded language: All computation is cast in the mold of array manipulation. Its practitioners point with pride at the conciseness of their programs; detractors point with scorn at the unreadability of the same programs. APL has long suffered from the fact that most of its operators are not normal ASCII symbols, so ordinary keyboards are not adequate for representing APL programs. Dialects such as J and APL/11 use several ASCII characters together to represent the unusual symbols. My examples expand unusual symbols into keywords to help you read them.

APL programs must be studied; they cannot simply be read. Not only does APL have an unusual character set, but it lacks control structures such as **while** and conditionals.

APL's greatest strength is its ability to handle arrays of any dimension with the same operators that apply to scalars (which are zero-dimensional arrays). The meaning is to apply the operator pointwise to each member of the array. The resulting uniformity, along with the wealth of arithmetic operators, makes it quite a powerful language. Another contributor to uniformity is that Booleans are represented (as in C) as numeric values: 0 means false and 1 means true. Arrays of Booleans can therefore be manipulated by the same means as arrays of numbers. Similarly, strings are treated as arrays of characters and can also be handled identically to numeric arrays.

If an operator requires both operands to have the same dimension, it is often valid to apply that operator to operands of different dimension. For example, x + y is the pointwise addition of elements of x with elements of y. Suppose that y is a matrix (that is, two-dimensional) with bounds 5 and 6, and that x is a scalar (zero-dimensional) with value 4. Then x will be coerced to two dimensions to conform to y, and each cell of the coerced matrix will have value 4. This kind of coercion is called **spreading**. The value x can be spread to conform to y only if the bounds of the dimensions of x match the bounds of the initial dimensions of y. In this example, x has no dimensions, so the condition is trivially met. Most APL implementations only allow one-dimensional quantities to be spread.

2.1 Operators and Meta-operators

APL is generally interpreted, not compiled. All operators are right-associative and have the same precedence. Most operator symbols can be used either as unary or as binary operators, often with different meanings. To keep things clear, I use different keywords for the two meanings. Besides ordinary operators such as + , APL has many unusual operators, including the following:

Operator	Meaning
x min y	min(x,y) -- lesser value
floor x	floor(x) -- greatest integer $\leq$ x
ceil x	ceiling(x) -- least integer $\geq$ x
recip x	1/x -- reciprocal
sign x	abs(x) / x -- sign of x
abs x	abs(x) -- absolute value
x max y	max(x,y) -- greater value
exp x	exp(x) -- e to power x
x power y	x $^\wedge$y -- x to power y
x log y	logarithm (base x) of y
ln x	logarithm (base e) of x
x comb y	C(y,x) -- number of combinations of y taken x at a time
fact x	factorial(x) -- x can be fractional

x **deal** y	x integers picked randomly (no replacement) from 1...y
rand x	random integer from 1..ceiling(x)
x **layout** y	array with dimensions x and initial value y
fill x	one-dimensional array with initial values 1...x
shape x	array of bounds of x
x **drop** y	remove first x elements of y
x **take** y	keep only first x elements of y
transpose x	reverse the order of dimensions of x
x **member** y	0 or 1, depending on whether x is found in y
x **cat** y	x concatenated with y (spread if necessary)
ravel x	array x reduced to one dimension (row-major)
x **rotate** y	array y left-rotated in first dimension by x places
x **matdiv** y	x / y, where both are matrices
matinv x	inverse(x), where x is a matrix
x **compress** y	only members of y in positions where x is true

If you call an operator a verb, then APL provides not only many verbs but also a few adverbs that modify verbs. You might call adverbs **meta-operators**, because they convert operators to new operators. Here are some meta-operators, where v and w are the operators on which they act.

Adverb	Meaning
x **outer** v y	outer product with operator v on x and y
x v **inner** w y	inner product with operators v and w on x and y
v **accumulate** x	apply operator v to one-dimensional array x repeatedly
v **scan** x	accumulate, generating all intermediate results
x v **rank** n y	operator v applied to n-dim cells of x and y
x v **birank** n m y	operator v applied to n-dim cells of x and m-dim cells of y
n **power** v x	operator v applied n times to x.

The operators v and w can be any binary operators, including programmer-defined procedures. This ability to create new operators out of old ones is quite powerful indeed. The **power** operator is equivalent in purpose to power loops, described in Chapter 2.

Figure 9.33 presents some examples to help clarify this welter of operators.

Figure 9.33

```
in:  3 4 5 -- one-dimensional array              1
out: 3 4 5                                        2


in:  a := 3 4 5                                   3
     recip a -- applies pointwise to each element 4
out: .333333333 .25 .2                            5


in:  3 + a -- 3 is spread to same dimension as a  6
out: 6 7 8                                        7


in:  + accumulate a -- like 3 + 4 + 5             8
out: 12                                           9


in:  - accumulate a -- like 3 - (4 - 5)          10
out: 4                                           11


in:  - scan a -- 3, 3-4, 3-(4-5)                 12
out: 3 -1 4                                      13


in:  max accumulate a                            14
out: 5                                           15


in:  * accumulate recip a -- .333333333 * .25 * .2  16
out: .0166666667                                 17


in:  a=a -- pointwise comparison                 18
out: 1 1 1                                       19


in:  ≠ accumulate a=a -- determine parity        20
out: 1                                           21


in:  fill 4                                       22
out: 1 2 3 4                                      23


in:  recip fill 4                                 24
out: 1 .5 .333333333 .25                          25


in:  (2 3) layout fill 6                          26
out: 1 2 3                                        27
     4 5 6                                        28
```

```
in:   a := (2 3) layout fill 6                               29
      a[1,1] := 9 -- indices start at 1                      30
      a[2,] := 8 -- entire row; 8 is spread                  31
      a[,2] := 7 -- entire column; 7 is spread               32
      a                                                      33
out:  9 7 3                                                  34
      8 7 8                                                  35


in:   (2 3) layout (5 6) -- last parens not needed           36
out:  5 6 5                                                  37
      6 5 6                                                  38


in:   + accumulate (2 3) layout (5 6)                        39
out:  16 17                                                  40


in:   + scan (2 3) layout (5 6)                              41
out:  5 11 16                                                42
      6 11 17                                                43


in:   1 rotate (3 2) layout fill 6                           44
out:  3 4                                                    45
      5 6                                                    46
      1 2                                                    47


in:   (fill 4) + inner * (fill 4)                            48
      -- sum of products; last parens not needed             49
out:  30                                                     50


in:   (fill 2) + inner * ((2 3) layout fill 6)               51
           -- sum of products                                52
out:  9 12 15                                                53


in:   (fill 2) * inner + ((2 3) layout fill 6)               54
           -- product of sums                                55
out:  12 21 32                                               56


in:   (fill 2) outer + (fill 2)                              57
out:  2 3                                                    58
      3 4                                                    59


in:   (fill 2) outer * (fill 2)                              60
out:  1 2                                                    61
      2 4                                                    62


in:   (1 2 3) cat (4 5 6)                                    63
out:  (1 2 3 4 5 6)                                          64
```

```
in:  (1 2 3) cat rank 0 (4 5 6)                              65
out: 1 4                                                     66
     2 5                                                     67
     3 6                                                     68
```

As you can see, APL allows a great many usual and unusual manipulations to be performed readily. The computations lend themselves to vector-processing hardware on modern supercomputers.

Although APL has no structured control structures, it does have **goto**, and the label can be computed, as in Figure 9.34.

Figure 9.34
```
goto ((a > 0) cat (a < 0) cat (a=0)) compress            1
     (positive cat negative cat zero)                    2
```

Line 2 builds an array of labels (I ignore how labels are declared). Line 1 compresses that array to one element based on a Boolean array only one of whose elements can be true. It then executes a **goto** to the selected label.

Figure 9.35 shows how to generate the first n Fibonacci numbers.

Figure 9.35
```
(n - 2) power                                               1
     (right cat + accumulate -2 take right) -- OneStep      2
     1 1                                                    3
```

The **power** meta-operator replicates the anonymous operator given in line 2 (let me call it OneStep) n-2 times and then applies the resulting operator to the array 1 1. OneStep uses the predeclared identifier right to refer to its right-hand operand, which is an initial Fibonacci string. Since it has no occurrence of left, OneStep is unary. OneStep takes the *last* two elements of the operand, since the left argument to **take** is a negative number. These last two elements are summed by the accumulation and are then concatenated to the previous sequence.

2.2 An APL Evaluator

One of the most delightful things about APL is that it lends itself to lazy evaluation. For example, **transpose** need not actually create a new array and fill it with data; it needs only to wait until one of its values is required. It can then convert the indices of the desired access into the nontransposed indices and fetch the value from its operand. Likewise, the **fill** operator need not actually build an array; it can easily return values when they are actually required. Although lazy evaluation will generally not be faster than full evaluation, it can avoid allocating large amounts of space.

A lazy evaluator can be written for APL in an object-oriented language. In Smalltalk nomenclature, the class Expression has instance variables dimension, bounds, and values. For example, (3 4) **layout** 4 can be represented by an object in which dimension = 2 and bounds = (3 4). The instance variable values caches the values that have already been computed, so they do not need to be computed again. The Expression class has a method **inRange:** that reports whether a given index expression is valid for the dimensions and bounds given. It also provides methods **store:at:** and **retrieve:at:** for caching computed values in values, a method **write** for displaying all values, and methods **dimension** and **bounds** to report these instance variables.

The Expression class has subclasses for every operator. Each subclass has methods for initialization (to set the dimension and bounds) and for access at any index. For example, Fill sets dimension = 1. It can compute the value at any valid index without needing to store any array. Subclasses like Matinv that wish to cache computed values may do so via **store:at:**. The Expression class has methods for creating and initializing an instance of each subclass. One final subclass of Expression is Spread, which is used to accomplish coercion to a higher dimension. It can be called explicitly, but it will also be called implicitly by operators such as Plus when necessary.

Some of the examples above could be cast as shown in Figure 9.36 into Smalltalk.

Figure 9.36

```
APL:  fill 5                                                    1
OOP:  Expression fill: 5                                        2

APL:  ≠ accumulate a=a                                          3
OOP:  Expression accumulate: NotEqual of:                       4
          (Expression equal: a and: a)                          5

APL:  (fill 4) + inner * (fill 4)                               6
OOP:  Expression inner: Plus with: Times of:                    7
          (Expression fill: 4) and: (Expression fill: 4)        8

APL:  (2 3) layout fill 6                                       9
OOP:  Expression layout: #(2 3) with:                          10
          (Expression fill: 6)                                 11
```

In Line 2, the **fill:** method in Expression returns an instance of the Fill subclass, suitably initialized. I have omitted an invocation to **write** that would display all the values of this object. In lines 4–5, the **accumulate:of:** method of Expression creates an instance of the Accumulate subclass and gives it both an operator, represented as the class NotEqual, and an expression to manipulate (all of line 5). If it needs to make calculations, it can instantiate NotEqual as many times as needed and initialize those instances to the appropriate values. Array literals such as #(2 3) (line 10) could be coerced to the appropriate constant Expression, or I could require that they be explicitly converted by saying Expression **constant:** #(2 3).

2.3 Incremental Evaluation

In some applications, the same program is executed repeatedly on slightly different inputs. For example, spreadsheet programs are often reevaluated with slightly different data. Functional programming languages have been designed that can quickly evaluate expressions given new data expressed as a modification of previous data [Yellin 91].

I want to show you how this idea can be embedded in an APL interpreter. To keep the discussion simple, I do not use a lazy interpreter, and I assume that the program is a single function with no internal variables. Given an old value and a new value, a **delta** represents how to change the old value to the new value. Of course, by value I mean an array of some shape. The delta and the old value together are enough to completely specify the new value.

Every operator instance records the most recent value it has produced. It provides that value to its caller as a delta. The ultimate caller is typically the outer-level write routine, which uses the delta it receives to display the value of the program. (It might even display the delta, if the user is interested in that representation instead of the fully expanded result.) The first time the program is run, the deltas show the difference between the void value (not even a zero-dimensional array!) and the initial value.

In order for this scheme to be efficient, incremental computation should usually not be more expensive than computing from scratch. If we are lucky, incremental computation is very inexpensive. An occasional inefficient recomputation is perfectly acceptable, though.

Achieving efficiency has two parts. First, the format for the deltas should not be longer than the new value. If a value has changed in major ways, it is better just to provide the new value outright. For APL arrays, a delta might indicate dimensions to delete, indices within a dimension to delete, particular values to change, and new indices within a dimension to add (with their values). For example, the delta from 1 3 4 5 7 to 1 2 4 5 might be represented as "change at index 2 to value 2, delete index 5."

Second, each operator and meta-operator should be implemented to take advantage of deltas. For example, the + operator generates an output delta that only includes indices where the input deltas indicate a change. The **accumulate** meta-operator could make use of an inverse to the operator it is given, if one exists, in order to remove the effects of any deleted array elements before adding the effects of inserted elements.

3 ◆ DATABASE LANGUAGES

Databases are much more varied in structure than strings or arrays. The range of languages designed for databases is also quite wide. Database languages tend to look like ordinary algebraic languages and are often Algol-based. They integrate database operations by providing additional data types and control constructs. Typically, programmers need to keep two "current locations" in mind: the current point of execution of the program, and the current record of a database. In some languages, it is also necessary to keep the current relation in mind.

3.1 Data Types

There are several ways to represent data in a database, known as hierarchical, network, and relational. I concentrate on relational databases, in which information is stored in **relations**, which are persistent homogeneous arrays of records.

My examples are taken from dBASE [Simpson 87], Sal [Sturgill 89], and a higher-level language, SQL. My examples will be based on the relations shown in Figure 9.37.

Figure 9.37

```
People : relation                                    1
     FirstName, LastName : string;                   2
     BirthYear : integer;                            3
end;                                                 4

Events : relation                                    5
     Place, What : string;                           6
     EventYear : integer;                            7
end;                                                 8
```

That is, People and Events are homogeneous persistent arrays of records with the fields as shown. I have not limited the length of the string fields (dBASE requires declaring the exact length; Sal does not, but does allow patterns that restrict valid values) nor the range of the integer fields (dBASE requires specifying the number of characters in a string version of the field; Sal allows explicit range specification). The data specifications, known as **schemata**, are usually stored in files, as are the relations themselves. Schemata are built either interactively (dBASE) or by a specification file (Sal).

In dBASE, a program that uses a relation opens it for use, at which time the field names become defined. dBASE is dynamic-typed. Runtime functions are available to determine the types of fields. In Sal, a program must read the relation into a local relation variable before using it and must specify which fields are to be read. Runtime type checking verifies that the specified fields actually exist and are consistent with the uses to which they are put.

Both dBASE and Sal allow the programmer to restrict attention to those records in a relation for which some Boolean expression holds. In dBASE, there are two techniques for restriction. First, a **filter** statement causes records to be invisible, as in Figure 9.38.

Figure 9.38

```
filter BirthYear < 1990 and LastName ≠ FirstName;
```

Until filtering is turned off, accesses to the currently open relation will not see any record for which field BirthYear ≥ 1990 or for which Last-Name = FirstName. This statement causes a runtime error if the currently open database does not have fields with the given names or if there is a type mismatch (for example, if BirthYear is not compatible with integer).

Second, control constructs that iterate through a relation can explicitly avoid certain records, as I describe shortly. In Sal, the statement to copy an external relation into an internal variable has an optional **where** clause to select appropriate records only. The advantage of Sal's approach is that the same relation can be read into multiple variables, possibly with different restrictions, after which each can be independently accessed. In dBASE, it is not possible to have two filters on the same relation, nor to have the same relation open multiple times. It is easy in Sal, but quite awkward in dBASE, to generate a list of all first names combined with all last names. The advantage of dBASE's approach is that entire relations do not need to be read into memory before access may begin. Large relations are not usable in Sal. Of course, Sal could be implemented to evaluate relation variables in a lazy fashion or to represent them on external store altogether.

Both languages allow the programmer to construct Boolean expressions involving the fields of a relation. In addition to arithmetic and string comparison, both have pattern matching. In dBASE, pattern matching is restricted to determining if one string expression is contained within another. dBASE also has an inexact string-comparison mode in which strings are considered equal if the first is a prefix of the second. Sal has a regular-expression pattern matcher.

In dBASE, multiple orders can be imposed on the records of a single relation. They include natural order (the order in which records have been added to the relation) and sorting (either increasing or decreasing) on any field or expression based on fields. These orders are built under program control, are given names, and persist after the program finishes, as shown in Figure 9.39.

Figure 9.39

```
open People; -- make the relation available and current      1
order BirthOrder; -- increasing BirthYear                    2
seek 1950; -- move to the first record matching expression   3
makeorder NameOrder := LastName + " " + FirstName;           4
order NameOrder; -- use the order                            5
seek "Newman Alfred"                                         6
```

In line 1, People is opened for use. Line 2 establishes which order is to be used. BirthOrder must already be part of the persistent representation of the relation. Line 3 moves the current-record mark to the first record for which 1950 is the value under the current order. The programmer needs to remember the expression that defines BirthOrder, since it is not given in the program. I am assuming it is simply the BirthYear field and is of type integer. Line 4 shows how a new order can be added to the relation and given a name. I use + for string concatenation. The success of the **seek** statement in lines 3 and 6 can be queried later by a library routine.

Some database languages, such as DMAWK [Sicheram 91], permit a field to have multiple values within a single record. Each field is an implicit zero-based array; the programmer can refer to FirstName[2], for example, to get a person's third name. DMAWK has the strange rule that omitting the subscript represents the last element of the array for R-values, but one past the end for L-values. Assigning a nil value to a field deletes the field. Therefore, in a record that is initially empty, Figure 9.40

Figure 9.40

```
FirstName := "Jones"; -- FirstName[0] := "Jones"            1
FirstName := FirstName; -- FirstName[1] := FirstName[0]     2
FirstName[1] := nil; -- delete FirstName[1]                 3
FirstName := "Hamzah"; -- FirstName[1] := "Hamzah"          4
```

would have the effect of setting FirstName[0] and FirstName[1] both to "Jones" (lines 1 and 2) before clearing the latter (line 3), later resetting the latter to "Hamzah" (line 4).

Since database languages deal heavily with string data, they can take advantage of the data structures and string operations discussed earlier in this chapter, particularly associative arrays and pattern matching. Sal, for example, has both.

3.2 Control Structures

Control structures are needed for setting the current-record mark and for iterating through all relevant records in a relation. Sal has no methods for explicitly moving the current-record mark; it only provides for iteration.

In dBASE, **seek** uses the current order to search quickly for a record whose order value matches the given expression. In addition, the programmer can undertake a search within a subset of the records for one whose fields match any Boolean expression. Such a search is slower than **seek**, because the order information allows an $O(\log n)$ binary search, where n is the number of records. Finally, dBASE provides a **goto** statement that sets the current-record mark to any given record by serial number in the natural order, and a **skip** statement that moves any number of records relative to the current record in the current order. There are predeclared routines that indicate the value of the current-record mark and the number of records in the relation.

Iteration is accomplished in Sal by a **foreach** statement. In Sal, **foreach** indicates which relation variable to use and names a control variable, as in Figure 9.41.

Figure 9.41

```
variable                                     1
    People : relation                        2
        FirstName, LastName : string;        3
        BirthYear : integer;                 4
    end;                                     5
    Person : tuple of People;                6

put FirstName, LastName                      7
    into People                              8
    from "People.data"                       9
    where BirthYear < 1990;                  10
foreach Person in People do                  11
    if LastName > "Jones" then               12
        write(FirstName, LastName);          13
    end;                                     14
end;                                         15
```

Lines 7–10 explicitly copy the external data into an internal variable. It is a runtime error if the declaration in lines 2–5 does not match the contents of file People.data at this time. A **tuple** (line 6) is a record in a relation.

In dBASE, the **scan** statement implicitly uses the currently open relation, as in Figure 9.42.

```
Figure 9.42          open People; -- make the relation available and current    1
                     filter BirthYear < 1990;                                    2
                     scan for LastName > "Jones" do                             3
                         write(FirstName, LastName);                            4
                     end;                                                        5
```

Natural order is used in lines 3–5, since no **order** statement was encountered.

Nested **scan** statements iterating over the same relation are useful. Figure 9.43 shows how to list all people by age category.

```
Figure 9.43          variable TheYear : integer;                                 1

                     open People; -- make the relation available and current    2
                     order BirthOrder; -- increasing BirthYear                   3

                     scan do -- each iteration covers one birth year            4
                         TheYear := BirthYear;                                   5
                         write("During ", TheYear);                             6
                         scan rest while BirthYear = TheYeardo                   7
                             write(FirstName, LastName);                        8
                         end;                                                    9
                         skip -1; -- don't ignore first record of next set      10
                     end;                                                        11
```

The **rest** keyword on line 7 prevents this **scan** statement from resetting the current-record mark to the start of the relation every time it begins to execute. The **while** clause indicates a stopping condition for this **scan** loop. The surprising code of line 10 is necessary because the **scan** statement of lines 7–9 leaves the current-record mark on the first record that does not match BirthYear = TheYear, but when control returns to line 4, the current-record mark will be advanced again.

Nested **scan** statements iterating over different relations are also quite useful. For example, the code of Figure 9.44 prints the events that occurred in every person's birth year:

```
Figure 9.44          variable TheYear : integer;                                 1

                     open People;                                                2
                     order BirthOrder; -- increasing BirthYear                   3

                     open Events;                                                4
                     order EventOrder; -- increasing EventYear                   5
```

```
use People; -- make relation current                       6
scan do -- each iteration covers one person                7
    write(FirstName, LastName);                             8
    TheYear := BirthYear;                                   9
    use Events; -- ready for nested scan                   10
    seek TheYear;                                          11
    scan rest while EventYear = TheYear do                 12
        write(What, Place);                                13
    end;                                                   14
    use People; -- ready for next iteration                15
end;                                                       16
```

Because only one relation is current, and the **scan** statements do not remember which relation they are scanning, I need to employ **use** to explicitly reestablish context before each **scan** (lines 6 and 10) and before each iteration (line 15). Luckily, the current-record mark, current order, and filtering information are retained independently for each relation. The **seek** in line 11 moves the current-record mark in Events efficiently to the first relevant record.

It is possible to link the People and Events relations to form a pseudorelation (not persistent) with fields from both, as in Figure 9.45.

Figure 9.45

```
variable ThePerson : string;                               1

open Events;                                               2
order EventOrder; -- increasing EventYear                  3
open People; -- natural order                              4
link Events on BirthYear;                                  5

scan do -- each iteration covers one person                6
    write(FirstName, LastName);                            7
    ThePerson := LastName + " " + FirstName;               8
    scan rest while LastName + " " + FirstName = ThePerson 9
    do -- each iteration covers one event                 10
        write(What, Place);                               11
    end;                                                  12
    skip -1; -- don't ignore first record of next set     13
end;                                                      14
```

The **link** statement in line 5 connects the currently open relation, People, with the stated relation, Events, using People.BirthYear (explicitly) and Events.EventYear (implicitly: that is the order field). Each record in the linked relation has fields FirstName, LastName, What, and Place. For every person, there are as many records as there are events that share the same date.

The Sal code for this algorithm, shown in Figure 9.46, has fewer surprises, although Sal has no concept of orders, cannot seek information efficiently, and has no concept of linking relations.

Figure 9.46

```
variable                                                       1
    People : relation                                          2
        FirstName, LastName : string;                          3
        BirthYear : integer;                                   4
    end;                                                       5
    Person : tuple of People;                                  6

    Events : relation                                          7
        Place, What : string;                                  8
        EventYear : integer;                                   9
    end;                                                      10
    Event : tuple of Events;                                  11

put FirstName, LastName, BirthYear                            12
    into People                                               13
    from "People.data";                                       14
put What, Place, EventYear                                    15
    into Events                                               16
    from "Events.data";                                       17

foreach Person in People do                                   18
    write(FirstName, LastName);                               19
    foreach Event in Events do                                20
        if Event.EventYear = Person.BirthYear then            21
            write(What, Place);                               22
        end; -- if                                            23
    end; -- foreach Event                                     24
end; -- foreach Person                                        25
```

3.3 Modifying Data

Sal is not intended for modifying data (there are related programs for that purpose in the package that contains Sal). dBASE modifies data in the current record by a **replace** statement, which indicates new field-value pairs. Fields that are not mentioned are left alone. New records are added to the end of the relation by an **append** statement, after which it is necessary to **replace** the values of all fields. The current record can be deleted or undeleted; a separate statement is needed to accomplish the fairly expensive operation of physically removing all records that have been deleted and rebuilding order information. dBASE is also capable of copying a relation (or a part of it based on Boolean expressions) to a new relation, with an option to sort the new relation in the process.

3.4 SQL

SQL (Structured Query Language) was developed during the mid-1970s and introduced commercially in 1979. Since then, it has become widely available. SQL is in a sense a single-minded language: All computation is cast in the mold of relation manipulation. This is just the right level of abstraction for many database operations. I concentrate on expressions that access existing relations; there are also commands that update existing relations. First, Figure 9.47 shows how to compute all people born before 1990 with distinct first and last names.

Figure 9.47

```
select *                                              1
    from People                                       2
    where BirthYear < 1990 and LastName ≠ FirstName;  3
```

This program fragment is an expression. If it stands by itself, the resulting data are be displayed; it can be placed in an assignment statement or anywhere else that a relation is expected. The `*` in line 1 indicates that the resulting relation is to contain all fields of the underlying relation, which in line 2 is specified to be `People`. Line 3 restricts which records are to be selected for the result.

Figure 9.48 shows how to find the names of people whose last name appears after "Jones" and were born before 1990.

Figure 9.48

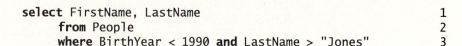

```
select FirstName, LastName                 1
    from People                            2
    where BirthYear < 1990 and LastName > "Jones"  3
```

Figure 9.49 shows how to find all people by age category.

Figure 9.49

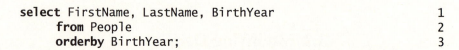

```
select FirstName, LastName, BirthYear      1
    from People                            2
    orderby BirthYear;                     3
```

The **orderby** clause in line 3 indicates that the resulting relation is to be sorted by birth year.

The code of Figure 9.50 will print the events that occurred in every person's birth year.

Figure 9.50
```
select FirstName, LastName, What, Place                1
    from People, Events                                2
    where EventYear = BirthYear                        3
    orderby LastName + FirstName;                      4
```

This example builds a single relation from multiple relations. Such a computation is known as a **join**. In this case, line 2 specifies that the fields of People and Events are to be combined. Line 3 restricts attention to those records where the EventYear is the same as the BirthYear. Such restriction is common, but not required. It is not necessary to build the restriction out of an equality test. Line 1 restricts attention to four of the resulting fields. Line 4 sorts the resulting relation by person. It shows that the sort condition can be any expression. One difference between this code and what I showed previously for dBASE is that people born in years without events are omitted from the result. Another difference is that the result is a relation, which can be manipulated further before printing.

SQL provides several accumulation operators, such as count, sum, min, max, and average. Figure 9.51 shows how to find the average birth year and the alphabetically last name of all people.

Figure 9.51
```
select average(BirthYear), max(LastName + FirstName)   1
    from People;                                       2
```

Accumulated values are particularly helpful in conjunction with grouping, since the accumulation is computed independently for each group. Figure 9.52 shows how to count how many people were born in each year.

Figure 9.52

```
select BirthYear, Count(*)                             1
    from People                                        2
    groupby BirthYear;                                 3
```

The * in line 1 refers to entire records instead of a particular field. The result of this expression is a relation with two fields: BirthYear and Count1 (the latter is automatically named). The relation has one record for each distinct value of BirthYear.

Individual groups can be suppressed by a **having** clause, much as individual records can be suppressed by a **where** clause. Figure 9.53 shows how to get the number of people born in each year, but only show those years where the number is greater than 100.

Figure 9.53

```
select BirthYear, Count(*)                          1
    from People                                     2
    groupby BirthYear                               3
    having Count(*) > 100;                          4
```

Expressions can be combined in several ways. The simplest is to take the **union** of two expressions. Those expressions must result in structurally equivalent relations (although the names of the fields may differ). Duplicate records are removed. Figure 9.54 shows how to get a relation with all first or last names, along with birth date.

Figure 9.54

```
select BirthYear, FirstName called Name             1
    from People                                     2
union                                               3
select BirthYear, LastName                          4
    from People;                                    5
```

Line 1 introduces a new name for the second field in the result.

A more complex way to join expressions is by subordinating one to another, as shown in Figure 9.55, which will find those people born after the average birth year.

Figure 9.55

```
select FirstName, LastName                          1
    from People                                     2
    where BirthYear > average(                      3
        select BirthYear from People                4
    );                                              5
```

Line 4 is an expression embedded inside the invocation of average. Similarly, Figure 9.56 shows how to find people born after Ramachandran.

Figure 9.56

```
select FirstName, LastName                          1
    from People                                     2
    where BirthYear > (                             3
        select BirthYear                            4
        from People                                 5
        where LastName = "Ramachandran"             6
    );                                              7
```

If there are several records with LastName = "Ramachandran", this expression will fail. In that case, I can modify the expression slightly, as in Figure 9.57.

Figure 9.57
```
select FirstName, LastName                              1
    from People                                         2
    where BirthYear > any(                              3
        select BirthYear                                4
        from People                                     5
        where LastName = "Ramachandran"                 6
    );                                                  7
```

The accumulator any in line 3 allows the **where** clause of line 3 to be satisfied for anyone born after even one of the several Ramachandrans. This accumulator is, in effect, an Icon iterator (described earlier in this chapter). A related iterating accumulator is all; if I had used it in line 3 instead of any, I would only get those people born after all Ramachandrans. Finally, the accumulator exists reduces the result of a subexpression to a Boolean indicating whether the subexpression's value contains any records.

The outer expression can communicate values to the inner expression. Figure 9.58 shows how to find all people born in the year the last occurrence of each event took place.

Figure 9.58
```
select FirstName, LastName                              1
    from People, Events called OuterEvents              2
    where BirthYear = (                                 3
        select max(EventYear)                           4
        from Events called InnerEvents                  5
        where InnerEvents.What = OuterEvents.What        6
    );                                                  7
```

Lines 2 and 5 give two aliases for Events, so that the two uses of this relation can be distinguished in line 6.

The **select** mechanism of SQL allows programmers to deal with data instead of control structures. The APL language discussed in the next section takes this idea to an extreme.

4 ◆ SYMBOLIC MATHEMATICS

Early languages like FORTRAN were intended primarily for numeric mathematical computation. A completely different class of languages has been developed for symbolic mathematical computation. The major novelty of these languages is that unbound identifiers can be treated as algebraic symbols to be manipulated. The best-known languages in this family are Macsyma, Maple, and Mathematica. These languages can simplify algebraic expressions, perform symbolic integration and differentiation, calculate limits, generate series and sequences, solve systems of equations, and produce graphs. They are almost always used inter-actively.

Since there are so many different mathematical manipulations possi-ble, mathematical programming languages tend to organize their func-tions into libraries that are dynamically loaded when they are needed. This organization reduces the amount of memory that a typical session will need. For example, Maple's linear algebra library contains routines for solving linear systems of equations, inverting matrices, and finding eigenvectors and eigenvalues. There are also libraries for combina-torics, for the simplex method, for trigonometric functions, and many other applications. Arrays can be manipulated much as in APL, includ-ing extraction of slices in any dimension, so operations like Gaussian elimination are easy to write. In fact, Mathematica has APL's **inner** and **outer** operators.

Figure 9.59 shows some examples of the manipulations possible in these languages.

Figure 9.59

```
in:    poly := 2*x^5 - 3*x^4 + 38*x^3 - 57*x^2 - 300*x+450;    1
       solve(poly=0,x); -- solve with respect to x              2
out:                      1/2      1/2                           3
       3/2, 5 I, - 5 I, 6    , - 6                               4

in:    e1 := a + b + c + d = 1;                                  5
       e2 := 2*a + 5*b + c + 4*d = 4;                            6
       e3 := -5*a + 4*b + 5*c - 3*d = -1;                        7
       e4 := b + 4*c - 5*d = 0;                                  8
       SolutSet := solve({e1,e2,e3,e4},{a,b,c,d});               9
out: SolutSet := {d = 0, c = -2/13, a = 7/13, b = 8/13}         10

in:    f:=x^2 - y^2;                                            11
       diff(f,x);                                               12
out: 2x                                                         13

in:    y^2 + 2*y;                                               14
       factor(%+1); -- % means previous expression             15
out:        2                                                   16
       (1+y)                                                    17
```

The output in lines 3–4 and lines 16–17 is carefully formatted over sev-eral lines to look like typeset mathematics. Matrices are also displayed in multiple lines. The identifier I in line 4 is the mathematical constant i, the square root of -1. Not only can Maple differentiate polynomials (and other sorts of expressions), it can also differentiate programmer-defined functions, as in Figure 9.60.

Figure 9.60

```
f := procedure (x);                              1
variable                                         2
    i : integer;                                 3
    result := 0;                                 4
begin                                            5
    for i := 1 to 2 do                           6
        result := result + x ^ i;                7
    end;                                         8
    return result;                               9
end;                                            10

g := differentiate(f);                          11
```

Line 11 assigns into g a procedure with the declaration shown in Figure 9.61.

Figure 9.61

```
procedure g(x);                                  1
variable                                         2
    i : integer;                                 3
    resultx := 0;                                4
begin                                            5
    for i := 1 to 2 do                           6
        resultx := resultx + i * x ^ (i - 1);    7
    end;                                         8
    return resultx;                              9
end;                                            10
```

Much more complicated examples are possible, involving trigonometric functions, for example. The ability to differentiate programmer-defined functions makes it possible to program Newton's method for finding roots of functions, as shown in Figure 9.62.

Figure 9.62

```
findRoot := procedure (f : procedure);           1
variable                                         2
    result := 0; -- or any other initial guess   3
    epsilon := 0.001; -- or any other desired precision  4
begin                                            5
    while abs(f(result)) > epsilon do            6
        result := result - f(a)/differentiate(f)(a);  7
    end;                                         8
    return result;                               9
end;                                            10
```

The data types available in mathematical languages include integer, real, arrays, strings, and lists, in addition to symbolic expressions. They also include arbitrarily large integers and fractions of arbitrarily large integers. Maple also provides associative arrays, which are useful for storing values of functions, and arrays with programmer-defined indexing functions, which can introduce structure such as symmetry or triangularity in matrices and can provide default values for arrays at indices that have not been given values. Maple implicitly associates an associative array called the remember table with every procedure. The programmer can request that values computed by the procedure be remembered in that array to short-circuit future evaluations with the same parameters. In other words, dynamic programming is trivial to add to any program, such as the one shown in Figure 9.63 for Fibonacci numbers.

Figure 9.63

```
Fibonacci := procedure[remember](n);                              1
begin                                                             2
      Fibonacci(n-1) + Fibonacci(n-2);                            3
end;                                                              4

Fibonacci(0) := 0; -- assigns to the remember table              5
Fibonacci(1) := 1; -- assigns to the remember table              6
```

The option **remember** in line 1 causes Fibonacci to store and use previously computed values. The assignments in lines 5 and 6 explicitly place values in Fibonacci's remember table, making it unnecessary to put special cases in the body of the procedure itself.

5 ◆ FINAL COMMENTS

Languages that are aimed at special applications tend to concentrate on particular aggregates in order to help the programmer write clear and efficient code. SNOBOL and Icon are particularly designed for applications that need to read and manipulate textual data. The related **scripting languages** are used to scan text files, extract information, print reports, construct input for other programs, and collect output from other programs. Such languages include command interpreters like Csh, stream editors like Awk and Sed, and interpreted languages such as Perl and Tcl. These languages generally have many features for manipulating strings. Extensions to Prolog (see Chapter 8) for dealing with strings are actively being researched, giving rise to languages such as CLP(Σ). The problem that string Prolog must grapple with is that unification over strings is intractable (it is at least NP hard, although it is decidable) [Rajasekar 94]. Which language to use depends, of course, on what is available (Csh is only available under Unix), how fast the program must run (interpreted programs are generally slower), and how sophisticated the string manipulations need to be.

SNOBOL has some excellent points. The fact that backtracking is built into the language frees the SNOBOL programmer from writing backtrack code, which is tricky to get right. Patterns free the programmer from worrying about maintaining an explicit variable for the focus of attention (the position in the subject string that is being matched). Patterns can be assigned to variables and used to build more complex patterns. In fact, the BNF for a context-free (and even a context-sensitive) language can be represented directly in SNOBOL, so it is easy to write parsers.

SNOBOL also has some unfortunate points.

1. There are many ways to build patterns, and it takes a significant amount of effort to learn how to use these methods. Patterns can grow so complex that they become difficult to understand, debug, and maintain.

2. The programmer must remember the difference between pattern-construction time and pattern-matching time. It is easy to write inefficient programs that construct patterns each time they are used instead of saving them in pattern variables. Variables used in a pattern often need to be marked for lazy evaluation.

3. The fact that side effects are an essential part of pattern application makes programs unclear, especially if the pattern is stored in a pattern variable and applied in a different part of the program.

4. Although patterns are something like procedures, they do not take parameters, and they do not introduce a name scope, so they are forced to communicate and perform local computations through global variables.

5. The pattern-matching part of SNOBOL is mostly divorced from the rest of the language. For example, a good way to find if the first comma in a string Subject is at least 10 characters from the beginning is shown in Figure 9.64 [Griswold 80].

Figure 9.64

```
Subject match ((break(",") @ here) & fence &              1
    (delay ge(here,10)));                                 2
```

The '@' operator assigns the position in Subject achieved by finding the first comma. It is prevented from finding a later comma by the **fence** operator. The ge integer-comparison procedure is invoked lazily to make sure that here is current when the parameters to ge are evaluated. This example shows how awkward it is to build programs that involve both pattern matching and arithmetic.

The two novel ideas of Icon, the concept of scanning strings by matching procedures and the idea of iterator expressions, are both unusual and powerful. However, this power has a price. The global nature of subject and pos, and the fact that matching procedures have side effects on these pseudovariables, can make programs hard to follow. It is possible to directly assign into both subject and pos, which can wreak havoc, especially in a **scan** body. Although Icon iterator expressions are as powerful as CLU iterators (and often easier to encode), they are not general-purpose coroutines. They cannot be used, for example, to solve the binary-tree equality puzzle from Chapter 2.

On the positive side, the concept of scanning strings is easily generalized to scanning other data structures, such as trees. A programmer may introduce matching procedures that inspect a subject of any type and modify position variables to indicate progress. Instead of using **scan**, which is specific to subject and pos, all that is needed is a new name scope with local variables properly initialized, as in Figure 9.65.

Figure 9.65

```
variable                                               1
    target : ... := ...; -- can be any data structure  2
    position : ... := ...; -- in any representation     3
begin                                                   4
    ... -- expression using matching procedures         5
end;                                                    6
```

In fact, **scan** is just a name scope with variables subject and pos automatically declared and initialized. It is not necessary to use **scan**, because all predeclared matching procedures have overloaded versions with more parameters that explicitly specify the subject. So everything that is done automatically by **scan** and the matching procedures could be done (maybe with increased clarity) by name scopes, explicit variables, and extra parameters. Some adjustment would be needed to pass parameters like pos by reference or value result mode; Icon only has value mode.

Arrays are primarily important in mathematical calculations. However, APL shows that adequately powerful array operations can take the place of control structures; it is possible to build very sophisticated non-mathematical programs in APL. These programs may appear to be inefficient to execute, with very large intermediate results, but clever evaluation techniques allow APL interpreters to work in limited memory. Unfortunately, the programs are difficult to read, especially in the natural APL syntax.

The simplest databases are just ASCII files, with one line per tuple. Scripting languages like Awk, Sed, Perl, and Tcl often suffice to manipulate these databases. More complex databases can be accessed through subroutines in other languages. It is quite common to embed SQL calls, for instance, in a C program. Commercial databases often come with their own languages. dBASE, for example, is a generally Algol-like language interwoven with specific constructs for accessing databases. Paradox, in contrast, is built on an object-oriented model.

Symbolic computation is important to mathematicians and engineers, and especially to students in these disciplines. Languages like Mathematica and Maple allow these users to construct symbolic equations, manipulate them, and view their behavior graphically.

There are other aggregates that I have not covered in this chapter. In particular, specialty languages are very important for statistics, controlling machine tools, and text formatting.

EXERCISES

Review Exercises

9.1   In Icon, is the expression tab(4 | 3) equivalent to tab(4) | tab(3)?

9.2   Write a regular expression that matches either "begin" or "end".

9.3   Write a regular expression that matches any word starting with "pre" and ending with "ion".

9.4   Modify the Icon program of example 21 on page 323 so that the final word in MyString may continue to the end of MyString without a final space character.

9.5   What is the Icon equivalent of SNOBOL's **fence** pattern?

9.6   In dBASE, it is quite awkward to generate a list of all first names combined with all last names in the People relation. Suggest how to manage such a feat.

9.7   Design an SQL expression that builds a relation containing the first name of everyone born before all earthquakes in San Francisco.

9.8   Write a SNOBOL pattern that prints all contiguous substrings of the subject and then fails.

Challenge Exercises

9.9   Referring to Figure 9.5 (page 313), design a variety of CharSearch that finds the second s in "sample string".

9.10 Write a regular expression that matches all words that can be typed by alternating hands on a standard qwerty keyboard.

9.11 Refer to Figure 9.11 (page 317), and suggest a better component type than Boolean for Present.

9.12 Write a SNOBOL program that has the same effect as the Icon program in Figure 9.20 (page 323).

9.13 Modify the Icon program of Figure 9.21 (page 323) so that it writes all words that contain telephone numbers, that is, sequences of only digits and an obligatory single hyphen.

9.14 The simple program for MatchDouble in Figure 9.23 (page 325) becomes more complex if it doesn't use concatenation. Show how to code it, using neither concatenation nor explicit reference to pos.

9.15 Write an Icon program that generates all binary trees on *n* nodes, similar to the ones written in C and CLU in Chapter 2.

9.16 Why is it impossible to write an Icon program that solves the binary-tree equality puzzle of Chapter 2?

9.17 Can Icon iterator expressions and iterator procedures be implemented with a single stack?

9.18 Show how to implement rest and last, mentioned on page 319, using the primitive substring operations.

9.19 Use primitive substring operations to implement Icon's upto matching procedure. Don't worry about integrating your result into Icon's backtracking mechanism.

9.20 Use primitive substring operations to build a function NewBase(x) that returns a substring that is equal to x, has a new base, has left set to the beginning of the new base, and right set to the end of the new base.

9.21 What is the subtle bug in Figure 9.45 (page 342)? How would you fix it?

9.22 Describe what the APL program in Figure 9.66 does.

Figure 9.66

```
in:  n := 30                                          1
     a := 1 ≠ or accumulate (1 1) drop               2
          (transpose 0 =                              3
          (fill n) outer mod fill n) -                4
          (fill n) outer = fill n                     5
     a compress 1 drop fill n                         6
out: 2  3  5  7 11 13 17 19 23 29                      7
```

9.23 In Figure 9.36 (page 335), the `accumulate` operator is represented by an instance of the Accumulate class. What would be the response of this instance to a `dimension` query and to a **bounds** query, given that the variable a is currently bound to the three-dimensional array with bounds 2 3 4?

9.24 Does it make sense in APL to turn a lazy evaluator into an incremental lazy evaluator?

Chapter 10

Formal Syntax and Semantics

1 ◆ SYNTAX

A programming language is defined by specifying its **syntax** (structure) and its **semantics** (meaning). Syntax normally means context-free syntax because of the almost universal use of context-free grammars as a syntax-specification mechanism. Syntax defines what sequences of symbols are valid; syntactic validity is independent of any notion of what the symbols mean. For example, a context-free syntax might say that A := B + C is syntactically valid, while A := B +; is not.

Context-free grammars are described by **productions** in **BNF** (Backus-Naur Form, or Backus Normal Form, named after John Backus and Peter Naur, major designers of Algol-60). For example, part of the syntax of Pascal is shown in Figure 10.1.

Figure 10.1

```
Program ::= program IDENTIFIER ( FileList ) ;                    1
        Declarations begin Statements end .                     2
FileList ::= IDENTIFIER | IDENTIFIER , FileList                 3
Declarations ::= ConstantDecs TypeDecs VarDecs ProcDecs        4
ConstantDecs ::= const ConstantDecList | ε                     5
ConstantDecList ::= IDENTIFIER = Value; ConstantDecList | ε   6
```

The identifiers on the left-hand sides of the rules are called **nonterminals**. Each rule shows how such a nonterminal can be expanded into a collection of nonterminals (which require further expansion) and **terminals**, which are lexical tokens of the programming language. In our example, **program** and IDENTIFIER are terminals, and Program and Statements are nonterminals. I use | to indicate alternatives and ε to indicate an empty string.

Sometimes, a clearer notation may be used for BNF; the purpose of notation, after all, is to specify ideas precisely and clearly. The FileList

357

and `ConstantDecList` productions use recursion to represent arbitrarily long lists. I can rewrite those productions as shown in Figure 10.2, introducing iteration for the recursion.

Figure 10.2

```
FileList ::= [ IDENTIFIER +,]                               1
ConstantDecList ::= [ IDENTIFIER = Value ; *]               2
```

Here I use brackets [and] to surround repeated groups. I end the group either with * , which means 0 or more times (line 2), with + , which means 1 or more times (line 1), or with neither, which means 0 or 1 time. Optionally, following the * or + is a string that is to be inserted between repetitions. So line 1 means that there may be one or more identifiers, and if there are more than one, they are separated by , characters. Line 2 means there may zero or more constant declarations; each is terminated by the ; character. This notation obscures whether the repeated items are to be associated to the left or to the right. If this information is important, it can be specified in some other way, or the productions can be written in the usual recursive fashion.

The BNF specification is helpful for each of the three software-tool aspects of a programming language.

1. It helps the programming language designer specify exactly what the language looks like.
2. It can be used by automatic compiler-generator tools to build the parser for a compiler.
3. It guides the programmer in building syntactically correct programs.

BNF is inadequate to describe the syntax for some languages. For example, Metafont dynamically modifies the meanings of input tokens, so that it is not so easy to apply standard BNF.

BNF also fails to cover all of program structure. Type compatibility and scoping rules (for example, that A := B + C is invalid if B or C is Boolean) cannot be specified by context-free grammars. (Although context-sensitive grammars suffice, they are never used in practice because they are hard to parse.) Instead of calling this part of program structure static semantics, as has become customary, let me call it **advanced syntax**. Advanced syntax augments context-free specifications and completes the definition of what valid programs look like. Advanced syntax can be specified in two ways:

1. Informally via a programming language report, as is done for most programming languages. An informal specification can be compact and easy to read but is usually imprecise.

2. Formally (for example, via two-level van Wijngaarten grammars or attribute grammars).

Attribute grammars are one popular method of formal specification of advanced syntax. They formalize the semantic checks often found in compilers. As an example of attribute grammars, the production E ::= E + T might be augmented with a type attribute for E and T and a predicate requiring type compatibility, as shown in Figure 10.3.

Figure 10.3

$$(E_2.\texttt{type} = \texttt{numeric}) \wedge (T.\texttt{type} = \texttt{numeric})$$

where E_2 denotes the second occurrence of E in the production. Attribute grammars are a reasonable blend of formality and readability, and they are relatively easy to translate into compilers by standard techniques, but they can still be rather verbose.

2 ◆ AXIOMATIC SEMANTICS

Semantics are used to specify what a program does (that is, what it computes). These semantics are often specified very informally in a language manual or report. Alternatively, a more formal **operational semantics** interpreter model can be used. In such a model, a program state is defined, and program execution is described in terms of changes to that state. For example, the semantics of the statement A := 1 is that the state component corresponding to A is changed to 1. The LISP interpreter presented in Chapter 4 is operational in form. It defines the execution of a LISP program in terms of the steps needed to convert it to a final reduced form, which is deemed the result of the computation. The Vienna Definition Language (VDL) embodies an operational model in which abstract trees are traversed and decorated to model program execution [Wegner 72]. VDL has been used to define the semantics of PL/I, although the resulting definition is quite large and verbose.

Axiomatic semantics model execution at a more abstract level than operational models [Gries 81]. The definitions are based on formally specified predicates that relate program variables. Statements are defined by how they modify these relations.

As an example of axiomatic definitions, the axiom defining var := exp usually states that a predicate involving var is true after statement execution if and only if the predicate obtained by replacing all occurrences of var by exp is true beforehand. For example, for y > 3 to be true after execution of the statement y := x + 1, the predicate x + 1 > 3 would have to be true before the statement is executed.

Similarly, y = 21 is true after execution of x := 1 if y = 21 is true before its execution, which is a roundabout way of saying that changing x doesn't affect y. However, if x is an alias for y (for example, if x is a formal reference-mode parameter bound to an actual parameter y), the axiom is invalid. In fact, aliasing makes axiomatic definitions much more complex. This is one reason why attempts to limit or ban aliasing are now common in modern language designs (for example, Euclid and Ada).

The axiomatic approach is good for deriving proofs of program correctness, because it avoids implementation details and concentrates on how relations among variables are changed by statement execution. In the assignment axiom, there is no concept of a location in memory being updated; rather, relations among variables are transformed by the assignment. Although axioms can formalize important properties of the semantics of a programming language, it is difficult to use them to define a language completely. For example, they cannot easily model stack overflow or garbage collection.

Denotational semantics is more mathematical in form than operational semantics, yet it still presents the notions of memory access and update that are central to von Neumann languages. Because they rely upon notation and terminology drawn from mathematics, denotational definitions are often fairly compact, especially in comparison with operational definitions. Denotational techniques have become quite popular, and a definition for all of Ada (excluding concurrency) has been written. Indeed, this definition was the basis for some early Ada compilers, which operated by implementing the denotational representation of a given program.[1] A significant amount of effort in compiler research is directed toward finding automatic ways to convert denotational representations to equivalent representations that map directly to ordinary machine code [Wand 82; Appel 85]. If this effort is successful, a denotational definition (along with lexical and syntactic definitions) may be sufficient to automatically produce a working compiler.

The field of axiomatic semantics was pioneered by C. A. R. Hoare [Hoare 69]. The notation

$$\{P\} \ S \ \{R\}$$

is a mathematical proposition about the semantics of a program fragment S. It means, "If predicate P is true before program S starts, and

---

[1] The first Ada implementation to take this approach was the NYU Ada/Ed system, infamous for its slowness. Its authors claim this slowness is due primarily to inefficient implementation of certain denotational functions.

program S successfully terminates, then predicate R will be true after S terminates."

The predicates (P and R) typically involve the values of program variables. P is called the **precondition** and R the **postcondition** of the proposition above. The precondition indicates the assumptions that the program may make, and the postcondition represents the result of correct computation. If P and R are chosen properly, such a proposition can mean that S is a **conditionally correct** program, which means it is correct if it terminates.

Relatively strong conditions hold for very few program states; relatively weak conditions hold for very many. The strongest possible condition is `false` (it holds for no program state); the weakest possible condition is `true` (it holds for every program state). A strong proposition is one with a weak precondition or a strong postcondition (or both); thus

```
{true} S {false}
```

is exceptionally strong. In fact, it is so strong that it is true only of nonterminating programs. It says that no matter what holds before S is executed, nothing at all holds afterward. Conversely,

```
{false} S {true}
```

is an exceptionally weak proposition, true of all programs. It says that given unbelievable initial conditions, after S finishes, one can say nothing interesting about the state of variables.

2.1 Axioms

The programming language designer can specify the meaning of control structures by stating axioms, such as the axiom of assignment in Figure 10.4.

Figure 10.4	**Axiom of assignment**	1
	`{P[x → y]} x := y {P}`	2
	`where`	3
	x is an identifier	4
	y is an expression without side effects, possibly containing x	5

This notation says that to prove P after the assignment, one must first prove a related predicate. $P[x \rightarrow y]$ means the predicate P with all references to x replaced by references to y. For instance,

$$\{y < 3 \land z < y\} \ x := y \ \{x < 3 \land z < y\}$$

is a consequence of this axiom.

In addition to axioms, axiomatic semantics contain **rules of inference**, which specify how to combine axioms to create provable propositions. They have the form:

if X **and** Y **then** Z

That is, if one already knows X and Y, then proposition Z is proven as well. Figure 10.5 shows some obvious rules of inference.

Figure 10.5	**Rules of consequence**	1
	if {P} S {R} **and** R $\Rightarrow$ Q **then** {P} S {Q}	2
	if {P} S {R} **and** Q $\Rightarrow$ P **then** {Q} S {R}	3

Since R $\Rightarrow$ S means "R is stronger than S," the rules of consequence say that one may always weaken a postcondition or strengthen a precondition. In other words, one may weaken a proposition that is already proven.

The easiest control structure to say anything about is the composition of two statements, as in Figure 10.6.

| Figure 10.6 | **Axiom of composition** | 1 |
| | **if** {P} S_1 {Q} **and** {Q} S_2 {R} **then** {P} S_1; S_2 {R} | 2 |

Iteration with a **while** loop is also easy to describe, as shown in Figure 10.7.

Figure 10.7	**Axiom of iteration**	1
	if {P $\land$ B} S {P} **then**	2
	{P} **while** B **do** S **end** {¬ B $\land$ P}	3

That is, to prove that after the loop B will be false and that P still holds, it suffices to show that each iteration through the loop preserves P, given that B holds at the outset of the loop. P is called an **invariant** of the loop, because the loop does not cause it to become false.

Figure 10.8 presents an axiom for conditional statements.

Figure 10.8

Axiom of condition   1
if {P ∧ B} S {Q} **and** {P ∧ ¬B} T {Q} **then**   2
          {P} **if** B **then** S **else** T **end** {Q}   3

2.2 A Simple Proof

I will now use these axioms to prove a simple program correct. The program of Figure 10.9 is intended to find the quotient and remainder obtained by dividing a dividend by a divisor. It is not very efficient.

Figure 10.9

```
remainder := dividend;                                  1
quotient := 0;                                          2
while divisor ≤ remainder do                            3
        remainder := remainder - divisor;              4
        quotient := quotient + 1                        5
end;                                                    6
```

I would like the predicate shown in Figure 10.10 to be true at the end of this program.

Figure 10.10

```
{FINAL: remainder < divisor ∧                          1
        dividend = remainder + (divisor * quotient)}   2
```

The proposition I must prove is {true} Divide {FINAL}. Figure 10.11 presents a proof.

Figure 10.11

```
true ⇒ dividend = dividend + divisor * 0 [algebra]     1

{dividend = dividend + divisor*0} remainder := dividend
        {dividend = remainder + divisor*0} [assignment]   2

{dividend = remainder + divisor*0} quotient := 0
        {dividend = remainder + divisor*quotient} [assignment]  3

{true} remainder := dividend {dividend = remainder+divisor*0}
        [consequence, 1, 2]                               4

{true} remainder := dividend; quotient := 0
        {dividend = remainder+divisor*quotient}
        [composition, 3, 4]                               5

dividend = remainder+divisor*quotient ∧ divisor ≤ remainder ⇒
        dividend=(remainder-divisor)+divisor*(1+quotient)
        [algebra]                                         6
```

```
{dividend=(remainder-divisor)+divisor*(1+quotient)}
    remainder := remainder-divisor
    {dividend=remainder+divisor*(1+quotient)} [assignment] 7
```

```
{dividend=remainder+divisor*(1+quotient)}
    quotient := quotient+1
    {dividend=remainder+divisor*quotient} [assignment]      8
```

```
{dividend=(remainder-divisor)+divisor*(1+quotient)}
    remainder := remainder-divisor; quotient := quotient+1
    {dividend=remainder+divisor*quotient}
    [composition, 7, 8]                                      9
```

```
{dividend = remainder+divisor*quotient ∧ divisor ≤ remainder}
    remainder := remainder-divisor; quotient := quotient+1
    {dividend=remainder+divisor*quotient}
    [consequence, 6, 9]                                     10
```

```
{dividend = remainder+divisor*quotient}
    while divisor≤remainder do
        remainder := remainder-divisor;
        quotient := quotient+1
    end
    {remainder < divisor ∧
        dividend=remainder+divisor*quotient}
    [iteration, 10]                                         11
```

```
{true} Divide {FINAL} [composition, 5, 11]                 12
```

This style of proof is not very enlightening. It is more instructive to decorate the program with predicates in such a way that an interested reader (or an automated theorem prover) can verify that each statement produces the stated postcondition given the stated precondition. Each loop needs to be decorated with an invariant. Figure 10.12 shows the same program with decorations.

Figure 10.12

```
{true}                                                      1
{dividend = dividend + divisor*0}                           2
remainder := dividend;                                      3
{dividend = remainder + divisor*0}                          4
quotient := 0;                                              5
{invariant: dividend = remainder + divisor*quotient}        6
```

```
while divisor ≤ remainder do                                    7
    {dividend = (remainder - divisor) +                         8
        divisor * (quotient+1)}                                 9
    remainder := remainder - divisor;                          10
    {dividend = remainder + divisor * (quotient + 1)}          11
    quotient := quotient + 1                                    12
    {dividend = remainder + divisor * quotient}                13
end;                                                            14
{remainder<divisor ∧                                           15
    dividend = remainder + (divisor*quotient)}                 16
```

Unfortunately, the program is erroneous, even though I have managed to prove it correct! What happens if dividend = 4 and divisor = -2? The **while** loop never terminates. The program is only conditionally, not totally, correct.

The idea of axiomatic semantics has proved fruitful. It has been applied not only to the constructs you have seen, but also to more complex ones such as procedure and function call, **break** from a loop, and even **goto**. Figure 10.13 shows two examples of concurrent programming constructs to which it has been applied [Owicki 76].

Figure 10.13

Parallel execution axiom   1
if $\forall 0 \leq i \leq n$, {P_i} S_i {Q_i},   2
and no variable free in P_i or Q_i is changed in $S_{j \neq i}$ 3
and all variables in I(r) belong to resource r,   4
then   5
    {$P_1 \wedge \ldots \wedge P_n \wedge$ I(r)}   6
      resource r: cobegin S_1 // ... // S_n **coend**   7
    {$Q_1 \wedge \ldots \wedge Q_n$}   8

Critical section axiom   9
if I(r) is the invariant from the **cobegin** statement   10
and {I(r) ∧ P ∧ B} S {I(r) ∧ Q)   11
and no variable free in P or Q is changed in   12
    another thread   13
then {P} **region** r **await** B **do** S **end** {Q}   14

The **cobegin** and **region** statements are described in Chapter 7. If the formal axiomatic specification of a construct would suffice to make it intelligible, this example should require no further clarification. However, it may help to point out several facts.

- A **resource** is a set of shared variables.
- The **region** statement may only appear in a **cobegin**.
- **Region** statements for the same resource may not be nested.

The axiomatic method has given rise to an attitude summarized in the following tenets:

1. Programmers should be aware of the propositions that are meant to hold at different stages of the program.
2. The precondition and the postcondition of each whole program should be stated explicitly.
3. Students learning to program should write out the loop invariant explicitly for each loop.
4. Language constructs that do not have simple axioms (such as **goto** and multiple assignment) should not be used.
5. Programmers should prove their programs correct.
6. Proof checkers should be built to assist programmers in proving their programs correct. Such checkers should understand the axioms and enough algebra so that only occasional decorations (such as loop invariants) should be needed.
7. Programmers should develop their programs by starting with the postcondition and working slowly backward, attempting to render it true.
8. Programming languages should allow the programmer to explicitly show loop invariants, preconditions and postconditions to procedure calls, and other decorations, and the compiler should include a proof checker.

This attitude has led to extensive research in programming language design (Alphard and Eiffel were designed with the last point in mind) and automatic theorem provers. However, these tenets are not universally accepted. The strong argument can be made, for example, that program proofs are only as good as the precondition/postcondition specification, and that it is just as easy to introduce a bug in the specifications as it is in the program. For example, a sorting routine might have a postcondition that specifies the result be sorted but might accidentally omit the requirement that the elements be a permutation of the values in the input. Furthermore, it is hard to put much faith in an automated proof that is so complex that no human is willing to follow it.

2.3 Weakest Preconditions

The suggestion that a program can itself be developed by attention to the axiomatic meaning of language constructs and that programmers should develop their programs backward was elucidated by Edsger W. Dijkstra [Dijkstra 75]. Instead of seeing the axioms as static relations between preconditions and postconditions, Dijkstra introduced the concept of weakest precondition. I will say that P = wp(S, Q) if the following statements hold:

- {P} S {Q}. That is, P is a precondition to S.
- S is guaranteed to terminate, given P. That is, S shows **total correctness**, not just conditional correctness.
- If {R} S {Q}, then R $\Rightarrow$ P. That is, P is the weakest precondition, so {P} S {Q} is the strongest proposition that can be made given S and Q.

Weakest preconditions satisfy several properties:

1. For any statement S, wp(S, false) = false (law of the excluded miracle).
2. If P $\Rightarrow$ Q, then wp(S, P) $\Rightarrow$ wp(S, Q) (related to the rules of consequence).
3. wp(S, P) $\wedge$ wp(S, Q) = wp(S, P $\wedge$ Q) (again, related to rules of consequence).

The axioms shown earlier can be restated in terms of wp, as shown in Figure 10.14.

Figure 10.14

Empty statement	1
wp(**skip**, R) = R	2
Assignment statement	3
wp(x := y, R) = R[x $\rightarrow$ y]	4
Composition	5
wp(S_1, S_2) = wp(S_1, wp(S_2))	6
Condition	7
wp(**if** B **then** S **else** T **end**, R) =	8
B $\Rightarrow$ wp(S, R) $\wedge \neg$ B $\Rightarrow$ wp(T, R)	9
Iteration	10
wp(**while** B **do** S **end**, R) =	11
$\exists i \geq 0$ such that $H_i(R)$	12
where	13
$H_0(R)$ = R $\wedge \neg$B	14
$H_k(R)$ = wp(**if** B **then** S **else skip end**, $H_{k-1}(R)$)	15

Given these axioms, it is possible to start at the end of the program with the final postcondition and to work backward attempting to prove the initial precondition. With enough ingenuity, it is even possible to design the program in the same order. Let us take a very simple example. I have two integer variables, x and y. I would like to sort them into the two variables a and b. A proposition R that describes the desired result is shown in Figure 10.15.

Figure 10.15   R = a ≤ b ∧ ((a = x ∧ b = y) ∨ (a = y ∧ b = x))

My task is to find a program P such that wp(P,R) = true; that is, the initial precondition should be trivial. In order to achieve equalities like a = x, I will need to introduce some assignments. But I need two alternative sets of assignments, because I can't force a to be the same as both x and y at once. I will control those assignments by a conditional statement. The entire program P will look like Figure 10.16.

Figure 10.16   P = **if** B **then** S **else** T **end**

I will determine B, S, and T shortly. The condition axiom gives me wp(P,R), as in Figure 10.17.

Figure 10.17   wp(P,R) = B ⇒ wp(S,R) ∧ ¬ B ⇒ wp(T,R)

I will now make a leap of faith and assume that S should contain assignment statements in order to force part of R to be true, as in Figure 10.18.

Figure 10.18   S = a := x; b := y;

The assignment statement axiom gives me wp(S,R), as shown in Figure 10.19.

Figure 10.19   wp(S,R) = x ≤ y ∧ ((x = x ∧ y = y) ∨ (x = y ∧ y = x))   1
                 = x ≤ y   2

This equation tells me that statement S alone would almost serve as my program, except that it would have a remaining precondition. A similar set of assignments can force the other part of R to be true, as in Figure 10.20.

Figure 10.20   T = a := y; b := x;   1
           wp(T,R) = y ≤ x ∧ ((y = x ∧ x = y) ∨ (y = y ∧ x = x))   2
                   = y ≤ x   3

I can now combine statements S and T into the conditional statement P, giving me Figure 10.21.

Figure 10.21   wp(P,R) = B ⇒ x ≤ y ∧ ¬ B ⇒ y ≤ x

I can now choose B to be x < y (it would also work if I chose x ≤ y). This choice allows me to demonstrate that wp(P,R) is true. The entire program P is shown in Figure 10.22.

Figure 10.22

```
if x < y then                1
      a := x;                2
      b := y;                3
else                         4
      a := y;                5
      b := x;                6
end                          7
```

Examples involving loops are even less intuitive. Although the concept of weakest precondition is mathematically elegant, it has not caught on as a tool for programmers.

3 ◆ DENOTATIONAL SEMANTICS

The study of denotational semantics was pioneered by Dana Scott and Christopher Strachey of Oxford University, although many individuals have contributed to its development. A denotational definition is composed of three components: a syntactic domain, a semantic domain, and a number of semantic functions. **Semantic functions** map elementary syntactic objects (for example, numerals or identifiers) directly to their semantic values (integers, files, memory configurations, and so forth). Syntactic structures are defined in terms of the composition of the meanings of their syntactic constituents. This method represents a structured definitional mechanism in which the meaning of a composite structure is a function of the meaning of progressively simpler constituents. As you might guess, unstructured language features (most notably **goto**s) are less easily modeled in a denotational framework than structured features.

The **syntactic domain** contains the elementary tokens of a language as well as an abstract syntax. The syntax specified by a conventional context-free grammar is termed a **concrete syntax** because it specifies the exact syntactic structure of programs as well as their phrase structure. That is, a concrete syntax resolves issues of grouping, operator associativity, and so forth. An **abstract syntax** is used to categorize the kinds of syntactic structures that exist. It need not worry about exact details of program representation or how substructures interact; these issues are handled by the concrete syntax. Thus, in an abstract syntax, an **if** statement might be represented by

Stmt → **if** Expr **then** Stmt **else** Stmt

without worrying that not all expressions or statements are valid in an **if** statement or that **if** statements are closed by **end** to deal with the dangling-**else** problem.

Semantic domains define the abstract objects a program manipulates. These include integers (the mathematical variety, without size limits), Booleans, and memories (modeled as functions mapping addresses to primitive values). Semantic functions map abstract syntactic structures to corresponding semantic objects. The meaning of a program is the semantic object produced by the appropriate semantic function. For simple expressions, this object might be an integer or real; for more complex programs it is a function mapping input values to output values, or a function mapping memory before execution to memory after execution.

Concrete examples will make this abstract discussion much clearer. I will build a denotational description of a programming language by starting with very simple ideas and enhancing them little by little. As a start, I present in Figure 10.23 the semantics of binary literals—sequences of 0s and 1s. Because syntactic and semantic objects often have a similar representation (for example, 0 can be a binary digit or the integer zero), I will follow the rule that syntactic objects are always enclosed by [and] . The syntactic domain will be named BinLit and defined by abstract syntax rules. The semantic domain will be N, the natural numbers. The semantic function will be named E (for "Expression") and will map binary literals into natural numbers. The symbol | separates alternative right-hand sides in productions.

Figure 10.23

Abstract syntax   1

    BN ∈ BinLit   2

    BN → Seq   3
    Seq → 0 | 1 | Seq 0 | Seq 1   4

Semantic domain   5

    N = {0,1,2, ...}   6

Semantic function   7

```
E: BinLit  → N                                                    8

E[0] = 0                                                          9
E[1] = 1                                                          10
E[Seq 0] = 2 × E[Seq]                                             11
E[Seq 1] = 2 × E[Seq] + 1                                         12
```

The operators used in the semantic function ($\times$, $+$, $=$) are standard integer operators.

I have made a small start at defining the semantics of a programming language. At the heart of each denotational-semantics definition is a set of semantic functions. The meaning of a program is, in general, a function (usually built up out of other functions) that maps program inputs to program outputs. In the simple example so far, the programming language has no input or output, so the semantic function just takes literals and produces numbers. I will refine this definition until I can describe a significant amount of a programming language.

A summary of all the syntactic and semantic domains and the semantic functions I introduce is at the end of this chapter for quick reference. First, however, I need to introduce some background concepts and notation.

3.1 Domain Definitions

Denotational semantics is careful to specify the exact domains on which semantic functions are defined. This specification is essential to guarantee that only valid programs are ascribed a meaning. I will use the term **domain** to mean a set of values constructed (or defined) in one of the ways discussed below. This careful approach allows me to talk about actual sets and functions as the denotations of syntactic objects while avoiding the paradoxes of set theory.

I will always begin with a set of **basic domains**. For a simple programming language, basic syntactic domains might include: Op, the finite domain of operators; Id, the identifiers; and Numeral, the numerals. Basic semantic domains include N, the natural numbers, and Bool, the domain of truth values. I can also define finite basic domains by enumeration (that is, by simply listing the elements). For example the finite domain {true, false} defines the basic semantic domain of Boolean values. I assume the basic domains are familiar objects whose properties are well understood.

New domains can be defined by applying **domain constructors** to existing domains. I will show three domain constructors corresponding to Cartesian product, disjoint union, and functions. For each

constructor, I will show an ML equivalent. All the denotational semantic specifications I will show can be coded (and tested) in ML (discussed
in Chapter 3).

3.2 Product Domains

Given domains D_1 and D_2, their **product domain**, $D = D_1 \otimes D_2$, consists
of ordered pairs of elements of the component domains. That is,

$$x \in D_1 \otimes D_2 \equiv x = \; < x_1, x_2 >$$

where $x_1 \in D_1$ and $x_2 \in D_2$.

Product domain D provides two selector functions, Hd_D (the head of a
tuple), and Tl_D (the tail). These behave in a fairly natural way, as
shown in Figure 10.24.

Figure 10.24

$$Hd_D(< x_1, x_2 >) = x_1 \qquad\qquad 1$$
$$Tl_D(< x_1, x_2 >) = x_2 \qquad\qquad 2$$

Again, $x_1 \in D_1$, and $x_2 \in D_2$. I will rarely need to mention these functions
explicitly.

The ML equivalent of a product domain is a tuple with two elements.
That is, if D_1 and D_2 are ML types, then the product type $D = D_1 \otimes D_2$ is
just $D_1 * D_2$. Instead of selectors, I will use patterns to extract components. The tuple constructor will serve as a domain constructor.

3.3 Disjoint-Union Domains

Let D_1 and D_2 be domains. Their **disjoint union**, $D_1 \oplus D_2$, consists of elements of either D_1 or D_2, where each value carries with it an indication
of which domain it came from. Formally, the elements of $D = D_1 \oplus D_2$ are

$$\{ < 1, x_1 > \; | \; x_1 \in D_1 \} \cup \{ < 2, x_2 > \; | \; x_2 \in D_2 \} \; .$$

Disjoint-union domain D provides two injection functions, InD_1 and
InD_2, as in Figure 10.25.

Figure 10.25

$$InD_1(x_1) = \; < 1, x_1 > \qquad\qquad 1$$
$$InD_2(x_2) = \; < 2, x_2 > \qquad\qquad 2$$

As usual, $x_1 \in D_1$, and $x_2 \in D_2$.

This form of disjoint union may seem unnecessarily complicated, but
it has the advantage that the meaning of $D_1 \oplus D_2$ is independent of

whether D_1 and D_2 are disjoint. For example, such obvious properties as

$$\forall x_1 \in D_1 \; \forall x_2 \in D_2 \,.\, InD_1(x_1) \neq InD_2(x_2)$$

remain true even if $D_1 = D_2$.

The ML equivalent of a disjoint union is a **datatype**. That is, if D_1 and D_2 are ML types, then Figure 10.26 shows the disjoint-union type $D = D_1 \oplus D_2$.

Figure 10.26

```
datatype D                                    1
    = FirstComponent of D₁                    2
    | SecondComponent of D₂;                  3
```

The ML notation allows me to introduce names for the two components, which will be helpful in testing from which underlying domain a member of the disjoint-union domain comes.

3.4 Function Domains

Given domains D_1 and D_2, their **function domain** $D_1 \rightarrow D_2$ is a set of functions mapping elements of D_1 to elements of D_2. For technical reasons, $D_1 \rightarrow D_2$ means not all functions from D_1 to D_2, but rather a subset of them, called the continuous ones. Every computable function (hence every function I will need) is continuous. If $f \in D_1 \rightarrow D_2$ and $x_1 \in D_1$, the application of f to x_1, written $f(x_1)$ or $f\,x_1$, is an element of D_2.

There are several ways to package multiple parameters to a function. Just as in ML, they can be packaged into a single tuple or curried. Function values can be parameters or returned results, just like values of any other type.

I will need notation for a few simple functions. First, there is the constant function. For example,

```
f(x:D) = 17
```

denotes the function in $D \rightarrow N$ that always produces the value 17.

Second, I will need a function that differs from an existing function on only a single parameter value. Suppose $f \in D_1 \rightarrow D_2$, $x_1 \in D_1$, and $x_2 \in D_2$. Then

$$f[x_1 \leftarrow x_2]$$

denotes the function that differs from f only by producing result x_2 on parameter x_1; that is:

$$f[x_1 \leftarrow x_2]\, y \;=\; \textbf{if}\ y = x_1\ \textbf{then}\ x_2\ \textbf{else}\ f\ y$$

This simple device allows me to build up all almost-everywhere-constant functions—functions that return the same result on all but finitely many distinct parameter values. This mechanism is particularly useful in modeling declarations and memory updates.

3.5 Domain Equations

I will define a collection of domains $D_1, \dots, D_k$ by a system of formal equations, as in Figure 10.27.

Figure 10.27

$$
\begin{aligned}
D_1 &= rhs_1 & &1\\
&\cdots & &2\\
D_k &= rhs_k & &3
\end{aligned}
$$

Each right-hand side rhs_i is a domain expression, built from basic domains (and possibly from some of the D_i themselves) using the domain constructors given above.

For technical reasons, it is important that I not treat these formal equations as meaning strict equality. Instead, I use a somewhat more liberal interpretation. I say that domains $D_1, \dots, D_k$ comprise a solution to the above system of domain equations if, for each i, D_i is isomorphic to the domain denoted by rhs_i; that is, there exists a one-to-one, onto function between them.

While I have not shown that this liberal interpretation of domain equations is technically necessary, you can certainly appreciate its convenience. Consider the single equation:

$$D = N \oplus Bool\ .$$

Intuitively, the set $N \cup Bool$ has all the properties required of a solution to this equation. The right-hand side of this equation denotes

$$N \oplus Bool \equiv \{\,<1, x>\ |\ x \in N\,\} \cup \{\,<2, y>\ |\ y \in Bool\,\}$$

which is clearly not equal to $N \cup Bool$. However, it is easy to see that the two sets are isomorphic, since N and $Bool$ are disjoint, so by the liberal interpretation of equations as isomorphisms, $N \cup Bool$ is a solution to the equation. Thus, as intuition suggests, if D_1 and D_2 are disjoint domains, no confusion results from taking $D_1 \oplus D_2$ to be $D_1 \cup D_2$ rather than using the full mechanism of the disjoint-union domain constructor.

3.6 Nonrecursive Definitions

I need to introduce just a bit more terminology. In a system of domain equations, each right-hand side is a domain expression, consisting of applications of domain constructors to basic domains and possibly to some of the domains D_i being defined by the system of equations. A right-hand side that uses no D_i, that is, one that consists entirely of applications of domain constructors to basic domains, is **closed**. A right-hand side rhs that is not closed has at least one use of a D_i; I will say that D_i **occurs free** in rhs. For example, in

$$D_{17} = D_{11} \oplus (D_{11} \otimes N) \oplus (D_{12} \otimes N)$$

rhs_{17} has two free occurrences of the name D_{11} and one free occurrence of the name D_{12}; no other names occur free in rhs_{17}.

A system S of domain equations is nonrecursive if it can be ordered as in Figure 10.28,

Figure 10.28

$D_1 = rhs_1$	1
...	2
$D_k = rhs_k$	3

where only the names $D_1, \ldots, D_{i-1}$ are allowed to appear free in rhs_i. In particular, this definition implies that rhs_1 is closed.

A solution to a nonrecursive system of domain equations S can be found easily by a process of repeated back substitution, as follows. Begin with the system S, in which rhs_1 is closed. Build a new system S^2 from S by substituting rhs_1 for every occurrence of the name D_1 in the right-hand sides of S. You should convince yourself of the following:

1. S^2 has no free occurrences of D_1.
2. S^2 is equivalent to S in the sense that every solution to S^2 is a solution to S, and conversely.
3. Both rhs_1^2 and rhs_2^2 are closed.

Now build system S^3 from S^2 by substituting rhs_2^2 for every occurrence of D_2 in the right-hand sides of S^2. Just as above, the following hold:

1. S^3 has no free occurrences of D_1 or D_2.
2. S^3 is equivalent to S^2 (and hence to S).
3. All of rhs_1^3, rhs_2^3, and rhs_3^3 are closed.

The pattern should now be clear: Repeat the substitution step to produce S^k, in which all of $rhs_1, \ldots, rhs_k$ are closed. There is an obvious solution to S^k: Evaluate all the right-hand sides.

A simple example may help. Let S be the nonrecursive system shown in Figure 10.29.

Figure 10.29

$D_1 = N \otimes N$	1
$D_2 = N \oplus D_1$	2
$D_3 = D_1 \otimes D_2$	3

Then S^2 is given in Figure 10.30.

Figure 10.30

$D_1 = N \otimes N$	1
$D_2 = N \oplus (N \otimes N)$	2
$D_3 = (N \otimes N) \otimes D_2$	3

Finally S^3 is given in Figure 10.31.

Figure 10.31

$D_1 = N \otimes N$	1
$D_2 = N \oplus (N \otimes N)$	2
$D_3 = (N \otimes N) \otimes (N \oplus (N \otimes N))$	3

Now all right-hand sides are closed.

3.7 Recursive Definitions

A system of domain equations is recursive if no matter how it is ordered there is at least one i such that rhs_i contains a free occurrence of D_j for some $j \geq i$. That is, a system is recursive if it cannot be reordered to eliminate forward references. Intuitively, such a system is an inherently circular definition.

BNF definitions for syntax can be recursive as well. The context-free grammar descriptions of typical programming languages routinely contain recursive production rules like:

```
Expr → Expr op Expr
```

Intuitively, this rule states that an expression can be built by applying an operator to two subexpressions. A recursive collection of grammar rules defines the set of all objects that can be constructed by finitely many applications of the rules. Such recursive rules are indispensable; they are the only way a finite set of context-free production rules can describe the infinite set of all valid programs. Similarly, if you try to define semantics with only nonrecursive domain equations, you will soon discover they are not powerful enough.

Unfortunately, interpreting a recursive system of domain equations can be subtle. In an ML representation of domain equations, I will just declare the equations with the **rec** modifier, so that they can depend on each other. I will ignore any problems that circularity might raise. But consider the innocuous-looking equation of Figure 10.32.

Figure 10.32 $$D = N \oplus (N \otimes D)$$

Interpreting this equation as if it were a production, you might conclude that the domain D consists of (or is isomorphic to) the set of all nonempty finite sequences of elements of N. However, the set D′ of all sequences (finite or infinite) over N is also a solution to Figure 10.32, since every (finite or infinite) sequence over N is either a singleton or an element of N followed by a (finite or infinite) sequence.

Where there are two solutions, it makes sense to look for a third. Consider the set of all (finite or infinite) sequences over N in which 17 does not occur infinitely often. This too is a solution. This observation opens the floodgates. Rather than 17, I can exclude the infinite repetition of any finite or infinite subset of N to get yet another solution to Figure 10.32—for example, the set of all sequences over N in which no prime occurs infinitely often.

By this simple argument, the number of distinct solutions to Figure 10.32 is at least as big as 2^N —the power set, or set of all subsets, of N. Which solution to Figure 10.32 is the right one? The one I want is the one that corresponds to a BNF-grammar interpretation—the set of finite sequences.

Any solution to Figure 10.32 need only satisfy the equation up to isomorphism; but I will find an exact solution. From Figure 10.32 I can determine the (infinite) set of all closed expressions denoting elements of D. A few of these are shown in Figure 10.33.

Figure 10.33
```
<1,0>                                                    1
<1,1>                                                    2
<1,2>                                                    3
<1,3>                                                    4
...                                                      5
<2,(0 ⊗ <1,0>>                                           6
<2,(1 ⊗ <1,0>>                                           7
<2,(2 ⊗ <1,0>>                                           8
<2,(3 ⊗ <1,0>>                                           9
...                                                     10
```

```
<2,(0 ⊗ <1,1>>                                              11
<2,(0 ⊗ <1,2>>                                              12
<2,(0 ⊗ <1,3>>                                              13
...                                                         14
```

The (infinite) set of the values of these expressions yields an exact solution to Figure 10.32. It can also be shown that this is the smallest solution, in that it is isomorphic to a subset of any other solution. In general, the solution to prefer when there are many possible solutions to a recursive system of domain equations is the smallest one.

Equations of the form of Figure 10.32 arise so frequently that their solutions have a notation: If D is already defined, then the solution to

$$D' = D \oplus (D \otimes D')$$

is called D^*.

Function domains cause problems in recursive systems of domain equations. Even a simple recursive equation like

$$D = \cdots \oplus (D \to D) \oplus \cdots$$

is suspect. Any solution to this equation would have the property that some subset of itself was isomorphic to its own function space. Unfortunately, if a set has more than one element, then the cardinality of its function space is strictly greater than the cardinality of the set itself, so no such isomorphism is possible!

Am I stuck? Not really. As mentioned above, I interpret $D \to D$ to mean not all functions from D to D, but just a distinguished set of functions called the continuous ones. There are sufficiently few continuous functions that the above cardinality argument does not apply, but sufficiently many of them that all functions computable by programming languages are continuous.

3.8 Expressions

Now that I have discussed domains, I can begin to create richer and more realistic semantic functions. I first extend my definition of binary literals to include infix operators; see Figure 10.34.

Figure 10.34   **Abstract syntax**   1

$T \in Exp$ 2

```
T → T + T                                  3
T → T - T                                  4
T → T * T                                  5
T → Seq                                    6
Seq → 0 | 1 | Seq 0 | Seq 1                7
```

Semantic domain   8

$N = \{0,1,2, \ldots, -1, -2, \ldots\}$ 9

Semantic function   10

$E: Exp \to N$ 11

$E[0] = 0$ 12
$E[1] = 1$ 13
$E[Seq\ 0] = 2 \times E[Seq]$ 14
$E[Seq\ 1] = 2 \times E[Seq] + 1$ 15

$E[T_1 + T_2] = E[T_1] + E[T_2]$ 16
$E[T_1 - T_2] = E[T_1] - E[T_2]$ 17
$E[T_1 * T_2] = E[T_1] \times E[T_2]$ 18

This example can be specified in ML as shown in Figure 10.35.

Figure 10.35

```
-- abstract syntax                                     1

    datatype Operator = plus | minus | times;          2
    datatype Exp                                       3
        = BinLit of int list -- [0,1] means 10 = 2     4
        | Term of Exp*Operator*Exp;                    5

-- semantic functions                                  6

    val rec E =                                        7
        fn BinLit([0]) => 0                            8
         | BinLit([1]) => 1                            9
         | BinLit(0 :: tail) => 2*E(BinLit(tail))      10
         | BinLit(1 :: tail) => 1+2*E(BinLit(tail))    11
         | Term(x, plus, y) => E(x) + E(y)             12
         | Term(x, minus, y) => E(x) - E(y)            13
         | Term(x, times, y) => E(x) * E(y);           14
```

Because it is easier to access the front of a list than the rear, I chose to let BinLits (line 4) store least-significant bits at the front of the list. A benefit of the ML description is that it can be given to an ML interpreter to check. For instance, I have checked the code shown in Figure 10.36.

Figure 10.36

```
in:   E(Term(BinLit([1,1]), plus,                          1
              BinLit([0,1])));  -- 3 + 2                    2
out:  5 : int                                              3
```

To include division, I must define what division by zero means. To do so, I augment the semantic domain with an error element, $\bot$. That is, I now have a domain of $R = N \oplus \{\bot\}$, where R represents "results." Because this is a disjoint-union domain, I can test which subdomain a given semantic element belongs to. I use the notation v?D to test if value v is in domain D. I also will use the following concise conditional-expression notation:

$$b \Rightarrow x,y \text{ means } \textbf{if } b \textbf{ then } x \textbf{ else } y$$

Errors must propagate through arithmetic operations, so I need to upgrade the semantic functions. Figure 10.37 presents the denotation of expressions with division.

Figure 10.37

Semantic domain	1
$\quad R = N \oplus \{\bot\}$	2
Semantic function	3
$\quad E: Exp \rightarrow R$	4
$\quad E[0] = 0$	5
$\quad E[1] = 1$	6
$\quad E[Seq\ 0] = 2 \times E[Seq]$	7
$\quad E[Seq\ 1] = 2 \times E[Seq] + 1$	8
$\quad E[T_1 + T_2] = E[T_1]?N \wedge E[T_2]?N \Rightarrow E[T_1] + E[T_2], \bot$	9
$\quad E[T_1 - T_2] = E[T_1]?N \wedge E[T_2]?N \Rightarrow E[T_1] - E[T_2], \bot$	10
$\quad E[T_1 * T_2] = E[T_1]?N \wedge E[T_2]?N \Rightarrow E[T_1] \times E[T_2], \bot$	11
$\quad E[T_1 / T_2] = E[T_1]?N \wedge E[T_2]?N \Rightarrow (E[T_2] = 0 \Rightarrow \bot, E[T_1] / E[T_2]), \bot$	12

This definition is unrealistic in that it ignores the finite range of computer arithmetic. Since I have an error value, I can use it to represent range errors. I will introduce a function range such that:

$$\text{range: } N \rightarrow \{\text{minInt..maxInt}\} \oplus \{\perp\}. \qquad 1$$
$$\text{range}(n) = \text{minInt} \leq n \leq \text{maxInt} \Rightarrow n, \perp \qquad 2$$

Figure 10.38 shows how to insert Range into the definition of E.

Figure 10.38   **Semantic function**   1

E: Exp → R   2

$E[0] = 0$ 3
$E[1] = 1$ 4
$E[\text{Seq } 0] = E[\text{Seq}]?N \Rightarrow \text{range}(2 \times E[\text{Seq}]), \perp$ 5
$E[\text{Seq } 1] = E[\text{Seq}]?N \Rightarrow \text{range}(2 \times E[\text{Seq}] + 1), \perp$ 6

$E[T_1 + T_2] = E[T_1]?N \wedge E[T_2]?N \Rightarrow \text{range}(E[T_1] + E[T_2]), \perp$ 7
$E[T_1 - T_2] = E[T_1]?N \wedge E[T_2]? \Rightarrow \text{range}(E[T_1] - E[T_2]), \perp$ 8
$E[T_1 * T_2] = E[T_1]?N \wedge E[T_2]?N \Rightarrow \text{range}(E[T_1] \times E[T_2]), \perp$ 9
$E[T_1/T_2] = E[T_1]?N \wedge E[T_2]?N \Rightarrow$ 10
$\qquad (E[T_2] = 0 \Rightarrow \perp, \text{range}(E[T_1] / E[T_2])), \perp$ 11

It is time to show the ML equivalent, given in Figure 10.39.

Figure 10.39   `-- tools`   1

```
val SayError = fn (str, result) => -- report error      2
(     output(std_out, str);                             3
      result -- returned                                4
);                                                      5

-- limits                                               6
val MaxInt = 1000; -- or whatever                       7
val MinInt = -1000; -- or whatever                      8

-- abstract syntax                                      9

datatype Operator = plus | minus | times | divide;      10
datatype Exp                                            11
    = BinLit of int list -- [0,1] means 10 = 2          12
    | Term of Exp*Operator*Exp;                         13

-- semantic domains                                     14

datatype R                                              15
    = NaturalR of int                                   16
    | ErrorR;                                           17
```

```
-- semantic functions                                         18

    val Range =                                               19
        fn NaturalR(a) =>                                     20
            if MinInt ≤ a and a ≤ MaxInt then                 21
                NaturalR(a)                                   22
            else                                              23
                SayError("overflow", ErrorR)                 24
         | _ => ErrorR;                                       25

    val Add =                                                 26
        fn (NaturalR(a),NaturalR(b)) => NaturalR(a+b);        27
    val Sub =                                                 28
        fn (NaturalR(a),NaturalR(b)) => NaturalR(a-b);        29
    val Mul =                                                 30
        fn (NaturalR(a),NaturalR(b)) => NaturalR(a*b);        31
    val Div =                                                 32
        fn (NaturalR(a),NaturalR(0)) =>                       33
                SayError("Divide by zero", ErrorR)            34
         | (NaturalR(a),NaturalR(b)) =>                       35
                NaturalR(floor(real(a)/real(b)));             36

    val rec E =                                               37
        fn BinLit([0]) => NaturalR(0)                         38
         | BinLit([1]) => NaturalR(1)                         39
         | BinLit(0 :: tail) =>                               40
            let val NaturalR(num) = E(BinLit(tail))           41
            in  NaturalR(2*num)                               42
            end                                               43
         | BinLit(1 :: tail) =>                               44
            let val NaturalR(num) = E(BinLit(tail))           45
            in  NaturalR(2*num + 1)                           46
            end                                               47
         | Term(x, plus, y) => Range(Add(E(x), E(y)))         48
         | Term(x, minus, y) => Range(Sub(E(x), E(y)))        49
         | Term(x, times, y) => Range(Mul(E(x), E(y)))        50
         | Term(x, divide, y) => Range(Div(E(x), E(y)));      51
```

I have introduced an error routine SayError (lines 2–5) so that a user can see exactly what sort of error has occurred instead of just getting a result of ⊥. The Range function (lines 19–25) not only checks ranges, but also makes sure that its parameter is a natural number. I have split out Add, Sub, Mul, and Div (lines 26–36), so that they can check the types of their parameters. I could have given them alternatives that return ⊥ if the types are not right. The semantic function E (lines 37–51) needs to convert parameters of type BinLit to results of type R.

Any realistic programming language will have more than one type, which I illustrate by adding the semantic domain Bool corresponding to Booleans. I also add the comparison operator = that can compare two integers or two Booleans. The additions I need to upgrade Figure 10.38 are given in Figure 10.40.

Figure 10.40	**Abstract syntax**	1
	$T \rightarrow T = T$	2
	Semantic domain	3
	$R = N \oplus Bool \oplus \{\bot\}$	4
	Semantic function	5
	$E[T_1 = T_2] = (E[T_1]?N \wedge E[T_2]?N) \vee (E[T_1]?Bool \wedge E[T_2]?Bool) \Rightarrow$	6
	$\quad (E[T_1] = E[T_2]), \bot$	7

3.9 Identifiers

I can now introduce predeclared identifiers, including true and false, maxint, minint, and so forth. Let Id be the syntactic domain of identifiers, and let L be a semantic lookup function such that L: Id $\rightarrow$ V, where V = N $\oplus$ Bool $\oplus$ {udef}. That is, L returns an integer or Boolean value, or udef if the identifier is undefined. The additions needed for Figure 10.40 are given in Figure 10.41.

Figure 10.41	**Abstract syntax**	1
	$I \in Id$	2
	$T \rightarrow I$	3
	Semantic domains	4
	$V = N \oplus Bool \oplus \{udef\}$	5
	Semantic functions	6
	$L: Id \rightarrow V$	7
	$E[I] = L[I]?\{udef\} \Rightarrow \bot, L[I]$	8

3.10 Environments

The next step is to introduce programmer-defined named constants. This step requires the concept of an environment that is updated when declarations are made. An **environment** is a function that maps identifiers (drawn from the syntactic domain) into results. I will denote the domain of environments as U, where $U = Id \rightarrow V$ and $V = N \oplus Bool \oplus \{udef\} \oplus \{\perp\}$, as in Figure 10.42. If $u \in U$ and $I \in Id$, then $u[I]$ is an integer, Boolean, udef, or $\perp$, depending on how and whether I has been declared. I can incorporate the definition of predeclared named constants by including them in u_0, a predefined environment. I no longer need the lookup function L.

Figure 10.42   **Semantic domain**   1

$$V = N \oplus Bool \oplus \{udef\} \oplus \{\perp\} \qquad\qquad 2$$
$$U = Id \rightarrow V \qquad\qquad 3$$

Semantic functions   4

$$E[I] = u_0[I]?\{udef\} \Rightarrow \perp, u_0[I] \qquad\qquad 5$$

The environment approach is useful because environments can be computed as the results of semantic functions (those that define the meaning of a local constant declaration).

It is time to expand my abstract syntax for a program into a sequence of declarations followed by an expression that yields the result of a program. I can specify whatever I like for the meaning of a redefinition of an identifier. In Figure 10.43, redefinitions will have no effect.

I will introduce two new semantic functions: D, which defines the semantic effect of declarations, and M, which defines the meaning of a program. D is curried; it maps a declaration and an old environment into a new environment in two steps. There is a major change to E; it now maps an expression and an environment into a result. Pr is the syntactic domain of all programs; $Decls$ is the syntactic domain of declarations.

Figure 10.43   **Abstract syntax**   1

$$P \in Pr \text{ -- a program} \qquad\qquad 2$$
$$T \in Exp \text{ -- an expression} \qquad\qquad 3$$
$$I \in Id \text{ -- an identifier} \qquad\qquad 4$$
$$Def \in Decls \text{ -- a declaration} \qquad\qquad 5$$

```
P → Def T                                              6
Def → ε -- empty declaration                           7
Def → I = T ; -- constant declaration                  8
Def → Def Def -- declaration list                      9
T → I -- identifier expression                         10
```

Semantic domains   11

```
R = N ⊕ Bool ⊕ {⊥} -- program results                 12
V = N ⊕ Bool ⊕ {udef} ⊕ {⊥} -- lookup values          13
U = Id → V -- environments                             14
```

Semantic functions   15

$$E: \ Exp \to U \to R \tag{16}$$
$$D: \ Decls \to U \to U \tag{17}$$
$$M: \ Pr \to R \tag{18}$$

$$M[Def\ T] = E[T]u \tag{19}$$
$$\textbf{where } u = D[Def]u_0. \tag{20}$$

$$D[\varepsilon]u = u \tag{21}$$
$$D[I = T]u = u[I]?\{udef\} \Rightarrow u[I \leftarrow e], u \tag{22}$$
$$\textbf{where } e = E[T]u. \tag{23}$$
$$D[Def_1\ Def_2]\ u = D[Def_2]v \tag{24}$$
$$\textbf{where } v = D[Def_1]u. \tag{25}$$

$$E[I] = u[I]?\{udef\} \Rightarrow \bot, u[I] \tag{26}$$
$$E[0]u = 0 \tag{27}$$
$$E[1]u = 1 \tag{28}$$
$$E[Seq\ 0]\ u = E[Seq]u?N \Rightarrow range(2 \times E[Seq]u), \bot \tag{29}$$
$$E[Seq\ 1]\ u = E[Seq]u?N \Rightarrow range(2 \times E[Seq]u + 1), \bot \tag{30}$$

$$E[T_1 + T_2]\ u = E[T_1]u?N \wedge E[T_2]u?N \Rightarrow \tag{31}$$
$$range(E[T_1]\ u + E[T_2]u), \bot \tag{32}$$
$$E[T_1 - T_2]\ u = E[T_1]u?N \wedge E[T_2]u?N \Rightarrow \tag{33}$$
$$range(E[T_1]\ u - E[T_2]u), \bot \tag{34}$$
$$E[T_1 * T_2]\ u = E[T_1]u?N \wedge E[T_2]u?N \Rightarrow \tag{35}$$
$$range(E[T_1]\ u \times E[T_2]u), \bot \tag{36}$$
$$E[T_1 / T_2]\ u = E[T_1]u?N \wedge E[T_2]u?N \Rightarrow \tag{37}$$
$$(E[T_2]\ u = 0 \Rightarrow \bot, range(E[T_1]\ u\ /\ E[T_2]u)), \bot \tag{38}$$
$$E[T_1 = T_2]u = (E[T_1]u?N \wedge E[T_2]u?N) \vee (E[T_1]u?Bool \wedge E[T_2]u?Bool) \Rightarrow \tag{39}$$
$$(E[T_1]u = E[T_2]u), \bot \tag{40}$$

Lines 19–20 define the meaning of a program to be the value of the expression T in the environment u formed by modifying the initial environment u_0 by the declarations. Lines 22–23 show how declarations modify a given environment u by substituting the meaning of T for the identifier I in u. Multiple declarations build the final environment in stages (lines 24–25).

Line 22 explicitly ignores attempts to redefine an identifier, but I can make the language a bit more realistic. I will let a redefinition of an identifier return an environment in which the identifier is bound to a new kind of error value named redef. E of a redefined identifier will yield ⊥. I extend the domain V of possible environment values to include redef. Figure 10.44 shows the differences.

Figure 10.44

Semantic domains   1

$$V = N \oplus \text{Bool} \oplus \{\bot\} \oplus \{\text{udef}\} \oplus \{\text{redef}\} \qquad 2$$

Semantic functions   3

$$D[I = T]u = u[I]?\{\text{udef}\} \Rightarrow u[I \leftarrow e], u[I \leftarrow \text{redef}] \qquad 4$$
$$\textbf{where } e = E[T]u. \qquad 5$$
$$E[I]u = u[I]?(\{\text{udef}\} \oplus \{\text{redef}\}) \Rightarrow \bot, u[I] \qquad 6$$

At this point I could add block structure, but since programs only compute a single expression, scoping isn't needed yet. Instead, I will put in variables.

3.11 Variables

I can model variables in several ways. The most general model employs an environment that maps identifiers to locations and a store that maps locations to values. This is how most languages are implemented, and it would allow me to model aliasing, reuse of storage, and so forth.

For the present, I'll use a simpler interpreter model and continue to use the environment function to map identifiers directly to values. I will also store a flag that indicates if a value can be changed (that is, if it's an L-value, not an R-value). An interpreter does roughly the same thing, maintaining a runtime symbol table for all program variables. From the semantic point of view, the distinction between interpreters and compilers is irrelevant—what is important is what the answer is, not how it's produced. The interpreter approach will allow interesting variations. For example, an untyped language (like Smalltalk) is just as easy to model as a strongly typed language.

I begin by extending the environment domain U as in Figure 10.45 to include an indication of how an identifier can be used:

$$U = Id \rightarrow \{var, const, uninit\} \otimes V$$

Uninit models the fact that after a variable is declared, it may be assigned to, but not yet used. After a variable is assigned a value, its flag changes from uninit to var. It is time to introduce statements. (In denotational formalisms, statements are usually called commands.) A statement maps an environment into a new environment (or ⊥). That is,

$$S: \ Stm \rightarrow U \rightarrow (U \oplus \{\bot\})$$

where S is the semantic function for statements, and Stm is the syntactic domain of statements.

I will first add only variable declarations and assignment statements to the programming language. Since there is no I/O, I will define the result of the program to be the final value of an identifier that is mentioned in the program header, as in Figure 10.45, which produces 1 as its result.

Figure 10.45

```
program(x)                                          1
      x : integer;                                  2
      x := 1;                                       3
end                                                 4
```

To simplify the definitions, I will use ∧ and ∨ as short-circuit operators: Only those operands needed to determine the truth of an expression will be evaluated. Thus,

$$e?N \wedge e > 0$$

is well defined even if e is a Boolean, in which case e > 0 is undefined.

Further, if some $e \in D$, where $D = (D_1 \otimes D_2) \oplus D_3$, and D_3 isn't a product domain, then $Hd(e)?D_1$ will be considered well defined (with the value false) if $e \in D_3$. That is, if e isn't in a product domain, I will allow Hd(e) or Tl(e) to be used in a domain test. This sloppiness should cause no confusion, since if e isn't in a product domain, then Hd(e) or Tl(e) isn't in any domain. Use of Hd(e) or Tl(e) in other than a domain test is invalid if e isn't in a product domain.

Figure 10.46 presents a new language specification, building on the one in Figure 10.43 (page 384).

Figure 10.46   **Abstract syntax**   1

    P ∈ Pr -- a program   2
    T ∈ Exp -- an expression   3
    I ∈ Id -- an identifier   4
    Def ∈ Decls -- a declaration   5
    St ∈ Stm -- a statement   6

    P → **program** (I) Def St **end** -- program   7
    Def → ε -- empty declaration   8
    Def → I = T; -- constant declaration   9
    Def → I : integer; -- integer variable declaration   10
    Def → I : Boolean; -- Boolean variable declaration   11
    Def → Def Def -- declaration list   12

    St → ε -- empty statement   13
    St → I := T -- assignment statement   14
    St → St St -- statement list   15

Semantic domains   16

    $R = N \oplus Bool \oplus \{\bot\}$ -- program results   17
    $V = N \oplus Bool \oplus \{\bot\} \oplus \{udef\} \oplus \{redef\}$ -- id value   18
    $U = Id \to \{var, const, uninit\} \otimes V$ -- environments   19

Semantic functions   20

    $E: Exp \to U \to R$ 21
    $D: Decls \to U \to U$ 22
    $M: Pr \to R$ 23
    $S: Stm \to U \to (U \oplus \{\bot\})$ 24

    $M[$**program** (I) Def St **end**$] = c?U \Rightarrow E[I]c, \bot$ 25
        where $u = D[Def]u_0; c = S[St]u.$ 26
    $D[\varepsilon]u = u$ 27
    $D[I = T]u = u[I]?\{udef\} \Rightarrow u[I \leftarrow f], u[I \leftarrow redef]$ 28
        where $e = E[T]u; f = e?\bot \Rightarrow \bot, <const, e>.$ 29
    $D[I:integer]u = u[I]?\{udef\} \Rightarrow u[I \leftarrow e], u[I \leftarrow redef]$ 30
        where $e = <uninit, InN(0)>$ 31
    $D[I:Boolean]u = u[I]?\{udef\} \Rightarrow u[I \leftarrow e], u[I \leftarrow redef]$ 32
        where $e = <uninit, InBool(true)>.$ 33
    $D[Def_1 \, Def_2]u = D[Def_2]v$ 34
        where $v = D[Def_1]u.$ 35
    $E[I]u = v?(\{redef\} \oplus \{udef\} \oplus \{\bot\}) \Rightarrow \bot,$ 36
        $(Hd(v) = uninit \Rightarrow \bot, Tl(v))$ 37
        where $v = u[I].$ 38

$$S[\varepsilon]u = u \qquad\qquad 39$$
$$S[I := T]u = v?(\{redef\} \oplus \{udef\} \oplus \{\bot\}) \vee (Hd(v) = const) \vee e?\{\bot\} \Rightarrow \quad 40$$
$$\bot, (e?N \wedge Tl(v)?N) \vee (e?Bool \wedge Tl(v)?Bool) \Rightarrow \qquad 41$$
$$u[I \leftarrow <var, e>], \bot \qquad\qquad 42$$
$$\textbf{where } e = E[T]u;\ v = u[I]. \qquad\qquad 43$$
$$S[St_1\ St_2]\ u = g?U \Rightarrow S[St_2]g, \bot \qquad\qquad 44$$
$$\textbf{where } g = S[St_1]u. \qquad\qquad 45$$

The easiest way to read the semantic functions is to first look at the **where** clauses to see the local shorthands. (These are like ML **let** blocks.) Then look at the definition itself, following the case where no errors are encountered. Much of each definition necessarily deals with checking for error situations, which tend to confuse the central issue. When I describe definitions, I will generally ignore all the error cases and concentrate on the usual case. Lastly, assure yourself that the functions are given parameters of the correct domains and produce results in the correct domains.

For example, lines 40–43 describe what an assignment does to the environment u. Start with line 43. The local variable e stands for the value of the right-hand side of the assignment in environment u, and v stands for the meaning of the identifier on the left-hand side. This meaning is evaluated in the same environment u, so if evaluating the right-hand side had a side effect (it can't yet, but it might later), that effect is ignored in determining the identifier's meaning. Then (line 40) given that v is properly declared and not a constant, given that e evaluates successfully, and given (line 41) that the expression and identifier are the same type, the statement creates a new environment (line 42) that is just like the old one with the identifier reassigned.

To check domain consistency, I will ignore all error cases and write out these few lines again in Figure 10.47.

Figure 10.47

$$S[I := T]u = u[I \leftarrow <var, e>] \qquad\qquad 1$$
$$\textbf{where } e = E[T]u. \qquad\qquad 2$$

Now I can painstakingly infer the type of S, as shown in Figure 10.48.

Figure 10.48

$$E: Exp \rightarrow U \rightarrow R \qquad\qquad 1$$
$$E[T]: U \rightarrow R \qquad\qquad 2$$
$$e = E[T]u: R \qquad\qquad 3$$
$$e: V,\ \text{since V is a superset of R} \qquad\qquad 4$$

$$u: U \qquad\qquad 5$$
$$u: Id \rightarrow \{var, const, uninit\} \otimes V \qquad\qquad 6$$
$$u[I]: \{var, const, uninit\} \otimes V \qquad\qquad 7$$

$$< var, e > : \{var, const, uninit\} \otimes V \qquad\qquad 8$$
$$u[I \leftarrow < var, e >]: U \qquad\qquad 9$$
$$u[I \leftarrow < var, e >]: U \oplus \{\perp\}, \text{ which is a superset of } U \qquad\qquad 10$$

$$S: Stm \rightarrow U \rightarrow (U \oplus \{\perp\}) \qquad\qquad 11$$
$$S[I := T]: U \rightarrow (U \oplus \{\perp\}) \qquad\qquad 12$$
$$S[I := T]u: U \oplus \{\perp\} \qquad\qquad 13$$

Line 10 shows the type of the right-hand side of the equation in line 1, and line 13 shows the type of the left-hand side. They match. It was necessary to raise several types; see lines 4 and 10. If this example were coded in ML, I would need to use explicit type converters.

Other notes on Figure 10.46: The value of 0 in line 31 is arbitrary since I don't allow access to variables with an uninit flag. In the definition of statement execution (lines 43–44), as soon as a statement yields $\perp$, all further statement execution is abandoned.

As I suggested earlier, my definitions can easily be modified to handle untyped languages like Smalltalk. I would of course modify the variable-declaration syntax to omit the type specification. A variable would assume the type of the object assigned to it. The definitions of E and S would be written as in Figure 10.49.

Figure 10.49

$$E[I]u = v?(\{redef\} \oplus \{udef\} \oplus \{\perp\}) \Rightarrow \perp, Tl(v) \qquad\qquad 1$$
$$\textbf{where } v = u[I]. \qquad\qquad 2$$

$$S[I := T]u = v?(\{redef\} \oplus \{\perp\}) \vee (Hd(v) = const) \vee e?\{\perp\} \Rightarrow \qquad\qquad 3$$
$$\perp, u[I \leftarrow < var, e >] \qquad\qquad 4$$
$$\textbf{where } e = E[T]u; v = u[I]. \qquad\qquad 5$$

3.12 Conditional and Iterative Statements

Conditional execution and iterative execution for a fixed number of iterations are readily modeled with the additions to the previous definition shown in Figure 10.50.

Figure 10.50

Abstract syntax   1

$$St \rightarrow \textbf{if } T \textbf{ then } St \textbf{ else } St \qquad\qquad 2$$
$$St \rightarrow \textbf{do } T \textbf{ times } St \qquad\qquad 3$$

Semantic functions 4

$$S[\textbf{if } T \textbf{ then } St_1 \textbf{ else } St_2]u = e?\text{Bool} \Rightarrow \quad 5$$
$$(e \Rightarrow S[St_1]u, S[St_2]u), \bot \quad 6$$
$$\textbf{where } e = E[T]u. \quad 7$$

$$S[\textbf{do } T \textbf{ times } St]u = e?N \Rightarrow v_m, \bot \quad 8$$
$$\textbf{where } e = E[T]u; m = \max(0, e); v_0 = u; \quad 9$$
$$v_{i+1} = v_i?U \Rightarrow S[St]v_i, \bot. \quad 10$$

In lines 8–10, v_i is the environment after i iterations of the loop.

The semantic definition of a **while** loop requires special care. The problem is that some **while** loops will never terminate, and I would like a mathematically sound definition of all loops. I might try to build on the definition for the **do** loop, but for nonterminating loops that would create an infinite sequence of intermediate environments (v_i's).

I will follow standard mathematical practice for dealing with infinite sequences and try to determine if a limit exists. I will then be able to conclude that infinite loops have a value of $\bot$, though the semantic function for **while** loops will not always be computable (because of decidability issues). Following Tennent, I will define a sequence of approximations to the meaning of a **while** loop [Tennent 81].

Let $p_0 \equiv \bot$. This formula represents a **while** loop whose Boolean expression has been tested zero times. Since a loop can't terminate until its Boolean expression has evaluated to false, p_0 represents the base state in which the definition hasn't yet established termination. Now I define p_{i+1} recursively, as in Figure 10.51.

Figure 10.51
$$p_{i+1}(u) = e?\text{Bool} \Rightarrow (e \Rightarrow (v?\{\bot\} \Rightarrow \bot, p_i(v)), u), \bot \quad 1$$
$$\textbf{where } e = E[T]u; v = S[St]u. \quad 2$$

If a **while** loop terminates without error after exactly one evaluation of the control expression (because the expression is initially false), $p_1(u)$ returns u (the environment after zero iterations through the loop). In all other cases, $p_1(u)$ returns $\bot$.

If a **while** loop terminates without error after at most two evaluations of the control expression, $p_2(u)$ returns v, the environment after loop termination. In all other cases, $p_2(u)$ returns $\bot$. In general, if a loop terminates after n iterations, $p_m(u)$ for $m \geq n$ will yield the environment after termination, given an initial environment u. For all terminating loops, the limit of $p_i(u)$ as $i \to \infty$ is the environment after loop termination. If the loop doesn't terminate or encounters a runtime error, then all p_i's return $\bot$, which is then trivially the limit as $i \to \infty$. The sequence of p_i's always converges, so the limit is always defined.

This leads to the definition of a **while** loop given in Figure 10.52.

Figure 10.52

$$S[\textbf{while } T \textbf{ do } St]u = \lim_{i \to \infty} p_i(u) \qquad\qquad 1$$
$$\textbf{where } p_{i+1}(w) = e?\text{Bool} \Rightarrow (e \Rightarrow (v?\{\bot\} \Rightarrow \bot, p_i(v)), w), \bot; \qquad 2$$
$$e = E[T]w; v = S[St]w. \qquad\qquad 3$$

In general, the above limit is not computable (because the halting problem is undecidable), but the limit can be computed for some infinite loops (and all finite loops). For example, it doesn't take an oracle to decide that the loop in Figure 10.53 has some problems.

Figure 10.53

```
while true do                                          1
    x := x + 1                                         2
```

What does the denotational definition say about this loop? Assuming true hasn't been redefined, the semantic function is shown in Figure 10.54.

Figure 10.54

$$p_{i+1}(u) = (\text{true} \Rightarrow (v?\{\bot\} \Rightarrow \bot, p_i(v)), u) = v?\{\bot\} \Rightarrow \bot, p_i(v) \qquad 1$$
$$\textbf{where } v = S[St]u. \qquad\qquad 2$$

Now, $p_{i+1}(u)$ is either equal to $\bot$ or $p_i(v)$. Similarly, $p_i(v)$ is either equal to $\bot$ or $p_{i-1}(v')$. But $p_0(s) \equiv \bot$ for all s, so each p_i must reduce to $\bot$, so $\bot$ is the limit of the sequence. The loop fails either because x overflows or because the loop doesn't terminate. Since both failings are represented by $\bot$, the denotational definition has correctly handled this example.

3.13 Procedures

I now consider simple procedures of the abstract form shown in Figure 10.55.

Figure 10.55

```
procedure I;                                           1
    St                                                 2
```

Procedures are invoked by a **call** statement (for example, **call** I). Since there are no scope rules yet, a procedure invocation is equivalent to macro substitution and immediate execution of the procedure's body. A procedure can call another procedure, but I will forbid recursion for now. Since a procedure name is a synonym for a list of statements, it represents a mapping from an environment to an updated environment or to $\bot$. The semantic domain for procedure declarations is given in Figure 10.56.

Figure 10.56

$$\text{Proc} = U \to (U \oplus \{\bot\})$$

I need to upgrade the environment domain to include procedures, as well as introduce a new flag $\texttt{opencall}$. I will set $\texttt{opencall}$ when a procedure call is in progress, but not yet completed. To prevent recursion, I will disallow invoking a procedure that has $\texttt{opencall}$ set. The environment domain U is now as shown in Figure 10.57.

Figure 10.57

```
V = N ⊕ Bool ⊕ Proc ⊕ {⊥} ⊕ {udef} ⊕{redef} -- id value          1
U = Id → {var, const, uninit, opencall} ⊗ V -- environments        2
```

These domain equations are recursive: U references Proc, and Proc references U. Before, I used $f[x \leftarrow y]$ to denote the function equal to f for all parameters except x, where y is to be returned. In the case that y is a member of a product domain, I will extend the notation;

$$f[Hd[x \leftarrow y]]$$

will denote the function equal to f for all parameters except x, where $Hd(f(x)) = y$, but $Tl(f(x))$ is unchanged; $f[Tl[x \leftarrow y]]$ will have an analogous definition. Figure 10.58 gives the new part of the definition, building on Figure 10.46 (page 388).

Figure 10.58

Abstract syntax   1

```
Def → procedure I; St                                              2
St → call I                                                        3
```

Semantic domains   4

```
Proc = U → (U ⊕ {⊥}) -- procedure declaration                     5
V = N ⊕ Bool ⊕ Proc ⊕ {⊥} ⊕ {udef} ⊕{redef} -- id value          6
U = Id → {var, const, uninit, opencall} ⊗ V -- environments        7
```

Semantic functions   8

```
D[procedure I; St]u = u[I]?{udef} ⇒ u[I ← c], u[I ← redef]         9
    where c = < const, InProc(S[St]) > .                          10

S[call I]u = Tl(v)?Proc ∧ Hd(v) = const ∧ w?U ⇒                   11
    w[Hd[I ← const]], ⊥                                           12
    where v = u[I]; w = Tl(v)(u[Hd[I ← opencall]]);               13
```

A procedure declaration (lines 9–10) updates the current environment u by calculating the meaning of the body St and converting the result to domain Proc (line 10). This result is used to build a meaning for I in the environment (line 9). The definition of procedure invocation in lines 11–13 first modifies I in the environment u to indicate the call is open, then applies the body of procedure I (Tl(v) in line 13), storing the resulting environment in w. It then returns w, but first restores the definition of I (line 12).

3.14 Functions

Functions, like procedures, execute a list of statements. They also return a value by evaluating an expression immediately prior to return. For the present, I will constrain functions to be nonrecursive. The abstract syntax of integer functions will be as shown in Figure 10.59.

Figure 10.59

```
integer function I;                                     1
    St;                                                 2
return(T)                                               3
```

Boolean functions have an analogous structure. Functions can be called to yield a value via the **eval** operator (for example, **eval** F).

Introducing function calls into the language raises the specter of side effects. Since I am building a definition, I can handle side effects pretty much as I wish. I might, for example, make them invalid and enforce this rule by comparing the environment after function invocation with that in place before invocation. Any changes would indicate side effects and yield an error result. Alternately, I could erase side effects by resuming execution after a function call with the same environment in place before the call. Although these alternatives are easy to denote, neither would be particularly easy for a compiler writer to implement, especially after the language definition includes I/O.

In the interests of realism, I will bite the bullet and allow side effects. The structure of the E function, which defines the meaning of expressions (which must now include function calls), will change. It will return not only the result value but also an updated environment. I add this facility by defining RR, the new domain of results:

$$RR = U \otimes (N \oplus Bool \oplus \{\perp\})$$

The semantic domain for function calls is:

$$Func = U \rightarrow RR$$

The semantic domain V is also extended to include Func.

The language allows constant declarations of the form I = T. Now that T includes function calls, the definition of constants is complicated by the fact that a call may induce side effects in the environment. This situation is undesirable (though it could be modeled, of course), so I will follow the lead of most languages and assume that a function call in this context is forbidden by the concrete syntax. Figure 10.60 shows what functions add to the definition of Figure 10.46 (page 388).

Figure 10.60

Abstract syntax	1
Def → Integer **function** I; St; **return**(T);	2
Def → Boolean **function** I; St; **return**(T);	3
T → **eval** I -- function invocation	4
Semantic domains	5
RR = U ⊗ (N ⊕ Bool ⊕ {⊥}) -- expression result	6
Func = U → RR	7
V = N ⊕ Bool ⊕ Proc ⊕ Func {⊥} ⊕ {udef} ⊕{redef} -- id value	8
U = Id → {var, const, uninit, opencall} ⊗ V -- environments	9
Semantic functions	10
E: Exp → U → RR	11
M[**program** (I) Def St **end**] = c?U ⇒ T1(E[I]c), ⊥	12
where u = D[Def]u₀; c = S[St]u.	13
D[I = T]u = u[I]?{udef} ⇒ u[I ← f], u[I ← redef]	14
where e = E[T]u; f = e?{⊥} ⇒ ⊥, < const, T1(e) > .	15
D[Integer **function** I; St; **return**(T)]u =	16
u[I]?{udef} ⇒ u[I ← f], u[I ← redef]	17
where f = < const, InFunc(v) > ; c = S[St]; e(w) = E[T](c(w));	18
v(w) = c(w)?{⊥} ∨ e(w)?{⊥} ⇒ ⊥, (T1(e(w))?N ⇒ e(w), ⊥).	19
D[Boolean **function** I; St; **return**(T)]u =	20
u[I]?{udef} ⇒ u[I ← f], u[I ← redef]	21
where f = < const, InFunc(v) > ; c = S[St]; e(w) = E[T](c(w));	22
v(w) = c(w)?{⊥} ∨ e(w)?{⊥} ⇒ ⊥, (T1(e(w))?Bool ⇒ e(w), ⊥).	23

Note: The subscript in u_0 appears as u₀ in line 13.

$$E[0]u = <u, 0>$$ 24

$$E[1]u = <u, 1>$$ 25

$$E[Seq\ 0]\ u = e?N \wedge range(2 \times e)?N \Rightarrow <u, 2 \times e>, \bot$$ 26

$$\textbf{where}\ e = Tl(E[Seq]u).$$ 27

$$E[Seq\ 1]\ u = e?N \wedge range(2 \times e + 1)?N \Rightarrow <u, 2 \times e + 1>, \bot$$ 28

$$\textbf{where}\ e = Tl(E[Seq]u).$$ 29

$$E[T_1 + T_2]\ u = Tl(e)?N \wedge Tl(f)?N \wedge$$ 30

$$range(Tl(e) + Tl(f))?N \Rightarrow <Hd(f), Tl(e) + Tl(f)>, \bot$$ 31

$$\textbf{where}\ e = E[T_1]u;\ f = E[T_2]Hd(e).$$ 32

$$E[T_1 - T_2]\ u = Tl(e)?N \wedge Tl(f)?N \wedge$$ 33

$$range(Tl(e) - Tl(f))?N \Rightarrow <Hd(f), Tl(e) - Tl(f)>, \bot$$ 34

$$\textbf{where}\ e = E[T_1]u;\ f = E[T_2]Hd(e).$$ 35

$$E[T_1 * T_2]\ u = Tl(e)?N \wedge Tl(f)?N \wedge$$ 36

$$range(Tl(e) \times Tl(f))?N \Rightarrow <Hd(f), Tl(e) \times Tl(f)>, \bot$$ 37

$$\textbf{where}\ e = E[T_1]u;\ f = E[T_2]Hd(e).$$ 38

$$E[T_1 / T_2]\ u = Tl(e)?N \wedge Tl(f)?N \wedge Tl(f) \neq 0 \wedge$$ 39

$$range(Tl(e) / Tl(f))?N \Rightarrow <Hd(f), Tl(e)/Tl(f)>, \bot$$ 40

$$\textbf{where}\ e = E[T_1]u;\ f = E[T_2]Hd(e).$$ 41

$$E[T_1 = T_2]\ u = (Tl(e)?N \wedge Tl(f)?N) \vee (Tl(e)?Bool \wedge Tl(f)?Bool) \Rightarrow$$ 42

$$<Hd(f), (Tl(e) = Tl(f))>, \bot$$ 43

$$\textbf{where}\ e = E[T_1]u;\ f = E[T_2]Hd(e).$$ 44

$$E[\textbf{eval}\ I]u = Tl(v)?Func \wedge Hd(v) = const \wedge w \neq \bot \Rightarrow$$ 45

$$w[Hd[I \leftarrow const]], \bot$$ 46

$$\textbf{where}\ v = u[I];\ w = Tl(v)(u[Hd[I \leftarrow opencall]]).$$ 47

$$E[I]u = v?(\{redef\} \oplus \{\bot\} \oplus \{udef\}) \Rightarrow \bot,$$ 48

$$(Hd(v) = uninit \Rightarrow \bot, <u, Tl(v)>)$$ 49

$$\textbf{where}\ v = u[I].$$ 50

$$S[I := T]u = v?(\{redef\} \oplus \{\bot\} \oplus \{udef\}) \vee$$ 51

$$(Hd(v) = const) \vee e?\{\bot\} \Rightarrow \bot,$$ 52

$$(Tl(e)?N \wedge Tl(v)?N) \vee (Tl(e)?Bool \wedge Tl(v)?Bool) \Rightarrow$$ 53

$$Hd(e)[I \leftarrow <var, Tl(e)>], \bot$$ 54

$$\textbf{where}\ e = E[T]u;\ v = u[I].$$ 55

$$S[\textbf{if}\ T\ \textbf{then}\ St_1\ \textbf{else}\ St_2]u =$$ 56

$$Tl(e)?Bool \Rightarrow (Tl(e) \Rightarrow S[St_1]Hd(e), S[St_2]Hd(e)), \bot$$ 57

$$\textbf{where}\ e = E[T]u.$$ 58

$$S[\textbf{do}\ T\ \textbf{times}\ St]u = Tl(e)?N \Rightarrow v_m(Hd(e)), \bot$$ 59

$$\textbf{where}\ e = E[T]u;\ m = max(0, Tl(e));$$ 60

$$v_0(w) = w;\ v_{i+1}(w) = v_i(w)?U \Rightarrow S[St]v_i(w), \bot.$$ 61

$$S[\textbf{while}\ T\ \textbf{do}\ St]u = \lim_{i \to \infty} p_i(u)$$ 62

$$\textbf{where}\ p_0(w) = \bot;$$ 63

$$p_{i+1}(w) = Tl(e)?Bool \Rightarrow$$ 64

$$(Tl(e) \Rightarrow (v?\{\bot\} \Rightarrow \bot, p_i(v)), Hd(e)), \bot;$$ 65

$$e = E[T]w;\ v = S[St]Hd(e).$$ 66

In line 14, I assume that the concrete syntax forbids function calls in the definition of a constant.

3.15 Recursive Routines

The danger in allowing recursive routines is that the definitions may become circular. As it stands, I define the meaning of a call in terms of the meaning of its body. If recursion is allowed, the meaning of a routine's body may itself be defined in terms of any calls it contains. My current definition breaks this potential circularity by forbidding calls of a routine (directly or indirectly) from its own body.

I will generalize the definition of a subroutine call to allow calls of bounded depth. The meaning of a routine with a maximum call depth of n will be defined in terms of the meaning of the subroutine's body with subsequent calls limited to a depth of $n-1$. The meaning of a call with a maximum depth of zero is $\perp$.

If a call to a routine will ever return, then it can be modeled by a call limited to depth n as long as n is sufficiently large. As n approaches ∞, the bounded-call-depth model converges to the unbounded-call model if the latter ever returns. But if a routine call doesn't ever return, then the bounded-call-depth model will always produce an error result $\perp$, which is a correct definition of an infinite recursion. Thus the limit as n approaches ∞ of the bounded-call-depth model is $\perp$, which I will take as the definition of the meaning of a call of unbounded depth that never returns. This approach parallels how I handled unbounded iteration, which isn't surprising, given the similarity of looping and subroutine call.

I will redefine U to replace the opencall flag with an integer representing the maximum depth to which a given procedure or function can be called. If this value is zero, the call is invalid. What used to be opencall is now represented by 0; the previous model always had a maximum call depth of 1. Figure 10.61 shows the necessary additions.

Figure 10.61

$$U = Id \rightarrow (\{var, const, uninit\} \oplus N) \otimes V \qquad\qquad 1$$

$$S[\textbf{call } I]u = Tl(v)?Proc \Rightarrow \lim_{i \to \infty} p_i(u, v), \perp \qquad\qquad 2$$

$$\textbf{where } v = u[I]; \qquad\qquad 3$$

$$p_0(u', v') = \perp; \qquad\qquad 4$$

$$p_{i+1}(u', v') = Hd(v') = const \Rightarrow (w?U \Rightarrow w[Hd[I \leftarrow const]], \perp), \qquad 5$$

$$Hd(v') > 0 \wedge y?U \Rightarrow y[Hd[I \leftarrow Hd(v')]], \perp; \qquad 6$$

$$w = Tl(v')(u'[Hd[I \leftarrow i]]); \qquad\qquad 7$$

$$y = Tl(v')(u'[Hd[I \leftarrow Hd(v') - 1]]). \qquad\qquad 8$$

$$E[\textbf{eval } I]u = Tl(v)?\text{Func} \Rightarrow \lim_{i \to \infty} p_i(u, v), \bot \qquad\qquad 9$$

$$\textbf{where } v = u[I]; \qquad\qquad 10$$

$$p_0(u', v') = \bot; \qquad\qquad 11$$

$$p_{i+1}(u', v') = Hd(v') = \text{const} \Rightarrow (w \neq \bot\{\bot\} \Rightarrow \{\bot\} \qquad\qquad 12$$

$$w[Hd[I \leftarrow \text{const}]], \bot), \qquad\qquad 13$$

$$Hd(v') > 0 \land y \neq \bot \Rightarrow y[Hd[I \leftarrow Hd(v')]], \bot; \qquad\qquad 14$$

$$w = Tl(v')(u'[Hd[I \leftarrow i]]); \qquad\qquad 15$$

$$y = Tl(v')(u'[Hd[I \leftarrow Hd(v') - 1]]). \qquad\qquad 16$$

3.16 Modeling Memory and Files

I am now ready to model variables more accurately. I will use a finite semantic domain Loc to name addressable memory locations. A semantic domain Mem will model memories as a mapping from Loc to an integer or Boolean value or to error values uninitInt, uninitBool, unalloc:

$$\text{Mem} = \text{Loc} \to N \oplus \text{Bool} \oplus \text{uninitInt} \oplus \text{uninitBool} \oplus \text{unalloc}$$

The uninitialized flag will now be in the memory mapping, not the environment mapping. Two different uninit flags are used to remember the type an uninitialized location is expected to hold. If a memory location is marked as unalloc, then it can be allocated for use (and possibly deallocated later). If m ∈ Mem, then I define alloc as follows:

$$\text{alloc}(m) = \text{any } l \in \text{Loc such that } m(l) = \text{unalloc}$$
$$= \bot \text{ if no such } l \text{ exists}$$

Alloc specifies no particular memory allocation pattern; this definition allows implementations the widest latitude in memory management.

I will model files as finite sequences over integers, Booleans, and eof, the end-of-file flag. I define the semantic domain File as:

$$\text{File} = (N \oplus \text{Bool} \oplus \text{eof}) *$$

That is, a file is a potentially infinite string of typed values. My definitions will never consider values in files following the first eof. Programs will now take an input file and produce an output file (or ⊥). To model this semantics, I will have a semantic domain State that consists of a memory and a pair of files:

$$\text{State} = \text{Mem} \otimes \text{File} \otimes \text{File}$$

At any point during execution, the current state is a combination of the current memory contents, what is left of the input file, and what has been written to the output file.

My definition of environments will now more nearly match the symbol tables found in conventional compilers. I will map identifiers to constant values, locations or routines:

$$V = N \oplus Bool \oplus Loc \oplus Proc \oplus Func \oplus \{\bot\} \oplus \{udef\} \oplus \{redef\}$$
$$U = Id \rightarrow V$$

Statements will take an environment and a state and will produce an updated state or an error value. Declarations will take an environment and state and will produce an updated environment and state (since memory allocation, performed by declarations, will update the original state). Figure 10.62 shows the additions and changes to the formal definition.

Figure 10.62

Abstract syntax   1

P → **program** Def St **end** -- program   2

St → **read** I -- read statement   3
St → **write** T -- write statement   4

Semantic domains   5

State = Mem ⊗ File ⊗ File   6
RR = State ⊗ (N ⊕ Bool ⊕ {⊥})   7
Proc = (U → State → (State ⊕ {⊥})) ⊗ Loc   8
Func = (U → State → RR) ⊗ Loc   9
Mem = Loc → N ⊕ Bool ⊕ {uninitInt} ⊕ {uninitBool} ⊕   10
    {unalloc}   11
File = (N ⊕ Bool ⊕ {eof}) *   12
V = N ⊕ Bool ⊕ Loc ⊕ Proc ⊕ Func ⊕ {⊥}⊕{udef}⊕{redef}   13
U = Id → V   14

Semantic functions   15

E: Exp → U → State → RR   16
D: Decls → (U ⊗ State) → (U ⊗ State)   17
M: Pr → File → File ⊕ {⊥}   18
S: Stm → U → State → (State ⊕ {⊥})   19

E[0] u s = < s, 0 >   20
E[1] u s = < s, 1 >   21

$$E[Seq0] \; u \; s = e?N \wedge range(2 \times e)?N \Rightarrow \; < s, 2 \times e >, \perp \qquad 22$$
$$\textbf{where} \;\; e = Tl(E[Seq] \; u \; s). \qquad 23$$
$$E[Seq1] \; u \; s = e?N \wedge range(2 \times e + 1)?N \Rightarrow \; < s, 2 \times e + 1 >, \perp \qquad 24$$
$$\textbf{where} \;\; e = Tl(E[Seq] \; u \; s). \qquad 25$$

$$E[I] \; u \; s = v?(\{\perp\} \oplus \{redef\} \oplus \{udef\}) \Rightarrow \perp, \qquad 26$$
$$v?Loc \Rightarrow (m(v)?(\{uninitInt\} \oplus \{uninitBool\}) \Rightarrow \perp, \qquad 27$$
$$< s, m(v) >), < s, v > \qquad 28$$
$$\textbf{where} \;\; v = u[I]; \; s = \; < m, i, o > . \qquad 29$$
$$E[T_1 + T_2] \; u \; s = Tl(e)?N \wedge Tl(f)?N \wedge \qquad 30$$
$$range(Tl(e) + Tl(f))?N \Rightarrow \; < Hd(f), Tl(e) + Tl(f) >, \perp \qquad 31$$
$$\textbf{where} \;\; e = E[T_1] \; u \; s; \; f = E[T_2] \; u \; Hd(e). \qquad 32$$
$$E[T_1 - T_2] \; u \; s = Tl(e)?N \wedge Tl(f)?N \wedge \qquad 33$$
$$range(Tl(e) - Tl(f))?N \Rightarrow \; < Hd(f), Tl(e) - Tl(f) >, \perp \qquad 34$$
$$\textbf{where} \;\; e = E[T_1] \; u \; s; \; f = E[T_2] \; u \; Hd(e). \qquad 35$$
$$E[T_1 * T_2] \; u \; s = Tl(e)?N \wedge Tl(f)?N \wedge \qquad 36$$
$$range(Tl(e) \times Tl(f))?N \Rightarrow \; < Hd(f), Tl(e) \times Tl(f) >, \perp \qquad 37$$
$$\textbf{where} \;\; e = E[T_1] \; u \; s; \; f = E[T_2] \; u \; Hd(e). \qquad 38$$
$$E[T_1 / T_2] \; u \; s = Tl(e)?N \wedge Tl(f)?N \wedge Tl(f) \neq 0 \wedge \qquad 39$$
$$range(Tl(e)/Tl(f))?N \Rightarrow \; < Hd(f), Tl(e)/Tl(f) >, \perp \qquad 40$$
$$\textbf{where} \;\; e = E[T_1] \; u \; s; \; f = E[T_2] \; u \; Hd(e). \qquad 41$$
$$E[T_1 = T_2] \; u \; s = (Tl(e)?N \wedge Tl(f)?N) \vee (Tl(e)?Bool \wedge Tl(f)?Bool) \Rightarrow \qquad 42$$
$$< Hd(f), (Tl(e) = Tl(f)) >, \perp \qquad 43$$
$$\textbf{where} \;\; e = E[T_1] \; u \; s; \; f = E[T_2] \; u \; Hd(e). \qquad 44$$
$$E[\textbf{eval} I] \; u \; s = v?Func \Rightarrow \lim_{i \to \infty} p_i(s, v), \perp \qquad 45$$
$$\textbf{where} \;\; v = u[I]; \; p_0(s', v') = \perp; \qquad 46$$
$$p_{i+1}(s', v') = m(l)?\{uninitInt\} \Rightarrow \qquad 47$$
$$(w?\{\perp\} \Rightarrow \perp, w[Hd(l \leftarrow uninitInt]]); \qquad 48$$
$$m(l) > 0 \wedge y?\{\perp\} \Rightarrow \perp, y[Hd(l \leftarrow m(l))]]; \qquad 49$$
$$s' = \; < m, I, O > ; \; v' = \; < f, l > ; \; w = fu < m[l \leftarrow i], I, O > ; \qquad 50$$
$$y = fu < m[l \leftarrow m(l) - 1], I, O > . \qquad 51$$

$$D[\varepsilon] < u, s > = \; < u, s > \qquad 52$$
$$D[I : integer] < u, s > = u[I]?\{udef\} \Rightarrow \qquad 53$$
$$(l?\{\perp\} \Rightarrow \; < u[I \leftarrow \perp], s >, \; < u[I \leftarrow l], \qquad 54$$
$$i < m[l \leftarrow uninitInt], i, o >>), < u[I \leftarrow redef], s > \qquad 55$$
$$\textbf{where} \;\; s = \; < m, i, o > ; \; l = alloc(m). \qquad 56$$
$$D[I : Boolean] < u, s > = u[I]?\{udef\} \Rightarrow \qquad 57$$
$$(l?\{\perp\} \Rightarrow \; < u[I \leftarrow \perp], s >, \qquad 58$$
$$< u[I \leftarrow l], < m[l \leftarrow uninitBool], i, o >>), \qquad 59$$
$$< u[I \leftarrow redef], s > \qquad 60$$
$$\textbf{where} \;\; s = \; < m, i, o > ; \; l = alloc(m). \qquad 61$$
$$D[Def_1 \; Def_2] < u, s > = D[Def_2] < v, t > \qquad 62$$
$$\textbf{where} \;\; < v, t > = D[Def_1] < u, s > . \qquad 63$$
$$D[I = T] < u, s > = u[I]?\{udef\} \Rightarrow \; < u[I \leftarrow f], s >, \qquad 64$$
$$< u[I \leftarrow redef], s > \qquad 65$$
$$\textbf{where} \;\; e = E[T] \; u \; s; \; f = e?\{\perp\} \Rightarrow \perp, Tl(e). \qquad 66$$

D[**procedure** I; St] < u, s > = u[I]?{udef} ⇒   67

    (l?{⊥} ⇒ < u[I ← ⊥], s > , < u[I ←< c, l >],   68

    < m[l ← uninitInt], i, o >>), < u[I ← redef], s >   69

    where c = S[St]; s = < m, i, o > ; l = alloc(m).   70

D[Integer **function** I; St; **return**(T)] < u, s > =   71

    u[I]?{udef} ⇒ (l?{⊥} ⇒ < u[I ← ⊥], s > ,   72

    < u[I ←< v, l >], < m[l ← uninitInt], i, o >>),   73

    < u[I ← redef], s >   74

    where s = < m, i, o > ; l = alloc(m); c = S[St];   75

    e(w, t) = E[T] w c(w, t);   76

    v(w, t) = c(w, t)?{⊥} ∨ e(w, t)?{⊥} ⇒ ⊥,   77

        (Tl(e(w, t))?N ⇒ e(w, t), ⊥).   78

D[Boolean **function** I; St; **return**(T)] < u, s > =   79

    u[I]?{udef} ⇒ (l?{⊥} ⇒ < u[I ← ⊥], s > ,   80

    < u[I ←< v, l >], < m[l ← uninitInt], i, o >>),   81

    < u[I ← redef], s >   82

    where s = < m, i, o > ; l = alloc(m); c = S[St];   83

    e(w, t) = E[T] w c(w, t);   84

    v(w, t) = c(w, t)?{⊥} ∨ e(w, t)?{⊥} ⇒ ⊥,   85

        (Tl(e(w, t))?Bool ⇒ e(w, t), ⊥).   86

M[**program** Def St **end**]i = c?{⊥} ⇒ ⊥, Tl(Tl(c))   87

    where < u, s > = D[Def] < u_0, < m_0, i, eof >> ;   88

    c = S[St] u   89

S[ε] u s = s   90

S[St_1 St_2] u s = g?{⊥} ⇒ ⊥, S[St_2] u g   91

    where g = S[St_1] u s.   92

S[I := T] u s = v?Loc ∧   93

    ((Tl(e)?N ∧ m(v)?N ⊕{uninitInt}) ∨   94

    (Tl(e)?Bool ∧ m(v)?Bool ⊕{uninitBool})) ⇒   95

    < m[v ← Tl(e) >], i, o > , ⊥   96

    where e = E[T] u s; Hd(e) = < m, i, o > ; v = u[I].   97

S[**read** I] u s = v?Loc ∧ i≠eof ∧   98

    ((Hd(i)?N ∧ m(v)?N ⊕{uninitInt}) ∨   99

    (Hd(i)?Bool ∧ m(v)?Bool ⊕{uninitBool})) ⇒   100

    < m[v ← Hd(i) >], Tl(i), o > , ⊥   101

    where s = < m, i, o > ; v = u[I].   102

S[**write** T] u s = e?{⊥} ⇒ ⊥, < m, i, append(o, < Tl(e), eof >) >   103

    where e = E[T] u s; Hd(e) = < m, i, o > .   104

S[**if** T **then** St_1 **else** St_2] u s =   105

    Tl(e)?Bool ⇒ (Tl(e) ⇒ S[St_1] u Hd(e), S[St_2] u Hd(e)), ⊥   106

    where e = E[T] u s.   107

S[**do** T **times** St] u s = Tl(e)?N ⇒ v_m(Hd(e)), ⊥   108

    where e = E[T] u s; m = max(0, Tl(e)); v_0(w) = w;   109

    v_{i+1}(w) = v_i(w)?{⊥} ⇒ ⊥, S[St] u v_i(w).   110

$$S[\textbf{while } T \textbf{ do } St] \; u \; s = \lim_{i \to \infty} p_i(s) \qquad\qquad 111$$

$$\textbf{where } \; p_0(w) = \bot; \qquad\qquad 112$$

$$p_{i+1}(w) = Tl(e)?Bool \Rightarrow (Tl(e) \Rightarrow \qquad\qquad 113$$

$$(v?\{\bot\} \Rightarrow \bot, p_i(v)), Hd(e)), \bot; \qquad\qquad 114$$

$$e = E[T] \; u \; w; \; v = S[St] \; u \; Hd(e). \qquad\qquad 115$$

$$S[\textbf{call } I] \; u \; s = v?Proc \Rightarrow \lim_{i \to \infty} p_i(s, v), \bot \qquad\qquad 116$$

$$\textbf{where } \; v = u[I]; \qquad\qquad 117$$

$$p_0(s', v') = \bot; \qquad\qquad 118$$

$$p_{i+1}(s', v') = m(l)?\{uninitInt\} \Rightarrow (w?\{\bot\} \Rightarrow \bot, \qquad\qquad 119$$

$$w[Hd[l \leftarrow uninitInt]]), \qquad\qquad 120$$

$$m(l) > 0 \land y?\{\bot\} \Rightarrow \bot, y[Hd[l \leftarrow m(l)]]]; \qquad\qquad 121$$

$$s' = \, < m, I, O >; \; v' = \, < f, l >; \; w = f \; u < m[l \leftarrow i], I, O >; \qquad\qquad 122$$

$$y = f \; u < m[l \leftarrow m(l) - 1], I, O > . \qquad\qquad 123$$

The syntax for programs (line 2) no longer needs an identifier in the header. I assume integers and Booleans each require one location in memory. I still forbid function calls in the definition of a constant. Append (line 102) concatenates two sequences, each terminated by eof. The initial memory configuration, in which all locations map to unalloc, is m_0 (line 87).

The location associated with procedures and functions (lines 8 and 9) is used to hold the depth count, which appears in the definition of procedure (lines 115–122) and function (lines 44–50) calls. This count is no longer kept in the environment, because expressions and statements now update states, not environments. If no calls of a routine are in progress, its associated memory location will contain uninitInt.

3.17 Blocks and Scoping

I will now model block structure and name scoping by adding a **begin-end** block to the syntax, as in Figure 10.63.

Figure 10.63   St → **begin** Def St **end**

As in most block-structured languages, declarations within a block are local to it, and local redefinition of a nonlocal identifier is allowed. Rather than a single environment, I will employ a sequence of environments, with the first environment representing local declarations, and the last environment representing the outermost (predeclared) declarations. The new semantic domain UU = U* will represent this sequence of environments. All definitions will be made in the head of the environment sequence, while lookup will proceed through the sequence of environments, using the functions Top and Find, shown in Figure 10.64.

Figure 10.64

$$Top: UU \to U \qquad \qquad 1$$
$$Top(u) = u?U \Rightarrow u, Hd(u) \qquad \qquad 2$$

$$Find: UU \to Id \to V \qquad \qquad 3$$
$$Find(u)[I] = Top(u)[I]?\{udef\} \Rightarrow \qquad \qquad 4$$
$$\qquad (u?U \Rightarrow \bot, Find(Tl(u))[I]), Top(u)[I] \qquad \qquad 5$$

Block structure introduces a memory-management issue. Most languages specify that memory for local variables is created (or allocated) upon block entry and released upon block exit. To model allocation, I create a function Free (Figure 10.65) that records the set of free memory locations.

Figure 10.65

$$Free: Mem \to 2^{Loc} \qquad \qquad 1$$
$$Free(m) = \{l \mid m(l) = unalloc\} \qquad \qquad 2$$

I will record free locations at block entry and reset them at block exit. Most implementations do this by pushing and later popping locations from a runtime stack. My definition, of course, does not require any particular implementation.

Figure 10.66 presents the definition of block structure, updating all definitions that explicitly use environments so that they now use sequences of environments. I also modify slightly the definition of the main program to put predeclared identifiers in a scope outside that of the main program.

Figure 10.66

Abstract syntax   1

$$St \to \textbf{begin}\ Def\ St\ \textbf{end} \qquad \qquad 2$$

Semantic domains   3

$$UU = U* \ \text{-- sequence of environments} \qquad \qquad 4$$
$$Proc = (UU \to State \to (State \oplus \{\bot\})) \otimes Loc \qquad \qquad 5$$
$$Func = (UU \to State \to RR) \otimes Loc \qquad \qquad 6$$

Semantic functions   7

$$E: Exp \to UU \to State \to RR \qquad \qquad 8$$
$$D: Decls \to (UU \otimes State) \to (UU \otimes State) \qquad \qquad 9$$
$$S: Stm \to UU \to State \to (State \oplus \{\bot\}) \qquad \qquad 10$$

$S[\textbf{begin } \text{Def St } \textbf{end}] \text{ u s} = c?\{\bot\} \Rightarrow \bot,$ 11

  $< m[\text{Free}(\text{Hd}(s)) \leftarrow \text{unalloc}], i, o >$ 12

  $\textbf{where } < v, t > = D[\text{Def}] << u_e, u >, s > ;$ 13

  $c = S[\text{St}] \text{ v } t = < m, i, o > .$ 14

$M[\textbf{program } \text{Def St } \textbf{end}] i = c?\{\bot\} \Rightarrow \bot, Tl(Tl(c))$ 15

  $\textbf{where } < u, s > = D[\text{Def}] << u_e, u_0 >, < m_0, i, \text{eof} >> ;$ 16

  $c = S[\text{St}] \text{ u s.}$ 17

$E[I] \text{ u s} = v?(\{\bot\} \oplus \{\text{redef}\} \oplus \{\text{udef}\}) \Rightarrow \bot,$ 18

  $v?\text{Loc} \Rightarrow (m(v)?(\{\text{uninitInt}\} \oplus \{\text{uninitBool}\})) \Rightarrow \bot,$ 19

  $< s, m(v) >), < s, v >$ 20

  $\textbf{where } v = \text{Find}(u)[I]; s = < m, i, o > .$ 21

$E[\textbf{eval } I] \text{ u s} = v?\text{Func} \Rightarrow \lim_{i \to \infty} p_i(s, v), \bot$ 22

  $\textbf{where } v = \text{Find}(u)[I];$ 23

  $p_0(s', v') = \bot;$ 24

  $p_{i+1}(s', v') = m(l)?\{\text{uninitInt}\} \Rightarrow (w?\{\bot\} \Rightarrow$ 25

   $\bot, w[\text{Hd}[l \leftarrow \text{uninitInt}]]),$ 26

   $m(l) > 0 \wedge y?\{\bot\} \Rightarrow \bot, y[\text{Hd}[l \leftarrow m(l)]]];$ 27

  $s' = < m, I, O > ; v' = < f, l > ;$ 28

  $w = f \text{ u} < m[l \leftarrow i], I, O > ;$ 29

  $y = f \text{ u} < m[l \leftarrow m(l) - 1], I, O > .$ 30

$D[I : \text{integer}] < u, s > = \text{Hd}(u)[I]?\{\text{udef}\} \Rightarrow$ 31

  $(l?\{\bot\} \Rightarrow < u[\text{Hd}[I \leftarrow \bot]], s >, < u[\text{Hd}[I \leftarrow l]],$ 32

  $< m[l \leftarrow \text{uninitInt}], i, o >>), < u[\text{Hd}[I \leftarrow \text{redef}]], s >$ 33

  $\textbf{where } s = < m, i, o > ; l = \text{alloc}(m).$ 34

$D[I : \text{Boolean}] < u, s > = \text{Hd}(u)[I]?\{\text{udef}\} \Rightarrow$ 35

  $(l?\{\bot\} \Rightarrow < u[\text{Hd}[[I \leftarrow \bot]], s >, < u[\text{Hd}[[I \leftarrow l]],$ 36

  $< m[l \leftarrow \text{uninitBool}], i, o >>), < u[\text{Hd}[[I \leftarrow \text{redef}]], s >$ 37

  $\textbf{where } s = < m, i, o > ; l = \text{alloc}(m).$ 38

$D[I = T] < u, s > = \text{Hd}(u)[I]?\{\text{udef}\} \Rightarrow < u[\text{Hd}[I \leftarrow f]], s >,$ 39

  $< u[\text{Hd}[I \leftarrow \text{redef}]], s >$ 40

  $\textbf{where } e = E[T] \text{ u s}; f = e?\{\bot\} \Rightarrow \bot, Tl(e).$ 41

$D[\textbf{procedure } I; \text{St}] < u, s > = \text{Hd}(u)[I]?\{\text{udef}\} \Rightarrow$ 42

  $(l?\{\bot\} \Rightarrow < u[\text{Hd}[I \leftarrow \bot]], s >, < u[\text{Hd}[I \leftarrow < c, l >]],$ 43

  $< m[l \leftarrow \text{uninitInt}], i, o >>), < u[\text{Hd}[I \leftarrow \text{redef}]], s >$ 44

  $\textbf{where } c = S[\text{St}]; s = < m, i, o > ; l = \text{alloc}(m).$ 45

$D[\text{Integer } \textbf{function } I; \text{St}; \textbf{return}(T)] < u, s > =$ 46

  $\text{Hd}(u)[I]?\{\text{udef}\} \Rightarrow (l?\{\bot\} \Rightarrow < u[\text{Hd}[I \leftarrow \bot]], s >,$ 47

  $< [\text{Hd}[I \leftarrow < v, l >]], < m[l \leftarrow \text{uninitInt}], i, o >>),$ 48

  $< u[\text{Hd}[I \leftarrow \text{redef}]], s >$ 49

  $\textbf{where } s = < m, i, o > ; l = \text{alloc}(m); c = S[\text{St}];$ 50

  $e(w, t) = E[T] \text{ w } c(w, t);$ 51

  $v(w, t) = c(w, t)?\{\bot\} \vee e(w, t)?\{\bot\} \Rightarrow$ 52

   $\bot, (Tl(e(w, t)))?N \Rightarrow e(w, t), \bot).$ 53

$$D[\text{Boolean } \textbf{function } I; St; \textbf{return}(T)] < u, s > = \tag{54}$$
$$Hd(u)[I]?\{udef\} \Rightarrow (l?\{\bot\} \Rightarrow < u[Hd[I \leftarrow \bot]], s > , \tag{55}$$
$$< u[Hd[I \leftarrow < v, l >]], < m[l \leftarrow uninitInt], i, o >>), \tag{56}$$
$$< u[Hd[I \leftarrow redef]], s > \tag{57}$$
$$\textbf{where } s = < m, i, o > ; l = alloc(m); c = S[St]; \tag{58}$$
$$e(w, t) = E[T] w c(w, t); \tag{59}$$
$$v(w, t) = c(w, t)?\{\bot\} \vee e(w, t)?\{\bot\} \Rightarrow \bot, \tag{60}$$
$$(Tl(e(w, t)))?Bool \Rightarrow e(w, t), \bot). \tag{61}$$

$$S[I := T] u s = \tag{62}$$
$$v?Loc \wedge ((Tl(e)?N \wedge m(v)?N \oplus \{uninitInt\}) \vee \tag{63}$$
$$(Tl(e)?Bool \wedge m(v)?Bool \oplus \{uninitBool\})) \Rightarrow \tag{64}$$
$$< m[v \leftarrow Tl(e) >], i, o > , \bot \tag{65}$$
$$\textbf{where } e = E[T] u s; Hd(e) = < m, i, o > ; v = Find(u)[I]. \tag{66}$$
$$S[\textbf{read } I] u s = v?Loc \wedge i \neq eof \wedge \tag{67}$$
$$((Hd(i)?N \wedge m(v)?N \oplus \{uninitInt\}) \vee (Hd(i)?Bool \wedge \tag{68}$$
$$m(v)?Bool \oplus \{uninitBool\})) \Rightarrow < m[v \leftarrow Hd(i) >], Tl(i), o > , \bot \tag{69}$$
$$\textbf{where } s = < m, i, o > ; v = Find(u)[I]. \tag{70}$$
$$S[\textbf{call } I] u s = v?Proc \Rightarrow \lim_{i \to \infty} p_i(s, v), \bot \tag{71}$$
$$\textbf{where } v = Find(u)[I]; \tag{72}$$
$$p_0(s', v') = \bot; \tag{73}$$
$$p_{i+1}(s', v') = m(l)?\{uninitInt\} \Rightarrow (w?\{\bot\} \Rightarrow \bot, \tag{74}$$
$$w[Hd[l \leftarrow uninitInt]]), \tag{75}$$
$$m(l) > 0 \wedge y?\{\bot\} \Rightarrow \bot, y[Hd[l \leftarrow m(l)]]; \tag{76}$$
$$s' = < m, I, O > ; v' = < f, l >; \tag{77}$$
$$w = f u < m[l \leftarrow i], I, O >; \tag{78}$$
$$y = f u < m[l \leftarrow m(l) - 1], I, O > . \tag{79}$$

In lines 13 and 16, u_e is the empty environment in which all identifiers map to udef.

3.18 Parameters

Now that I have scoping, I will turn my attention to procedures and functions. As defined above, procedures and functions execute in the environment of the call, not the environment of definition. No environment is stored with a procedure or function definition; rather, they use an environment provided at the point of call. In other words, I have provided dynamic scoping and shallow binding, which is common in interpreted, but not in compiled, languages. I will now refine the model to use the more common static model of scoping.

I will also include reference-mode parameters to illustrate how parameter definition and binding are handled. The approach will be similar to that used with blocks. However, when a procedure or function is called, I will provide an initial local environment in which parameter names have been bound to the locations associated with corresponding actual parameters. This approach allows the possibility of aliasing. I will be careful therefore not to release storage associated with formal parameters, since this storage will belong to the actual parameters (which persist after the call). However, other local definitions will be treated like locals declared in blocks and released after the call.

Figure 10.67 extends the syntax of routine definitions and calls to include parameters:

Figure 10.67

Abstract syntax   1

Actuals ∈ Aparms	2
Formals ∈ Fparms	3
Def → **procedure** I (Formals); **begin** Def St **end**	4
Def → Integer **function** I (Formals);	5
Def St **return**(T);	6
Def → Boolean **function** I (Formals);	7
Def St **return**(T);	8
St → **call** I (Actuals)	9
T → **eval** I (Actuals)	10
Formals → I : integer;	11
Formals → I : Boolean;	12
Formals → ε	13
Formals → Formals Formals	14
Actuals → ε	15
Actuals → I	16
Actuals → Actuals Actuals	17

In the concrete syntax, a routine with no parameters may well omit parentheses, and actuals will be separated by commas. I don't have to worry about such details at the level of abstract syntax.

I will also create two new semantic functions, FP and AP, to define the meaning of formal and actual parameters. Figure 10.68 shows the changes to the definition.

Figure 10.68

Semantic domains   1

$Parms = ((N \oplus Bool) \otimes Id \oplus eol)\ast$	2
$Proc = (UU \to State \to (State \oplus \{\bot\})) \otimes Loc \otimes Parms$	3
$Func = (UU \to State \to RR) \otimes Loc \otimes Parms$	4

Semantic functions   5

$$FP: Fparms \rightarrow Parms \rightarrow Parms \ -- \ Formals \qquad\qquad 6$$
$$AP: Aparms \rightarrow (UU \otimes Parms) \rightarrow State \rightarrow ((UU \otimes Parms) \oplus \{\bot\}) \qquad 7$$
$$\qquad\qquad -- \ Actuals \qquad\qquad\qquad\qquad\qquad\qquad\qquad 8$$

$$FP[I: integer]p = append(p, << 0, I >, eol >) \qquad\qquad 9$$
$$FP[I: Boolean]p = append(p, << false, I >, eol >) \qquad\quad 10$$
$$FP[\varepsilon]p = p \qquad\qquad\qquad\qquad\qquad\qquad\qquad\qquad\qquad 11$$
$$FP[Formals_1 \ Formals_2] \ p = FP[Formals_2]q \qquad\qquad 12$$
$$\textbf{where} \ \ q = FP[Formals_1]p. \qquad\qquad\qquad 13$$

$$AP[I] < u, p > s = v?Loc \wedge p \neq eol \wedge \qquad\qquad\qquad 14$$
$$\quad ((Hd(pp)?N \wedge m(v)?N \oplus \{uninitInt\}) \vee (Hd(pp)?Bool \wedge \qquad 15$$
$$\quad m(v)?Bool \oplus \{uninitBool\})) \Rightarrow \qquad\qquad\qquad 16$$
$$\quad < u[Hd(Tl(pp) \leftarrow v]], Tl(p) >, \bot \qquad\qquad\qquad 17$$
$$\quad \textbf{where} \ \ v = Find(Tl(u))[I]; \ pp = Hd(p); \ s = < m, i, o >. \qquad 18$$
$$AP[\varepsilon] < u, p > s = < u, p > \qquad\qquad\qquad\qquad 19$$
$$AP[Actuals_1 \ Actuals_2] < u, p > s = q?\{\bot\} \Rightarrow \bot, \qquad\qquad 20$$
$$\quad AP[Actuals_2] \ q \ s \qquad\qquad\qquad\qquad\qquad 21$$
$$\quad \textbf{where} \ \ q = AP[Actuals_1] < u, p > s. \qquad\qquad 22$$

$$D[\textbf{procedure} \ I \ (Formals); \ Def \ St] < u, s > = \qquad\qquad 23$$
$$\quad Hd(u)[I]?\{udef\} \Rightarrow (l?\{\bot\} \Rightarrow < u[Hd[I \leftarrow \bot]], s >, \qquad 24$$
$$\quad < uu, < m[l \leftarrow uninitInt], i, o >>), < u[Hd[I \leftarrow redef]], s > \qquad 25$$
$$\quad \textbf{where} \ \ f(v, t) = S[St]v't'; < v', t' > = D[Def] << v, uu >, t >; \qquad 26$$
$$\quad s = < m, i, o >; l = alloc(m); \qquad\qquad\qquad 27$$
$$\quad uu = u[Hd[I \leftarrow < f, l, p >]]; p = FP[Formals]eol. \qquad\qquad 28$$
$$D[Integer \ \textbf{function}(Formals) \ I; \ Def \ St \ \textbf{return}(T)] \qquad\qquad 29$$
$$\quad < u, s > = Hd(u)[I]?\{udef\} \Rightarrow \qquad\qquad\qquad 30$$
$$\quad (l?\{\bot\} \Rightarrow < u[Hd[I \leftarrow \bot]], s >, \qquad\qquad\qquad 31$$
$$\quad < uu, < m[l \leftarrow uninitInt], i, o >>), < u[Hd[I \leftarrow redef]], s > \qquad 32$$
$$\quad \textbf{where} \ \ s = < m, i, o >; l = alloc(m); e(w, r) = E[T](w \ c(w, r)); \qquad 33$$
$$\quad c(v, t) = S[St]v't'; < v', t' > = D[Def] << v, uu >, t >; \qquad\quad 34$$
$$\quad f(vv, tt) = c(vv, tt)?\{\bot\} \vee e(vv, tt)?\{\bot\} \Rightarrow \qquad\qquad 35$$
$$\quad\quad \bot, (Tl(e(vv, tt))?N \Rightarrow e(vv, tt), \bot); \qquad\qquad 36$$
$$\quad uu = u[Hd[I \leftarrow < f, l, p >]]; p = FP[Formals]eol. \qquad\qquad 37$$
$$D[Boolean \ \textbf{function}(Formals) \ I; \ Def \ St \ \textbf{return}(T)] \qquad\qquad 38$$
$$\quad < u, s > = Hd(u)[I]?\{udef\} \Rightarrow \qquad\qquad\qquad 39$$
$$\quad (l?\{\bot\} \Rightarrow < u[Hd[I \leftarrow \bot]], s >, \qquad\qquad\qquad 40$$
$$\quad < uu, < m[l \leftarrow uninitInt], i, o >>), < u[Hd[I \leftarrow redef]], s > \qquad 41$$
$$\quad \textbf{where} \ \ s = < m, i, o >; l = alloc(m); e(w, r) = E[T](w \ c(w, r)); \qquad 42$$
$$\quad c(v, t) = S[St]v't'; < v', t' > = D[Def] << v, uu >, t >; \qquad\quad 43$$
$$\quad f(vv, tt) = c(vv, tt)?\{\bot\} \vee e(vv, tt)?\{\bot\} \Rightarrow \qquad\qquad 44$$
$$\quad\quad \bot, (Tl(e(vv, tt))?Bool \Rightarrow e(vv, tt), \bot); \qquad\qquad 45$$
$$\quad uu = u[Hd[I \leftarrow < f, l, p >]]; p = FP[Formals]eol. \qquad\qquad 46$$

$$S[\textbf{call } I(Actuals)] \text{ u s} = v?Proc \wedge \tag{47}$$

$$q \neq \bot \wedge Tl(q) = eol \Rightarrow \lim_{i \to \infty} p_i(s, Hd(Hd(q))), \bot \tag{48}$$

$$\textbf{where } v = Find(u)[I] = <f, l, r>; \tag{49}$$

$$p_0(s', u') = \bot; \tag{50}$$

$$p_{i+1}(s', u') = m(l)?\{uninitInt\} \Rightarrow (w?\{\bot\} \Rightarrow \bot, ww), \tag{51}$$

$$m(l) > 0 \wedge y?\{\bot\} \Rightarrow \bot, yy; \tag{52}$$

$$q = AP[Actuals] << u_e, u>, r> s; \tag{53}$$

$$s' = <m, I, O>; \tag{54}$$

$$w = f \ u' <m[l \leftarrow i], I, O>; \tag{55}$$

$$ww = w[Hd[l \leftarrow uninitInt]][Hd[Free(m) \leftarrow unalloc]]; \tag{56}$$

$$y = f \ u' <m[l \leftarrow m(l) - 1], I, O>; \tag{57}$$

$$yy = y[Hd[l \leftarrow m(l)]][Hd[Free(m) \leftarrow unalloc]]. \tag{58}$$

$$E[\textbf{eval } I(Actuals)] \text{ u s} = v?Func \wedge q \neq \bot \wedge Tl(q) = eol \Rightarrow \tag{59}$$

$$\lim_{i \to \infty} p_i(s, Hd(Hd(q))), \bot \tag{60}$$

$$\textbf{where } v = Find(u)[I] = <f, l, r>; \tag{61}$$

$$p_0(s', u') = \bot; \tag{62}$$

$$p_{i+1}(s', u') = m(l)?\{uninitInt\} \Rightarrow (w?\{\bot\} \Rightarrow \bot, ww), \tag{63}$$

$$m(l) > 0 \wedge y?\{\bot\} \Rightarrow \bot, yy; \tag{64}$$

$$q = AP[Actuals] << u_e, u>, r> s; \tag{65}$$

$$s' = <m, I, O>; \tag{66}$$

$$w = f \ u' <m[l \leftarrow i], I, O>; \tag{67}$$

$$ww = w[Hd[l \leftarrow uninitInt]][Hd[Free(m) \leftarrow unalloc]]; \tag{68}$$

$$y = f \ u' <m[l \leftarrow m(l) - 1], I, O>; \tag{69}$$

$$yy = y[Hd[l \leftarrow m(l)]][Hd[Hd[Free(m) \leftarrow unalloc]]]. \tag{70}$$

The eol in line 2 represents "end of list."

3.19 Continuations

The denotational approach is very structured; the meaning of a construct is defined in terms of a composition of the meanings of the construct's constituents. The meaning of a program can be viewed as a top-down traversal of an abstract syntax tree from the root (the program nonterminal) to the leaves (identifiers, constants, and so forth). The meanings associated with the leaves are then percolated back up to the root, where the meaning of the whole program is determined.

This structured approach has problems with statements such as **break** or **goto** that don't readily fit the composition model. Further, it forces values to percolate throughout the whole tree, even if this action is unnecessary. Consider, for example, a **stop** statement. When **stop** is executed, I would like to discontinue statement evaluation and immediately return to the main program production, where the final result (the output file) is produced. But I can't; the meaning of **stop** must be composed with that of the remaining statements (even though **stop** means one must ignore the remaining statements!). As it stands, my definition of the meaning of a statement sequence (see lines 90–91 in Figure 10.62, page 401) checks for error on the first statement before evaluating the second. I could add another sort of value, like $\perp$, that indicates that execution should stop, even though there is no error. This device would work but would be rather clumsy, as I would model **stop** not by stopping but by continuing to traverse program statements while ignoring them.

Continuations were invented to remedy these problems. A **continuation** is a function passed as a parameter to every semantic function. The semantic function determines its value as usual and then calls (directly or indirectly) the continuation with its value as a parameter. This approach is quite clever but is much less intuitive than the structured approach I have presented so far.

I will first consider expression continuations, which have a semantic domain EC, defined as:

$$EC = (N \oplus Bool) \rightarrow State \rightarrow R$$

The expression continuation takes a value and a state (since side effects in evaluating the expression can change the state) and produces a result. The E semantic function will now include an expression continuation as a parameter:

$$E: Exp \rightarrow UU \rightarrow State \rightarrow EC \rightarrow R$$

E now produces a result rather than a state-result pair because state changes are included in the continuation component. Figure 10.69 now redefines the meaning of simple integer-valued bit strings. The expression continuation, k, uses the value and state computed by the semantic function E.

Figure 10.69	**Semantic functions**	1

$$E[0] \; u \; s \; k = k(0, s) \qquad\qquad\qquad\qquad 2$$
$$E[1] \; u \; s \; k = k(1, s) \qquad\qquad\qquad\qquad 3$$
$$E[Seq \; 0] \; u \; s \; k = E[Seq] \; u \; s \; k_1 \qquad\qquad 4$$
$$\qquad \textbf{where} \; k_1(r, t) = range(2 \times r)?\{\perp\} \Rightarrow \perp, k(2 \times r, t). \qquad 5$$
$$E[Seq \; 1] \; u \; s \; k = E[Seq] \; u \; s \; k_1 \qquad\qquad 6$$
$$\qquad \textbf{where} \; k_1(r, t) = range(2 \times r + 1)?\{\perp\} \Rightarrow \perp, k(2 \times r + 1, t). \qquad 7$$

It is no longer necessary to test if a construct produces $\perp$; if it does, the construct returns $\perp$ immediately. Otherwise, it calls its continuation parameter with values it knows to be valid. To see how evaluation proceeds, consider the following example. Evaluate $E[111]u_e \; s_0 \; K$, where u_e

and s_0 are the empty environment and initial state, and $K(r,s)=r$ returns the final result.

1. $E[111]u_e\ s_0\ K = E[11]u_e\ s_0\ k_1$, where
    $k_1(r_1,s_1) = range(2\times r_1+1)?\{\perp\} \Rightarrow \perp, K(2\times r_1+1,s_1)$.
2. $E[11]u_e\ s_0\ k_1 = E[1]u_e\ s_0\ k_2$, where
    $k_2(r_2,s_2) = range(2\times r_2+1)?\{\perp\} \Rightarrow \perp, k_1(2\times r_2+1,s_2)$.
3. $E[1]u_e\ s_0\ k_2 = k_2(1,s_0) = range(2\times 1+1)?\{\perp\} \Rightarrow \perp, k_1(2\times 1+1,s_0) =$
    $k_1(3,s_0) = range(2\times 3+1)?\{\perp\} \Rightarrow \perp, K(2\times 3+1,s_0) = K(7,s_0) = 7$.

Figure 10.70 shows how the binary operators are handled.

Figure 10.70   **Semantic functions**   1

$E[T_1+T_2]\ u\ s\ k = E[T_1]\ u\ s\ k_1$ 2
$\quad$ **where** $k_1(r_1,s_1) = r_1?N \Rightarrow E[T_2]\ u\ s_1\ k_2, \perp;$ 3
$\quad k_2(r_2,s_2) = r_2?N \wedge range(r_1+r_2)?N \Rightarrow k(r_1+r_2,s_2), \perp$.   4

Consider this example: Compute $E[22+33]u_e\ s_0\ K$, where again $K(r,s)=r$.

1. $E[22+33]u_e\ s_0\ K = E[22]u_e\ s_0\ k_1$, where
    $k_1(r_1,s_1) = r_1?N \Rightarrow E[33]\ u\ s_1\ k_2, k_2(r_2,s_2) = r_2?N$ and
    $range(r_1+r_2)?N \Rightarrow k(r_1+r_2,s_2), \perp$.
2. $E[22]u_e\ s_0\ k_1 = k_1(22,s_0) = 22?N \Rightarrow E[33]u_e\ s_0\ k_2, \perp =$
    $E[33]u_e\ s_0\ k_2 = k_2(33,s_0) = 33?N$ and
    $range(22+33)?N \Rightarrow K(22+33,s_0), \perp = K(55,s_0) = 55$.

The rest of the binary operators are similar in form, as shown in Figure 10.71.

Figure 10.71   **Semantic functions**   1

$E[T_1-T_2]\ u\ s\ k = E[T_1]\ u\ s\ k_1$ 2
$\quad$ **where** $k_1(r_1,s_1) = r_1?N \Rightarrow E[T_2]\ u\ s_1\ k_2, \perp;$ 3
$\quad k_2(r_2,s_2) = r_2?N \wedge range(r_1-r_2)?N \Rightarrow k(r_1-r_2,s_2), \perp$.   4
$E[T_1*T_2]\ u\ s\ k = E[T_1]\ u\ s\ k_1$ 5
$\quad$ **where** $k_1(r_1,s_1) = r_1?N \Rightarrow E[T_2]\ u\ s_1\ k_2, \perp;$ 6
$\quad k_2(r_2,s_2) = r_2?N \wedge range(r_1\times r_2)?N \Rightarrow k(r_1\times r_2,s_2), \perp$. 7
$E[T_1/T_2]\ u\ s\ k = E[T_1]\ u\ s\ k_1$ 8
$\quad$ **where** $k_1(r_1,s_1) = r_1?N \Rightarrow E[T_2]\ u\ s_1\ k_2, \perp;$ 9
$\quad k_2(r_2,s_2) = r_2?N \wedge r_2\neq 0 \wedge range(r_1/r_2)?N \Rightarrow k(r_1/r_2,s_2), \perp$. 10
$E[T_1=T_2]\ u\ s\ k = E[T_1]\ u\ s\ k_1$ 11
$\quad$ **where** $k_1(r_1,s_1) = E[T_2]\ u\ s_1\ k_2;$ 12
$\quad k_2(r_2,s_2) = (r_1?N \wedge r_2?N) \vee (r_1?Bool \wedge r_2?Bool) \Rightarrow$ 13
$\qquad k(r_1=r_2,s_2), \perp$.   14

Identifier lookup is straightforward; see Figure 10.72.

Figure 10.72

$$E[I] u s k = v?(\{\bot\} \oplus \{redef\} \oplus \{udef\}) \Rightarrow \bot, \qquad\qquad 1$$
$$v?Loc \Rightarrow (m(v)?(\{uninitInt\} \oplus \{uninitBool\})) \Rightarrow \qquad 2$$
$$\bot, k(m(v), s)), k(v, s) \qquad\qquad 3$$
$$\textbf{where } v = Find(u)[I]; s = <m, i, o>. \qquad\qquad 4$$

To see how side effects are handled, I will introduce an assignment expression similar to that found in C: $I \leftarrow T$ is an expression that evaluates to T and (as a side effect) sets I to T, as in Figure 10.73.

Figure 10.73

$$E[I \leftarrow T] u s k = E[T] u s k_1 \qquad\qquad 1$$
$$\textbf{where } k_1(r, t) = v?Loc \wedge \qquad\qquad 2$$
$$((r?N \wedge m(v)?N \oplus \{uninitInt\}) \vee \qquad 3$$
$$(r?Bool \wedge m(v)?Bool \oplus \{uninitBool\})) \Rightarrow \qquad 4$$
$$k(r, <m[v \leftarrow r], i, o>), \bot. \qquad\qquad 5$$
$$t = <m, i, o>; v = Find(u)[I]. \qquad\qquad 6$$

Consider this example: Compute $E[I + I \leftarrow 0]u_0 s_0 K$, where u_0 and s_0 contain a variable I with value 10 and $K(r, s) = r + Hd(s)(u_0[I])$ adds the final value of I to the value of the expression.

1. $E[I + I \leftarrow 0]u_0 s_0 K = E[I]u_0 s_0 k_1$, where
   $k_1(r_1, s_1) = r_1?N \Rightarrow E[I \leftarrow 0] u s_1 k_2, \bot. k_2(r_2, s_2) = r_2?N.$
   $range(r_1 + r_2)?N \Rightarrow K(r_1 + r_2, s_2), \bot.$

2. $E[I]u_0 s_0 k_1 = v?(\{\bot\} \oplus \{redef\} \oplus \{udef\}) \Rightarrow \bot.$
   $v?Loc \Rightarrow (m(v)?(\{uninitInt\} \oplus \{uninitBool\}) \Rightarrow \bot, k_1(m(v), s_0)), k_1(v, s_0),$
   where $v = Find(u_0)[I], s_0 = <m, i, o>.$

3. $E[I]u_0 s_0 k_1 = k_1(m(v), s_0) = k_1(10, s_0) = 10?N \Rightarrow$
   $E[I \leftarrow 0] u s_0 k_2, \bot = E[I \leftarrow 0] u s_0 k_2.$

4. $E[I \leftarrow 0]u_0 s_0 k_2 = E[0]u_0 s_0 k_3$, where
   $k_3(r, t) = v?Loc \wedge ((r?N \wedge m(v)?N \oplus \{uninitInt\}) \vee$
   $(r?Bool \wedge m(v)?Bool \oplus \{uninitBool\})) \Rightarrow k_2(r, <m[v \leftarrow r], i, o>), \bot.$
   $t = <m, i, o>, v = Find(u)[I].$

5. $E[0] u s_0 k_3 = k_3(0, s_0) = v?Loc \wedge ((0?N \wedge m(v)?N \oplus \{uninitInt\}) \vee$
   $(0?Bool \wedge m(v)?Bool \oplus \{uninitBool\})) \Rightarrow k_2(0, <m[v \leftarrow 0], i, o>), \bot.$
   $s_0 = <m, i, o>. v = Find(u)[I].$

6. $E[0] u s_0 k_3 = k_2(0, <m[v \leftarrow 0], i, o>) = k_2(0, ss_0)$, where
   $ss_0 = <m[v \leftarrow 0], i, o>. k_2(0, ss_0) = 0?N.$
   $range(10 + 0)?N \Rightarrow K(0 + 10, ss_0), \bot = K(0 + 10, ss_0).$

7. $K(10, ss_0) = 10 + Hd(ss_0)(u_0[I]) = 10 + 0 = 10.$

Continuations execute in the state that is current when they are evaluated, not in the state that is current when they are defined (that's why they take state as a parameter).

3.20 Statement Continuations

I am now ready to consider statement continuations, which are particularly useful because they allow me to handle nonstructured control flows. I will first define SC, the semantic domain of statement continuations (see Figure 10.74). I will also slightly alter EC, the semantic domain of expression continuations. In both cases, the continuations will return Ans, the domain of program answers, reflecting the fact that expressions and statements are not executed in isolation, but rather in contexts in which they contribute to the final answer to be computed by the whole program.

Figure 10.74

Semantic domains 1

$$Ans = File \oplus \{\bot\}$$ 2
$$EC = (N \oplus Bool) \rightarrow State \rightarrow Ans$$ 3
$$SC = State \rightarrow Ans$$ 4

Statement continuations take only one parameter because the only program component updated by a statement is the state. Figure 10.75 extends the S semantic function to include a statement continuation parameter. All semantic functions now return Ans because they all execute by evaluating (directly or indirectly) some continuation function. The values that change during the computation of a semantic function (a result, environment, or state) are now parameters to a continuation function.

Figure 10.75

Semantic functions 1

$$E: Exp \rightarrow UU \rightarrow State \rightarrow EC \rightarrow Ans$$ 2
$$S: Stm \rightarrow UU \rightarrow State \rightarrow SC \rightarrow Ans$$ 3

To see the utility of statement continuations, consider the definition of statement composition in Figure 10.76.

Figure 10.76

$$S[St_1 \ St_2] \ u \ s \ c = S[St_1] \ u \ s \ c'$$ 1
$$\textbf{where} \ c'(s') = S[St_2] \ u \ s'c.$$ 2

The statement continuation has a fairly intuitive interpretation: what to execute after the current statement. The advantage of the continuation approach is now evident. A statement need not execute its continuation if an abnormal transfer of control is indicated. A **stop** statement executes by returning an answer (the current value of the output file).

Similarly, **goto** executes by looking up (and executing) a statement continuation stored in the environment as the value of the label!

I can now consider other statements, as shown in Figure 10.77.

$$S[\varepsilon] \; u \; s \; c = c(s) \qquad\qquad 1$$
$$S[I := T] \; u \; s \; c = E[T] \; u \; s \; k \qquad\qquad 2$$
$$\textbf{where} \;\; k(r, t) = v?Loc \land \qquad\qquad 3$$
$$((r?N \land m(v)?N \oplus \{uninitInt\}) \lor \qquad\qquad 4$$
$$(r?Bool \land m(v)?Bool \oplus uninitBool)) \Rightarrow \qquad\qquad 5$$
$$c(< m[v \leftarrow r], i, o >), \bot; \qquad\qquad 6$$
$$t = < m, i, o > ; v = Find(u)[I]. \qquad\qquad 7$$
$$S[\textbf{read} \; I] \; u \; s \; c = v?Loc \land i \neq eof \land \qquad\qquad 8$$
$$((Hd(i)?N \land m(v)?N \oplus uninitInt) \lor \qquad\qquad 9$$
$$(Hd(i)?Bool \land m(v)?Bool \oplus uninitBool)) \Rightarrow \qquad\qquad 10$$
$$c(< m[v \leftarrow Hd(i)], Tl(i), o >), \bot \qquad\qquad 11$$
$$\textbf{where} \;\; s = < m, i, o > ; v = Find(u)[I]. \qquad\qquad 12$$
$$S[\textbf{write} \; T] \; u \; s \; c = E[T] \; u \; s \; k \qquad\qquad 13$$
$$\textbf{where} \;\; k(r, t) = c(< m, i, append(o, < r, eof >) >); t = < m, i, o > \;\; 14$$
$$S[\textbf{if} \; T \; \textbf{then} \; St_1 \; \textbf{else} \; St_2] \; u \; s \; c = \qquad\qquad 15$$
$$E[T] \; u \; s \; k \qquad\qquad 16$$
$$\textbf{where} \;\; k(r, t) = r?Bool \Rightarrow (r \Rightarrow S[St_1] \; u \; t \; c, S[St_2] \; u \; t \; c), \bot. \;\; 17$$
$$S[\textbf{do} \; T \; \textbf{times} \; St] \; u \; s \; c = E[T] \; u \; s \; k \qquad\qquad 18$$
$$\textbf{where} \;\; k(r, t) = r?N \Rightarrow v_m(t), \bot; \qquad\qquad 19$$
$$m = max(0, r); v_0(s') = c(s'); v_{i+1}(s') = S[St] \; u \; s' v_i. \qquad\qquad 20$$
$$S[\textbf{while} \; T \; \textbf{do} \; St] \; u \; s \; c = \lim_{i \to \infty} p_i(s) \qquad\qquad 21$$
$$\textbf{where} \;\; p_0(s') = \bot; p_{i+1}(s') = E[T] \; u \; s' \; k_{i+1}; \qquad\qquad 22$$
$$k_{i+1}(r, t) = r?Bool \Rightarrow (r \Rightarrow S[St] \; u \; t \; p_i, c(t)), \bot \qquad\qquad 23$$

3.21 Declaration Continuations

A declaration continuation will map an environment and state into an answer. The D function will now take a declaration continuation from the domain DC, as in Figure 10.78.

$$DC = UU \to State \to Ans \qquad\qquad 1$$
$$D: Decls \to UU \to State \to DC \to Ans \qquad\qquad 2$$

$$D[I:\text{integer}]\ u\ s\ d = Hd(u)[I]?\{udef\} \Rightarrow \qquad 3$$
$$(l?\{\bot\} \Rightarrow d(u[Hd[I \leftarrow \bot]], s), \qquad 4$$
$$d(u[Hd[I \leftarrow l]], < m[l \leftarrow \text{uninitInt}], i, o >)), \qquad 5$$
$$d(u[Hd[I \leftarrow \text{redef}]], s) \qquad 6$$
$$\textbf{where}\ s = < m, i, o > ; l = \text{alloc}(m). \qquad 7$$
$$D[I:\text{Boolean}]\ u\ s\ d = Hd(u)[I]?\{udef\} \Rightarrow \qquad 8$$
$$(l?\{\bot\} \Rightarrow d(u[Hd[I \leftarrow \bot]], s), \qquad 9$$
$$d(u[Hd[I \leftarrow l]], < m[l \leftarrow \text{uninitBool}], i, o >)), \qquad 10$$
$$d(u[Hd[I \leftarrow \text{redef}]], s) \qquad 11$$
$$\textbf{where}\ s = < m, i, o > ; l = \text{alloc}(m). \qquad 12$$
$$D[I = T]\ u\ s\ d = E[T]\ u\ s\ k \qquad 13$$
$$\textbf{where}\ k(r, t) = Hd(u)[I]?\{udef\} \Rightarrow \qquad 14$$
$$d(u[Hd[I \leftarrow r]], t), d(u[Hd[I \leftarrow \text{redef}]], t). \qquad 15$$

The expression T (line 13) can be allowed to contain function calls. If evaluation of T faults, E will simply return $\bot$; otherwise, it executes the declaration continuation (d) with the value that T returns and a possibly updated state. Other definitions are given in Figure 10.79.

Figure 10.79

$$D[\varepsilon]\ u\ s\ d = d(u, s) \qquad 1$$
$$D[Def_1\ Def_2]\ u\ s\ d = D[Def_1]\ u\ s\ d' \qquad 2$$
$$\textbf{where}\ d'(v, t) = D[Def_2]\ v\ t\ d. \qquad 3$$

$$S[\textbf{begin}\ Def\ St\ \textbf{end}]\ u\ s\ c = D[Def] < u_e, u > s\ d \qquad 4$$
$$\textbf{where}\ d(v, t) = S[St]\ v\ t\ c'; \qquad 5$$
$$c'(t') = c(t'[Hd[Free(Hd(s)) \leftarrow \text{unalloc}]]). \qquad 6$$

3.22 Procedures, Functions, and Parameters

I now define routines and parameters in the new continuation notation. First, declarations need to be handled, using D, DC, FP, and FC (formal parameter continuation), as shown in Figure 10.80.

Figure 10.80

$$FC = Parms \rightarrow Ans \qquad 1$$

$$FP: Fparms \rightarrow Parms \rightarrow FC \rightarrow Ans \qquad 2$$

$$FP[I : \text{integer}]\ p\ f = f(\text{append}(p, << 0, I >, \text{eol} >)) \qquad 3$$
$$FP[I : \text{Boolean}]\ p\ f = f(\text{append}(p, << \text{false}, I >, \text{eol} >)) \qquad 4$$
$$FP[\varepsilon]\ p\ f = f(p) \qquad 5$$
$$FP[Formals_1\ Formals_2]\ p\ f = FP[Formals_1]\ p\ f' \qquad 6$$
$$\textbf{where}\ f'(p') = FP[Formals_2]p'f. \qquad 7$$

Procedures are generalizations of statements, and, like all statements, take a statement continuation as a parameter. This continuation is essentially the return point of the procedure; see Figure 10.81.

Figure 10.81

$$Proc = (U \rightarrow State \rightarrow SC \rightarrow Ans) \otimes Loc \otimes Parms \qquad 1$$

D[**procedure** I (Formals); Def St] u s d =	2
FP[Formals]eol f,	3
where f(p) = Hd(u)[I]?{udef} $\Rightarrow$	4
(l?{$\perp$} $\Rightarrow$ d(u[Hd[I $\leftarrow \perp$]], s),	5
d(uu, < m[$l \leftarrow$ uninitInt], i, o >)),	6
d(u[Hd[I $\leftarrow$ redef]], s);	7
s = < m, i, o > ; l = alloc(m); uu = u[Hd[I $\leftarrow$< r, l, p >]];	8
r(v, t, cc) = D[Def] < v, uu > t d';	9
d'(v', t') = S[St]v't'c';	10
c'(tt) = cc(tt[Hd[Free(t) $\leftarrow$ unalloc]]).	11

Since functions are a generalization of expressions, they will now include an expression continuation that represents the mechanism through which the function's value is returned, as in Figure 10.82.

Figure 10.82

$$Func = (U \rightarrow State \rightarrow EC \rightarrow Ans) \otimes Loc \otimes Parms \qquad 1$$

D[Integer **function**(Formals) I; St; **return**(T)] u s d =	2
FP[Formals]eol f,	3
where f(p) = Hd(u)[I]?{udef} $\Rightarrow$	4
(l?{$\perp$} $\Rightarrow$ d(u[Hd[I $\leftarrow \perp$]], s),	5
d(uu, < m[$l \leftarrow$ uninitInt], i, o >)),	6
d(u[Hd[I $\leftarrow$ redef]], s);	7
s = < m, i, o > ; l = alloc(m); uu = u[Hd[I $\leftarrow$< r, l, p >]];	8
r(u', s', ec) = D[Def] < u', uu > s'd';	9
d'(v, t) = S[St] v t c;	10
c(v', t') = E[T]v't'k;	11
k(r, tt) = r?N $\Rightarrow$ ec(r, tt[Hd[Free(s') $\leftarrow$ unalloc]]), $\perp$.	12
D[Boolean **function**(Formals) I; St; **return**(T)] u s d =	13
FP[Formals]eol f,	14
where f(p) = Hd(u)[I]?{udef} $\Rightarrow$	15
(l?{$\perp$} $\Rightarrow$ d(u[Hd[I $\leftarrow \perp$]], s),	16
d(uu, < m[$l \leftarrow$ uninitInt], i, o >)),	17
d(u[Hd[I $\leftarrow$ redef]], s);	18
s = < m, i, o > ; l = alloc(m); uu = u[Hd[I $\leftarrow$< r, l, p >]];	19
r(u', s', ec) = D[Def] < u', uu > s' d';	20
d'(v, t) = S[St] v t c;	21
c(v', t') = E[T]v' t' k;	22
k(r, tt) = r?Bool $\Rightarrow$ ec(r, tt[Hd[Free(s') $\leftarrow$ unalloc]]), $\perp$.	23

It is time to consider actual-parameter evaluation and procedure and function calls; see Figure 10.83. AC is the semantic domain of actual-parameter continuations.

Figure 10.83

$$AC = UU \rightarrow Parms \rightarrow Ans \qquad\qquad 1$$

$$AP: Aparms \rightarrow UU \rightarrow Parms \rightarrow State \rightarrow AC \rightarrow Ans \qquad 2$$

$$AP[I]\ u\ p\ s\ a = v?Loc \wedge p \neq eol \wedge \qquad\qquad 3$$
$$((Hd(pp)?N \wedge m(v)?N \oplus uninitInt) \vee \qquad\qquad 4$$
$$(Hd(pp)?Bool \wedge m(v)?Bool \oplus uninitBool)) \Rightarrow \qquad 5$$
$$a(u[Hd[Tl(pp) \leftarrow v]], Tl(p)), \bot \qquad\qquad 6$$
$$\mathbf{where}\ v = Find(Tl(u))[I];\ pp = Hd(p);\ s = <m, i, o>. \qquad 7$$
$$AP[\varepsilon]\ u\ p\ s\ a = a(u, p) \qquad\qquad 8$$
$$AP[Actuals_1\ Actuals_2]\ u\ p\ s\ a = \qquad\qquad 9$$
$$AP[Actuals_1]\ u\ p\ s\ a' \qquad\qquad 10$$
$$\mathbf{where}\ a'(u', p') = AP[Actuals_2]u'\ p'\ s\ a. \qquad 11$$

$$S[\mathbf{call}\ I(Actuals)]\ u\ s\ c = v?Proc \Rightarrow \qquad\qquad 12$$
$$AP[Actuals] < u_e, u > r\ sa, \bot \qquad\qquad 13$$
$$\mathbf{where}\ a(u', q) = (q = eol) \Rightarrow \qquad\qquad 14$$
$$\lim_{i \rightarrow \infty} p_i(s, Hd(u')), \bot; \qquad\qquad 15$$
$$v = Find(u)[I] = < f, l, r >; \qquad\qquad 16$$
$$p_0(s', w) = \bot; \qquad\qquad 17$$
$$p_{i+1}(s', w) = m(l) = uninitInt \Rightarrow \qquad\qquad 18$$
$$f\ w < m[l \leftarrow i], I, O > c_1, \qquad\qquad 19$$
$$m(l) > 0 \Rightarrow f\ w < m[l \leftarrow m(l) - 1], I, O > c_2, \bot; \qquad 20$$
$$s' = < m, I, O >; \qquad\qquad 21$$
$$c_1(t_1) = c(t_1[Hd[l\ \texttt{<-}\ uninitInt]]); \qquad\qquad 22$$
$$c_2(t_2) = c(t_2[Hd[l\ \texttt{<-}\ m(l)]]). \qquad\qquad 23$$

$$E[\mathbf{eval}\ I\ (Actuals)]\ u\ s\ k = v?Func \Rightarrow \qquad\qquad 24$$
$$AP[Actuals] < u_e, u > r\ sa, \bot \qquad\qquad 25$$
$$\mathbf{where}\ a(u', q) = (q = eol) \Rightarrow \qquad\qquad 26$$
$$\lim_{i \rightarrow \infty} p_i(s, Hd(u')), \bot; \qquad\qquad 27$$
$$v = Find(u)[I] = < f, l, r >; \qquad\qquad 28$$
$$p_0(s', w) = \bot; \qquad\qquad 29$$
$$p_{i+1}(s', w) = m(l) = uninitInt \Rightarrow \qquad\qquad 30$$
$$f\ w < m[l \leftarrow i], I, O > k_1, \qquad\qquad 31$$
$$m(l) > 0 \Rightarrow f\ w < m[l \leftarrow m(l) - 1], I, O > k_2, \bot; \qquad 32$$
$$s' = < m, I, O >; \qquad\qquad 33$$
$$k_1(r_1, t_1) = k(r_1, t_1[Hd[l \leftarrow uninitInt]]); \qquad\qquad 34$$
$$k_2(r_2, t_2) = k(r_1, t_2[Hd[l \leftarrow m(l)]]). \qquad\qquad 35$$

Finally, I redefine the M function using continuations, as shown in Figure 10.84.

Figure 10.84

$$M: Pr \to File \to Ans \qquad\qquad 1$$

$$M[\textbf{program}\ Def\ St\ \textbf{end}]\ i = \qquad\qquad 2$$
$$D[Def] < u_e, u_0 > < m_0, i, eof > d \qquad\qquad 3$$
$$\textbf{where}\ d(v, t) = S[St]\ v\ tc;\ c(t') = Tl(Tl(t')). \qquad\qquad 4$$

3.23 Flow of Control

Now that I have the machinery of continuations in place, I can illustrate how to implement statements that alter the flow of control. I begin with the **stop** statement, which forces immediate termination of execution. Figure 10.85 shows the semantic function.

Figure 10.85

$$S[\textbf{stop}]\ u\ s\ c = Tl(Tl(s))$$

Stop returns the output file component of the current state. It avoids the normal flow of control by ignoring its continuation parameter.

A more interesting illustration is **break**, which I will use to exit any of the structured statements in the language (**if**, **do**, **while**, **begin-end**). I will let any of these statements be optionally labeled with an identifier, which will follow normal scoping rules. I define **break** I to cause execution to immediately break out of the structure labeled with I and then to continue execution with the normal successor to the labeled statement. If I isn't declared as a label in the scope of the break, the statement produces an error value.

I extend V, the domain of environment contents, to include statement continuations:

$$U = Id \to V$$
$$V = N \oplus Bool \oplus Loc \oplus Proc \oplus Func \oplus SC \oplus \{\bot\} \oplus \{udef\} \oplus \{redef\}$$

The meaning of a label on a structured statement will be the continuation associated with that statement. Figure 10.86 adds definitions for structured statements with labels (the definitions for unlabeled statements are, of course, retained).

Figure 10.86

$$S[I: \textbf{if}\ T\ \textbf{then}St_1\ \textbf{else}\ St_2]\ u\ s\ c = E[T]\ uu\ s\ k \qquad\qquad 1$$
$$\textbf{where}\ k(r, t) = r?Bool \Rightarrow (r \Rightarrow S[St_1]\ uu\ t\ c,\ S[St_2]\ uu\ t\ c), \bot; 2$$
$$uu = Hd(u)[I]?\{udef\} \Rightarrow u[Hd[I \leftarrow c']],\ u[Hd[I \leftarrow redef]]; \qquad 3$$
$$c'(t') = c(t'[Hd[Free(Hd(s)) \leftarrow unalloc]]). \qquad\qquad 4$$

$$S[I: \textbf{do } T \textbf{ times } St] \text{ u s c} = E[T] \text{ uu s k} \qquad 5$$
$$\textbf{where } k(r, t) = r?N \Rightarrow v_m(t), \bot; \qquad 6$$
$$m = max(0, t); v_0(s') = c(s'); \qquad 7$$
$$v_{i+1}(s') = S[St] \text{ uu s'} v_i; \qquad 8$$
$$uu = Hd(u)[I]?\{udef\} \Rightarrow u[Hd[I \leftarrow c']], u[Hd[I \leftarrow redef]]; \qquad 9$$
$$c'(t') = c(t'[Hd[Free(Hd(s)) \leftarrow unalloc]]). \qquad 10$$
$$S[I: \textbf{while } T \textbf{ do } St] \text{ u s c} = \lim_{i \to \infty} p_i(s) \qquad 11$$
$$\textbf{where } p_0(s') = \bot; p_{i+1}(s') = E[T] \text{ uu s'} k_{i+1}; \qquad 12$$
$$k_{i+1}(r, t) = r?Bool \Rightarrow (r \Rightarrow S[St] \text{ uu t } p_i, c(t)), \bot; \qquad 13$$
$$uu = Hd(u)[I]?\{udef\} \Rightarrow u[Hd[I \leftarrow c']], u[Hd[I \leftarrow redef]]; \qquad 14$$
$$c'(t') = c(t'[Hd[Free(Hd(s)) \leftarrow unalloc]]); \qquad 15$$
$$S[I: \textbf{begin } Def \; St \; \textbf{end}] \text{ u s c} = \qquad 16$$
$$D[Def] < u_e, uu > s \; d, \qquad 17$$
$$\textbf{where } d(v, t) = S[St] \text{ v t c'}; \qquad 18$$
$$c'(t') = c(t'[Hd[Free(Hd(s)) \leftarrow unalloc]]); \qquad 19$$
$$uu = Hd(u)[I]?\{udef\} \Rightarrow u[Hd[I \leftarrow c']], u[Hd[I \leftarrow redef]]. \qquad 20$$

Break looks up its identifier, and if it is bound to a statement continuation, it executes that continuation in the current state; see Figure 10.87.

Figure 10.87

$$S[\textbf{break } I] \text{ u s c} = v?SC \Rightarrow v(s), \bot \qquad 1$$
$$\textbf{where } v = Find(u)[I]. \qquad 2$$

3.24 Summary of Syntactic and Semantic Domains and Semantic Functions

The domains used in the denotational definitions in this chapter have been upgraded during the progression of examples. Figure 10.88 lists the most recent meanings.

Figure 10.88

Syntactic domains   1

BinLit: binary literals; nonterminals BN, Seq   2
Exp: expressions; nonterminal T   3
Id: identifiers; nonterminal I   4
Pr: programs; nonterminal P   5
Decls: declarations; nonterminal Def   6
Stm: statements; nonterminal St   7

Semantic domains   8

Basic: 9
    N = {0, 1, 2, ...} (natural numbers)   10
    Bool = {false, true} (Boolean values)   11

```
        Complex:                                                     12
            Loc = {0, 1, ···} -- finite domain of memory locations 13
            Mem = Loc → N ⊕ Bool ⊕ {uninitInt} ⊕ {uninitBool} ⊕     14
                {unalloc} -- memory location                         15
            File = (N ⊕ Bool ⊕ {eof})* -- contents of a file        16
            R = N ⊕ Bool ⊕ {⊥} -- value of an expression            17
            RR = State ⊗ (N ⊕ Bool ⊕ {⊥})                           18
                -- result of function                               19
            State = Mem ⊗ File ⊗ File -- program state              20
            Ans = File ⊕ {⊥} -- program result                      21
            V = N ⊕ Bool ⊕ Loc ⊕ Proc ⊕ Func ⊕ SC ⊕ {⊥} ⊕ {udef} ⊕ 22
                {redef} -- value of an identifier                   23
            U = Id → V -- environment                               24
            UU = U* -- sequence of environments                     25
            Proc = (U → State → SC → Ans) ⊗ Loc ⊗ Parms             26
                -- procedure                                        27
            Func = (U → State → EC → Ans) ⊗ Loc ⊗ Parms             28
                -- function                                         29
            Parms = ((N ⊕ Bool) ⊗ Id ⊕ eol)* -- parameters         30
            SC = State → Ans -- statement continuation              31
            EC = (N ⊕ Bool) → State → Ans -- expression contin.     32
            DC = UU → State → Ans -- declaration continuation       33
            AC = UU → Parms → Ans -- actual parameter contin.       34
            FC = Parms → Ans -- formal parameter continuation       35
```

Semantic functions   36

```
        L: Id → V -- lookup                                         37
        E: Exp → UU → State → EC → Ans -- expression                38
        S: Stm → UU → State → SC → Ans -- statement                 39
        D: Decls → UU → State → DC → Ans -- declaration             40
        M: Pr → File → Ans -- program                               41
        FP: Fparms → Parms → Parms -- formal parameters             42
        AP: Aparms → UU → Parms → State → AC → Ans                  43
            -- actual parameters                                    44
```

4 ◆ FINAL COMMENTS

This long (and somewhat tedious) exercise shows that it is possible to specify exactly what a programming language designer allows in the syntax and means by the constructs of the language. Such a specification can guide the designer (to make sure that all cases are properly covered), the implementer (to make sure that the compiler and runtime support live up to the specifications), and the programmer (to make sure that language constructs are used as intended).

Formal specification can also be used to evaluate the clarity of a language. If the axiomatic semantics of a construct are hard to build and hard to understand, then perhaps the construct itself is hard to understand. For example, a multiple assignment statement has this structure:

```
x, y, z := 13, 16, x + 3;
```

Three assignments are made simultaneously. However, x + 3 on the right-hand side depends on x, which is on the left-hand side. The order of evaluation makes a difference. It is not easy in axiomatic semantics to specify the rule for multiple assignment for this reason. Perhaps that complexity is a symptom that multiple assignment is itself an unclear concept.

As my brief forays into ML have shown, the specification can even be written in a programming language so that it can be checked for syntax and meaning. (Have you really read all the specifications? Did you find any mistakes?) Such a specification can even be used to interpret programs (written in abstract syntax, of course), more as a way of debugging the specification than understanding the meaning of the programs.

However, the fact that the specification is in a language, albeit a programming language, seems to reduce the question of formally specifying one language (the target) to specifying another (ML, for example). It requires that someone who wants to understand the target language specification needs to learn and understand some fairly complex notions, such as domain equations. There is no guarantee that every error case has been dealt with, and the notation is complex enough that such an omission would probably pass unnoticed.

The fact that I have succeeded in denoting standard features of a programming language gives me no particular confidence that I could handle such constructs as CLU coroutines (Chapter 2), ML higher-level functions (Chapter 3), Prolog resolution (Chapter 8), Post guardians (Chapter 6), SNOBOL patterns (Chapter 9), or Modula monitors (Chapter 7). An enormous amount of cleverness is required to build denotational semantic definitions. As you have seen, introducing a single concept into a language is likely to modify the definitions for everything else. A typical modification involves making functions like E even higher-order. The result is anything but straightforward.

Several excellent books deal with programming language semantics. I can especially recommend Tennent [Tennent 81] and Pagan [Pagan 81].

EXERCISES

Review Exercises

10.1 Describe the language (that is, the set of strings) generated by this BNF grammar:

$$S ::= (S) S \mid \varepsilon$$

10.2 Show a different BNF grammar that generates exactly the same language as the grammar in Exercise 10.1.

10.3 Write BNF productions for **if** statements.

10.4 An **ambiguous grammar** is one that generates strings that have more than one parse tree. Is the grammar of Figure 10.89 ambiguous? Does it have any other problems?

Figure 10.89

```
Expression ::=                                              1
        Expression + Expression |                          2
        Expression * Expression |                          3
        INTEGER                                            4
```

10.5 Prove the program in Figure 10.90 correct.

Figure 10.90

```
{a < 3}                                                    1
if a < 4 then x := 2 else x := 10 end;                     2
{x = 2}                                                    3
```

10.6 Compute:

```
wp(if a < 4 then x := 2 else x := 10 end, x = 2)
```

Challenge Exercises

10.7 In Figure 10.43 (page 384), I specify that redefinition of an identifier has no effect. Show how to modify the example so that redefinition hides the previous definition.

10.8   In line 25 of Figure 10.46 (page 388), why check that c is a member of U? What else could it be?

10.9   On page 386, I introduce redef. Why not just use udef for this purpose?

10.10 How would you code the semantics of a **while** loop (see Figure 10.52, page 392) in ML?

Appendix:
Languages Mentioned

This appendix lists the languages mentioned in the text, along with information you may find helpful if you want to investigate further. Many of the language names are registered trademarks.

When I say a language is "based on" another, I mean to say that it is in the same general family, even though it may have evolved a great distance from its forebear. Many languages include features from disparate language families and are therefore difficult to categorize. Some are clearly extensions or hybrids of other languages.

Whenever I can, I provide not only pointers to the literature but also URLs (universal resource locators) for getting more information via WWW (the World-Wide Web). These pointers direct you to documentation, examples, compilers, and other language-related information. Several URLs of general interest are `http://union.ncsa.uiuc.edu/-HyperNews/get/computing/lang-list.html`, which lists many languages with pointers to more information for each, and `http://cuiwww.unige.ch/langlist`, which lets you interactively search for particular languages. Unfortunately, the WWW changes constantly, so the pointers I provide here may not be valid when you try them.

In a few cases, I describe the syntax and some helpful routines in the language so that you can write small programs and run them.

ABC. Small, interactive, strong typing, indentation for grouping, strings, and exact arithmetic. In use [Pemberton 91]. `http://www.cwi.nl/~guido/ftp/steven/www/abc.html`.

Ada. Large, imperative, compiled, strong typing, concurrent; based on Pascal. In slowly increasing use. Has an ANSI standard. A revision called Ada 95 was published in 1995 (ISO 8652:1995); it includes object orientation [Ada 1983]. `http://lglwww.epfl.ch/Ada/9X/9X.html`.

AL. Imperative, control of a robot arm. Experimental; in use during the 1970s and 1980s at Stanford University [Finkel 76].

ALBA. Object-oriented, concurrent. Experimental [Hernández 93].

ALF. Multiparadigm: object-oriented and logic; based on Smalltalk. Experimental [Mellender 88]. `ftp://ftp.germany.eu.net/pub/-programming/languages/LogicFunctional`.

Algol. Imperative, static types, modern control structures. Pioneered free format, compound statements, variables declared with type, recursion, value-mode parameters. Hoare says that Algol-60 was "a language so far ahead of its time, that it was not only an improvement on its predecessors, but also on nearly all its successors" [Hoare 73]. In use in the 1960s, particularly in Europe. Algol-68, Algol-W, and Jovial are independent developments that grew out of Algol-60; they were in moderate use in the 1960s and 1970s [Naur 63; van Wijngaarden 75].

Alphard. Strongly typed, imperative, pre- and postconditions for procedures. Experimental [Wulf 77].

Amber. Strongly typed, dynamic and static typing, structural equivalence. Experimental [Cardelli 86].

APL. Matrices, interpreted. In widespread but sparse use since the 1960s [Iverson 62, 87; IBM Corporation 87]. `http://www.acm.org/-sigapl`.

Argus. Imperative, concurrent, strongly typed, compiled, transactions; based on CLU. Experimental [Liskov 83a, 83b].

Awk. Strings, interpreted. In widespread use, particularly on Unix [Aho 78]. Available in the GNU software suite as gawk. `ftp://netlib.att.com/research/awk*`.

C. Imperative, systems programming; based on Algol. In heavy and increasing use since the 1970s. Has an ANSI standard [Kernighan 88; Harbison 87]. `http://www.cis.ohio-state.edu/hypertext/faq/-usenet/C-faq/top.html`. Available in the GNU software suite and ported to a great number of platforms.

C++. Object-oriented, extends C. In heavy use [Ellis 90; Meyers 92]. Available in the GNU software suite. For MS-DOS, a nice and inexpensive implementation is available from Borland International, 1800 Green Hills Road, Box 660001, Scotts Valley, CA 95067.

Canopy. Concurrent, extends C. In use at Fermilab in Illinois [Hockney 92].

Charm. Concurrent, extends C. Experimental, primarily at the University of Illinois [Kalé 90]. `ftp://a.cs.uiuc.edu/pub/CHARM`.

CLP(*R*). "Constraint Logic Programming (Real domain)." Extends Prolog. In use; available on internet [Heintze 92; Fruhwirth 92]. http://www.cs.cmu.edu/Web/Groups/AI/html/faqs/ai/constraints/-top.html.

CLOS. "Common LISP Object System." Object-oriented, extends Common LISP [Bobrow 88]. http://www.cis.ohio-state.edu/hypertext/-faq/usenet/lisp-faq/part5/faq.html.

CLU. Imperative, strongly typed; based on Algol. Pioneered iterators. In occasional use, particularly at MIT [Liskov 81]. ftp://ftp.lcs.mit.edu/pub/pclu.

Concurrent C. Imperative, concurrent; based on C. Includes Ada rendezvous, with guards that can reference formal parameters and sorting expressions. In increasing use [Gehani 89].

CSP. "Communicating Sequential Processes." Concurrent. Not implemented (but see Occam) [Hoare 78]. http://www.comlab.ox.ac.uk/-archive/csp.html.

CST. Concurrent Smalltalk. Object-oriented, concurrent, extends Smalltalk. Experimental [Dally 89].

dBASE. Database. Several dialects (dBASE II, dBASE III, dBASE IV) in heavy use [Simpson 87].

DC++. Concurrent, object-oriented, extends C++. Experimental [Carr 93].

DP. "Distributed Processes." Imperative, concurrent. Not implemented [Brinch Hansen 78].

Edison. Imperative, concurrent; based on DP. Experimental [Brinch Hansen 80].

Eiffel. Object-oriented, statically typed, has assertions for axiomatic correctness checking. In use [Meyer 88, 92]. http://www.eiffel.com/-doc/eiffel.html. Available from Interactive Software Engineering (ISE).

Eiffel Linda. Object-oriented, concurrent, extends Eiffel and Linda. Experimental [Jellinghaus 90].

Euclid. Imperative, strongly typed, for systems programming and formal verification; based on Pascal. Several dialects (April Euclid, Small Euclid) in use during the 1980s [Lampson 77].

Distributed Eiffel. Object-oriented, concurrent, extends Eiffel. Experimental [Gunaseelan 92].

FORTRAN. "Formula Translator." Imperative, typed, no block structure, weak control structures. Designed at IBM in 1954 under the direction of John Backus. Pioneered arrays, **for** loops, and branching **if** statements. Various dialects (FORTRAN II, FORTRAN IV, WatFor, WatFive, FORTRAN 66 (ANSI X3.9-1966), FORTRAN 77 (ANSI X3.9-1978), FORTRAN 90 (ISO 1539-1991, ANSI X3.198-1992)) in heavy use since the late 1950s, especially for scientific computing. `http://www.cis.ohio-state.edu/hypertext/faq/usenet/-fortran-faq/faq.html`.

FP. Functional. Some experimental dialects (FP*, FP*/88N, Berkeley FP) have been implemented [Backus 78; Radensky 87; Baden 84]. `http://www.nectec.or.th/pub/archives/comp.sources.unix/-volume20/fpc`.

G-2. Multiparadigm, dynamically typed, compiled. Experimental [Placer 92].

Gedanken. Clear separation of functional and imperative parts. Not implemented [Reynolds 70].

Gödel. Logic. Experimental [Hill 94]. `ftp://ftp.cs.kuleuven.ac.be/pub/logic-prgm/goedel`.

Icon. Imperative, strings, backtracking. In use [Griswold 80, 90]. `http://www.cs.arizona.edu/icon/www/index.html`.

[incr Tcl]. Scripting, strings, object-oriented, interpreted. Extension of Tcl. In use. `http://www.wn.com/biz/itcl`.

Intercal. Humorous. Implemented [Woods 73]. `http://www.nectec.or.th/pub/archives/comp.sources.misc/-volume16/intercal.programming language`.

Io. Continuations. Not implemented [Levien 89].

Leda. Multiparadigm, strongly typed, compiled. Experimental [Budd 95]. `http://www.cs.orst.edu/~budd/leda.html`.

Linda. Concurrent, meant to be embedded in other languages. Embedded in various packages and in use [Gelernter 85]. `http://www.cs.yale.edu/HTML/YALE/CS/Linda/linda.html`.

LISP. "List Processing Language." Functional, homoiconic. Pioneered garbage collection. In widespread use since the 1960s [McCarthy 62;

Hughes 86; Teitelman 81; Steele Jr. 90; Abelson 85]. There are many dialects of LISP, such as MacLISP, InterLISP, Common LISP, and Scheme. Scheme was designed by Guy Steele and Gerald Sussman. `http://www-swiss.ai.mit.edu/scheme-home.html`. It has an exceptionally clear and simple semantics and few different ways to form expressions. Common LISP, also developed by Guy Steele, contains a great deal that is not mentioned in Chapter 4, including default parameters, exception handling, a type mechanism, and data structures like strings, arrays, records, and hash tables. `http://www.cs.rmit.edu.au/docs/-cltl/cltl2.html`. Like Scheme, Common LISP uses static, not dynamic, scope rules. The form for defining a function is (**defun** name (param list) (body)). Lambda forms should be quoted: '(**lambda** (x) (+ x 1)); they are invoked by the **funcall** form. Comments start with ; and continue to the end of the line. The `print` function outputs its parameter. Static scope rules are like those in ML; a scope looks like (**let** ((var1 val1) ...) (body)); use **let*** for recursive declarations.

Lucid. Functional with iteration. Lucid started as a simple, nonprocedural temporal language; it has developed into a programming paradigm called **intensional programming** [Ashcroft 77]. `http://www.csl.sri.com/Lucid.html`.

Lucinda. Linda-Russell hybrid. Experimental [Butcher 91].

Lynx. Imperative, concurrent, strongly typed; based on Algol. Experimental [Scott 84].

Macsyma. Mathematical, interactive. Heavily used during the 1970s and 1980s; still in use and commercially available. `http://www.macsyma.com/` [Heller 91].

Madcap. Experimental. A descendent, Modcap, is in use at New Mexico State University [Wells 63].

Maple. Mathematical, interactive. Widely used; commercially available [Char 93]. `http://www.maplesoft.com/Maple/`.

Mathematica. Mathematical, interactive. Widely used. Commercially available [Gaylord 93; Shaw 94]. `http://www.wri.com/`.

Mesa. Imperative, strongly typed, concurrent; based on Pascal. Used heavily at Xerox Palo Alto Research Center during the 1970s and 1980s [Lampson 80].

Metafont. Font specification. Widely used [Knuth 86]. `http://etna.mcs.kent.edu/TeX/TeX-FAQ` Part of almost every TeX distribution.

Miranda. Functional, polymorphic types, lazy evaluation. Experimental, in increasing use; commercially available [Turner 85a, 86; Thompson 86]. `http://www.cs.nott.ac.uk/Department/Staff/mpj/-faq.html#Miranda(TM)`.

ML. "MetaLanguage." Functional, type inference with polymorphic types, interactive; based on Edinburgh Logic for Computable Functions (LCF). Pioneered type inference. Experimental, in increasing use. ML has evolved into Standard ML [Harper 89; Reade 89; Appel 91; Paulson 92; Ramsey 90]. `ftp://pop.cs.cmu.edu/usr/rowan/-sml-archive/faq.txt`. New Jersey Standard ML is interactive, expecting the user to type in expressions, just as shown in Chapter 3. Each expression is terminated by `;` . Comments are surrounded by `(*` and `*)` . Some useful predefined functions are:

```
use = fn : (string list) -> unit
print = 'a -> 'a
```

Use allows you to read in a program from a list of files. Print allows you to output values. Unit is a type with one value, used as void in C is used. The unary negation operator is ~ .

Modula. Imperative, concurrent, compiled, strong typing; based on Pascal. No longer used [Wirth 77].

Modula-2. Imperative, concurrent, compiled, strong typing; based on Modula and Pascal. In widespread use [Wirth 85]. `http://www.cis.ohio-state.edu/hypertext/faq/usenet/-Modula-2-faq/faq.html`.

Modula-3. Imperative, concurrent, compiled, strong typing with structural equivalence, objects; based on Modula-2. Experimental, in increasing use [Nelson, G. 1991]. `http://www.research.digital.com/SRC/modula-3/html/home.html`

Oberon. Imperative, strong typing, for students; based on Modula-2. In increasing use [Reiser 92]. `http://www.cis.ohio-state.edu/-hypertext/faq/usenet/Oberon-Lang-FAQ/faq.html`; also, `http://huxley.inf.ethz.ch/~marais/Spirit.html`.

Occam. Concurrent, extension of CSP. In use [May 83]. `http://www.comlab.ox.ac.uk/archive/occam.html`.

OPS5. Rule-based. In use [Brownston 86]. `http://www.nectec.or.th/pub/archives/comp.sources.unix/-volume12/ops5`.

Pascal. Imperative, typed, block-structured; based on Algol-60. In heavy use since the 1970s. Has an ANSI standard [Jensen 74; ANSI 83]. `http://www.yahoo.com/Computers/Languages/Pascal`.

Perl. "Practical Extraction and Report Language." Scripting, strings, interpreted. In use [Wall 91; Schwartz 94]. `http://www.cis.ufl.edu/-perl`.

Post. Dataflow. Not fully implemented [Ravishankar 89].

Prolog. Declarative, logic, patterns, backtrack. In widespread use [Clocksin 81]. `http://www.cs.cmu.edu/afs/cs.cmu.edu/Web/Groups/-AI/html/faqs/lang/prolog/top.html`. SICStus Prolog 2.1 is a portable implementation of Prolog; inquiries can be addressed to `sicstus-request@sics.se`. SWI-Prolog comes from the University of Amsterdam. SWI-Prolog is interactive. It begins in query mode, showing a prompt `?-`. To switch to a mode in which facts can be entered, give the query `[user]`. To return to query mode, type an end-of-file. To read facts from a file, give the query `[filename]`. The query `trace` causes prolog to show the rules it tries as the evaluator solves queries. The unary predicate `print` outputs its parameter. The comment delimiters are `/*` and `*/`. To get a bag of all solutions to a query, try bagof((list of output variables), query, bagname).

Russell. Types as first-class values. Experimental [Demers 79; Boehm 86]. `ftp://arisia.xerox.com/pub/russell/russell.tar.Z`.

SAIL. Imperative with some AI structures; based on Algol-W and Leap (a language with associative store). Heavily used at Stanford in the 1970s.

SAL. Imperative, systems administration, database. In use, primarily at the University of Kentucky [Sturgill 89].

Sed. A stream editor standard with all Unix implementations.

Simula. Imperative, types, classes, coroutines; based on Algol. Pioneered abstract data types and object orientation. Various dialects (starting with Simula 67) in heavy use in the 1970s [Birtwistle 73]. `http://remarque.berkeley.edu/~muir/free-compilers/TOOL/-Simula67-1.html`.

Sisal. "Streams and Iteration in a Single-Assignment Language." Dataflow; based on Val. in use [McGraw 83]. `http://www.llnl.gov/-sisal/`.

Smalltalk. Object-oriented. Various dialects (mainly of Smalltalk-80) are in use [Ingalls 78; Goldberg 83; LaLonde 90]. `http://st-www.cs.uiuc.edu/other_st.html`. A version of Smalltalk 1.0 is available in the Gnu software suite. It is interactive, expecting the user to type in expressions as if they were the body of an anonymous method. The body is terminated by `!`. Comments are surrounded by double quotes. Some useful predefined classes and methods:

```
(FileStream open: 'file name' mode: 'r') fileIn !          1
    "read and execute a program from a file"              2
anObject class inspect !                                   3
    "show class, superclass, subclasses, methods,         4
    variables"                                            5
anObject printNl !                                        6
    "print the object with a trailing newline"           7
```

Version 3 of Little Smalltalk is a portable implementation intended for a wide range of machines. It is in the public domain and can be distributed; it is available in `msdos/misclang/stv3-dos.zip` from many sites. Details are available from Tim Budd, Department of Computer Science, Oregon State University, Corvallis, OR 97331. Smalltalk-80 Version 2 is available from ParcPlace Systems, 999 E. Arques Avenue, Sunnyvale, CA 94086-4593, which markets implementations for a wide variety of machines.

SNOBOL. "StriNg Oriented symbOLic Language." Strings, patterns, dynamic typing, dynamic scope. Pioneered pattern matching. Various dialects (mainly SNOBOL4 and Spitbol) in widespread use in the 1970s [Griswold 71]. `ftp://cs.arizona.edu/snobol4`.

Specint. Logic, goal-directed. Experimental [Darlington 90].

SR. Imperative, concurrent; based on Algol. Experimental, in increasing use [Andrews 88]. `ftp://cs.arizona.edu/sr/sr.tar.Z`.

SQL. "Structured Query Language." Relational database. Has an ANSI standard (X3.135-1992). In widespread use. `http://waltz.ncsl.nist.gov/~len/sql_info.html`.

Tcl. Scripting, strings, interpreted. In use [Ousterhout 94]. `http://www.x.co.uk/of_interest/tcl/Tcl.html`.

Val. Dataflow. Obsolete [McGraw 82; Gehani 80].

Glossary

Many standard English words are used in a technical sense in this book. Careful and consistent use of these terms is a worthwhile habit to cultivate. Alternative expressions that you might find in the literature are also given here. This glossary should be taken as a guide to the sense in which I have used these terms rather than as a prescription for their proper use.

Abort. To close a transaction unsuccessfully. (p. 238)

Abstract data types. A set of values and a set of procedures that manipulate those values. (p. 71)

Abstract syntax. A categorization of the kinds of syntactic structures that exist in a programming language. (p. 369)

Abstraction. Quality of language design that provides a way to factor out recurring patterns. (p. 4)

Abstractions. In lambda calculus, terms of the form (λ x . T), representing a function of one parameter x with body T. (p. 152)

Activation records. Regions of the runtime stack that hold information for individual procedure instances. Also called **stack frames**. (p. 26)

Active objects. Instances of Simula classes that have not completed their initialization code. (p. 37)

Actual parameters. Expressions passed at the point of invocation to procedures. (p. 16)

Advanced syntax. The context-sensitive parts of the syntactical component of a programming language. Also called **static semantics**. (p. 358)

Aggregate types. See **structured types**. (p. 6)

Aggregates. Data structured according to some generally useful organization, such as strings, arrays, and databases. (p. 311)

Aggregates. See **constructors**. (p. 8)

Aliasing. Referencing the same memory cell by more than one name. (p. 203)

Alpha (α) conversion. In lambda calculus, the rule that identifiers may be renamed in a consistent fashion. (p. 154)

Ambiguous grammars. Grammars that generate strings that have more than one parse tree. (p. 421)

Ancestors. See **superclasses**. (p. 176)

Anonymous functions. Functions not bound to names. (p. 124)

Applications. In lambda calculus, terms of the form (F T), representing invocation of the function F with actual parameter T. (p. 152)

Applicative languages. See **functional languages**. (p. 119)

Applicative-order evaluation. See **strict evaluation**. (p. 139)

Arguments. See **parameters**. (p. 16)

Arity. The number of operands expected by an operator (p. 8)

Array slices. Subarrays of an array. (p. 7)

Assignment compatibility. A condition defined by rules that determine when an expression of one type may be assigned to a variable of another type. (p. 67)

Assignment-compatible types. A variable of one type may be assigned a value of the other. (p. 9)

Associative arrays. Arrays indexed by strings instead of by integers or other scalar types. (p. 316)

Asynchronous data structures. Structures that need not be entirely computed before any computed part can be used. (p. 207)

Asynchronous message passing. Message passing in which the sender does not wait for the destination. Opposite of **synchronous** message passing. (p. 250)

Atomic operations. See **indivisible operations**. (p. 220)

Atomic types. See **primitive types**. (p. 6)

Atoms. The fundamental values of LISP: numbers and symbols. (p. 120)

Axiomatic semantics. A formal semantics model that describes the effect each statement has by logical predicates that show how the statement modifies relations among program variables. (p. 359)

BNF. (Backus-Naur Form, or Backus Normal Form) A way to present the formal syntax of a programming language. (p. 357)

Backtracking. An algorithm in which alternative possibilities are tried (recursively) if particular possibilities fail. (p. 272)

Barriers. A synchronization type with a **meet** operation. (p. 235)

Base classes. See **superclasses**. (p. 176)

Basic domains. In denotational semantics, the fundamental domains out of which more complex ones are built. (p. 371)

Basic types. See **primitive types**. (p. 6)

Beta (β) reduction. In lambda calculus, the rule that defines the meaning of applying a function to an actual parameter. (p. 153)

Binary selectors. Message selectors with one parameter. (p. 171)

Binary semaphores. Semaphores used for mutual exclusion. (p. 221)

Binding. Associating attributes such as types to identifiers. Binding that takes place at compile time is usually called **static**, and binding that takes place at runtime is called **dynamic**. (p. 63)

Block statements. Statements composed of other statements, possibly with local declarations. (p. 11)

Block-structured languages. Languages in which procedures introducing name scopes can nest. (p. 21)

Blocked. A thread is blocked if it is waiting for some synchronization. (p. 219)

Blocks. Program structures that introduce new **name scopes**. (p. 20)

Body. The statements contained in a block or procedure. (p. 16)

Bottom-up evaluation. In logic programming, starting with facts and working toward goals. Opposite of **top-down evaluation**. (p. 294)

Bound identifiers. In lambda calculus, x is bound in (λ x . T). Opposite of **free identifiers**. (p. 152)

Bounded buffers. Arrays filled by producer threads and emptied by consumer threads. (p. 222)

Brands. String literals associated with derived types to identify them. (p. 68)

Busy waiting. Repeatedly testing to see if the conditions are right to continue computation. (p. 222)

Cactus stacks. Stacks built out of segments that form a tree, connected by static chains to the root. (p. 219)

Case analysis. An ordered sequence of pattern-action pairs. (p. 89)

Casting. Explicitly converting data types. (p. 9)

Central stack. Runtime data structure holding activation records of active procedures. (p. 26)

Choice types. Structured types with a single component value corresponding to any of the component types. Also called **disjoint unions**, **variant records**, and **discriminant records**. (p. 7)

Clarity. Quality of language design in which mechanisms are well defined and the outcome of code can be easily predicted. (p. 4)

Class methods. Methods belonging to a class object. (p. 176)

Class variables. Data shared by all instances of a class. (p. 176)

Classes. Records in Simula that include procedure fields. (p. 167)

Client processes. Processes that receive assistance to other processes. See **server processes**. (p. 253)

Client threads. Threads that make procedure calls into other threads. (p. 241)

Clients, type. The parts of a program that use an abstract data type. (p. 71)

Closed equation. In denotational semantics, a domain equation whose right-hand side consists entirely of applications of domain constructors to basic domains. (p. 375)

Closed-world assumption. In logic, the rule that whatever cannot be proven true is thereby false. (p. 269)

Closures. Procedures along with their nonlocal referencing environments, or label targets along with their activation records. (p. 22)

Clusters. See **modules**. (p. 72)

Coarse-grain parallelism. A style of concurrent computing in which different computers interact with each other only at long intervals. Also called **large-grain parallelism**. Opposite of **fine-grain parallelism**. (p. 261)

Code. Compiled program instructions. (p. 26)

Combinators. In lambda calculus, terms with no free identifiers (p. 155)

Commands. See **statements**. (p. 11)

Commit. To close a transaction successfully. (p. 238)

Completeness. See **expressiveness**. (p. 4)

Components. The building blocks of a structured type. (p. 6)

Composite types. See **structured types**. (p. 6)

Compound statements. Statements built of other statements. Also called **structured statements**. Opposite of **simple statements**. (p. 11)

Compound types. See **structured types**. (p. 6)

Concrete syntax. Specification of the exact syntactic structure of a language, including the phrase structure. (p. 369)

Concurrent programming. Multiple computations occurring simultaneously in cooperation with each other. Also called **parallel programming** (usually for shared memory) and **distributed programming** (usually for nonshared memory). (p. 217)

Condition type. A synchronization type with operations `signal` and `wait`. (p. 224)

Conditional correctness. Correctness of a program given that it successfully terminates. Also called **partial correctness**. See **total correctness**. (p. 361)

Conditional expressions. Expressions built with an `if` construct. (p. 10)

Conjunct. In logic, a predicate joined to others by the **and** operator. (p. 270)

Constrained. In constraint-logic programming, a status for identifiers that lies between bound and free. (p. 294)

Constructed types. See **structured types**. (p. 6)

Constructed types. Types for which constructors are available. (p. 99)

Constructive negation. In logic programming, constructing a list of bindings that satisfy a negation. (p. 291)

Constructors. See **initializers**. (p. 187)

Constructors. In algebraic specification of abstract data types, operations that result in values of the abstract data type. See also: **destructors** and **inspectors**. (p. 279)

Constructors. Operators that build structured values from components. Opposite of **selectors** (which extract the components) and of **destructors** (which deallocate the values). Also called **aggregates**. (p. 8)

Continuations. In denotational semantics, a function passed to every semantic function that is to be invoked after that semantic function. (p. 409)

Continuations. Procedure-valued parameters to be invoked after a called procedure is finished in lieu of returning. (p. 50)

Coroutines. Execution threads that can pass control to each other without losing their current execution environment. (p. 37)

Currying functions. Converting functions that take several parameters to ones that take just the first parameter and return a function that takes the others. (p. 97)

Dangling-procedure problem. If a non-top-level procedure is a first-class value, it can be assigned to a variable that persists after the nonlocal referencing environment of the procedure is deallocated. Subsequent invocation of the procedure has dangling pointers to its nonlocal referencing environment. Also called the **functional argument problem** or **funarg problem**. (p. 77)

Data encapsulation. One object may only examine or modify another object in ways defined by the latter object's protocol. (p. 164)

Data members. See **instance variables**. (p. 170)

Data-driven evaluation. See **speculative evaluation**. (p. 144)

Data-parallel computing. A style of concurrent computing in which machines work in parallel using the same algorithm on different parts of a single, large data set. (p. 261)

Database. In logic programming, a set of facts and rules of inference. (p. 267)

Dataflow graphs. Data-dependency graphs that represent the partial order of evaluation imposed by data dependencies. (p. 197)

Deadlock. A group of threads is blocked waiting for resources (such as mutexes) held by other members of the group. Also called **deadly embrace**. (p. 237)

Deadly embrace. See **deadlock**. (p. 237)

Declaration equivalence. See **name equivalence**. (p. 66)

Declarative languages. Languages in which programs state goals and rules, but do not explicitly invoke rules to derive the goals. Also called **nonprocedural languages**. Opposite of **procedural languages**. (p. 267)

Deep binding. See **deep search**. (p. 133)

Deep binding. Binding the nonlocal referencing environment of a procedure at the time it is elaborated. Also called **funarg binding**. Opposite of **shallow binding**. (p. 25)

Deep copy operation. Copying a record structure, recursively copying pointers contained in it. (p. 180)

Deep search. In dynamically scoped languages, storing all bindings in a single association list. Also called **deep binding**. (p. 133)

Deferred binding. In object-oriented programming, delaying until runtime binding a method invocation to a particular method. (p. 166)

Deferred methods. See **virtual methods**. (p. 185)

Delayed evaluation. See **lazy evaluation**. (p. 139)

Delegation. Forwarding a request from one object to another to respond to directly. (p. 250)

Delta. Given two values, a representation of how to change the old value to the new value. (p. 336)

Demand-driven evaluation. See **lazy evaluation**. (p. 139)

Denotational semantics. A formal semantics model that describes the effect of a program by building a mathematical function that is equivalent to the program. (p. 360)

Dereferencing operators. Unary operators that produce the value pointed to by a pointer. (p. 8)

Derived classes. See **subclasses**. (p. 176)

Derived types. Type-inequivalent versions of another type. (p. 68)

Descendents. See **subclasses**. (p. 176)

Destructors. See **finalizers**. (p. 187)

Destructors. In algebraic specification of abstract data types, constructors that reduce the amount of information. (p. 279)

Difference list. A data structure for Prolog that represents a list in two parts, the initial portion and the rest. (p. 282)

Dimensions. Typelike attributes that can be manipulated by multiplication and division. (p. 70)

Discriminant records. See **choice types**. (p. 7)

Disjoint unions. See **choice types**. (p. 7)

Disjoint-union domains. In denotational semantics, elements of either of the component domains. (p. 372)

Distributed programming. See **concurrent programming**. (p. 217)

Domain constructors. In denotational semantics, methods of building domains from other domains. (p. 371)

Domains. In denotational semantics, a set of values constructed according to a particular set of rules. (p. 371)

Don't-care patterns. Patterns that match any value but create no new bindings. (p. 34)

Don't-care results. Internal temporary names for unbound results in logic programs. (p. 278)

Dummy parameters. See **formal parameters**. (p. 16)

Dynamic chain. List of activation records on the central stack, each of which points to the activation record of its invoker. (p. 26)

Dynamic scope rules. Identifiers are accessible in a procedure if they were accessible at the point of invocation. Opposite of **static scope rules**. (p. 26)

Dynamic semantics. See **Semantics**. (p. 357)

Dynamic-sized arrays. Arrays whose declared bounds depend on runtime values of the bounds expressions. (p. 7)

Dynamic-typed languages. Languages in which types are bound to identifiers at runtime. Also called **untyped languages**. Opposite of **static-typed languages**. (p. 64)

Edited strings. Strings formed by insertion of expressions of arbitrary type within an ordinary string. (p. 312)

Efficiency. Quality of language design that allows efficient code to be produced, possibly with the assistance of the programmer. (p. 5)

Elaboration time. The time at which a declaration takes effect. (p. 20)

Entries. Exported identifiers that may be invoked from outside a module. (p. 241)

Environments. In denotational semantics, functions mapping identifiers in the syntactic domain into results. (p. 384)

Error values. Pseudovalues that indicate results of erroneous computations. (p. 35)

Eta (η) conversion. In lambda calculus, the rule that allows a function to be written without the λ notation. (p. 155)

Event counts. A synchronization type with operations **advance, read,** and **await**. (p. 232)

Exceptions. A data type with the **raise** operation (also called **throw**) for dealing with runtime errors. (p. 32)

Execution semantics. See **Semantics**. (p. 357)

Explicit return. The **return** statement includes the value being returned. Alternative to **implicit return** and **identifier return**. (p. 19)

Exporting identifiers. Making identifiers elaborated within a module visible to the surrounding scope. (p. 72)

Expression-based languages. Languages in which conditionals, declarations, procedures, and so forth are packaged as expressions that yield values. (p. 81)

Expressions. Literals, constructors, constants, variables, invocations of value-returning procedures, or operators with operands that are themselves expressions. (p. 8)

Expressiveness. Quality of language design that allows a wide variety of programs to be expressed. Also called **completeness**. (p. 4)

Extensions. New types that enlarge the set of values available in an old type. Opposite of **reductions**. (p. 69)

Facts. In logic programming, predicates that are assumed true. Also called **hypotheses**. (p. 269)

Fields of a record. Selectors for components of a record type. (p. 7)

Final algebra. In algebraic specification of abstract data types, an algebra that equates all elements that the inspectors cannot distinguish. See also **initial algebra**. (p. 279)

Finalizers. Procedures invoked when objects are deallocated. Also called **destructors**. (p. 187)

First-class values. Value that can be passed as parameters, can be the return value of a procedures, and can be assigned into variables. (p. 75)

Fixed-point operators. In lambda calculus, combinators Y with the property that Y g = g (Y g). (p. 155)

Flexible arrays. Arrays without declared bounds; only those components that have been given values at runtime may be accessed. Also called **unconstrained arrays**. (p. 7)

Form. A functionlike construct treated as a special case by the translator. (p. 123)

Formal parameters. Identifiers declared as parameters in a procedure header. Also called **dummy parameters**. (p. 16)

Free identifiers. In lambda calculus, identifiers in a term that are not bound. Opposite of **bound identifiers**. (p. 152)

Funarg binding. See **deep binding**. (p. 25)

Function application. Invoking a function with parameters. (p. 83)

Function domains. In denotational semantics, a domain of functions mapping elements of one component domain to the other. (p. 373)

Functional argument (funarg) problem. See **dangling-procedure problem**. (p. 77)

Functional languages. Programming languages in which there are no variables, no assignment statements, no iterative constructs, and no side effects in procedures. Also called **applicative languages**. (p. 119)

Functions. Procedures that return a value. (p. 15)

Functors. In logic programming, names of structures. (p. 268)

Generic modules. Modules parameterized by types. (p. 78)

Generic types. See **polymorphic types**. (p. 77)

Global identifiers. Identifiers that belong to the outermost block of the program. See **local** and **nonlocal identifiers**. (p. 21)

Goals. See **queries**. (p. 269)

Guarded commands. See **nondeterministic statements**. (p. 12)

Guardians. Implementation of shared data in Post. (p. 210)

Guards. The conditions on the branches of a conditional or **case** statement. (p. 12)

Heaps. Runtime-store regions used for dynamic allocation of values accessed through pointers. (p. 27)

Higher-order functions. Functions that return other functions. (p. 79)

Homogeneous. Structures with all components of the same type. Opposite of **heterogeneous**. (p. 7)

Homoiconic languages. Languages in which programs and data are represented in the same way. (p. 123)

Hypotheses. See **facts**. (p. 269)

Identifier return. A procedure returns a value to the caller by assigning it to a variable mentioned in the procedure header. Alternative to **explicit return** and **implicit return**. (p. 19)

Imperative languages. Languages in which programs execute commands sequentially, use variables to organize memory, and update variables with assignment statements. (p. 119)

Implementation part of module. Part of a module that contains the bodies of procedures and other declarations that are private to the module. See also **specification part**. (p. 73)

Implicit return. A procedure returns a value to the caller by assigning it to a pseudovariable with the same name as the procedure. Alternative to **explicit return** and **identifier return**. (p. 19)

Importing identifiers. Inheriting nonlocal identifiers into a name scope. (p. 72)

Incremental compilers. Compilers that can translate new code (typically new procedures) and integrate it into already-compiled code. (p. 79)

Index types. The types of values used to index an array. (p. 7)

Indivisible operations. Operations that execute in a thread instantaneously so far as other threads are concerned. Also called **atomic operations** and **serializable operations**. (p. 220)

Infinite overtaking. See **starvation**. (p. 236)

Information hiding. Quality of language design that allows program units to access only the information they require. (p. 4)

Inheritance. Defining a class as an extension of another. (p. 164)

Initial algebra. In algebraic specification of abstract data types, an algebra that equates only those elements that the axioms force to be equal. See also **final algebra**. (p. 279)

Initializers. Procedures invoked when objects are allocated. Also called **constructors**. (p. 187)

Input guards. A guard that ends with a **receive** statement. (p. 251)

Inspectors. In algebraic specification of abstract data types, operations that do not result in values of the abstract data type. See also **constructors**. (p. 279)

Instance methods. Methods belonging to all instances of a class. (p. 176)

Instance variables. Data local to an instance of a class. Also called **data members**. (p. 170)

Instantiation. Creating an instance of a module or a class. (p. 78)

Interactive languages. Programming languages in which a session is a dialogue of questions (posed by the user) and answers (provided by the language). (p. 79)

Iterators. Procedures that return intermediate values via **yield** in order to control loops. (p. 39)

Join. In relational databases, a relation constructed from several other relations. (p. 345)

Keyword parameters. Parameters that indicate which formal parameter each actual matches by naming the formal. Opposite of **positional parameters**. (p. 18)

Keyword selectors. Message selectors with any number of parameters. (p. 171)

L-value. The runtime address of a variable. See **R-value**. (p. 9)

Large-grain parallelism. See **coarse-grain parallelism**. (p. 261)

Lazy evaluation. Postponing evaluation of an expression until it is needed. Most often applies to actual parameters. Also called **delayed**, **normal-order**, **demand-driven** and **output-driven evaluation**. Alternative to **strict** and **speculative evaluation**. (p. 139)

Lexical scope rules. See **static scope rules**. (p. 26)

Links. A communication type that represents a two-way channel between address spaces. (p. 253)

Lists. A kind of LISP S-expression. (p. 122)

Literals. Values of primitive types expressly denoted in a program. (p. 8)

Local identifiers. Identifiers introduced within a particular name scope are **local** to it. See **nonlocal** and **global**. (p. 21)

Local referencing environment. The set of identifier bindings introduced in a procedure and referred to from within that procedure. (p. 15)

Loops. Iterative statements. (p. 12)

Macro mode. A parameter-passing mode in which every use of the formal parameter causes the text of the actual parameter to be freshly evaluated. (p. 17)

Mapping. Associating an attribute with an identifier, often as a result of a declaration. (p. 20)

Member functions. See **methods**. (p. 170)

Members. Instance variables and methods. (p. 170)

Messages. Requests sent from one object to another to perform an operation, in an object-oriented programming language. (p. 163)

Meta-operators. Operators that take operator parameters. (p. 331)

Metacircular interpreter. An interpreter for a language written in the language itself and available at runtime. See **homoiconic languages**. (p. 137)

Metaclasses. Classes whose members are themselves classes. (p. 173)

Metaprogramming. Programming an evaluator for expressions with the language of those expressions. (p. 298)

Methods. Procedures available to instances of a class that define the properties of an object. (p. 163)

Methods. Procedures exported by classes. Also called **member functions**. (p. 170)

Modularity. Quality of language design that allows the interactions between programming units to be stated explicitly. (p. 4)

Modules. Name scopes that allow the programmer to control what identifiers are imported and exported from or to the surrounding name scope. Modules are used to implement abstract data types. Also called **clusters** and **packages**. (p. 72)

Monomorphic types. Types that do not contain type identifiers. Also called **monotypes**. Opposite of **polymorphic types**. (p. 91)

Monotypes. See **monomorphic types**. (p. 91)

Multilevel statement. A **break**, **next**, or **redo** statement that affects an iterative statement outside the one in which it is placed. (p. 13)

Multiple inheritance. Allowing a class to be the direct subclass of more than one superclass. Also called **repeated inheritance**. (p. 183)

Mutual exclusion. While one thread is executing instructions that deal with shared variables, all other threads are excluded from such instructions. (p. 219)

Name equivalence. Two types are equivalent if they are declared by the same type name, or, in a looser definition, by the same type constructor. Also called **declaration** and **named equivalence**. See **structural equivalence**. (p. 66)

Name mode. A parameter-passing mode in which every use of the formal parameter causes the actual parameter to be freshly evaluated. (p. 17)

Name scopes. Regions of a program in which particular identifiers are bound to particular meanings, either as variables of some type, or as types, constants, labels, or procedures. (p. 20)

Named equivalence. See **name equivalence**. (p. 66)

Nested-monitor problem. The question whether a call from one monitor to another should release exclusion on the first monitor. (p. 228)

Nondeterministic statements. Statements that make arbitrary choices among branches. Also called **guarded commands**. (p. 12)

Nonlocal identifiers. Identifiers inherited by a particular name scope are **nonlocal** to it. See **local** and **global**. (p. 21)

Nonlocal referencing environment. The set of nonlocal identifier bindings dynamically in force during program execution (p. 22)

Nonmonotonic reasoning. In logic, the property that adding information can reduce the number of conclusions that can be proved. (p. 291)

Nonprocedural languages. See **declarative languages**. (p. 267)

Nonterminals. In BNF, identifiers on the left-hand sides of productions. (p. 357)

Normal form. In lambda calculus, a term that cannot be reduced by β reductions. (p. 155)

Normal-order evaluation. See **lazy evaluation**. (p. 139)

Object-oriented languages. Languages following a paradigm in which programs and data are all objects that interact through messages. (p. 163)

Objects. Encapsulations of data and program in object-oriented languages. (p. 163)

Occurring free. In denotational semantics, a left-hand side of a domain equation that occurs in the right-hand side of a domain equation is said to occur free in that right-hand side. (p. 375)

Operational semantics. A formal semantics model that interprets the changes a program makes to the program state during execution. (p. 359)

Operators. Parts of an **expression**; value-returning procedures. (p. 8)

Orthogonality. Quality of language design that allows independent functions to be controlled by independent mechanisms. (p. 4)

Output guards. A guard that ends with a **send** statement. (p. 251)

Overloading. Binding multiple procedure declarations to the same name, with the compiler choosing the correct one based on arity and type information. Also called **polymorphism**. (p. 8)

Overriding. Providing a new declaration for an identifier that has already been declared, rendering the old identifier inaccessible during the scope of the new declaration. (p. 20)

Own variables. Variables declared within a procedure that retain their values from one invocation to the next. Also called **static variables**. (p. 195)

Packages. See **modules**. (p. 72)

Parallel programming. See **concurrent programming**. (p. 217)

Parameter-passing modes. Specifications of how formal parameters are bound to actual parameters. (p. 16)

Parameters. Inputs and outputs to procedures. Also called **arguments**. (p. 16)

Parametric types. See **polymorphic types**. (p. 77)

Partial application. Providing only some of the expected parameters of a function. (p. 96)

Partial correctness. See **conditional correctness**. (p. 361)

Patterns. Expressions that serve to bind their component identifiers when they match other expressions (p. 89)

Persistence root. The root of the tree of persistent values. (p. 148)

Persistent values. Values that are retained after the program that created them has terminated. (p. 148)

Pervasive identifiers. Identifiers that are automatically imported into all nested name scopes. (p. 73)

Polychronous data structures. Structures that are partly synchronous and partly asynchronous. (p. 207)

Polymorphic types. Types that contain type identifiers and may be further specified later. Also called **polytypes**, **generic types**, and **parametric types**. Opposite of **monomorphic types**. (p. 77)

Polymorphism. See **overloading**. (p. 8)

Polytypes. See **polymorphic types**. (p. 77)

Positional parameters. Parameters that indicate which formal parameter each actual matches by the order in which the actual parameters are placed. Opposite of **keyword parameters**. (p. 18)

Postconditions. Predicates that should be true after a program executes. (p. 361)

Postfix operators. Unary operators that follow their expressions. Opposite of **prefix operators**. (p. 8)

Power loops. A control construct whereby n loops can be nested. (p. 57)

Precedence of operators. A property of an operator that determines the way the expression is grouped in the absence of parentheses. (p. 8)

Preconditions. Predicates that a program may assume before executing. (p. 361)

Predicates. In logic programming, identifiers with parameters that indicate a fact (actual or to be proven) that relates values of their parameters. Also called **relations**. (p. 268)

Primitive types. Types not built out of other types. Also called **simple**, **basic**, and **atomic types**. Opposite of **structured types**. (p. 6)

Principle of uniform reference. Clients should not be able to discover algorithmic details of exporting modules. (p. 75)

Procedural languages. Languages in which programs are organized around control structures such as iteration and procedure invocation. Opposite of **declarative languages**. (p. 267)

Procedure header. An indication of a procedure name, its parameters, and return type. (p. 15)

Procedures. Groups of statements that can be invoked from elsewhere in the program; contain a header, declarations, and a body. Also called **subroutines** and **functions**. (p. 15)

Processes. See **threads**. (p. 217)

Product domains. In denotational semantics, ordered pairs of elements of the component domains. (p. 372)

Productions. Rules in BNF notation composed of a nonterminal (the left-hand side) and a regular expression (the right-hand side). (p. 357)

Programming by classification. Organizing abstract data types into a tree, with the most abstract at the root, and modifying programs by introducing new subclasses. (p. 193)

Promises. See **Suspensions**. (p. 139)

Protocol. The set of messages that instances of a class will respond to (its interface). (p. 163)

Pseudovariables. Readonly variables with a language-specific meaning. (p. 175)

Pure virtual methods. Methods that are not implemented in a class, so they must be overridden by methods in each subclass. (p. 185)

Qualified identifiers. Identifiers with a prefix to indicate which class instance, module, or name scope is intended. (p. 168)

Queries. In logic programming, requests to prove or disprove assertions. Also called **goals**. (p. 269)

Quoting. Preventing evaluation. (p. 123)

R-value. The value of a literal, constructor, variable, or expression. See **L-value**. (p. 9)

Readers-writers problem. Some threads (the readers) need to read shared data, and others (the writers) need to write those data. (p. 230)

Readonly mode. A parameter-passing mode in which either value or reference mode is actually used, but the compiler ensures that the formal parameter is never used on the left-hand side of an assignment. (p. 17)

Receiver. An object that is sent a message. (p. 171)

Recoverable. An action that can be undone in case of failure. (p. 238)

Recursive procedures. Procedures that invoke themselves, either directly or indirectly. (p. 16)

Reduction semantics. The meaning of a program is defined by repeatedly reducing the program by finding a function application and evaluating it. (p. 147)

Reductions. New types that reduce the set of values available in an old type. Opposite of **extensions**. (p. 69)

Reference mode. A parameter-passing mode in which the L-value of the formal parameter is set to the L-value of the actual parameter. (p. 16)

Referencing operators. Operators that produce a pointer to an expression with an L-value (p. 16)

Referential transparency. In functional programming, the characteristic that all references to a particular identifier always produce the same results. (p. 151)

Regular expressions. Strings used for matching, in which most characters match themselves, but some characters and character combinations have special meanings. (p. 315)

Regularity. See **uniformity**. (p. 4)

Relations. See **predicates**. (p. 268)

Relations. In databases, persistent homogeneous arrays of records. (p. 337)

Remote procedure call (RPC). A procedure call between address spaces that is handled not by **accept** statements, but rather by an ordinary exported procedure. (p. 245)

Rendezvous. A thread explicitly accepting calls from another thread (p. 241)

Repeated inheritance. See **multiple inheritance**. (p. 183)

Resolution. A general inference rule in logic that allows two implications to derive a new implication. (p. 285)

Result mode. A parameter-passing mode in which the value of the formal parameter is copied into the actual parameter at return (p. 16)

Rule body. In logic programming, the part of a rule that implies the head of the rule. See **rule head**. (p. 271)

Rule head. In logic programming, the predicate implied by the body of a rule. See **rule body**. (p. 271)

Rules of inference. Rules that specify how to combine axioms to create provable propositions. (p. 362)

Rules. In logic programming, a definition of one predicate in terms of other predicates. (p. 270)

Runtime semantics. See **Semantics**. (p. 357)

S-expressions. LISP data structures. (p. 120)

Safety. Quality of language design that allows semantic errors to be detected. (p. 4)

Schemata. Data specifications in databases. (p. 337)

Scope rules. Rules that determine which syntactic entity is bound to an identifier, particularly when there are several competing meanings. (p. 25)

Scripting languages. Languages for scanning text files, constructing input for other programs, and collecting output from other programs. (p. 350)

Second-class values. Values that can be passed as parameters but cannot be the return values of procedures or assigned into variables. (p. 75)

Selective receive. The acceptance only of incoming messages that satisfy some condition based on sender or contents. (p. 250)

Selector operators. Operators that extract a component of a structure. Opposite of **constructors**. (p. 87)

Semantic domains. In denotational semantics, the abstract objects manipulated by programs. (p. 370)

Semantic functions. Functions in denotational semantics that map syntactic objects to their semantic values. (p. 369)

Semantics. A specification of what programs will compute when they run. Also called **execution semantics**, **dynamic semantics**, and **runtime semantics**. (p. 357)

Semaphore. A synchronization type with **up** and **down** operations. (p. 220)

Sequencer. A synchronization type with a `ticket` operation. (p. 233)

Serializable operations. See **indivisible operations**. (p. 220)

Serialized classes. Classes whose objects allow only one thread at a time to be executing methods. (p. 258)

Server processes. Processes that provide assistance to other processes. See **client processes**. (p. 253)

Server threads. Threads that receive procedure calls from other threads. (p. 241)

Shallow binding. See **shallow search**. (p. 134)

Shallow binding. Binding the nonlocal referencing environment of a procedure at the time it is invoked. Opposite of **deep binding**. (p. 25)

Shallow copy operation. Copying a record structure, but not recursively copying pointers contained in it. (p. 180)

Shallow search. In dynamically scoped languages, storing the most recent binding of an atom in its property list. Also called **shallow binding**. (p. 134)

Shared variables. Data global to all instances of all classes or global to several threads. (p. 173)

Short-circuit operators. Versions of **and** or **or** that only evaluate their second operand if the value of the first operand so dictates. (p. 10)

Side effects. Modifications to the environment, such as changing variable values, caused by a procedure call. (p. 79)

Simple statements. Statements not built of other statements. Opposite of **compound statements**. (p. 11)

Simple types. See **primitive types**. (p. 6)

Simplicity. Quality of language design that uses a minimal number of basic concepts. (p. 4)

Software tools. Interfaces between humans and lower-level facilities. (p. 2)

Software tools. Program packages such as editors, data transformers, operating systems, and programming languages with an interface between clients and implementation. (p. 2)

Specification part of module. Part of a module with declarations visible to clients of the module. See also **implementation part**. (p. 73)

Speculative evaluation. See **strict evaluation**. (p. 139)

Speculative evaluation. Evaluation of expressions whose values are not yet needed. Also called **data-driven evaluation**. Alternative to **strict** and **lazy evaluation**. (p. 144)

Spreading. Coercing an array to a higher dimension. (p. 330)

Stack frames. See **activation records**. (p. 26)

Starvation. A condition in which a thread fails to make progress, even though other threads are executing, because of scheduling decisions. Also called **infinite overtaking**. (p. 236)

Statements. Units of runtime execution. Also called **commands**. See **simple** and **compound** statements. (p. 11)

Static chain. List of activation records on the central stack, each of which points to the activation record of its nonlocal referencing environment. (p. 26)

Static scope rules. Rules according to which the compiler can determine the declaration associated with each identifier based on position in the program. Also called **lexical scope rules**. Opposite of **dynamic scope rules**. (p. 26)

Static semantics. See **advanced syntax**. (p. 358)

Static variables. See **own variables**. (p. 195)

Static-typed languages. Languages in which types are bound to identifiers at compile time. Opposite of **dynamic-typed languages**. (p. 63)

Streams. Unbounded homogeneous sequences of values. (p. 207)

Strict evaluation. Evaluating actual parameters entirely before a procedure is invoked. Also called **applicative-order evaluation** and **eager evaluation**. Alternative to **lazy** and **speculative evaluation**. (p. 139)

Strongly typed languages. Programming languages that provide rules that allow the type of every value to be determined. (p. 64)

Structural equivalence. Two types are equivalent if, after all type identifiers are replaced by their definitions, the same structure is obtained. See **name equivalence**. (p. 65)

Structured statements. See **compound statements**. (p. 11)

Structured types. Types built out of other types. Also called **aggregate**, **compound**, **composite**, and **constructed types**. Opposite of **primitive types**. (p. 6)

Stub compiler. A program that takes a specification of exported procedures and builds suitable code for both the client and the server of RPC calls. (p. 246)

Subclasses. Classes that inherit members from their superclasses. Also called **derived classes** and **descendents**. (p. 176)

Subroutines. See **procedures**. (p. 15)

Subtypes. Type-equivalent restrictions of other type (p. 68)

Superclasses. Classes that export members to their subclasses. Also called **base classes** and **ancestors**. (p. 176)

Suspensions. Expressions that can be evaluated later by a lazy evaluator. Also called **promises**. (p. 139)

Synchronous data structures. Structures that must be entirely computed before any part can be used. (p. 207)

Synchronous message passing. Message passing in which the sender waits for a reply. Opposite of **asynchronous** message passing. (p. 250)

Syntactic domains. Parts of a denotational definition containing the elementary tokens of the language and an abstract syntax. (p. 369)

Syntax. The structure of a language, determining whether a program is valid or invalid. (p. 357)

Terminals. In BNF, lexical tokens of the programming language. (p. 357)

Terms. Elementary values composed of literals, variables, and structures. (p. 268)

Third-class values. Values that cannot be passed as a parameter, be the return value of a procedure, or be assigned into a variable. (p. 75)

Threads. Sequential computations that may interact with other simultaneous computations. Also called **processes**. (p. 217)

Tokens. Decorations that carry data along arcs of a dataflow graph. (p. 198)

Top-down evaluation. In logic programming, starting with the goal and working to subgoals. Opposite of **bottom-up evaluation**. (p. 294)

Total correctness. A statement that a program terminates and is conditionally correct. See **conditional correctness**. (p. 367)

Transactions. Sets of operations undertaken by threads that are indivisible and recoverable. (p. 238)

Type coercion. Implicitly converting values of one type into another. (p. 9)

Type constraints. Type expressions that restrict the polymorphism of expressions. (p. 98)

Type constructors. Expressions that yield a type. (p. 66)

Type domains. The sets of all values of the given types. (p. 98)

Type identifiers. Symbols standing for any type. (p. 80)

Type inference. Ability of a compiler to infer the types of identifiers from the ways they are used. (p. 80)

Type-safe languages. Languages in which whenever a program passes the type-checking rules, no runtime type error is possible. (p. 95)

Types. Sets of values and operations that may be applied to those values. (p. 6)

Unary selectors. Message selectors with no parameters. (p. 171)

Unconstrained arrays. See **flexible arrays**. (p. 7)

Unification. In logic programming, matching parameters from a goal with parameters of the head of a rule, binding free variables in the rule. (p. 272)

Unification. Finding the strongest common constraint for partially constrained values. (p. 93)

Uniformity. Quality of language design according to which the basic concepts are applied consistently and universally. Also called **regularity**. (p. 4)

Unityped languages. See **dynamic-typed languages**. (p. 64)

Value mode. A parameter-passing mode in which the value of the actual parameter is copied into the formal parameter at invocation (p. 16)

Value result mode. A parameter-passing mode combining the semantics of value mode and result mode. (p. 16)

Valves. In dataflow graphs, nodes that control the flow of tokens within the graphs. (p. 198)

Variables. Identifiers bound to a value that can be changed dynamically by an assignment statement. (p. 120)

Variables. Named memory locations. (p. 6)

Variant records. See **choice types**. (p. 7)

Virtual methods. Methods that are expected to be overridden by methods in a subclass. Also called **deferred methods**. (p. 185)

References

[Abadi 91] MARTIN ABADI, LUCA CARDELLI, BENJAMIN PIERCE, AND GORDON PLOTKIN, "Dynamic typing in a statically typed language," *ACM TOPLAS* **13**(2) pp. 237-268 (April 1991).

[Abelson 85] H. ABELSON AND GERALD J. SUSSMAN, *Structure and Interpretation of Computer Programs*, Cambridge, MA: MIT Press (1985).

[Ackerman 80] W. B. ACKERMAN, *Axiomatic Verification in Single Assignment Languages*, CSG memo, Laboratory for Computer Science, Massachusetts Institute of Technology (September 1980).

[Ada 1983] UNITED STATES DEPARTMENT OF DEFENSE, "Reference Manual for the Ada Programming Language," *ANSI/NIL-STD 1815A-1983* (1983).

[Aho 78] ALFRED V. AHO, BRIAN W. KERNIGHAN, AND PETER J. WEINBERGER, *AWK: A Pattern Scanning and Processing Language* (2nd edition), Murray Hill, NJ: Bell Laboratories (September 1978).

[Andrews 88] GREGORY R. ANDREWS, RONALD A. OLSSON, MICHAEL COFFIN, IRVING ELSHOFF, K. NILSEN, TITUS PURDIN, AND G. TOWNSEND, "An overview of the SR language and implementation," *ACM Transactions on Programming Languages and Systems* **10**(1) pp. 51-86 (January 1988).

[ANSI 83] ANSI, *American National Standard Pascal Computer Programming Language* (ANSI/IEEE 770X3.97), New York: American National Standards Institute (1983).

[Appel 85] ANDREW W. APPEL, "Semantics-Directed Code Generation," *12th POPL Conference* pp. 315-324 (1985).

[Appel 91] ANDREW W. APPEL AND DAVID B. MACQUEEN, "Standard ML of New Jersey," *Third International Symposium on Programming Language Implementation and Logic Programming* (August 1991).

[Artsy 89] YESHAYAHU ARTSY AND RAPHAEL FINKEL, "Designing a process migration facility — The Charlotte Experience," *IEEE Computer* **22**(9) pp. 47-56 (September 1989).

[Arvind 89] ARVIND, R. S. NIKHIL, AND K. K. PINGALI, "I-Structures: Data Structures for Parallel Computing," *ACM Transactions on Programming Languages and Systems* **11** pp. 568-632 (October 1989).

[Ashcroft 77] E. A. ASHCROFT AND W. W. WADGE, "Lucid, a nonprocedural language with iteration," *CACM* **20**(7) pp. 519-526 (July 1977).

[Backus 78] JOHN W. BACKUS, "Can programming be liberated from the von Neumann style? A functional style and its algebra of programs," *Communications of the ACM* **21** pp. 613-641 (1978).

[Baden 84] SCOTT BADEN, "Berkeley FP User's Manual," in *Ultrix-32 Supplementary Documents, Volume II*, (Revised) Merrimack, NH: Digital Equipment Corporation, pp. 2.359-2.391 (1984).

[Baker 82] T. P. BAKER, "A one-pass algorithm for overload resolution in Ada," *ACM TOPLAS* **4**(4) pp. 601-614 (October 1982).

[Birtwistle 73] G. M. BIRTWISTLE, OLE-JOHAN DAHL, B. MYHRHAUG, AND KRISTEN NYGAARD, *Simula Begin*, Philadelphia: Auerback Press (1973).

[Bobrow 88] DANIEL G. BOBROW, LINDA G. DEMICHIEL, RICHARD P. GABRIEL, SONYA E. KEENE, GREGOR KICZALES, AND DAVID A. MOON, "Common LISP object system specification," *ACM SIGPLAN Notices* **23**(9) (September 1988).

[Boehm 86] HANS-JUERGAN BOEHM AND ALAN DEMERS, "Implementing Russell," *ACM SIGPLAN Notices* **21**(7) (July 1986).

[Brinch Hansen 78] PER BRINCH HANSEN, "Distributed processes: A concurrent programming concept," *CACM* **21**(11) pp. 934-941 (November 1978).

[Brinch Hansen 80] PER BRINCH HANSEN, *Edison: A Multiprocessor Language*, Technical Report, University of Southern California Computer Science Department (September 1980).

[Bron 89] C. BRON AND EDSGER W. DIJKSTRA, "A better way to combine efficient string length encoding and zero-termination," *ACM SIGPLAN Notices* **24**(6) pp. 11-19 (June 1989).

[Brownston 86] L. BROWNSTON, R. FARRELL, F. KANT, AND N. MARTIN, *Programming Expert Systems in OPS5*, Reading, MA: Addison-Wesley (1986).

[Budd 95] TIMOTHY A. BUDD, *Multiparadigm Programming in Leda*, Reading, MA: Addison-Wesley (1995).

[Butcher 91] PAUL BUTCHER AND HUSSEIN ZEDAN, "Lucinda — An overview," *ACM SIGPLAN Notices* **26**(8) pp. 90-100 (August 1991).

[Byrd 80] L. BYRD, "Understanding the control flow of Prolog programs," in *Proceedings of the 1st International Workshop on Logic Programming*, ed. S. Tarlund, ISBN 0-12-1755-207, pp. 127-138 (1980).

[Calliss 91] FRANK W. CALLISS, "A comparison of module constructs in programming languages," *ACM SIGPLAN Notices* **26**(1) pp. 38-46 (January 1991).

[Cardelli 86] LUCA CARDELLI, "Amber," in *Combinators and Functional Programming Languages*, ed. G. Cousineau, P. L. Courien, and B. Robinet, New York: Springer-Verlag (1986).

[Carr 93] HAROLD CARR, ROBERT KESSLER, AND MARK SWANSON, "Distributed C++," *ACM SIGPLAN Notices* **28**(1) p. 81 (January 1993).

[Char 93] CHAR, GEDDES, GONNET, LEONG, MONOGAN, AND WATT, *Maple V Language Reference Manual*, New York: Springer-Verlag (1993).

[Church 41] ALONZO CHURCH, *The Calculi of Lambda Conversion*, Princeton, NJ: Princeton University Press (1941).

[Clement 92] BRUCE CLEMENT, "ADD 1 TO COBOL GIVING COBOL," *ACM SIGPLAN Notices* **27**(4) pp. 90-91 (April 1992).

[Clocksin 81] W. F. CLOCKSIN AND C. S. MELLISH, *Programming in PROLOG*, New York: Springer-Verlag (1981).

[Dahl 72] OLE-JOHAN DAHL, EDSGER W. DIJKSTRA, AND C. A. R. HOARE, *Structured Programming*, New York: Academic Press (1972).

[Dally 89] W. J. DALLY AND A. A. CHIEN, "Object-oriented concurrent programming in CST," *Proceedings of the ACM SIGPLAN Workshop on Object-Based Concurrent Programming: ACM SIGPLAN Notices* **24**(4) pp. 28-31 (April

1989).

[Darlington 90] JARED L. DARLINGTON, "Search direction by goal failure," *ACM TOPLAS* **12**(2) pp. 224-252 (April 1990).

[Demers 79] ALAN DEMERS AND J. DONAHUE, *Revised Report on Russell*, Cornell CS Department Technical Report TR 79-389 (1979).

[Dennis 77] J. B. DENNIS, C. K. LEUNG, AND D. P. MISUNAS, *A Highly Parallel Processor Using a Dataflow Machine Language*, CSG memo 134-1, Massachusetts Institute of Technology (January 1977).

[Dijkstra 75] EDSGER W. DIJKSTRA, "Guarded commands, nondeterminacy and formal derivation of programs," *CACM* **18**(8) pp. 453-457 (August 1975).

[Ellis 90] MARGARET ELLIS AND BJARNE STROUSTRUP, *The Annotated C++ Reference Manual*, Reading, MA: Addison-Wesley (1990).

[Finkel 76] RAPHAEL A. FINKEL, *Constructing and debugging manipulator programs*, Stanford AI Laboratory memo AIM-284, Stanford Computer Science Department report STAN-CS-76-567 (August 1976).

[Fruhwirth 92] T. FRUHWIRTH, A. HEROLD, AND V. KUCHENHOFF, *Constraint Logic Programming — An informal introduction*, Berlin: Springer-Verlag (1992).

[Gauthier 92] MICHEL GAUTHIER, "Noised or filtered programming?" *ACM SIGPLAN Notices* **27**(4) pp. 37-40 (April 1992).

[Gaylord 93] GAYLORD, KAMIN, AND WELLIN, *Introduction to Programming with Mathematica*, New York: Springer-Verlag (1993).

[Gehani 80] NAHRAIN GEHANI AND C. WETHERELL, *Denotational Semantics for the Dataflow Language VAL*, Murray Hill, NJ: Internal memo, Bell Laboratories (July 1980).

[Gehani 89] NAHRAIN H. GEHANI AND W. D. ROOME, *The Concurrent C programming language*, Summit, NJ: Silicon Press (1989).

[Gelernter 85] DAVID GELERNTER, "Generative communication in Linda," *ACM TOPLAS* **7**(1) pp. 80-112 (January 1985).

[Goldberg 83] ADELE GOLDBERG AND DAVID ROBSON, *Smalltalk-80, The Language and Its Implementation*, Reading, MA: Addison-Wesley (1983).

[Goodenough 75] J. B. GOODENOUGH, "Exception handling: Issues and a proposed notation," *CACM* **18**(12) pp. 683-696 (December 1975).

[Gries 81] DAVID GRIES, *The Science of Programming*, Berlin: Springer-Verlag (1981).

[Griswold 71] RALPH E. GRISWOLD, J. POAGE, AND I. POLONSKY, *The Snobol4 Programming Language* (2nd edition), Englewood Cliffs, NJ: Prentice-Hall (1971).

[Griswold 80] RALPH E. GRISWOLD AND DAVID R. HANSON, "An alternative to the use of patterns in string processing," *ACM TOPLAS* **2**(2) pp. 153-172 (April 1980).

[Griswold 90] RALPH E. GRISWOLD AND M. T. GRISWOLD, *The Icon Programming Language* (2nd edition), Englewood Cliffs, NJ: Prentice-Hall (1990).

[Gunaseelan 92] L. GUNASEELAN AND RICHARD J. LEBLANC, JR., "Distributed Eiffel: A language for programming multi-granular distributed objects on the Clouds operating system," *Proceedings IEEE 1992 International Conference on Computer Languages* (April 1992).

[Gupta 89] R. GUPTA, "The fuzzy barrier: A mechanism for high speed synchronization of processors," *Proceedings of the Third ASPLOS* pp. 54-63 (April 1989).

[Gurd 85] J. GURD, C. KIRKHAM, AND I. WATSON, "The Manchester Prototype Dataflow Computer," *CACM* **28**(1) pp. 34-52 (January 1985).

[Guttag 77] JOHN V. GUTTAG, "Abstract data types and the development of data structures," *CACM* **20**(6) pp. 396-404 (June 1977).

[Haddon 77] B. HADDON, "Nested Monitor Calls," *Operating systems review* **11**(10) pp. 18-23 (October 1977).

[Hansen 92] WILFRED J. HANSEN, "Subsequence references: First-class values for substrings," *ACM TOPLAS* **14**(4) pp. 471-489 (October 1992).

[Harbison 87] SAMUEL P. HARBISON AND GUY L. STEELE, *C: A Reference Manual* (2nd edition), Englewood Cliffs, NJ: Prentice-Hall (1987).

[Harper 89] ROBERT HARPER, ROBIN MILNER, AND MADS TOFTE, *The Definition of Standard ML* (Version 2), Cambridge, MA: MIT Press (1989).

[Heintze 92] N. HEINTZE, J. JAFFAR, AND S. MICHAYLOV, *The CLP(R) Programmer's Manual, Version 1.2*, IBM Thomas J. Watson Research Center (1992).

[Heller 91] HELLER, *MACSYMA for Statisticians*, New York: John Wiley and Sons (1991).

[Hernández 93] J. HERNÁNDEZ, P. DE MIGUEL, M. BARRENA, J. M. MARTÍNEZ, A. POLO, AND M. NIETO, "ALBA, a parallel language based on actors," *ACM SIGPLAN Notices* **28**(4) pp. 11-20 (April 1993).

[Herrin 93] ERIC HERRIN, *Dynamic Service Rebalancing*, Ph.D. Thesis, Technical report 235-93, University of Kentucky, Lexington, KY (1993).

[Hill 94] P. M. HILL AND J. W. LLOYD, *The Gödel Programming Language*, Cambridge, MA: MIT Press (1994).

[Hoare 69] C. A. R. HOARE, "An axiomatic basis for computer programming," *CACM* **12**(10) pp. 576-580 (October 1969).

[Hoare 73] C. A. R. HOARE, *Hints on Programming Language Design*, Stanford CS Department Technical Report STAN-CS-73-403 (December 1973).

[Hoare 74] C. A. R. HOARE, "Monitors: An operating system structuring concept," *CACM* **17**(10) pp. 549-557 (October 1974).

[Hoare 78] C. A. R. HOARE, "Communicating Sequential Processes," *CACM* **21**(8) pp. 666-677 (August 1978).

[Hockney 92] GEORGE HOCKNEY, PAUL MACKENZIE, AND MARK FISCHLER, *Canopy Version 5.0*, Fermi National Accelerator Laboratory (February 1992).

[Horn 77] FRANK HORN AND MARTY HONDA, Personal Communication (1977).

[Hughes 86] SHEILA HUGHES, *Lisp*, London: Pitman Publishing Limited (1986).

[IBM Corporation 87] IBM CORPORATION, *APL2 Programming: Language Reference* (SH20-9227) (1987).

[Ingalls 78] DANIEL H. INGALLS, "The Smalltalk-76 programming system design and implementation," *Fifth Annual ACM Symposium on Principles of Programming Languages* (1978).

[ISO/IEC 94] ISO/IEC, *Language Independent Datatypes* (Language Bindings Working Group JTC1/SC22 WG11), DIS 11404 (1994).

[Iverson 62] KENNETH E. IVERSON, *A Programming Language*, New York: John Wiley and Sons (1962).

[Iverson 87] KENNETH E. IVERSON, "A Dictionary of APL," *(ACM) APL Quote Quad* **18**(1) (September 1987).

[Jaffar 92] JOXAN JAFFAR, SPIRO MICHAYLOV, PETER J. STUCKEY, AND ROLAND H. C. YAP, "The CLP(R) Language and System," *ACM TOPLAS* **14**(3) pp. 339-395 (July 1992).

[Jellinghaus 90] ROBERT JELLINGHAUS, "Eiffel Linda: An object-oriented Linda Dialect," *ACM SIGPLAN Notices* **25**(12) pp. 70-84 (December 1990).

[Jensen 74] K. JENSEN AND NIKLAUS WIRTH, "Pascal: User manual and report," *Lecture Notes in Computer Science* (18) Springer-Verlag (1974).

[Jonsson 89] DAN JONSSON, "Pancode assessed," *ACM SIGPLAN Notices* **24**(12) pp. 17-20 (December 1989).

[Kalé 90] L. V. KALÉ, "The Chare-Kernel parallel programming language and system," *Proceedings of the International Conference on Parallel Processing* pp. 17-25 (August 1990).

[Karp 66] RICHARD M. KARP AND RAYMOND E. MILLER, "Properties of a model for parallel computation: Determinacy, termination, queuing," *SIAM Journal of App. Math* pp. 1390-1411 (November 1966).

[Katzenelson 92] JACOB KATZENELSON, SHLOMIT S. PINTER, AND EUGIN SCHENFELD, "Type matching, type graphs, and the Schanuel conjecture," *ACM TOPLAS* **14**(4) pp. 574-588 (October 1992).

[Kennedy 94] ANDREW KENNEDY, "Dimension types," *Proceedings of the 5th European Symposium on Programming* (In *Springer Lecture Notes in Computer Science*, vol. 788) Springer-Verlag (1994).

[Kernighan 88] BRIAN W. KERNIGHAN AND DENNIS M. RITCHIE, *The C Programming Language* (2nd edition), Englewood Cliffs, NJ: Prentice-Hall (1988).

[Knuth 71] DONALD E. KNUTH AND ROBERT W. FLOYD, "Notes on avoiding goto statements," *Information Processing Letters* **1** pp. 23-31 (1971).

[Knuth 86] DONALD E. KNUTH AND DUANE R. BIBBY, *The METAFONTbook* (volume C of *Computers and Typesetting*), American Mathematical Society (1986).

[Kowalski 79] ROBERT KOWALSKI, "Algorithm = logic + control," *CACM* **22**(7) (1979).

[LaLonde 90] WILF R. LALONDE AND JOHN R. PUGH, *Inside Smalltalk*, Englewood Cliffs, NJ: Prentice-Hall (1990).

[Lampson 77] BUTLER W. LAMPSON, JIM J. HORNING, R. L. LONDON, JAMES G. MITCHELL, AND GARY J. POPEK, "Report on the programming language Euclid," *Sigplan Notices* **12**(2) pp. 1-79 (February 1977).

[Lampson 80] BUTLER W. LAMPSON AND D. D. REDELL, "Experience with processes and monitors in Mesa," *CACM* **23**(2) pp. 105-117 (February 1980).

[Levien 89] RAPHAEL L. LEVIEN, "Io: A new programming notation," *ACM SIGPLAN Notices* **24**(12) pp. 24-31 (December 1989).

[Liskov 81] BARBARA LISKOV, R. ATKINSON, T. BLOOM, E. MOSS, J. C. SCHAFFERT, R. SCHEIFLER, AND A. SNYDER, *CLU Reference Manual*, Berlin: Springer-Verlag (1981).

[Liskov 83a] BARBARA LISKOV AND R. SCHEIFLER, "Guardians and actions: Linguistic support for robust, distributed programs," *ACM Transactions on Programming Languages and Systems* **5**(3) pp. 381-404 (July 1983).

[Liskov 83b] BARBARA LISKOV ET AL., *Preliminary Argus reference manual*, Programming Methodology Group Memo 39, MIT Laboratory for Computer Science, Cambridge, MA (October 1983).

[Louden 93] KENNETH C. LOUDEN, *Programming Languages: Principles and Practice*, Boston: PWS-Kent (1993).

[Mandl 90] ROBERT MANDL, "On 'PowerLoop' constructs in programming languages," *ACM SIGPLAN Notices* **25**(4) pp. 73-82 (April 1990).

[May 83] D. MAY, "OCCAM," *ACM SIGPLAN Notices* **18**(4) pp. 69-79 (Relevant correspondence appears in volume 19, number 2 and volume 18, number 11) (April 1983).

[McCarthy 62] JOHN MCCARTHY ET AL., *Lisp 1.5 Programmer's Manual*, , MIT Press, Cambridge, MA (1962).

[McGraw 82] JAMES R. MCGRAW, "The VAL language: Description and analysis," *ACM TOPLAS* **4**(1) (January 1982).

[McGraw 83] JAMES R. MCGRAW AND STEPHEN SKEDZIELEWSKI ET AL., *SISAL: Streams and Iteration in a Single-Assignment Language*, Lawrence Livermore National Laboratories, Report M-146 (July 1983).

[McNally 91] DAVID J. MCNALLY AND ANTONY J. T. DAVIE, "Two models for integrating persistence and lazy functional languages," *ACM SIGPLAN Notices* **26**(5) (May 1991).

[Meek 94] BRIAN L. MEEK, "A taxonomy of datatypes," *ACM SIGPLAN Notices* **29**(9) pp. 159-167 (September 1994).

[Mellender 88] FRED MELLENDER, "An integration of logic and object-oriented programming," *ACM SIGPLAN Notices* **23**(10) pp. 181-185 (October 1988).

[Meyer 88] BERTRAND MEYER, *Object-Oriented Software Construction*, Englewood Cliffs, NJ: Prentice Hall (1988).

[Meyer 92] BERTRAND MEYER, *Eiffel: The language*, Englewood Cliffs, NJ: Prentice Hall (1992).

[Meyers 92] SCOTT MEYERS, *Effective C++*, Reading, MA: Addison-Wesley (1992).

[M. Nelson 91] MICHAEL L. NELSON, "Concurrency and Object-Oriented Programming," *ACM SIGPLAN Notices* **26**(10) pp. 63-72 (October 1991).

[Morrison 90] R. MORRISON AND M. P. ATKINSON, "Persistent Languages and Architectures," in *Security and Persistence*, New York: Springer-Verlag, pp. 9-28 (1990).

[Naur 63] PETER NAUR, "Revised report on the algorithmic language Algol 60," *CACM* **6**(1) pp. 1-17 (1963).

[Nelson 81] BRUCE J. NELSON, *Remote Procedure Call*, Ph.D. Thesis, Technical report CMU-CS-81-119, Carnegie Mellon University, Philadelphia, PA (1981).

[Nelson, G. 1991] GREG NELSON, *Systems Programming with Modula-3*, Englewood Cliffs, NJ: Prentice Hall (1991).

[Ousterhout 94] JOHN OUSTERHOUT, *Tcl and the Tk Toolkit*, Reading, MA: Addison-Wesley (1994).

[Owicki 76] SUSAN OWICKI AND DAVID GRIES, "Verifying properties of parallel programs: An axiomatic approach," *CACM* **19**(5) pp. 279-285 (May 1976).

[Paaki 90] JUKKA PAAKI, ANSSI KARHINEN, AND TOMI SILANDER, "Orthogonal type extensions and reductions," *ACM SIGPLAN Notices* **25**(7) pp. 28-38 (July 1990).

[Pagan 81] FRANK G. PAGAN, *Semantics of Programming Languages: A Panoramic Primer*, Englewood Cliffs, NJ: Prentice Hall (1981).

[Paulson 92] LAWRENCE C. PAULSON, *ML for the Working Programmer*, Cambridge: Cambridge University Press (1992).

[Pemberton 91] STEVEN PEMBERTON, "A short introduction to the ABC language," *ACM SIGPLAN Notices* **26**(2) pp. 11-16 (February 1991).

[Placer 92] JOHN PLACER, "Integrating destructive assignment and lazy evaluation in the multiparadigm language G-2," *ACM SIGPLAN Notices* **27**(2) pp. 65-74 (February 1992).

[Pratt 96] TERRENCE W. PRATT AND MARVIN V. ZELKOWITZ, *Programming Languages: Design and Implementation* (3rd edition), Englewood Cliffs, NJ: Prentice Hall (1996).

[Radensky 87] A. RADENSKY, "Lazy evaluation and nondeterminism make Backus' FP-systems more practical," *ACM SIGPLAN Notices* **22**(4) pp. 33-40 (April 1987).

[Rajasekar 94] ARCOT RAJASEKAR, "Applications in constraint logic programming with strings," *Proceedings of Principles and Practice of Constraint Programming* pp. 109-122 Springer-Verlag (1994).

[Ramsey 90] NORMAN RAMSEY, *Concurrent Programming in ML*, CS-TR-262-90, Princeton University, Department of Computer Science (1990).

[Ravishankar 89] CHINYA V. RAVISHANKAR AND RAPHAEL FINKEL, *Linguistic Support for Dataflow*, Computer Sciences Technical Report 136-89 (Also The University of Michigan Electrical Engineering and Computer Science Technical report CSE-TR-14-89, February 1989), University of Kentucky–Lexington (January 1989).

[Reade 89] CHRIS READE, *Elements of Functional Programming*, Reading, MA: Addison-Wesley (1989).

[Reed 79] D. P. REED AND R. K. KANODIA, "Synchronization with eventcounts and sequencers," *CACM* **22**(2) pp. 115-123 (February 1979).

[Reiser 92] MARTIN REISER AND NIKLAUS WIRTH, *Programming in Oberon — Steps Beyond Pascal and Modula*, Reading, MA: Addison-Wesley (1992).

[Reynolds 70] JOHN C. REYNOLDS, "Gedanken," *CACM* **13**(5) pp. 308-319 (May 1970).

[Rubin 88] F. RUBIN, "'GOTO considered harmful' considered harmful," *CACM* **30**(3) (March 1988).

[Schwartz 94] RANDAL L. SCHWARTZ, *Learning Perl*, Sebastopol, CA: O'Reilly & Associates, Inc. (August 1994).

[Scott 84] MICHAEL L. SCOTT AND RAPHAEL A. FINKEL, "LYNX: A dynamic distributed programming language," *1984 International Conference on Parallel Processing* (August 1984).

[Scott 86] MICHAEL L. SCOTT, *Lynx Reference Manual*, BPR 7, Computer Science Department, University of Rochester (March 1986).

[Scott 88] MICHAEL L. SCOTT AND RAPHAEL A. FINKEL, "A simple mechanism for type security across compilation units," *IEEE Transactions on Software Engineering* **14**(8) pp. 1238-1239 (August 1988).

[Sebesta 93] ROBERT W. SEBESTA, *Concepts of Programming Languages* (2nd edition), Redwood City, CA: Benjamin/Cummings (1993).

[Sethi 89] RAVI SETHI, *Programming Languages: Concepts and Constructs*, Reading, MA: Addison-Wesley (1989).

[Shapiro 89] EHUD Y. SHAPIRO, "The family of concurrent logic programming languages," *ACM Computing Surveys* **21**(3) pp. 413-510 (September 1989).

[Shaw 94] SHAW AND TIGG, *Applied Mathematica, Getting Started, Getting It Done*, Reading, MA: Addison-Wesley (1994).

[Sicheram 91] G. L. SICHERAM, "An Algorithmic Language for Database Operations," *ACM SIGPLAN Notices* **26**(5) pp. 53-58 (May 1991).

[Simpson 87] ALAN SIMPSON, *dBASE III Programmer's Reference Guide*, Alameda, CA: Sybex, Inc. (1987).

[Solomon 80] MARVIN H. SOLOMON AND RAPHAEL A. FINKEL, "A note on enumerating binary trees," *JACM* **27**(1) (January 1980).

[Stamos 90] JAMES W. STAMOS AND DAVID K. GIFFORD, "Remote evaluation," *ACM TOPLAS* **12**(4) pp. 537-565 (October 1990).

[Steele Jr. 90] GUY L. STEELE JR., *Common Lisp — The Language* (2nd edition), Bedford, MA: Digital Press (1990).

[Sterling 94] LEON STERLING AND EHUD Y. SHAPIRO, *The Art of Prolog*, Cambridge, MA: MIT Press (1994).

[Sturgill 89] BRIAN STURGILL AND RAPHAEL FINKEL, *System Administration Tools: The SAT Package*, Computer Sciences Technical Report 147-89, University of Kentucky–Lexington (July 1989).

[Sunderam 89] VAIDY S. SUNDERAM, "Large grained parallel processing on workstation networks," *Proc. IEEE Conf. on High-Speed LANs* (November 1989).

[Teitelman 81] WARREN TEITELMAN AND LARRY MASINTER, "The Interlisp programming environment," *IEEE Computer* **14**(4) pp. 25-33 (1981).

[Tennent 81] R. D. TENNENT, *Principles of Programming Languages*, Englewood Cliffs, NJ: Prentice-Hall International (1981).

[Thompson 86] S. J. THOMPSON, "Laws in Miranda," *Proceedings of the 4th ACM International Conference on LISP and Functional Programming* (August 1986).

[Turner 85a] DAVID A. TURNER, "Miranda: A non-strict functional language with polymorphic types," *Proceedings IFIP International Conference on Functional Programming Languages and Computer Architecture* (In *Springer Lecture Notes in Computer Science*, vol. 201) (September 1985).

[Turner 85b] DAVID A. TURNER, "Functional languages as executable specifications," in *Mathematical Logic and Programming Languages*, ed. Hoare and Shepherdson, Englewood Cliffs, NJ: Prentice Hall (1985).

[Turner 86] DAVID A. TURNER, "An Overview of Miranda," *ACM SIGPLAN Notices* **21**(12) pp. 158-166 (December 1986).

[van Wijngaarden 75] A. VAN WIJNGAARDEN, B. J. MAILLOUX, J. L. PECK, C. H. A. KOSTER, M. SINTZOFF, C. H. LINDSEY, L. G. L. T. MEERTENS, AND R. G. FISKER, "Revised report on the algorithmic language ALGOL 68," *Acta Informatica* **5**(1-3) pp. 1-236 (1975).

[Walinsky 89] C. WALINSKY, "CLP(Σ*): Constraint logic programming with regular sets," *Proceedings of the International Conference of Logic Programming* pp. 181-196 (1989).

[Wall 91] LARRY WALL AND RANDAL I. SCHWARTZ, *Programming Perl*, Sebastopol, CA: O'Reilly and Associates (1991).

[Wand 82] MITCHELL WAND, "Deriving target code as a representation of continuation semantics," *ACM TOPLAS* **4**(3) (July 1982).

[Wegner 72] PETER WEGNER, "The Vienna Definition Language," *Computing Surveys* **4**(1) pp. 5-63 (1972).

[Weihl 90] WILLIAM E. WEIHL, "Linguistic support for atomic data types," *ACM TOPLAS* **12**(2) pp. 178-202 (April 1990).

[Wells 63] MARK B. WELLS, "Recent improvements in Madcap," *CACM* **6**(11) pp. 674-678 (June 1963).

[Wetherell 83] CHARLES S. WETHERELL AND W. STANLEY BROWN, "A numeric error algebra," *Proceedings of 6th Symposium on Computer Arithmetic* pp. 86-91 (June 1983).

[Wirth 76] NIKLAUS WIRTH, *Algorithms + Data Structures = Programs*, Englewood Cliffs, NJ: Prentice-Hall (1976).

[Wirth 77] NIKLAUS WIRTH, "Modula: A language for modular multiprogramming," *Software Practice and Experience* **7**(1) pp. 3-35 (1977).

[Wirth 85] NIKLAUS WIRTH, *Programming in Modula-2* (3rd corrected edition), New York: Springer-Verlag (1985).

[Wong 90] LIMSOON WONG AND B. C. OOI, "Treating failure as state," *ACM SIGPLAN Notices* **25**(8) pp. 24-26 (August 1990).

[Woods 73] DONALD R. WOODS AND JAMES M. LYON, *The Intercal Programming Language Reference Manual* (Not published) (1973).

[Wulf 77] W. A. WULF, R. L. LONDON, AND MARY SHAW, "Abstraction and verification in Alphard: Defining and specifying iteration and generators," *CACM* **20**(8) pp. 553-563 (August 1977).

[Yellin 91] DANIEL M. YELLIN AND ROBERT E. STROM, "INC: A language for incremental computations," *ACM TOPLAS* **13**(2) pp. 211-236 (April 1991).

[Yuen 91] C. K. YUEN, "Which model of programming for Lisp: sequential, functional, or mixed?" *ACM SIGPLAN Notices* **26**(10) pp. 83-92 (October 1991).

Index